THE
Expositor's
Bible
Commentary

with The New International Version

LUKE

THE
Expositor's
Bible
Commentary

with The New International Version

LUKE

Walter L. Liefeld

ZondervanPublishingHouse

Grand Rapids, Michigan

A Division of HarperCollinsPublishers

General Editor:

FRANK E. GAEBELEIN

Former Headmaster, Stony Brook School
Former Coeditor, *Christianity Today*

Associate Editors:

J. D. DOUGLAS

Editor, *The New International
Dictionary of the Christian Church*

RICHARD P. POLCYN

Luke
Copyright © 1995 by Walter L. Liefeld

Requests for information should be addressed to:
    Zondervan Publishing House
    Grand Rapids, Michigan 49530

Library of Congress Cataloging-in-Publication Data

The expositor's Bible commentary : with the New International Version of the Holy Bible /
    Frank E. Gaebelein, general editor of series.
        p.   cm.
    Includes bibliographical references and index.
        Contents: v. 1–2. Matthew / D. A. Carson — Mark / Walter W. Wessel — Luke / Walter
    L. Liefeld — John / Merrill C. Tenney — Acts / Richard N. Longenecker — Romans / Everett
    F. Harrison — 1 and 2 Corinthians / W. Harold Mare and Murray J. Harris — Galatians and
    Ephesians / James Montgomery Boice and A. Skevington Wood
        ISBN: 0-310-50001-X (softcover)
        1. Bible N.T. — Commentaries. I. Gaebelein, Frank Ely, 1899–1983.
    BS2341.2.E96 1995
    220.7-dc 00   94-47450
                                                                                        CIP

Printed in the United States of America

95 96 97 98 99 00 / ❖ DH / 10 9 8 7 6 5 4 3 2

CONTENTS

PREFACE

The title of this work defines its purpose. Written primarily by expositors for expositors, it aims to provide preachers, teachers, and students of the Bible with a new and comprehensive commentary on the books of the Old and New Testaments. Its stance is that of a scholarly evangelicalism committed to the divine inspiration, complete trustworthiness, and full authority of the Bible. Its seventy-eight contributors come from the United States, Canada, England, Scotland, Australia, New Zealand, and Switzerland, and from various religious groups, including Anglican, Baptist, Brethren, Free, Independent, Methodist, Nazarene, Presbyterian, and Reformed churches. Most of them teach at colleges, universities, or theological seminaries.

No book has been more closely studied over a longer period of time than the Bible. From the Midrashic commentaries going back to the period of Ezra, through parts of the Dead Sea Scrolls and the Patristic literature, and on to the present, the Scriptures have been expounded. Indeed, there have been times when, as in the Reformation and on occasions since then, exposition has been at the cutting edge of Christian advance. Luther was a powerful exegete, and Calvin is still called "the prince of expositors."

Their successors have been many. And now, when the outburst of new translations and their unparalleled circulation have expanded the readership of the Bible, the need for exposition takes on fresh urgency.

Not that God's Word can ever become captive to its expositors. Among all other books, it stands first in its combination of perspicuity and profundity. Though a child can be made "wise for salvation" by believing its witness to Christ, the greatest mind cannot plumb the depths of its truth (2 Tim. 3:15; Rom. 11:33). As Gregory the Great said, "Holy Scripture is a stream of running water, where alike the elephant may swim, and the lamb walk." So, because of the inexhaustible nature of Scripture, the task of opening up its meaning is still a perennial obligation of biblical scholarship.

How that task is done inevitably reflects the outlook of those engaged in it. Every biblical scholar has presuppositions. To this neither the editors of these volumes nor the contributors to them are exceptions. They share a common commitment to the supernatural Christianity set forth in the inspired Word. Their purpose is not to supplant the many valuable commentaries that have preceded this work and from which both the editors and contributors have learned. It is rather to draw on the resources of contemporary evangelical scholarship in producing a new reference work for understanding the Scriptures.

A commentary that will continue to be useful through the years should handle contemporary trends in biblical studies in such a way as to avoid becoming outdated when critical fashions change. Biblical criticism is not in itself inadmissible, as some have mistakenly thought. When scholars investigate the authorship, date, literary characteristics, and purpose of a biblical document, they are practicing biblical criticism. So also when, in order to ascertain as nearly as possible the original form of the text, they deal with variant readings, scribal errors, emendations, and other phenomena in the manuscripts. To do these things is essential to responsible exegesis and exposition. And always there is the need to distinguish hypothesis from fact, conjecture from truth.

The chief principle of interpretation followed in this commentary is the grammatico-historical one—namely, that the primary aim of the exegete is to make clear the meaning of the text at the time and in the circumstances of its writing. This endeavor to understand what in the first instance the inspired writers actually said must not be confused with an inflexible literalism. Scripture makes lavish use of symbols and figures of speech; great portions of it are poetical. Yet when it speaks in this way, it speaks no less truly than it does in its historical and doctrinal portions. To understand its message requires attention to matters of grammar and syntax, word meanings, idioms, and literary forms—all in relation to the historical and cultural setting of the text.

The contributors to this work necessarily reflect varying convictions. In certain controversial matters the policy is that of clear statement of the contributors' own views followed by fair presentation of other ones. The treatment of eschatology, though it reflects differences of interpretation, is consistent with a general premillennial position. (Not all contributors, however, are premillennial.) But prophecy is more than prediction, and so this commentary gives due recognition to the major lode of godly social concern in the prophetic writings.

THE EXPOSITOR'S BIBLE COMMENTARY is presented as a scholarly work, though not primarily one of technical criticism. In its main portion, the Exposition, and in Volume 1 (General and Special Articles), all Semitic and Greek words are transliterated and the English equivalents given. As for the Notes, here Semitic and Greek characters are used but always with transliterations and English meanings, so that this portion of the commentary will be as accessible as possible to readers unacquainted with the original languages.

It is the conviction of the general editor, shared by his colleagues in the Zondervan editorial department, that in writing about the Bible, lucidity is not incompatible with scholarship. They are therefore endeavoring to make this a clear and understandable work.

The translation used in it is the New International Version (North American Edition). To The International Bible Society thanks are due for permission to use this most recent of the major Bible translations. The editors and publisher have chosen it because of the clarity and beauty of its style and its faithfulness to the original texts.

Walter C. Kaiser, Jr. and Dr. Bruce K. Waltke for the Old Testament, and Dr. James Montgomery Boice and Dr. Merrill C. Tenney for the New Testament—the general editor expresses his gratitude for their unfailing cooperation and their generosity in advising him out of their expert scholarship. And to the many other contributors he is indebted for their invaluable part in this work. Finally, he owes a special debt of gratitude to Dr. Robert K. DeVries, publisher, The Zondervan Corporation; Richard P. Polcyn, manuscript editor; and Miss Elizabeth Brown, secretary, for their continual assistance and encouragement.

Whatever else it is—the greatest and most beautiful of books, the primary source of law and morality, the fountain of wisdom, and the infallible guide to life—the Bible is above all the inspired witness to Jesus Christ. May this work fulfill its function of expounding the Scriptures with grace and clarity, so that its users may find that both Old and New Testaments do indeed lead to our Lord Jesus Christ, who alone could say, "I have come that they may have life, and have it to the full" (John 10:10).

FRANK E. GAEBELEIN

ABBREVIATIONS

A. General Abbreviations

A	Codex Alexandrinus
Akkad.	Akkadian
א	Codex Sinaiticus
Ap. Lit.	Apocalyptic Literature
Apoc.	Apocrypha
Aq.	Aquila's Greek Translation of the Old Testament
Arab.	Arabic
Aram.	Aramaic
b	Babylonian Gemara
B	Codex Vaticanus
C	Codex Ephraemi Syri
c.	*circa*, about
cf.	*confer*, compare
ch., chs.	chapter, chapters
cod., codd.	codex, codices
contra	in contrast to
D	Codex Bezae
DSS	Dead Sea Scrolls (see E.)
ed., edd.	edited, edition, editor; editions
e.g.	*exempli gratia*, for example
Egyp.	Egyptian
et al.	*et alii*, and others
EV	English Versions of the Bible
fem.	feminine
ff.	following (verses, pages, etc.)
fl.	flourished
ft.	foot, feet
gen.	genitive
Gr.	Greek
Heb.	Hebrew
Hitt.	Hittite
ibid.	*ibidem*, in the same place
id.	*idem*, the same
i.e.	*id est*, that is
impf.	imperfect
infra.	below
in loc.	*in loco*, in the place cited
j	Jerusalem or Palestinian Gemara
Lat.	Latin
LL.	Late Latin
LXX	Septuagint
M	Mishnah
masc.	masculine
mg.	margin
Mid	Midrash
MS(S)	manuscript(s)
MT	Masoretic text

n.	note
n.d.	no date
Nestle	Nestle (ed.) *Novum Testamentum Graece*
no.	number
NT	New Testament
obs.	obsolete
OL	Old Latin
OS	Old Syriac
OT	Old Testament
p., pp.	page, pages
par.	paragraph
Pers.	Persian
Pesh.	Peshitta
Phoen.	Phoenician
pl.	plural
Pseudep.	Pseudepigrapha
Q	Quelle ("Sayings" source in the Gospels)
qt.	quoted by
q.v.	*quod vide*, which see
R	Rabbah
rev.	revised, reviser, revision
Rom.	Roman
RVm	Revised Version margin
Samar.	Samaritan recension
SCM	Student Christian Movement Press
Sem.	Semitic
sing.	singular
SPCK	Society for the Promotion of Christian Knowledge
Sumer.	Sumerian
s.v.	*sub verbo*, under the word
Syr.	Syriac
Symm.	Symmachus
T	Talmud
Targ.	Targum
Theod.	Theodotion
TR	Textus Receptus
tr.	translation, translator, translated
UBS	Tha United Bible Societies' Greek Text
Ugar.	Ugaritic
u.s.	*ut supra*, as above
v., vv.	verse, verses
viz.	*videlicet*, namely
vol.	volume
vs.	versus
Vul.	Vulgate
WH	Westcott and Hort, *The New Testament in Greek*

ix

B. Abbreviations for Modern Translations and Paraphrases

AmT	Smith and Goodspeed, *The Complete Bible, An American Translation*	Mof	J. Moffatt, *A New Translation of the Bible*
ASV	American Standard Version, American Revised Version (1901)	NAB	The New American Bible
		NASB	New American Standard Bible
		NEB	The New English Bible
Beck	Beck, *The New Testament in the Language of Today*	NIV	The New International Version
		Ph	J. B. Phillips *The New Testament in Modern English*
BV	Berkeley Version (The Modern Language Bible)	RSV	Revised Standard Version
		RV	Revised Version — 1881–1885
JB	The Jerusalem Bible	TCNT	Twentieth Century New Testament
JPS	*Jewish Publication Society Version of the Old Testament*		
		TEV	Today's English Version
KJV	King James Version	Wey	*Weymouth's New Testament in Modern Speech*
Knox	R.G. Knox, *The Holy Bible: A Translation from the Latin Vulgate in the Light of the Hebrew and Greek Original*	Wms	C. B. Williams, *The New Testament: A Translation in the Language of the People*
LB	The Living Bible		

C. Abbreviations for Periodicals and Reference Works

AASOR	*Annual of the American Schools of Oriental Research*	BASOR	*Bulletin of the American Schools of Oriental Research*
AB	*Anchor Bible*	BC	Foakes-Jackson and Lake: *The Beginnings of Christianity*
AIs	de Vaux: *Ancient Israel*		
AJA	*American Journal of Archaeology*	BDB	Brown, Driver, and Briggs: *Hebrew-English Lexicon of the Old Testament*
AJSL	*American Journal of Semitic Languages and Literatures*		
		BDF	Blass, Debrunner, and Funk: *A Greek Grammar of the New Testament and Other Early Christian Literature*
AJT	*American Journal of Theology*		
Alf	Alford: *Greek Testament Commentary*		
		BDT	Harrison: *Baker's Dictionary of Theology*
ANEA	*Ancient Near Eastern Archaeology*		
		Beng.	Bengel's *Gnomon*
ANET	Pritchard: *Ancient Near Eastern Texts*	BETS	*Bulletin of the Evangelical Theological Society*
ANF	Roberts and Donaldson: *The Ante-Nicene Fathers*	BH	*Biblia Hebraica*
		BHS	*Biblia Hebraica Stuttgartensia*
ANT	M. R. James: *The Apocryphal New Testament*	BJRL	*Bulletin of the John Rylands Library*
A-S	Abbot-Smith: *Manual Greek Lexicon of the New Testament*	BS	*Bibliotheca Sacra*
		BT	*Babylonian Talmud*
AThR	*Anglican Theological Review*	BTh	*Biblical Theology*
BA	*Biblical Archaeologist*	BW	*Biblical World*
BAG	Bauer, Arndt, and Gingrich: *Greek-English Lexicon of the New Testament*	CAH	*Cambridge Ancient History*
		CanJTh	*Canadian Journal of Theology*
		CBQ	*Catholic Biblical Quarterly*
BAGD	Bauer, Arndt, Gingrich, and Danker: *Greek-English Lexicon of the New Testament* 2nd edition	CBSC	*Cambridge Bible for Schools and Colleges*
		CE	*Catholic Encyclopedia*
		CGT	*Cambridge Greek Testament*

CHS	Lange: *Commentary on the Holy Scriptures*	IDB	*The Interpreter's Dictionary of the Bible*
ChT	*Christianity Today*	IEJ	*Israel Exploration Journal*
DDB	*Davis' Dictionary of the Bible*	Int	*Interpretation*
Deiss BS	Deissmann: *Bible Studies*	INT	E. Harrison: *Introduction to the New Testament*
Deiss LAE	Deissmann: *Light From the Ancient East*	IOT	R. K. Harrison: *Introduction to the Old Testament*
DNTT	*Dictionary of New Testament Theology*	ISBE	*The International Standard Bible Encyclopedia*
EBC	*The Expositor's Bible Commentary*	ITQ	*Irish Theological Quarterly*
EBi	*Encyclopaedia Biblica*	JAAR	*Journal of American Academy of Religion*
EBr	*Encyclopaedia Britannica*	JAOS	*Journal of American Oriental Society*
EDB	*Encyclopedic Dictionary of the Bible*		
EGT	Nicoll: *Expositor's Greek Testament*	JBL	*Journal of Biblical Literature*
EQ	*Evangelical Quarterly*	JE	*Jewish Encyclopedia*
ET	*Evangelische Theologie*	JETS	*Journal of Evangelical Theological Society*
ExB	*The Expositor's Bible*		
Exp	*The Expositor*	JFB	Jamieson, Fausset, and Brown: *Commentary on the Old and New Testament*
ExpT	*The Expository Times*		
FLAP	Finegan: *Light From the Ancient Past*		
GKC	Gesenius, Kautzsch, Cowley, *Hebrew Grammar*, 2nd Eng. ed.	JNES	*Journal of Near Eastern Studies*
		Jos. Antiq.	Josephus: *The Antiquities of the Jews*
GR	*Gordon Review*	Jos. War	Josephus: *The Jewish War*
HBD	*Harper's Bible Dictionary*	JQR	*Jewish Quarterly Review*
HDAC	Hastings: *Dictionary of the Apostolic Church*	JR	*Journal of Religion*
		JSJ	*Journal for the Study of Judaism in the Persian, Hellenistic and Roman Periods*
HDB	Hastings: *Dictionary of the Bible*		
HDBrev.	Hastings: *Dictionary of the Bible*, one-vol. rev. by Grant and Rowley	JSOR	*Journal of the Society of Oriental Research*
		JSS	*Journal of Semitic Studies*
HDCG	Hastings: *Dictionary of Christ and the Gospels*	JT	*Jerusalem Talmud*
		JTS	*Journal of Theological Studies*
HERE	Hastings: *Encyclopedia of Religion and Ethics*	KAHL	Kenyon: *Archaeology in the Holy Land*
HGEOTP	Heidel: *The Gilgamesh Epic and Old Testament Parallels*	KB	Koehler-Baumgartner: *Lexicon in Veteris Testament Libros*
HJP	Schurer: *A History of the Jewish People in the Time of Christ*	KD	Keil and Delitzsch: *Commentary on the Old Testament*
		LSJ	Liddell, Scott, Jones: *Greek-English Lexicon*
HR	Hatch and Redpath: *Concordance to the Septuagint*	LTJM	Edersheim: *The Life and Times of Jesus the Messiah*
HTR	*Harvard Theological Review*	MM	Moulton and Milligan: *The Vocabulary of the Greek Testament*
HUCA	*Hebrew Union College Annual*		
IB	*The Interpreter's Bible*		
ICC	*International Critical Commentary*	MNT	Moffatt: *New Testament Commentary*

xi

MST	McClintock and Strong: *Cyclopedia of Biblical, Theological, and Ecclesiastical Literature*	SJT	*Scottish Journal of Theology*
NBC	Davidson, Kevan, and Stibbs: *The New Bible Commentary*, 1st ed.	SOT	Girdlestone: *Synonyms of Old Testament*
		SOTI	Archer: *A Survey of Old Testament Introduction*
NBCrev.	Guthrie and Motyer: *The New Bible Commentary*, rev. ed.	ST	*Studia Theologica*
		TCERK	Loetscher: *The Twentieth Century Encyclopedia of Religious Knowledge*
NBD	J. D. Douglas: *The New Bible Dictionary*	TDNT	Kittel: *Theological Dictionary of the New Testament*
NCB	*New Century Bible*	TDOT	*Theological Dictionary of the Old Testament*
NCE	*New Catholic Encyclopedia*		
NIC	*New International Commentary*	THAT	*Theologisches Handbuch zum Alten Testament*
NIDCC	Douglas: *The New International Dictionary of the Christian Church*		
		ThT	*Theology Today*
NovTest	*Novum Testamentum*	TNTC	*Tyndale New Testament Commentaries*
NSI	Cooke: *Handbook of North Semitic Inscriptions*		
		Trench	Trench: *Synonyms of the New Testament*
NTS	*New Testament Studies*		
ODCC	*The Oxford Dictionary of the Christian Church*, rev. ed.	TWOT	*Theological Wordbook of the Old Testament*
Peake	Black and Rowley: *Peake's Commentary on the Bible*	UBD	*Unger's Bible Dictionary*
		UT	Gordon: *Ugaritic Textbook*
PEQ	*Palestine Exploration Quarterly*	VB	Allmen: *Vocabulary of the Bible*
PNFl	P. Schaff: *The Nicene and Post-Nicene Fathers* (1st series)		
		VetTest	*Vetus Testamentum*
		Vincent	Vincent: *Word-Pictures in the New Testament*
PNF2	P. Schaff and H. Wace: *The Nicene and Post-Nicene Fathers* (2nd series)		
		WBC	*Wycliffe Bible Commentary*
		WBE	*Wycliffe Bible Encyclopedia*
PTR	*Princeton Theological Review*	WC	*Westminster Commentaries*
RB	*Revue Biblique*	WesBC	*Wesleyan Bible Commentaries*
RHG	Robertson's *Grammar of the Greek New Testament in the Light of Historical Research*	WTJ	*Westminster Theological Journal*
		ZAW	*Zeitschrift für die alttestamentliche Wissenschaft*
RTWB	Richardson: *A Theological Wordbook of the Bible*	ZNW	*Zeitschrift für die neutestamentliche Wissenschaft*
SBK	Strack and Billerbeck: *Kommentar zum Neuen Testament aus Talmud und Midrasch*	ZPBD	*The Zondervan Pictorial Bible Dictionary*
		ZPEB	*The Zondervan Pictorial Encyclopedia of the Bible*
SHERK	*The New Schaff-Herzog Encyclopedia of Religious Knowledge*	ZWT	*Zeitschrift für wissenschaftliche Theologie*

D. Abbreviations for Books of the Bible, the Apocrypha, and the Pseudepigrapha

OLD TESTAMENT

Gen	2 Chron	Dan
Exod	Ezra	Hos
Lev	Neh	Joel
Num	Esth	Amos
Deut	Job	Obad
Josh	Ps(Pss)	Jonah
Judg	Prov	Mic
Ruth	Eccl	Nah
1 Sam	S of Songs	Hab
2 Sam	Isa	Zeph
1 Kings	Jer	Hag
2 Kings	Lam	Zech
1 Chron	Ezek	Mal

NEW TESTAMENT

Matt	1 Tim
Mark	2 Tim
Luke	Titus
John	Philem
Acts	Heb
Rom	James
1 Cor	1 Peter
2 Cor	2 Peter
Gal	1 John
Eph	2 John
Phil	3 John
Col	Jude
1 Thess	Rev
2 Thess	

APOCRYPHA

1 Esd	1 Esdras	Ep Jer	Epistle of Jeremy
2 Esd	2 Esdras	S Th Ch	Song of the Three Children (or Young Men)
Tobit	Tobit		
Jud	Judith	Sus	Susanna
Add Esth	Additions to Esther	Bel	Bel and the Dragon
Wisd Sol	Wisdom of Solomon	Pr Man	Prayer of Manasseh
Ecclus	Ecclesiasticus (Wisdom of Jesus the Son of Sirach)	1 Macc	1 Maccabees
		2 Macc	2 Maccabees
Baruch	Baruch		

PSEUDEPIGRAPHA

As Moses	Assumption of Moses	Pirke Aboth	Pirke Aboth
2 Baruch	Syriac Apocalypse of Baruch	Ps 151	Psalm 151
3 Baruch	Greek Apocalypse of Baruch	Pss Sol	Psalms of Solomon
1 Enoch	Ethiopic Book of Enoch	Sib Oracles	Sibylline Oracles
2 Enoch	Slavonic Book of Enoch	Story Ah	Story of Ahikar
3 Enoch	Hebrew Book of Enoch	T Abram	Testament of Abraham
4 Ezra	4 Ezra	T Adam	Testament of Adam
JA	Joseph and Asenath	T Benjamin	Testament of Benjamin
Jub	Book of Jubilees	T Dan	Testament of Dan
L Aristeas	Letter of Aristeas	T Gad	Testament of Gad
Life AE	Life of Adam and Eve	T Job	Testament of Job
Liv Proph	Lives of the Prophets	T Jos	Testament of Joseph
MA Isa	Martyrdom and Ascension of Isaiah	T Levi	Testament of Levi
		T Naph	Testament of Naphtali
3 Macc	3 Maccabees	T 12 Pat	Testaments of the Twelve Patriarchs
4 Macc	4 Maccabees		
Odes Sol	Odes of Solomon	Zad Frag	Zadokite Fragments
P Jer	Paralipomena of Jeremiah		

E. Abbreviations of Names of Dead Sea Scrolls and Related Texts

CD	Cairo (Genizah text of the) Damascus (Document)	1QSa	Appendix A (Rule of the Congregation) to 1Qs
DSS	Dead Sea Scrolls	1QSb	Appendix B (Blessings) to 1QS
Hev	Nahal Hever texts	3Q15	Copper Scroll from Qumran Cave 3
Mas	Masada Texts		
Mird	Khirbet mird texts	4QExod a	Exodus Scroll, exemplar "a" from Qumran Cave 4
Mur	Wadi Murabba'at texts		
P	Pesher (commentary)	4QFlor	Florilegium (or Eschatological Midrashim) from Qumran Cave 4
Q	Qumran		
1Q, 2Q, etc.	Numbered caves of Qumran, yielding written material; followed by abbreviation of biblical or apocryphal book.	4Qmess ar	Aramaic "Messianic" text from Qumran Cave 4
QL	Qumran Literature	4QpNah	Pesher on portions of Nahum from Qumran Cave 4
1QapGen	Genesis Apocryphon of Qumran Cave 1	4QPrNab	Prayer of Nabonidus from Qumran Cave 4
1QH	*Hodayot* (Thanksgiving Hymns) from Qumran Cave 1	4QpPs37	Pesher on portions of Psalm 37 from Qumran Cave 4
1QIsa a,b	First or second copy of Isaiah from Qumran Cave 1	4QTest	Testimonia text from Qumran Cave 4
1QpHab	Pesher on Habakkuk from Qumran Cave 1	4QTLevi	Testament of Levi from Qumran Cave 4
1QM	*Milhamah* (War Scroll)	4QPhyl	Phylacteries from Qumran Cave 4
1QpMic	Pesher on portions of Micah from Qumran Cave 1	11QMelch	Melchizedek text from Qumran Cave 11
1QS	*Serek Hayyahad* (Rule of the Community, Manual of Discipline)	11QtgJob	Targum of Job from Qumran Cave 11

TRANSLITERATIONS

Hebrew

א = '		ד = $\underline{d}$		י = y		ס = s		ר = r
בּ = b		ה = h		כּ = k		ע = '		שׂ = $\acute{s}$
ב = $\underline{b}$		ו = w		כ ך = $\underline{k}$		פּ = p		שׁ = $\check{s}$
גּ = g		ז = z		ל = l		פ ף = $\underline{p}$		תּ = t
ג = $\underline{g}$		ח = ḥ		ם מ = m		צ ץ = ṣ		ת = $\underline{t}$
דּ = d		ט = ṭ		ן נ = n		ק = q		

(הָ) ָ = $\hat{a}$ (h)	ָ = $\bar{a}$	ַ = a	ֲ = ^{a}
ֵי = $\hat{e}$	ֵ = $\bar{e}$	ֶ = e	ֱ = ^{e}
ִי = $\hat{i}$	ֹ = $\bar{o}$	ִ = i	ְ = ^{e} (if vocal)
וֹ = $\hat{o}$		ָ = o	ֳ = ^{o}
וּ = $\hat{u}$		ֻ = u	

Aramaic

' b g d h w z ḥ ṭ y k l m n s ' p ṣ q r ś š t

Arabic

' b t ṯ ǧ ḥ ḫ d ḏ r z s š ṣ ḍ ṭ ẓ ' ġ f q k l m n h w y

Ugaritic

' b g d ḏ h w z ḥ ḫ ṭ ẓ y k l m n s ṣ ' ġ p ṣ q r š t ṯ

Greek

α	—	a	π	—	p	αι	—	ai
β	—	b	ρ	—	r	αυ	—	au
γ	—	g	σ,ς	—	s	ει	—	ei
δ	—	d	τ	—	t	ευ	—	eu
ε	—	e	υ	—	y	ηυ	—	ēu
ζ	—	z	φ	—	ph	οι	—	oi
η	—	ē	χ	—	ch	ου	—	ou
θ	—	th	ψ	—	ps	υι	—	hui
ι	—	i	ω	—	ō			
κ	—	k				ῥ	—	rh
λ	—	l	γγ	—	ng	ʽ	—	h
μ	—	m	γκ	—	nk			
ν	—	n	γξ	—	nx	ᾳ	—	ā
ξ	—	x	γχ	—	nch	ῃ	—	ē
ο	—	o				ῳ	—	ō

LUKE

Walter L. Liefeld

LUKE

Introduction

Had modern methods of book publishing been available in the first century, the books of Luke and Acts might have been found standing side by side in paperback editions on a bookseller's shelf. Possibly they would have been bound together in one hardback volume. Though Acts has some characteristics of the ancient novel, this need not be understood as impugning its historical value. One can picture a Gentile reader going from adventure to adventure, delighting in the story of Paul's shipwreck and learning something of the gospel through reading the various speeches. Likewise the Gospel of Luke contains narratives and sayings of Jesus cast in a variety of literary forms. No doubt among its readers would have been the "God-fearers," those Gentiles who had already been convinced of Jewish monotheism and of Jewish ethical standards.[1] They, in turn, would have interested their friends in reading Luke-Acts.

1. Literary Genre

It is difficult for us today to know with what literary genre, if any, the first-century reader would have identified the Gospels. There has been much discussion of this in recent years. R.H. Gundry has evaluated the literature up to the early 1970s in "Recent Investigations into the Literary Genre 'Gospel.'"[2] More recently David E. Aune has provided an excellent discussion of some of the alleged first-century parallels to the Gospels, as well as a critical evaluation of twentieth-century

---

[1]See, however, Max Wilcox, "The God-Fearers in Acts-A Reconsideration," *Journal for the Study of the New Testament* 13 (1981): 102–22.

[2]In *New Dimensions in New Testament Study*, pp. 97–114. See also Frank E. Gaebelein, "The Bible as Literature," ZPEB, 3:944.

approaches, in his article "The Problem of Genre of the Gospels: A Critique of C. H. Talbert's *What Is a Gospel?* "[3]

2. Distinctive Features

Before proceeding further it will be helpful at least to recognize some of the distinctive features of Luke's Gospel, especially in comparison with other Gospels. Among these are Jesus' concern for all people, especially those who were social outcasts—the poor, women, and those who were known as "sinners"; Luke's universal scope; his alteration of some of the terminology of Mark to facilitate the understanding of Luke's readers—e.g., the Greek term for "lawyer" (*nomikos*) instead of the Hebrew term "scribe" (*grammateus*); an emphasis on Jesus' practical teaching (e.g., chs. 12 and 16 deal with finances); Luke's sense of purpose, fulfillment, and accomplishment; his sense of joy and praise to God for his saving and healing work; Jesus' strong call to discipleship; Jesus' dependence on the Holy Spirit and prayer; and many examples of the power of God.

In the first century, when pagans had not only long since turned from the traditional gods but had also wrestled unsuccessfully with issues of luck and fate and had turned to the false hopes of the so-called Eastern or mystery religions, such a narrative as Luke's doubtless had a genuine appeal. Here was a "Savior" who actually lived and cared about people. He was here among people; he was crucified and actually raised from the dead. And Luke tells all this with a conviction and verisimilitude that brought assurance to Theophilus and continues to bring assurance down to our day.

3. Authorship

The unique relation of Luke to Acts sets the authorship of Luke apart from the problem of the authorship of the other Gospels. The following facts are important: (1) both Luke and Acts are addressed to an individual named Theophilus (Luke 1:3; Acts 1:1); (2) Acts refers to a previous work (1:1), presumably Luke; (3) certain stylistic and structural characteristics, such as the use of chiasm and the device of focusing on particular individuals, are common to both books and point to a single author; and (4) not only do the two volumes have a number of themes in common, but some of these receive a distinctive emphasis in this third Gospel that are not found elsewhere in the NT. These things point to a common author.

The author of the Gospel indicated that he was a second-generation Christian who was in a position to investigate the traditions about Jesus. As for the Book of Acts, the author associated himself with Paul in the well-known "we-passages" (Acts 16:10–17; 20:5–15; 21:1–18; 27:1–28:16). The use of the first person plural in the "we passages" certainly does not prove that Luke was the author of Acts, but it does accord with other data pointing in this direction.[4] Paul mentioned Luke as a

---

[3]In R.T. France and D. Wenham, edd., *Gospel Perspectives*, 2:9–60.

[4]See V.K. Robbins, "The We–Passages in Acts and Ancient Sea Voyages," *Biblical Research* 20 (1975): 5–18, for a negative assessment; R.N. Longenecker, "Acts," EBC, 9:235–38 in support of Lukan authorship.

Acts written by Luke?

companion in Colossians 4:14, Philemon 24, and 2 Timothy 4:11 (assuming a genuine tradition of Paul here).

The tradition of the early church is consistent in attributing the third Gospel to Luke. Thus the Muratorian Canon (c. A.D. 180) says, "The third book of the Gospel, according to Luke, Luke that physician, who after the ascension of Christ, when Paul had taken him with him as companion of his journey, composed in his own name on the basis of report." But even before this, the heretic Marcion (c. A.D. 135) acknowledged Luke as the author of the third Gospel. This tradition of authorship was continued by Irenaeus and successive writers.

As seen in the above quotation from the Muratorian Canon, tradition also held that Luke was a physician (cf. 4:14). In 1882 Hobart attempted to prove that Luke and Acts "were written by the same person, and that the writer was a medical man" (p. xxix). His study of the alleged medical language is informed, rich, and still useful; but it does not necessarily prove his point. Cadbury argued that though the terminology cited by Hobart was used by medical writers in the ancient world, others who were by no means physicians also used it.[5] Cadbury's work does not, of course, disprove that Luke was a physician, much less that he wrote Luke and Acts; but it does weaken the linguistic evidence for the former assumption.

Irenaeus not only attested to Luke's authorship of the Gospel but also said that Luke was Paul's "inseparable" companion (Adversus Haereses 3.14.1). While there were periods of time when Luke was not with Paul, their relationship was deep and lasting. Taking 2 Timothy 4:11 as a genuine comment of Paul's, only Luke was with him during his final imprisonment. Paul's comment in Colossians 4 leads us to assume Luke was a Gentile, because in vv.10–11 Paul listed several friends and said, "These are the only Jews among my fellow workers for the kingdom of God." Then he mentioned Luke (v.14). This, however, falls short of a direct statement that Luke was a Gentile. Some have held that he was a Jewish Christian, even (according to an early church tradition) one of the seventy-two disciples in Luke 10:1. The Semitic elements of style in Luke, especially in chapters 1–2 and in the Jerusalem narrative in Acts (chs. 1–15), might also suggest that he was a Jewish Christian. But as we shall note below, there are other possible reasons for these stylistic traits. There is a church tradition that Luke came from Antioch in Syria. It is generally accepted, not on its own authority, but because of Luke's involvement with the church in Antioch. This would mean, of course, that Luke was not (as some think) the "man of Macedonia" Paul saw in his vision at Troas (Acts 16:8–9).[6]

4. Purpose

Can we discern a single purpose for the Gospel of Luke? The answer must be based on a consideration of the prologue to the Gospel (1:1–4),[7] of the apparent purposes of Acts (cf. Longenecker, "Acts," EBC, 9:216–21), of the major themes and

---

[5]Henry J. Cadbury, The Style and Literary Method of Luke, pp. 39–72.

[6]For more detail and a citation of scholars on each side of this question, see Joseph A. Fitzmyer, The Gospel According to Luke I–IX (Garden City: Doubleday, 1981), pp. 35–53, 59–61.

[7]Schuyler Brown, "The Role of the Prologue in Determining the Purpose of Luke-Acts," in Talbert, Perspectives, pp. 99–111.

theology of the book, and of its life situation. The following proposals are worth weighing.

a. Evangelism

The centrality of the theme and theology of salvation and the frequent proclamation of Good News, both in Luke and in Acts, make the evangelization of non-Christians a possible purpose for Luke-Acts.

b. Confirmation of the factual basis for faith

This is supported by the prologue (Luke 1:1–4), the historical references throughout the two books, the references to eyewitnesses (e.g., Luke 1:2; Acts 10:39), and the apologetic value of proof from prophecy (e.g., Acts 10:43).

c. Personal assurance

Confirmation of the factual basis for faith is not sufficient unless it brings a corresponding conviction and assurance within the reader. Luke 1:4 says that Luke wrote so that Theophilus might "know the certainty of the things" he had "been taught."

d. Narration of history

Did Luke write simply because he sensed the need of preserving the record of the origin and growth of the early church? Few, if any, ancient writers wrote history simply to preserve a chronicle of events. Also, it would be difficult to explain the disproportionate space given to early events and figures in the life of the church if Luke were merely doing a historical chronicle. Fitzmyer (*Gospel of Luke*, p. 9) sees value in Nils Dahl's proposal that this is a "continuation of biblical history" in that it shows the validity of apostolic tradition as part of that continuity and locus of salvation truth. But see further at "f" below.

e. An apologetic

One version of this purpose, which was occasionally proposed in an earlier generation, was that Luke wrote Acts as a brief for Paul's trial at Rome. The contents are too broad for that purpose, and it does not explain the Gospel of Luke. A more likely proposal is that the Gospel is an apologetic for Christianity as a religious sect. Jews had certain rights under the Roman Empire, and Luke may have written to demonstrate that Christianity should also have such rights as a *religio licita* ("legitimate religion") along with Pharisaism and the other sects of Judaism. At his trials Paul tried to identify himself with Judaism, especially Pharisaism. He himself called Christianity a "sect" in Acts 24:14, a term used in the accusation against him in v.5.

f. Solution of a theological problem

It has been common in recent years to assume that Luke was writing to explain the delay of the Parousia. According to this theory, proposed by Conzelmann and others, the early Christians were troubled because Christ did not return immediately as they had expected; and they therefore needed both assurance and some explanation for this delay. This is questionable and will be dealt with below (cf. 11.k). Another possible problem relates to the identity of the Christian church with

Israel. Is the church a new entity? Are all Christians to be considered part of Israel spiritually, or is there some other way to view this new group (cf. below at 11.j)?

g. Conciliation

The well-known contention of F.C. Baur and the so-called Tübingen School was that the Book of Acts was an example of the Hegelian principle of thesis, antithesis, and synthesis. Baur and his group saw Peter and Paul as representing opposing parties, with Luke trying to bring the antithetical viewpoints together in a synthesis of organized, normative Christianity. That there were differences is obvious, and Luke may well have written in part to show that these differences were not unresolvable. But the process as described by Tübingen scholars does not fit the facts and requires too long a period of time.

h. Defense against heresy

During the period when Gnosticism was being proposed as a problem dealt with by several NT books, C.H. Talbert proposed a short-lived hypothesis that Luke was written against this heresy. Not only is there insufficient evidence in Luke's writings to support this, but it also leaves unanswered the question as to why so much else is included in these books that is not relevant to the Gnostic issue.

i. Instruction

This is a very general proposal, which covers a great deal of what we have in these writings. As a generality the proposal is valid but lacks focus.

j. Dealing with social problems

Recent works have made a good deal of the prominence of the theme of poverty and wealth in both Luke and Acts (cf. n.34). This concern was hardly large enough in comparison to other more major matters to be considered a major purpose for Luke's writing, but it does call for a response from the reader.

k. Multiple purposes

If none of the above qualifies as *the* purpose for the writing of Luke-Acts, is it then wrong to seek a single overarching purpose in Luke? Should we think instead of primary and secondary purposes? If we take this approach, almost everything mentioned above has value. In this case we may take the prologue to the Gospel as articulating the primary purpose of not only the Gospel but, at least to an extent, of Acts as well, providing enough information about Jesus to supplement the instruction Theophilus had already received, to confirm him in his faith. By extrapolation we may assume that Luke wrote to bring the gospel, and the assurance of salvation that follows its acceptance, to a larger audience than Theophilus. This certainly does not exclude subsidiary purposes, especially in the second volume (Acts). Since Luke clearly distinguishes the second volume from the first, there is no reason why he could not have accomplished his purpose mainly in the first volume and then continued the story of "all that Jesus began to do and teach" in the second one to accomplish yet further objectives.

If in addition to winning and establishing individual converts, Luke is concerned with forwarding the Christian movement, such subsidiary aims as establishing the legitimacy of that movement as a true sect of Judaism, demonstrating the innocence of Jesus and Paul at their trials, clarifying the relationship of Jewish and Gentile believers to Israel, and rooting the Gospel record in Jewish and secular history all have their place. It was important for Luke to deal with specific problems, whether eschatological or social, if such problems threatened to hinder the forward movement of the church. Far from producing a simplistic or a fragmented work, the author (Luke) brings together all the data and addresses all the issues he feels it necessary to deal with in order to advance Christ's cause throughout the world.

5. Intended Readership

Any conclusions as to the readership of the Gospel must be drawn primarily from the prologue (1:1–4) and secondarily from conclusions about the purpose of the Gospel. As to the first, see the commentary on 1:1–4 for remarks about Theophilus. From our brief survey of theories about Luke's purpose, it would appear that while Luke-Acts had an appeal to the non-Christian, Luke expected and desired it to be read by Christians, especially new converts. Some of the characteristics of the Gospel, such as its orientation to the secular world, its references to Judaism, its Septuagintisms, along with the prominence of God-fearers in both books, make it plausible that Luke had those God-fearers in mind. They were Gentiles (though see n.1), at home in secular society but monotheistic by conviction; and they were accustomed to hearing the Jewish Scriptures read in the synagogue, though not familiar with Palestinian geography and society. Like the God-fearers reached through Paul's mission (cf. the Acts narrative), they formed an ideal bridge from the synagogue to the Gentile world. It is possible, though unprovable, that Luke himself had been a God-fearer. While it is impossible to restrict Luke's readership to the God-fearers, it is difficult to imagine him writing without at least having them in mind.[8]

6. Literary Characteristics

Moulton called Luke "the only *littérateur* among the authors of NT books."[9] He said this mainly because of Luke's rare use of the optative. To Moulton, Luke was a Greek who had the "native instinct" not only to write well but to vary his style scene by scene. While there is no uniform agreement today regarding Luke's background or the reasons for his distinctive style, nevertheless his writings are generally held to be superb in style and in structure.[10]

---

[8]Maddox (p. 187) says, "[Luke] writes to reassure the Christians of his day that their faith in Jesus is no aberration, but the authentic goal towards which God's ancient dealings with Israel were driving."

[9]James Hope Moulton, *A Grammar of New Testament Greek*, vol. 2, *Accidence and Word-Formation*, ed. W.F. Howard (Edinburgh: T. & T. Clark, 1929), p. 7.

[10]Cf. Cadbury, *Style and Method of Luke*, who demonstrates the excellence of Luke's style. Among Luke's distinctive words are many with a literary flavor, medical terms (see earlier on Hobart's theory and Cadbury's response), and distinctive theological terms. The following are the major sources for word statistics: Gaston, *Horae Synopticae Electronicae*; Hawkins, *Horae Synopticae*; R. Morgenthaler, *Statistik des neutestamentlichen Wortschatzes*.

As to the linguistic and syntactical idioms of Luke's Gospel, we find a mystifying combination of literary Greek and Semitic style. The latter includes expressions characteristic of Hebrew, Aramaic, or both, and Septuagintisms. This "translation Greek" betrays its Hebrew or Aramaic original. Some of these characteristics can be easily seen in familiar KJV expressions such as "he answering said" (where the participle "answering" is redundant, e.g., 1:19; 4:12; 5:5, 22, 31), "before the face of" (e.g., 2:31), the use of the verb *egeneto* with a finite verb (familiar from the KJV "it came to pass that . . ."), and the intensive "with desire I have desired" (22:15), to name a few. (NIV's idiomatic renderings generally eliminate these awkward expressions.)

These characteristics occur more often in Luke 1 and 2 and in Acts 1–15 than in the rest of the books. There are fewer such in the "we passages," which leads Turner to suggest that these are from a diary Luke wrote earlier than he did the rest of the work, before he was exposed to Septuagintal idioms through Paul.[11]

Among the theories advanced to explain this occurrence of Hebrew and Aramaic "interference" in Luke's fine Greek style and the traces of Septuagintal influence are (1) Luke was actually Jewish; (2) he was a Gentile but had a long exposure to Semitic idioms; (3) he was a Greek who perhaps unconsciously adopted a Septuagintal style, possibly through association with Paul; (4) he artificially affected a Semitic style to give a ring of genuineness to certain sections of his works; and (5) at times he was using a source with a tradition that went back to a Semitic original. Though these idioms occur in some places more heavily than in others, they are found scattered throughout Luke's works. Of the theories mentioned above, the most likely are (2), supported by Fitzmyer, or (3), supported by Turner, with (5) applying in certain parts. The idea of a Semitic source behind Luke 1–2 has received recent cautious support from S.C. Farris's "On Discerning Semitic Sources in Luke 1–2,"[12] based on the research of R.A. Martin.

As to structure, Luke also shows literary skill. Talbert (*Literary Patterns*) has demonstrated Luke's ability to use the device of chiasm (a sequence of topics repeated in reverse order) as a major structural means of presenting his message. Talbert notes other examples of this in some of the finest Greek writings. It is widely acknowledged that the two books attributed to Luke exhibit a unit of structure (which, as noted above, is significant with regard to the issue of authorship). Cadbury has observed two striking pairs of stylistic characteristics.[13] The first is "repetition and variation," i.e., Luke at times has obvious repetitions—e.g., "the growth of a child in Luke 1:80; 2:40; 2:52" (to which we could add the growth of the church under the favor of God and of people, Acts 2:47). The second pair of characteristics is "distribution and concentration." By this he means the tendency to use a term frequently in a passage or in a sequence of passages, only to use it rarely or never elsewhere. All in all it is evident that Luke's writings are rich in linguistic, stylistic, and structural creativity.

---

[11]James Hope Moulton, *A Greek Grammar of the New Testament*, vol. 4, *Style*, Nigel Turner (Edinburgh: T. & T. Clark, 1976), p. 55, cf. p. 61. The most useful survey of data is by Fitzmyer, *Gospel of Luke*, pp. 107–25. For a useful survey of scholarship on this matter, see Fred Horton, "Reflections on the Semitisms of Luke-Acts," in Talbert, *Perspectives*, pp. 1–23.

[12]In France and Wenham, *Gospel Perspectives*, vol. 2. The Semitic character of Luke 1–2 also forms a significant step in establishing the historicity of the Virgin Birth in Machen, pp. 62–101.

[13]Henry J. Cadbury, "Four Features of Lucan Style," in Keck and Martyn, pp. 87–102.

7. Method of Composition

Since the synoptic problem and the proposed frameworks for its solution involve some of the same data for Matthew as for Luke, the reader should consult the introduction to Donald A. Carson's commentary on Matthew in this volume (see also "The Synoptic Gospels" by J. Julius Scott, Jr., EBC, 1:501–14).

The first written Gospel in the NT form was probably Mark. Matthew apparently had access to Mark, as well as other traditions that contained sayings of Jesus. These other traditions are referred to by scholars as "Q," but whether or not that was a written collection is now impossible to determine. Scholars have been increasingly reluctant to accept the hypothesis of the relation of Matthew and Luke to the two sources of Mark and "Q"; but it still seems to be, with modifications, the most satisfactory hypothesis at this time. In the reconstruction of synoptic traditions by Streeter,[14] he called the other material known to Luke beside Mark and "Q" by the letter "L." Although this terminology is less used today, it is customary to assume that, in addition to other materials, Luke had one main special source. The parts of the Gospel unique to Luke include 1:5–2:52 (birth and childhood narratives); 3:10–14 (John the Baptist's ethical teaching); 7:12–17 (the raising of the widow of Nain's son); a good deal of the material in 9:51–19:44; and a number of incidents in the passion narrative, along with other small sections.[15] Whether, as Streeter and others have supposed, Luke wrote an earlier Gospel (which Streeter called "Proto-Luke") before he became acquainted with Mark or with the content of his first two chapters is extremely doubtful.

Since publication of Conzelmann's work *Die Mitte der Zeit* in 1953 (English tr., *The Theology of St. Luke*), major attention has been given to the redaction criticism of Luke. The term comes from the German *Redaktionsgeschichte* and has to do with the analysis of the editorial work of an author as he shaped the written or oral materials that came to his hand. To some this implies creativity to the extent of changing or slanting the materials received for the purpose of imposing the editor's theological viewpoint on that material. Such a radical handling of sources is, however, not a necessary presupposition to a redactional study of the synoptic Gospels. There is no question but that each of the Gospels contributes a distinctive perspective on the life and teachings of the Lord Jesus. It is to the enrichment of our total understanding of the person and work of Christ that we thoroughly investigate these distinct contributions. But extreme caution is needed lest we superimpose on the Gospel the supposed conditions of the church communities at the time Luke wrote and to do this so as to alter what Jesus actually taught. The same caution applies to superimposing our own schemes of theology on the Gospel.[16]

In 1971 Schramm[17] showed that much of the distinctive material in Luke was due not so much to his redactional activity as to his use of sources different from those available to Matthew and Mark. Also it has long been assumed that many of the differences in Luke are due to his stylistic improvements of Mark. Various scholars have analyzed individual pericopes (sections) of Luke to determine the extent of his

---

[14]B.H. Streeter, *The Four Gospels* (New York: Macmillan), 1930.

[15]For a fuller list, a useful discussion of the entire matter of Luke's sources, and a full bibliography, see Fitzmyer, *Gospel of Luke*, pp. 63–106.

[16]See also section 11 below on "Themes and Theology."

[17]T. Schramm, *Der Markus-Stoff bei Lukas*.

redaction A recent example is Bruce Chilton's "Announcement in Nazara: An Analysis of Luke 4:16–21."[18] The most detailed study of the passion narrative was done in a series of studies originally published as separate monographs by H. Schürmann.[19] There are, in summary, three main reasons why a passage in Luke may be different from parallel passages in Matthew or Mark: theology, literary style, and source material.

Those who have engaged in redaction criticism of Luke have not necessarily followed the radical conclusions of Conzelmann. One of the first full-scale responses was that of Helmut Flender. His work included a fascinating study of the dialectical structure of Luke-Acts, which has not received complete acceptance. Robinson employed a redactional approach but criticized Conzelmann and proposed a geographical scheme for Luke's theology.[20] Another major study that counters some of Conzelmann's ideas is Schuyler Brown's *Apostasy and Perseverance*. Brown debates Conzelmann's theory that between the temptation of Jesus and the betrayal of Judas, Satan was not actively opposing the ministry of Jesus. Brown answers this by reexamining the meaning of *peirasmos* ("temptation" or "trial") in Luke.

The negative assessment Conzelmann made of Luke's knowledge of Palestinian geography and of historical matters has also been challenged by a number of writers. The finest assessment of Luke as both a theologian and a historian is Marshall's *Luke: Historian and Theologian*. Nevertheless a good deal of skepticism about Luke's accuracy persists, and unfortunately redaction criticism is often carried on under such negative assumptions.

One of the more recent approaches to the material in the Gospels is that of structuralism. This does not pertain uniquely to Luke; and it is a large, complex, and much-debated approach. Structuralism seeks to understand reality—relating to sociology and a number of other disciplines as well as to linguistics and literature—in what might be called universal terms. Scholars using it construct theoretical structural models to explain particular linguistic and literary elements, such as the roles and actions within a narrative or parable.[21]

A final comment on Luke's method of composition relates to the central section of the Gospel (9:51–19:44). This part has no parallel in the other Gospels, though some of the stories and parables within it do. It has long been a matter of debate whether Luke is merely following some literary or historical procedure in the composition of this section, or whether he has some theological purpose in mind. The most persistent supposition is that he is consciously constructing a parallel to Deuteronomy.

---

[18] In France and Wenham, *Gospel Perspectives*, 2:147–72.

[19] *Der Paschamahlbericht, Der Einsetzungsbericht* (Münster: Aschendorffsche Verlagsanstalt, 1955), and *Jesu Abschiedsrede*.

[20] W.C. Robinson, Jr., *Der Weg des Herrn*.

[21] The following works are useful for understanding structuralism: R. Barthes et al., *Structural Analysis and Biblical Exegesis: Interpretational Essays*, tr. A.M. Johnson, Jr., Pittsburgh Theological Monograph Series Number 3 (Pittsburgh: Pickwick, 1974); Daniel Patte, *What is Structural Exegesis?* New Testament Guides to Biblical Scholarship Series (Philadelphia: Fortress, 1976); Daniel and Aline Patte, *Structural Exegesis: From Theory to Practice* (Philadelphia: Fortress, 1978); R.M. Polzin, *Biblical Structuralism: Method and Subjectivity in the Ancient Texts* (Philadelphia: Fortress, 1977); V.S. Poythress, "Structuralism and Biblical Studies," JETS 21 (1978); Robert W. Funk, ed., "A Structuralist Approach to the Parables," *Semeia* 1 (1978); A.C. Thiselton, "Keeping Up With Recent Studies: II. Structuralism and Biblical Studies: Method or Ideology?" ExpT 89 (1977–78): 329–35. On the state of parable research in particular, see Carson's introduction to Matthew in this volume.

(For further remarks and a bibliography on this subject, see the introduction to that section in the commentary.)

8. Text

There are some textual problems in Luke that demand the attention of the exegete, though not so many as in Acts. In general the so-called Alexandrian tradition of the text has proved reliable, especially since the discovery in 1961 of the papyrus P[75]. In some cases (e.g., Luke 22:19b–20; 24:3, 6, 12, 36, 40, 51–52) the omission of words from the so-called Western text, which tends to add rather than omit words, was so unusual that these omissions were considered significant. Recent studies have challenged that assessment,[22] and it is fairly certain that the inclusion of the wording in question in the Alexandrian text tradition is correct. See remarks on the verses in question in the Notes portions of the commentary.[23]

9. History and Geography

Discussion of the historical value of Luke usually proceeds along one or more of the following lines: (1) Luke's careful observation of the historical setting of his narratives; (2) the question as to whether a work so tendential, so committed to establishing certain theological conclusions, can possibly be historically objective; (3) the authenticity and accuracy of Luke's sources; (4) his own claim to historical accuracy in his introduction; (5) problems caused by apparent errors (e.g., his reference to the census under Quirinius in 2:1–2; see commentary in loc.); and (6) apparent discrepancies between Luke and the other Gospels.

The first of these has to do with the kind of data collected by W.M. Ramsay in his well-known works[24] and by A.N. Sherwin-White.[25] Cassidy (p. 13) calls these data "empire history," that is, things "within the broad category of political affairs . . . [such as] the description of rulers and officials . . . the dating of specific events in relation to other events more widely known throughout the empire" and so on. It is important to recognize that where Luke can be checked historically (except for the few problem texts under 8 above), his accuracy has been validated. We should, however, acknowledge that this does not in itself guarantee Luke's accuracy in everything he relates.

Second, as indicated earlier, Luke's theological intentions should not be taken as invalidating his historical accuracy. Even so careful a scholar as Fitzmyer assumes that Luke's theological concern sets him apart from both ancient and modern historians, noting that his introduction "reveals his historical concern as subordinate to a theological one" (*Gospel of Luke*, p. 16). But it does not logically follow that

---

[22]So K. Snodgrass, "Western Non-Interpolations."

[23]See also Gordon D. Fee, "The Textual Criticism of the New Testament," EBC, 1:419–33, and Fitzmyer, *Gospel of Luke*, pp. 128–33.

[24]E.g., *St. Paul the Traveller and the Roman Citizen* (New York: Putnam, 1898); *Was Christ Born in Bethlehem?*; *The Bearing of Recent Discovery on the Trustworthiness of the New Testament* (1915, reprint, Grand Rapids: Baker, 1953).

[25]*Roman Society and Roman Law*.

because historical concern is subordinate, error must result.[26] Likewise we must remember that other ancient historians were seeking to establish certain viewpoints as they wrote their histories.

Third, the matter of sources was briefly discussed under Method of Composition above. So was the question of whether Luke's use of Semitic constructions indicates Semitic source material (cf. Literary Characteristics). If it does, the presence of such sources (with the tradition handed down either in the original Semitic idiom or in Septuagintal Greek) points to an early Palestinian origin of the book. Though this does not guarantee authenticity or accuracy, it certainly increases their probability. It appears that in some instances Luke follows an even earlier tradition than Matthew or Mark does. An example is the tradition of the institution of the Lord's Supper, where the wording in Luke is close to that found in 1 Corinthians 11, which had probably been committed to writing earlier than Matthew or Mark. Apparently both Luke and Paul had access to a very early tradition.

Fourth, the terminology of Luke's prologue (1:1–4) certainly implies careful historical research. Such a claim to historical accuracy does not in itself prove accuracy. But the honesty of the writer in distinguishing himself from the eyewitnesses and the care he took to provide an orderly, accurate account cannot be overlooked. Historians in the ancient world were, contrary to what many have thought, interested in accurate reporting.[27]

Fifth, there are indeed several serious historical problems in Luke's writings, such as the reference to Quirinius (Luke 2:2) and the reference to Theudas (Acts 5:36–37). A few others are more easily handled. Nevertheless, as the commentary shows, there are possible solutions that obviate extreme skepticism as to Luke's historical accuracy.

Sixth, the issues involved in the apparent discrepancies between the Gospels are so complex as to preclude brief discussion of them here. However, it must at least be said that, unfortunately, attempts at reasonable reconciliation are often summarily dismissed as "harmonization," as though any attempt to give the benefit of the doubt to one of two parallel ancient documents was somehow unworthy. To think that one can either "prove" or "disprove" the historical value of an ancient historical work on the basis of the slight amount of information we have about the remote events it deals with is presumptuous.

10. Date

The dating of Luke depends largely on four factors: (1) the date of Mark and Luke's relationship to it, (2) the date of Acts, (3) the reference to the destruction of Jerusalem in chapter 21, and (4) the theological and ecclesiastical tone of Luke-Acts.

First, the date of Mark is, of course, relevant only if Luke used Mark as one of his sources. That probability is strong enough to assume here. With rare exceptions, scholars today hold that Mark was written about A.D. 70, probably just a few years before that date, which was marked by the destruction of Jerusalem. Yet there is no compelling reason why it could not have been written a few years earlier, toward

---

[26]See the strong comments on this topic by Martin Hengel in *Acts and the History of Earliest Christianity*, tr. J. Bowden (Philadelphia: Fortress, 1979), pp. 59–68.

[27]See A.W. Mosley, "Historical Reporting in the Ancient World," NTS 12 (1965–66): 10–26.

A.D. 60. At this time it is not possible to be certain about this (cf. Introduction to Mark in this volume).

Second, the issues surrounding the date of Acts are more complex (cf. Longenecker, "Acts," EBC, 9:235–38). Presumably Luke completed his Gospel before writing Acts, though this has been debated. Apart from its connection with the writing of the Gospel and the implications of the theological climate of the two books, which will be discussed below, the main considerations in the dating of Acts relate to the time of Paul's imprisonment and the date of the Neronian persecution. Acts 28:30 takes leave of Paul with a reference to his two-year imprisonment at Rome. This is generally agreed to have taken place around A.D. 60 to 62. This provides a *terminus a quo* for the date of Acts. The fact that there is no record in Acts of the subsequent persecution under Nero in A.D. 65 and of Paul's death at about that time suggests that Luke wrote Acts before these events. There is no hint of further hostilities between the Jews and the Romans or of the climax in A.D. 70. One might have expected Luke to cite the destruction of Jerusalem in his attempt to show the innocence of Christianity and the culpability of the Jewish rulers. On the ground of these historical matters alone, Acts can be dated anywhere between A.D. 61 and 65, probably around A.D. 63 or 64.

Third, Luke's reference to the destruction of Jerusalem in his version of the Olivet Discourse (21:8–36) complicates the problem of dating the Gospel. Most scholars see it as a *vaticinium ex eventu,* a "prophecy" given after the event. In that case Luke would have added sufficient detail to the discourse in Mark 13, once the event had occurred, to show his readers what he thought Jesus must have intended. An obvious response to this, though not in itself conclusive, is that one cannot assume that Jesus did not, or could not, actually have included Jerusalem in his prediction. Also, if Luke had adapted the prediction to the event, it is strange that he did not also modify the prediction of the accompanying apocalyptic events, including the coming of the Son of Man. These did not happen in A.D. 70, at least in the literal sense in which Luke probably would have understood them (cf. Morris, *Luke,* p. 23). But the conventional apocalyptic terminology does stand in Luke 21, and the passage has very little additional detail about the destruction of Jerusalem, as might be expected were it written after the event. Furthermore, if Jesus had, either explicitly or implicitly, referred in the Olivet Discourse to the destruction of Jerusalem, why was Luke the only one of the synoptic writers to include that specific reference, unless he were indeed writing after the event? The answer would seem to be that it is only Luke who throughout his Gospel stresses Jerusalem as the city of destiny. His Gospel opens with a scene in the temple in Jerusalem; Jesus is constantly pressing toward Jerusalem (see commentary passim); and Luke includes a lament of Jesus over the city (19:41–44). It is natural that he would pick up any tradition of Jesus' words about the fate of that city, even before the event occurred. The question of whether Jesus specifically predicted the Fall of Jerusalem and whether Luke wrote chapter 21 before or after the event should, therefore, not be decided subjectively.

Fourth, another reason why many date Acts and also Luke later (even as late as the early second century) is that they believe Acts reflects a theological climate and ecclesiastical situation nonexistent in the 60s or 70s. They base their view largely on the assumption that the author of Acts shows little knowledge of the apostle Paul as the early epistles portray him and also that the author reflects a view of the church more in common with the later Pastoral Epistles and "early Catholicism." On this complex matter, see I. Howard Marshall's " 'Early Catholicism' in the New Testament," in Longenecker and Tenney (*New Dimensions*, pp. 217–31), and Longenecker's Introduction to Acts (EBC, 9:235–38). Longenecker offers several internal evidences for an early date for Acts. See also the discussion in Ellis, *Gospel of Luke* (pp. 44–51), and his treatment of the date of Luke (pp. 55–60). Among other points, Ellis sees evidences in Luke of a troublesome time such as that begun by the Neronian persecution. He prefers a date around A.D. 70 for Luke. In my judgment the only compelling reason for assigning a date much earlier than this would be the lack of allusions in Acts to the death of Paul and to the Neronian persecution. Even this conclusion is based on the assumption that Luke would have alluded to such events had he written later—though he might not have done so if he had intended to write a third volume covering that period. All things considered, then, it seems preferable to date the completion of Luke's two works somewhere in the decade of A.D. 60–70.

11. Themes and Theology

A word of caution is necessary on beginning this section. Fitzmyer (*Gospel of Luke*, pp. 6ff.) has warned against superimposing a "thesis" about Lukan theology on the data of Luke and Acts themselves. Though his warning is directed largely against Conzelmann's *Theology of Luke* and J.C. O'Neill's *The Theology of Acts in Its Historical Setting*, rev. ed. (London: SPCK, 1970), it applies to other works as well and serves as a warning to all expositors. It is constantly necessary to check one's understanding of an author against the actual data in his work. But what constitutes evidence for biblical theology? It is one thing to exegete the propositions in the logical argument of an epistle (and even here there is much room for disagreement); it is another thing to reconstruct the theology of a narrator such as Luke. The evidence ranges from overall patterns of structure (cf. Talbert's *Literary Patterns*) to the possible significance of (e.g., the use or nonuse of) an article before the word "mountain" in Matthew or Luke. Word frequency is certainly one valuable clue. Yet it is not enough to make a simple word count and draw conclusions from it. As Gaston has shown in *Horae Synopticae Electronicae*, it is necessary to use modern statistical methodology, such as standard deviation, to assess the significance of word counts. We also need to bear in mind the source of the material under consideration. If a word appears frequently in one of Luke's special sources (assuming that we know when he is using such a source), should we use that as evidence for Luke's own theological viewpoint? Does the very fact that he selected that source indicate that he wanted to express its theology? One would assume this to be the case and that Luke was being divinely led in weaving together his materials into a cohesive theology.

Moreover, those passages in the Gospel that are of most theological weight must be taken into account, namely, not only passages that contain specific teachings, but also those that contain a confluence of significant Lukan terminology. For example, Jesus' conversation with Zacchaeus in 19:1–10 includes the word "today" (bis), "salvation," "save," and the name "Abraham." Such terminology is relatively frequent in Luke. Also, Zacchaeus, who was a tax collector and so was called a "sinner" by the people, exemplifies the kind of people Luke uses to show God's grace. This incident is of high significance (see commentary).

Jesus' preaching at Nazareth (4:16–21) exemplifies the kerygmatic (proclamation) theme in Luke and provides a programmatic statement regarding Jesus' ministry (see commentary).

While the proper use of redaction criticism in discerning the theology of a Gospel author must depend on careful comparison with parallel passages in the other Gospels, the coherence of themes *within* a Gospel is as important as a comparison of themes *between* the Gospels. For example, the messiahship of Jesus and the kingdom of God must be recognized as important themes in Luke's theology whether or not they appear with unusual frequency as compared with Matthew and Mark.

History and geography play an important part in Luke's theology (we object to the criticism that this implies that Luke is less reliable in these areas). Luke's "empire history" (to use Cassidy's term) as well as the local context of events in his Gospel demonstrate the reality and importance of salvation-history in time and space. The providence of God in history has an important relation to the sequence of events in Luke-Acts.

In Luke's central section (9:51–18:14), we can discern a theological motif in the way Jesus orients his thinking and his ministry toward Jerusalem, the city of destiny, which would be the scene of the passion and ascension of Christ (9:51). That Luke, in contrast to the other Gospels, does not describe the actual entrance of Jesus into Jerusalem itself is significant. (See comments on 19:28–44. Other historical and geographical matters of theological importance will be treated in loc. See also remarks on Luke's scheme of history as understood by Conzelmann, under "Eschatology" below [k].)

The following are some of the more significant topics in Luke.

a. Christology

The Gospel opens with a series of birth narratives alternating between Jesus and John the Baptist. Among other purposes, these narratives effect a contrast between the two figures, both of whom are identified in Luke as prophets.[28] From the beginning it is apparent that Jesus is also the Son of God, born of a virgin (1:26–33). The atmosphere of chapters 1–2 is that of the OT. In them Jesus is presented in terms of messiahship (cf. 1:32b–33, 68–75). Simeon and Anna give testimony to the baby Jesus in the temple and announce that God's day of redemption has dawned, since the coming of the Savior means light to the Gentiles and glory to Israel (2:25–38). At the age of twelve, Jesus expresses his filial consciousness—his unique awareness that God is his Father (2:49).

There are hints throughout the Gospel that Jesus came as a "prophet" (e.g., 4:24; 13:33; 24:19). Luke effectively focuses on the messiahship of Jesus (unlike Mark) by taking the reader directly from the question of Herod—"Who, then, is this I hear such things about?" (9:9)—to the messianic act of feeding the five thousand (9:10–17) and then immediately to Peter's affirmation that Jesus is "the Christ of God" (9:20).

Unlike the other Gospels, Luke's narrative concludes with the ascension of Jesus. This marks both the conclusion of the Gospel and the beginning of Acts and is thus also pivotal in the two-volume work. Moreover, Luke makes mention of the Ascension in 9:51, at the beginning of the central section of his Gospel.

---

[28]Minear, *Heal and Reveal*, pp. 95–96; cf. Marshall, *Luke: Historian and Theologian*, pp. 125–28.

16

b. Doxology

The prominence of the Ascension in Luke contributes to his "theology of glory." It has often been observed that Luke has emphasized the resurrection, ascension, and vindication of Christ (taking into account also the early chapters of Acts). The descriptive term "glory" (*doxa*) is also appropriate because there is a sense of doxology—i.e., of ascribing glory to God—throughout Luke's work. Those who observe or benefit from the healing power of Christ are filled with wonder and bring glory to God (e.g., Luke 5:25–26; Acts 3:8–10). Other examples of praising and blessing God in Luke are 1:46–55, 68–79; 2:13–14, 20, 28–32; 7:16; 10:21; 18:43; 19:37–38; 24:53.

c. Soteriology

If Luke has a theology of glory, this does not mean he lacks a theology of the Cross. It is true that the gospel as proclaimed in the first chapters of Acts does not feature the doctrine of the atonement as we have come to understand it from Paul. Nevertheless the Cross is central. Even before the first passion prediction of Luke 9:22, there are foreshadowings of Jesus' sufferings (2:35; 5:35). Jesus is clearly moving toward the Cross in 13:33. His words instituting the Last Supper must not be overlooked as evidence of his understanding of the Cross (22:19–20).

d. Salvation

"The central theme in the writings of Luke is that Jesus offers salvation to men." This is the thesis of Marshall in *Luke: Historian and Theologian* (p. 116). This offer of salvation is not to be dissociated from the concept of salvation-history that, properly understood, has a significant place in Luke and elsewhere in Scripture. It does, however, focus on the person and the saving work of the Lord Jesus Christ, rather than a scheme of history (as in Conzelmann). *Sōzō* ("save") occurs in Luke 6:9; 7:50; 8:12, 36, 48, 50; 9:24, 56 mg.; 13:23; 17:19; 18:26, 42; 19:10; 23:35, 37, 39; *sōtēr* ("Savior") in 1:47; 2:11; *sōtēria* ("salvation") in 1:69, 71, 77; 19:9; and *sōtērion* in 2:30; 3:6.

We observed above that one of the key passages in Luke is 19:1–10, which concludes with the statement that the Son of Man "came to seek and to save what was lost." The entire Gospel of Luke pictures Jesus as reaching out to the lost in forgiveness. We see this exemplified in the beautiful story of the sinful woman (7:36–50). In the well-known parables in Luke 15, Jesus, in contrast with the attitude of the Pharisees, identifies himself with the heavenly Father in rejoicing over the return of those who are lost. See Marshall's *Luke: Historian and Theologian* (pp. 116–44) for a fine discussion of Jesus' ministry of salvation. Also, see further under "Sense of Destiny" below (h).

e. The Holy Spirit

The prominence of the Holy Spirit in Luke-Acts has received considerable attention. It is through the overshadowing spirit and power of God that Mary conceives the one who will be called the Son of God (1:35). The same Spirit would fill John the Baptist (1:15) and his mother, Elizabeth (1:41). The Spirit was on Simeon, and through the Spirit he gave testimony to the Messiah (2:25–35). Jesus was full of the Spirit and was led by the Spirit at the time of his temptation (4:1). The great passage from Isaiah that Jesus quoted in the synagogue at Nazareth begins: "The Spirit of the Lord is on me" (4:18). Furthermore, Jesus promised the Holy Spirit both as an answer to prayer (11:13) and in anticipation of Pentecost (24:49; Acts 1:4). The Holy Spirit, of course, has a major place throughout Acts.

f. Prayer

Not only was prayer significant throughout Jesus' life and in the early church, but it seems to have been especially important in times of transition and crisis. Only Luke records that Jesus was praying at his baptism when the Holy Spirit descended on him (3:21). He prayed before choosing the twelve apostles (6:12). Again only Luke records that Jesus was praying on the Mount of Transfiguration (9:29). Luke 11:1–13 and 18:1–8 contain his special teaching and parables on prayer. Other instances of Jesus praying in Luke are 5:16; 9:18; 11:1.

g. Miracles

All four Gospels record miracles of Christ. In Luke, as noted above, the performance of miracles often results in expressions of praise to God. The word *dynamos* ("power") occurs frequently in Luke, though not significantly more than in Matthew or Mark. It also occurs a number of times in Acts.

h. Sense of destiny

The word *dei* ("it is necessary") is prominent in Luke and in Acts. Jesus "had to" be in his Father's house (2:49); he "must preach the good news of the kingdom of God," because that "is why I was sent" (4:43); he "must suffer" (9:22; cf. Matt 16:21; Mark 8:31); he must finish the way appointed to him, the way that culminated in the Cross (13:33); and it was necessary for the Son of Man to be betrayed and crucified, suffering first before entering his glory (24:7, 26, 44–47). In this way Jesus occupies the central place in salvation history, fulfilling the plan of God.

i. Prophecy and fulfillment

God's plan in Christ was in accordance with OT prophecy. Although Luke does not use the fulfillment formulas of Matthew, the idea is in his Gospel. This is especially notable in the programmatic statement in 4:16–21. The quotation of Isaiah 61:1–2, which Jesus concluded with the words "the year of the Lord's favor," became contemporary as Jesus said, "Today this scripture is fulfilled in your hearing" (4:21).[29] The theme of fulfillment also has apologetic value in Luke. "Proof from prophecy" is significant, especially in Luke 24 and in the early chapters of Acts.[30]

j. Israel and the people of God

The term *laos* ("people") is to be distinguished, as Minear ("Jesus' Audiences," pp. 81–109) points out, from the more general *ochlos* ("crowd"). In his Gospel, Luke uses it to describe believers and sympathetic Jews. In Acts it seems at one or two

---

[29]For the significance of this in connection with the OT Year of Jubilee, see Robert B. Sloan, Jr., *The Favorable Year of the Lord* (Austin: Schola, 1977).

[30]Cf. Nils A. Dahl, "The Story of Abraham in Luke-Acts," in Keck and Martyn; cf. also Tiede.

18

points to include potential believers among Gentiles. Whereas the crowds are some-times hostile to Jesus, the "people" are responsive. But what happens to the Jewish people who become believers in Christ? Once they are part of the Christian church, are they separated from Israel? Or, at the other extreme, is the entire church to be considered "Israel"? Richardson has shown that the term "Israel of God" (Gal 6:16) does not refer to the church itself but rather to "those within Israel to whom God will show mercy."[31] Jervell (pp. 41–74) likewise refrains from applying the term "Israel" to the church as a whole. There is a group of repentant Jews who have accepted the gospel. The Gentile mission grows out of the fulfillment of the biblical promises to Israel. Jervell's view is consistent with the emphasis in Acts on the conversion of great numbers of Jews, even Jewish priests. See especially the summary in Acts 21:20: "many thousands of Jews have believed."

k. Eschatology

The continuity of the true people of God and the mission to the Gentiles are part of the plan of God that, as many have seen, is a major theme in Luke. The opening chapters of Luke emphasize the messianic promises, especially through the songs of Mary (1:46–55) and Zechariah (1:68–79). The ultimate fulfillment of these still lies in the future. Luke, in common with the other synoptic Gospels, contains teachings of Jesus about his return and about the glorification of the Son of Man.[32] It has been common to picture Luke, however, as writing at a time when Christians were despairing over the return of Christ, which they had expected immediately. This "delay of the Parousia" was of such major concern to Luke that he devised a scheme that divided history into three phases. The first of these was the OT period, the second the life of Jesus, and the third the period of the church. This idea is set forth in Conzelmann's *Theology of Luke*, the German title of which—*Die Mitte der Zeit* (i.e., the central point in time)—reflects his theory. But one of the problems with Conzelmann's idea is that it makes Luke distort the traditions of Jesus' sayings regarding his return by superimposing on them a concept of an extended period of the church in which life is to go on without the return of Christ.

A number of studies have addressed this issue, maintaining the importance of those eschatological teachings that Luke does incorporate and that were not reinter-preted as radically as Conzelmann had thought.[33] It is possible to see stages in the fulfillment of predictions made both in the OT and by Jesus, with a partial fulfillment now and a consummation later. The problem, says Ellis (*Eschatology in Luke*, p. 19), is "not the delay of the parousia . . . but false apocalyptic speculation that has misapplied the teachings of Jesus and threatens to pervert the church's mission." Thus Luke contains vivid warnings against coming judgment, an encouragement to watchfulness (e.g., 12:40), and the description of the coming of the Son of Man (17:22–37), but warns against misguided speculation (17:20–21). Faithfulness is needed during the time the Master is away (12:42–48; 19:11–27). In another response to Conzelmann, which seeks to maintain the eschatological

---

[31]Peter Richardson, *Israel in the Apostolic Church* (Cambridge: Cambridge University Press, 1969), p. 82.

[32]See the excursus on "Son of Man" in Carson's commentary in this volume at Matt 8:17.

[33]E.g., I.H. Marshall, *Eschatology and the Parables;* cf. Ellis, *Eschatology in Luke;* and Mattill, *Luke and the Last Things.*

element in Luke, Franklin sees the ascension and proclamation of Jesus as Lord as an eschatological climax.

There are other subjects related to eschatology that cannot be discussed here. The concept of present and future stages in the fulfillment of prophecy naturally includes the idea of the kingdom of God with its present or "inaugurated" aspects and its later consummation. Likewise, we see Luke's emphasis on the present reality of God's work in the use of the word "today" (*sēmeron*), alluded to earlier. The following passages are significant: 2:11; 4:21; 5:26; 12:28; 13:32–33; 19:5–9; 22:34, 61; 23:43. "Today" also occurs nine times in Acts.

I. *Discipleship and the Christian in the world*

This topic covers a multitude of subjects that cannot be discussed in this brief introduction but which have occasioned much attention in recent years. Only Luke contains the narrative of 9:57–62 on would-be disciples and the teaching of Jesus on the cost of discipleship in 14:25–35.

A major question in Luke is whether Jesus requires the sacrifice of material possessions for salvation or for discipleship, or whether he just presents it as an ideal for those who are especially devoted. The first idea is not taught in Luke. The case of the rich ruler (18:18–30) is unique (see commentary). Likewise those who want to be disciples should *yield* up all their possessions but not necessarily *disperse* them (see commentary on 14:33). But if this is an ideal, it is an ideal strongly taught. Luke includes Jesus' woes as well as blessings (6:24–26), which speak strongly against the wealthy. He also addresses the matter of possessions in chapter 12 and in chapter 16. In addition Acts not only mentions but emphasizes the sacrificial giving of the early church (2:45; 3:6; 4:32–37; 5:1–11).[34]

Recent attention to the social and political teachings of Jesus has focused on their implications for possible political revolution.[35] Cassidy, dealing particularly with the Gospel of Luke in *Jesus, Politics and Society*, concludes that Luke gives an accurate description of Jesus' social and political stance, and that, though he rejected the use of violence, Jesus challenged the social status quo under the Roman Empire. Cassidy holds that the teachings of Jesus as found in the Gospel of Luke would, if carried out widely, have seriously challenged the principles of the Roman government. He bases his conclusions on Jesus' social teachings in general and on specific texts such as Luke 20:23–25, the familiar "give to Caesar what is Caesar's, and to God what is God's."

---

[34]A number of recent works have addressed the theme of poverty and wealth in the NT. See especially Martin Hengel, *Property and Riches in the Early Church* (Philadelphia: Fortress, 1974); Luke T. Johnson, *The Literary Function of Possessions in Luke-Acts*; R.J. Karris, "Poor and Rich: The Lukan *Sitz im Leben*," in Talbert, *Perspectives on Luke-Acts*; G.W.E. Nickelsburg, "Riches, the Rich and God's Judgment in 1 Enoch 92–105 and the Gospel According to Luke"; Walter E. Pilgrim, *Good News to the Poor*. Regarding the understanding of the early church on biblical teachings, see L. Wm. Countryman, *The Rich Christian in the Church of the Early Empire* (New York and Toronto: Edwin Mellon, 1980).

[35]Oscar Cullmann, *The State in the New Testament* (New York: Scribner's, 1956); id., *Jesus and the Revolutionaries* (New York: Harper and Row, 1970); Martin Hengel, *Was Jesus a Revolutionist?* tr. W. Klassen (Philadelphia: Fortress, 1971). For a different position, see S.G.F. Brandon, *Jesus and the Zealots* (Manchester: Manchester University Press, 1967). See the critical review of Brandon's book by Martin Hengel in JSS 14 (1969): 231–40. See also Harold J. Yoder, *The Politics of Jesus* (Grand Rapids: Eerdmans, 1972).

m. *The word of God*

This is a more important theme in Luke than is generally realized. The first appearance of *logos* is in 1:2: "servants of the word." Luke emphasizes the graciousness and effectiveness of Jesus' word in 4:22, 32, 36. The term is prominent in the parable of the sower (8:4–15). It is those who "hear the word, retain it, and by persevering produce a crop" who are truly related to Jesus. We also learn from Luke that, not only is the word of God in the OT fulfilled in the life of Jesus, but also that Jesus' own words are fulfilled (e.g., 19:32: "just as he had told them"). Thus we have the prophetic word, the authoritative word of Jesus, and the inspired word that is the Gospel of Luke itself.[36]

12. Bibliography

Books

Arndt, William F. *The Gospel According to St. Luke*. St. Louis: Concordia, 1956.
Bailey, Kenneth. *Poet and Peasant: A Literary-Cultural Approach to the Parables in Luke*. Grand Rapids: Eerdmans, 1977.
_____. *Through Peasant Eyes*. Grand Rapids: Eerdmans, 1980.
Barrett, C.K. *Luke, the Historian in Recent Study*. Facet Books, Biblical Series 24. Philadelphia: Fortress, 1970.
Black, Matthew. *An Aramaic Approach to the Gospels and Acts*. 3rd ed. Oxford: Clarendon, 1967.
Bode, E.G. *The First Easter Morning*. Rome: Biblical Institute Press, 1970.
Brown, R.E. *The Birth of the Messiah: A Commentary on the Infancy Narratives in Matthew and Luke*. Garden City: Doubleday, 1977.
Brown, Schuyler. *Apostasy and Perseverance in the Theology of Luke*. Rome: Pontifical Biblical Institute, 1969.
Cadbury, Henry J. *The Making of Luke-Acts*. New York: Macmillan, 1927.
_____. *The Style and Literary Method of Luke*. Cambridge: Harvard, 1920.
Cassidy, Richard J. *Jesus, Politics, and Society. A Study of Luke's Gospel*. Maryknoll, N.Y.: Orbis, 1978.
Conzelmann, Hans. *The Theology of St. Luke*. Translated by Geofrey Buswell. New York: Harper and Row, 1960.
Creed, J.M. *The Gospel According to St. Luke. A Commentary on the Third Gospel*. London: Macmillan, 1930.
Danker, F.W. *Jesus and the New Age According to St. Luke. A Commentary on the Third Gospel*. St. Louis: Clayton, 1972.
_____. *Luke*. Proclamation Commentaries. Philadelphia: Fortress, 1976.
Dillon, R.J. *From Eyewitnesses to Ministers of the Word*. Rome: Biblical Institute Press, 1978.

---

[36]Since the writing of this Introduction, two significant works have appeared. Charles H. Talbert's *Reading Luke* has important insights and information on fulfillment of prophecy and miracles. But his concept of martyr theology (pp. 221–25) has been heavily critiqued by Robert J. Karris in a paper, unpublished at this date, delivered at the Chicago Society for Biblical Research, on 16 April, 1983. Eduard Schweizer, *Luke*, says that Luke's christology is "far from being clear" (p. 43) and that his usage of "Son of God" is "chaotic" (p. 44). Schweizer's insistence that one's approach to theology should be molded by the approach of a biblical author (e.,g., Luke) shows the importance of rightly understanding Luke.

Drury, John. *Tradition and Design in Luke's Gospel*. London: Daston, Longman and Todd, 1976.

Edwards, O.C., Jr. *Luke's Story of Jesus*. Philadelphia: Fortress, 1981.

Ellis, E.E. *The Gospel of Luke*. NCB. New York: Nelson, 1966.

————. *Eschatology in Luke*. Facet Books. Biblical Series 30. Philadelphia: Fortress, 1972.

Fitzmyer, Joseph A. *Essays on the Semitic Background of the New Testament*. Missoula, Mont.: Scholars, 1974.

Flender, Helmut. *St. Luke: Theologian of Redemptive History*. Translated by R.H. and I. Fuller. Philadelphia: Fortress, 1967.

France, R.T., and Wenham, D., edd. *Gospel Perspectives*, 2 vols. Sheffield: J.S.O.T., 1981.

Franklin, Eric. *Christ the Lord: A Study in the Purpose and Theology of Luke-Acts*. Philadelphia: Westminster, 1975.

Gaston, Lloyd. *Horae Synopticae Electronicae; Word Statistics of the Synoptic Gospels*. Missoula, Mont.: Society of Biblical Literature, 1973.

Geldenhuys, Johannes Norval. *Commentary on the Gospel of Luke*. NIC. Grand Rapids: Eerdmans, 1951.

Godet, Frederic. *A Commentary on the Gospel of St. Luke*. Translated by E.W. Shalders and M.D. Cusin. Edinburgh: T. & T. Clark, 1893.

Grundmann, Walter. *Das Evangelium nach Lukas*. Berlin: Evangelische Verlagsanstalt, 1974.

Hawkins, John Caesas. *Horae Synopticae; Contributions to the Study of the Synoptic Problem*. 1909. Reprint. Grand Rapids: Baker, 1968.

Hendriksen, William. *Exposition of the Gospel According to Luke*. Grand Rapids: Baker, 1978.

Hobart, William K. *The Medical Language of St. Luke*. Reprint. Grand Rapids: Baker, 1954.

Hoehner, H.W. *Chronological Aspects of the Life of Christ*. Grand Rapids: Zondervan, 1977.

Jeremias, Joachim. *The Parables of Jesus*. Rev. ed. Translated by S.H. Hooke. New York: Scribner, 1963.

Jervell, J. *Luke and the People of God. A New Look at Luke-Acts*. Minneapolis: Augsburg, 1972.

Johnson, L.T. *The Literary Function of Possessions in Luke-Acts*. Society of Biblical Literature Dissertation Series no. 39. Missoula, Mont.: Scholars, 1977.

Keck, Leander, and Martyn, J. Louis, edd. *Studies in Luke-Acts*. New York: Abingdon, 1966.

Leaney, A.R.C. *A Commentary on the Gospel According to St. Luke*. Harper's New Testament Commentaries. New York: Harper and Brothers, 1958.

Longenecker, R.N., and Tenney, M.C., edd. *New Dimensions in New Testament Study*. Grand Rapids: Zondervan, 1974.

Machen, J. Gresham. *The Virgin Birth of Christ*. Reprint. Grand Rapids: Baker, 1965.

Maddox, Robert. *The Purpose of Luke-Acts*. Göttingen: Vandenhoeck und Ruprecht, 1982.

Manson, T.W. *The Sayings of Jesus*. London: SCM, 1949.

Marshall, I. Howard. *Eschatology and the Parables*. London: Tyndale, 1963.

————. *Luke: Historian and Theologian*. Grand Rapids: Zondervan, 1971.

————. *The Gospel of Luke: A Commentary on the Greek Text*. Grand Rapids: Eerdmans, 1978.

Mattill, A.J., Jr. *Luke and the Last Things*. Dillsboro, N.C.: Western North Carolina, 1979.

Minear, Paul S. *To Heal and to Reveal*. New York: Seabury, 1976.

Morgenthaler, R., *Die lukanische Geschichtsschreibung als Zeugnis. Gestalt und Gehalt der Kunst des Lukas*. 2 vols. Abhandlung zur Theologie des Alten und Neuen Testaments, 14–15. Zürich, 1949.

————. *Statistik des neutestamentlichen Wortschatzes*. Zürich: Gotthelf, 1973.

Morris, Leon. *The Gospel According to St. Luke*. TNTC. Grand Rapids: Eerdmans, 1974.

Navone, J. *Themes of St. Luke*. Rome: Gregorian University, 1970.

Nineham, D.E., ed. *Studies in the Gospels*. Naperville, Ill.; Allenson, 1955.

Pilgrim, W.E. *Good News to the Poor*. Minneapolis: Augsburg, 1981.

Plummer, Alfred. *A Critical and Exegetical Commentary on the Gospel According to St. Luke*. ICC. 5th ed. Edinburgh: T. & T. Clark, 1922.

Ramsay, W.M. *Was Christ Born in Bethlehem? A Study on the Credibility of St. Luke*. New York: Putnam, 1898.

Robinson, W.C. *Der Weg des Herrn: Studien zur Geschichte und Eschatologie im Lukas-Evangelium: Ein Gespräch mit Hans Conzelmann*. Theologische Forschung, 36. Hamburg-Bergstedt: H. Reich, 1964.

Schramm, T. *Der Markus-Stoff bei Lukas. Eine literarkritische und redaktionsgeschichtliche Untersuchung*. Society for New Testament Studies Monograph Series 15. New York and Cambridge: Cambridge University Press, 1971.

Schürmann, H. *Das Lukasevangelium. Erster Teil: Kommentar zu Kap. 1.1—9.50*. Herders Theologischer Kommentar zum Neuen Testament. Bank III. Freiburg-Vienna: Herder, 1969.

———. *Der Paschamahlbericht*. Münster: Aschendorffsche Verlagsanstalt, 1953.

———. *Jesu Abschiedsrede*. Münster: Aschendorffsche Verlagsanstalt, 1957.

Schweizer, E. *Luke: A Challenge to Present Theology*. Atlanta: John Knox, 1982.

Sherwin-White, A.N. *Roman Society and Roman Law in the New Testament*. Oxford: Clarendon, 1963.

Sloan, R.B. *The Favorable Year of the Lord*. Austin: Schola, 1977.

Stanton, G.H. *Jesus of Nazareth in New Testament Preaching*. SNTS Monograph Series 27. London: Cambridge University Press, 1974.

Stonehouse, Ned B. *The Witness of Luke to Christ*. Grand Rapids: Eerdmans, 1951.

Summers, R. *Commentary on Luke*. Waco: Word, 1972.

Talbert, Charles H. *Luke and the Gnostics*. New York: Abingdon, 1966.

———. *Literary Patterns, Theological Themes and the Genre of Luke-Acts*. Society of Biblical Literature Monograph Series 20. Missoula, Mont.: Scholars, 1974.

———, ed. *Perspectives on Luke-Acts*. Edinburgh: T. & T. Clark, 1978.

———. *Reading Luke: A Literary and Theological Commentary on the Third Gospel*. New York: Crossroad, 1982.

Thompson, G.H.P. *The Gospel According to Luke*. Oxford: Clarendon, 1972.

Tiede, David L. *Prophecy and History in Luke-Acts*. Philadelphia: Fortress, 1980.

Wilcock, Michael. *Savior of the World. The Message of Luke's Gospel*. Downers Grove, Ill.: Inter-Varsity, 1979.

Articles

Only articles that bear significantly on more than one part of the Gospel of Luke are listed here. Others will be found at the appropriate passages.

Minear, Paul S. "Jesus' Audiences, According to Luke." Nov Test 16 (1974): 81–109.

Nickelsburg, G.W.E. "Riches, the Rich and God's Judgment in 1 Enoch 92–105 and the Gospel According to Luke." NTS 25 (1979): 324–44.

Snodgrass, K. "Western Non-Interpolations." JBL 91 (1972): 369–79.

Talbert, Charles H. "Shifting Sands: the recent study of the Gospel of Luke." Int 30, 4 (October 1976): 381–95.

13. Outline

I. Introduction (1:1–4)
II. Birth and Childhood Narratives (1:5–2:52)
    A. Anticipation of Two Births (1:5–56)
        1. The birth of John the Baptist foretold (1:5–25)
        2. The birth of Jesus foretold (1:26–38)
        3. Mary's visit to Elizabeth (1:39–45)
        4. Mary's song: The Magnificat (1:46–56)
    B. Birth Narratives (1:57–2:20)
        1. The birth of John the Baptist (1:57–66)
        2. Zechariah's song: The Benedictus (1:67–80)
        3. The birth of Jesus (2:1–7)
        4. The announcement to the shepherds (2:8–20)
    C. Jesus' Early Years (2:21–52)
        1. Presentation of Jesus in the temple (2:21–40)
        2. The boy Jesus at the temple (2:41–52)
III. Preparation for Jesus' Ministry (3:1–4:13)
    A. The Ministry of John the Baptist (3:1–20)
    B. The Baptism of Jesus (3:21–22)
    C. Jesus' Genealogy (3:23–38)
    D. The Temptation of Jesus (4:1–13)
IV. The Galilean Ministry (4:14–9:50)
    A. Initial Phase (4:14–6:16)
        1. First approach and rejection at Nazareth (4:14–30)
        2. Driving out an evil spirit (4:31–37)
        3. Healing many (4:38–44)
        4. Calling the first disciples (5:1–11)
        5. The man with leprosy (5:12–16)
        6. Healing a paralytic (5:17–26)
        7. Calling Levi (5:27–32)
        8. The question about fasting (5:33–39)
        9. Sabbath controversies (6:1–11)
      10. Choosing the twelve apostles (6:12–16)
    B. Jesus' Great Sermon (6:17–49)
        1. Blessings and woes (6:17–26)
        2. Love for enemies (6:27–36)
        3. Judging others (6:37–42)
        4. A tree and its fruit (6:43–45)
        5. The wise and foolish builders (6:46–49)
    C. Ministry to Various Human Needs (7:1–9:17)
        1. The faith of the centurion (7:1–10)
        2. Raising a widow's son (7:11–17)
        3. Jesus and John the Baptist (7:18–35)
        4. Anointed by a sinful woman (7:36–50)
        5. Parable of the sower (8:1–15)
        6. Parable of the lamp (8:16–18)
        7. Jesus' true family (8:19–21)
        8. Calming the storm (8:22–25)

Text and Exposition

I. Introduction

1:1–4

> [1]Many have undertaken to draw up an account of the things that have been fulfilled among us, [2]just as they were handed down to us by those who from the first were eyewitnesses and servants of the word. [3]Therefore, since I myself have carefully investigated everything from the beginning, it seemed good also to me to write an orderly account for you, most excellent Theophilus, [4]so that you may know the certainty of the things you have been taught.

The introduction to Luke is a long, carefully constructed sentence in the tradition of the finest historical works in Greek literature. It stands in contrast to the genealogical table of Matthew, the concise opening sentence of Mark, and the theological prologue of John. It was customary among the great Greek and Hellenistic historians, including the first-century Jewish writer Josephus, to explain and justify their work in a preface. Their object was to assure the reader of their capability, thorough research, and reliability. While such a weighty introduction does not in itself guarantee the honesty of the writer, neither should its conventional form be dismissed as a merely formal pretension.

The classical literary style of the preface contrasts with the remainder of the Gospel, in which Semitisms abound (cf. comment in Introduction in loc.; cf. also introductory comments on vv.5–25).

1 The preface opens with the Greek word *epeidēper* (KJV, "forasmuch as"; RSV, "inasmuch as"), a classical word used only here in the NT but found in such major authors as Thucydides, Philo, and Josephus. It stands in stylistic contrast to the colloquial *egeneto* ("there was"), which in v.5 opens the narrative. NIV omits *epeidēper* for the sake of concise English style, adding "therefore" in v.3. This clarifies the meaning—that Luke's account was written after those of many others.

"Many have undertaken" implies that by the time Luke wrote there was considerable interest in data about Jesus and his ministry. Luke does not say he himself actually reproduced material from any of the existing accounts, though that could be assumed from this and subsequent evidence. The choice of the word "undertaken" (*epecheirēsan*) need not mean that earlier attempts to write gospel narratives had failed (cf. MM, pp. 250–51). Obviously Luke would not be writing if there were no need for something further, but this does not necessarily reflect adversely on his predecessors. "To draw up an account" (*anataxasthai diēgēsin*) means to write a report or narrative, relating events in an orderly way (cf. MM, p. 38). The verbal form of *diēgēsis* ("accounts") occurs in Luke 8:39; 9:10; Acts 9:27; 12:17.

"Fulfilled" is a better translation of *peplērophorēmenōn* than "most surely believed" (KJV) in this context. The word and its cognate *plērophoria* can be translated "full assurance" or "assurance," when their basic reference is to the confident attitude of a person (cf. Rom 4:21; 14:5; Col 2:2; Heb 6:11; 10:22). Otherwise, and especially with reference to things rather than people, the idea of accomplishment or completion is foremost. (See "discharge all the duties" and "fully proclaimed" in 2 Tim 4:5, 17.) Further, if the accomplishment of the purposes of God in the life and ministry of Jesus is one of Luke's themes, it is appropriate for the preface to reflect this.

2 "Just as they were handed down" stresses the validity of the tradition of Jesus' words and deeds. The same emphasis occurs in Paul, who was careful to pass on to others what had been "handed down" to him (1 Cor 11:23; 15:3; cf. also O. Cullmann, *The Early Church: Studies in Early Christian History and Theology* [Philadelphia: Westminster, 1956], pp. 59–75).

Although the "eyewitnesses and servants" may have included some of the "many" (v.1), they are mostly to be distinguished from them because they were prior to them. Luke is establishing the validity of the information both he and his predecessors included in their narratives. Witnesses are important to Luke. While the concept of "witness" is not as prominent in Luke as in John (see esp. John 5:31–47), it is integral to Luke's historical and theological purposes.

The words "from the first" (probably meaning from the early days of Jesus' ministry) are tied to the word "eyewitnesses" as closely as grammar permits—viz., "the from-the-first witnesses" (*hoi ap' archēs autoptai*). These were not passive observers but "servants of the word." Luke is probably referring primarily to the apostles, whose authority he upholds throughout Luke-Acts. In Acts 10:39–42, Peter speaks as one of those who were both witnesses and preachers.

"Word" (*logos*) here means the message of the Gospel, especially as embodied in the words and deeds of Jesus. Ancient Greek writers often stressed the importance of matching one's words with appropriate deeds. In Acts 1:1, Luke combines the words "do" and "teach" when he describes Jesus' ministry. This is essential to the fulfillment mentioned in v.1. While all four Gospels use the term *logos* (with particular significance in John 1:1, 14), Luke uses it surprisingly often. This is especially true in passages unique to Luke (see Gaston, pp. 64, 76; Hawkins, pp. 20, 43). In summary, v.2 makes a serious claim regarding careful historical research that has weighty implications for our estimate of the entire Gospel.

3 The opening words in the Greek order are "it seemed good also to me" (*edoxe kamoi*). This establishes a balance and pattern of comparison between vv.1–2 and 3–4: "Many have undertaken" and "it seemed good also to me"; "to draw up an account" and "to write an orderly account"; "handed down to us" and "so that you may know."

Luke now describes his own work of investigation and writing. The word "everything" may partially explain how his work differed from that of the "many" (v.1) and also from that of Mark—namely, in its greater comprehensiveness. "From the beginning" translates *anōthen*, which can mean, according to the context, either "above" or "again." Here in its relation to historical research, it has a temporal sense. Luke did his research "carefully" (*akribōs*, lit., "accurately") and wrote an "orderly" (*kathexēs*) account. We cannot determine from this preface alone whether Luke is referring to a chronological or to a thematic order. He does not specifically claim to have aimed at chronological sequence. Perhaps he may have followed an order found in his sources. If so, this could explain his occasional differences from Matthew and Mark. Or he may have rearranged his sources according to another pattern. Taken alone the prologue is not conclusive as to these possibilities. In any event Luke intended his claim of working in an orderly way to inspire confidence in his readers.

The identity of Theophilus is unknown. The name ("friend of God") might be either a symbol or a substitute for the true name of Luke's addressee. Theophilus was, however, a proper name, and "most excellent" naturally suggests an actual person of some distinction. He may have been Luke's literary patron or publisher, after the custom of the times (cf. E.J. Goodspeed, "Some Greek Notes: I. Was Theophilus Luke's Publisher?" JBL 73 [1954]: 84).

4 Though it is not clear whether Theophilus was a believer, he had doubtless received some instructions in the faith. The genitive plural (*logōn*) of *logos* ("word") is here translated by NIV as "things," a legitimate extended use. Theophilus has learned of both the words and the deeds of Jesus. "Taught" (*katēchēthēs*) may refer to formal church teaching (Gal 6:6), but not necessarily. For some reason Theophilus needed assurance, or "certainty" (*asphaleian*), as to the truth of the things taught him. Possibly he was troubled by denials of the Resurrection and other historical foundations of the faith that Gnostic speculation was challenging. Such are not to be countered by mere speculation but by the factual narrative Luke is about to write. His book will set forth evidences and purposes ancillary to the one he has stated in this preface.

According to the prologue, Luke's purpose in writing was to assure Theophilus of the "certainty" of the Gospel tradition. His Gospel can still fulfill that purpose. This does not exclude other purposes for Luke-Acts (cf. Introduction: Purpose).

Notes

1–4 Among the many useful articles on the Lukan prologue and the method of his historical investigation, see Stonehouse, *The Witness to Christ*, pp. 24–25, in which he especially surveys the contributions of H.J. Cadbury. Supplementary to this is Stonehouse's *Origins of the Synoptic Gospels* (Grand Rapids: Eerdmans, 1963), pp. 113–31. For more recent perspectives, see D.J. Sneen, "An Exegesis of Luke 1:1–4 with Special Regard to Luke's Purpose as a Historian," ExpT 83 (1971–72): 40–43, and I.I. du Plessis, "Once More: The Purpose of Luke's Prologue," NovTest 16 (1974): 259–71 (contains useful comparisons with other ancient historical introductions, and S. Brown, "The Role of the Prologues in Determining the Purpose of Luke–Acts," in C.H. Talbert, ed., *Perspectives on Luke–Acts*). A most important recent work on the purpose of Luke is Maddox's *Purpose of Luke-Acts*.

II. Birth and Childhood Narratives (1:5–2:52)

A. *Anticipation of Two Births* (1:5–56)

1. *The birth of John the Baptist foretold* (1:5–25)

> [5]In the time of Herod king of Judea there was a priest named Zechariah, who belonged to the priestly division of Abijah; his wife Elizabeth was also a descendant of Aaron. [6]Both of them were upright in the sight of God, observing all the Lord's commandments and regulations blamelessly. [7]But they had no children, because Elizabeth was barren; and they were both well along in years.
> [8]Once when Zechariah's division was on duty and he was serving as priest

before God, [9]he was chosen by lot, according to the custom of the priesthood, to go into the temple of the Lord and burn incense. [10]And when the time for the burning of incense came, all the assembled worshipers were praying outside.

[11]Then an angel of the Lord appeared to him, standing at the right side of the altar of incense. [12]When Zechariah saw him, he was startled and was gripped with fear. [13]But the angel said to him: "Do not be afraid, Zechariah; your prayer has been heard. Your wife Elizabeth will bear you a son, and you are to give him the name John. [14]He will be a joy and delight to you, and many will rejoice because of his birth, [15]for he will be great in the sight of the Lord. He is never to take wine or other fermented drink, and he will be filled with the Holy Spirit even from birth. [16]Many of the people of Israel will he bring back to the Lord their God. [17]And he will go before the Lord, in the spirit and power of Elijah, to turn the hearts of the fathers to their children and the disobedient to the wisdom of the righteous—to make ready a people prepared for the Lord."

[18]Zechariah asked the angel, "How can I be sure of this? I am an old man and my wife is well along in years."

[19]The angel answered, "I am Gabriel. I stand in the presence of God, and I have been sent to speak to you and to tell you this good news. [20]And now you will be silent and not able to speak until the day this happens, because you did not believe my words, which will come true at their proper time."

[21]Meanwhile, the people were waiting for Zechariah and wondering why he stayed so long in the temple. [22]When he came out, he could not speak to them. They realized he had seen a vision in the temple, for he kept making signs to them but remained unable to speak.

[23]When his time of service was completed, he returned home. [24]After this his wife Elizabeth became pregnant and for five months remained in seclusion. [25]"The Lord has done this for me," she said. "In these days he has shown his favor and taken away my disgrace among the people."

This narrative introduces a section in Luke unparalleled in the other Gospels (cf. Introduction for critical and stylistic issues). Its distinctive characteristics include (1) an atmosphere reminiscent of the OT, with a grammatical and stylistic Semitic cast; (2) an alternation of focus on John the Baptist and on Jesus; (3) the awesomeness of heavenly beings appearing to humans; and (4) a note of joy, especially as heard in four songs: Mary's (1:46–55), Zechariah's (1:68–79), the angels' (2:14), and Simeon's (2:29–32).

1. The Semitic style fits the religious and historical connection Luke is establishing between the OT and NT periods. Luke does not use the fulfillment formulas Matthew used but shows that OT predictions stand behind the events he describes. This he does by giving his style and vocabulary a flavor of the LXX. He also takes pains to ground the Christian message in Jerusalem and in its temple. Machen (pp. 62–101) uses the Semitic style in his arguments for the Virgin Birth.

2. To make this connection with the OT, Luke also uses a pattern of alternation, in which attention shifts back and forth between John the Baptist and Jesus. Far from being a confusion of sources, as is sometimes supposed, this alternation is a literary device to focus attention successively on each person (cf. G.N. Stanton, *Jesus of Nazareth in New Testament Preaching*, SNTS Monograph Series 27 [London: Cambridge University Press, 1974], pp. 55–56). Luke clearly identifies John as a successor to the OT prophets. Through his alternating presentations, Luke links John and Jesus, whom Luke apparently also identifies as a prophet (Minear, *Heal and Reveal*, pp. 95–96). Since he also sees in Jesus far more than a prophet, Luke's device of alternation goes beyond comparison to contrast, with Jesus presented as "Son of the Most High" and messianic Deliverer (1:32–33, 69, 76; 2:11, 30). The

structure of the section then is (1) the announcement of John's coming birth, (2) the announcement of Jesus' coming birth, (3) Elizabeth's blessing of Mary, (4) Mary's praise to God, (5) John's birth, and (6) Jesus' birth, which is acclaimed by angels in heaven and by saintly Jews in the temple.

3. The appearance of angels is likewise appropriate for an account that teaches that God has acted decisively in the history of his people to accomplish our salvation. Some reject this supernatural activity, attempting to explain the narratives as an accretion of legends. To do so deprives the event of an effective cause. Actually the appearance of an angel is no more remarkable than the Incarnation itself.

4. The theme of joy finds expression not only in the songs but in the tone of the whole passage. The gospel is always "good news of great joy" (2:10). Moreover, the passage realistically includes a reminder both of the pain of sin and of the cost of our deliverance, as Simeon's allusion to the ultimate death of Mary's son (2:35) shows.

Another pattern of themes may be seen in the repetition of the phrase "Most High": (1) Jesus is the "Son of the Most High" (1:32); (2) Mary's conception by the Holy Spirit is said to be by the "power of the Most High" (1:35); and (3) John is called a "prophet of the Most High" (1:76) (H.H. Oliver, "The Lucan Birth Stories and the Purpose of Luke-Acts," NTS 10 [1963–64]: 215–26).

While the phrases just outlined do not occur in close sequence, they should probably be taken together as relating to three major themes in Luke's Gospel: (1) John is the final prophet of the OT period, the forerunner of the Messiah, and the first proclaimer of the kingdom; (2) Jesus is the unique Son of God, the true eschatological prophet and Messiah; and (3) the Holy Spirit's ministry both validates and empowers the ministry of Jesus. (The Holy Spirit is mentioned frequently in this section; viz., 1:15, 35, 41, 67, 80; 2:25–27.) Other themes prominent in Luke occur in these opening narratives and will be pointed out in the exposition.

5 As has already been said, the style of this section is different from the classical style of vv. 1–4. Likewise, the method of dating differs from that used later in 3:1, where Luke is interested in establishing a more precise point of historical reference. In this verse his only concern is to locate the events in the reign of Herod (king of Judea 37–4 B.C.).

Luke emphasizes the Jewish roots of Christianity by mentioning that, not only was Zechariah (whose name means "God remembers") a priest, but that his wife had also been born into the priestly line. (See comment on v.8 for the functioning of this "priestly division.")

6 This is a description of a truly pious couple wholly devoted to God. The language of the verse "implies a religious rather than a purely ethical character" (Marshall, *Gospel of Luke*, p. 53). Marshall remarks that v.6 shows that their childlessness did not imply any sin. The OT would use the Hebrew *tām* or *tāmîm* to describe such a couple (tr. "blameless" in Gen 6:9; Job 1:8).

7 To be childless brought sorrow and often shame. At her advanced age, Elizabeth could no longer entertain the hope of each Jewish woman to be the mother of the Messiah. While her situation and the subsequent intervention of God had its precedents in the OT (cf. Sarah, Gen 17:16–17; Hannah, 1 Sam 1:5–11), no other woman had such a total reversal in fortune as to bear the forerunner of the Messiah.

31

8–9 The "division" (v.8; cf. v.5) was one of twenty-four groups of priests divided by families and structured after the pattern of 1 Chronicles 23 and 24 (note Abijah, Zechariah's ancestor [1 Chron 24:10]). The Exile had interrupted the original lines of descent; so the divisions were regrouped, most of them corresponding to the original in name only. Each of the twenty-four divisions served in the temple for one week, twice a year, as well as at the major festivals (J. Jeremias, *Jerusalem in the Time of Jesus* [London: SCM, 1969], pp. 198–207). An individual priest, however, could offer the incense at the daily sacrifice (cf. Notes) only once in his lifetime (v.9), since there were so many priests. Therefore this was the climactic moment of Zechariah's priestly career, perhaps the most dramatic moment possible for the event described to have occurred. God was breaking into the ancient routine of Jewish ritual with the word of his decisive saving act. Considering his interest in the Jewish origin of Christianity, Luke probably viewed this dramatic moment not so much as a judgment against Judaism as an appropriate and significant context for the new revelation.

10 Mention of the worshipers outside not only heightens the suspense but prepares the reader for vv.21–22. They were probably pious Jews who loved to be near the temple when sacrifices were offered. NIV's "assembled worshipers" obscures the important word *laos* ("people"; cf. comments on v.27).

11–12 The suddenness of the appearance of the angel (v.11) accords with other supernatural events in Luke and elsewhere in Scripture (cf. 2:9, 13). Luke does not describe the angel, but the fact that he tells exactly where the angel appeared shows the reality of the vision. Only a heavenly being had the right to appear in the Holy Place with the priest. "Startled" (v.12) represents a word of deep emotion (from *tarassō*) and is coupled with the descriptive phrase "gripped with fear." This is not only a natural reaction to such an appearance but is also consistent with what the Gospels say about the response of the disciples and others to the presence of the supernatural (e.g., 5:8–10). Sometimes this betrayed unbelief. But this was certainly not true of Mary (v.38). Rather her attitude (v.29) showed her genuine awe and quite natural trepidation at being confronted by the heavenly visitor.

13 This is the first indication of prayer on the part of Zechariah. The word Luke used (*deēsis*) indicates a specific petition. If this was for a child (probably a son), the aorist tense in the phrase "has been heard" refers to Zechariah's lifelong prayer. Otherwise, his just-offered prayer in the temple was probably for the messianic redemption of Israel. Actually, the birth of his child was bound up with redemption in a way far beyond anything Zechariah expected. That the prayer included a petition for a son is substantiated by the further description of the child, beginning with his name. "John" (*Iōannēs*) combines in its Hebrew form the name of God with the word *ḥānan* ("to show favor" or "be gracious"). God did indeed answer Zechariah's prayer. That the child was named before his birth stresses God's sovereignty in choosing him to be his servant.

14–15 The description of the child's mission has a counterpart in Gabriel's words to Mary (vv.32–33). This is part of the literary device that connects and compares the roles of Jesus and John.

The "joy" (v.14) so characteristic of the day of God's salvation and so prominent in

Luke came first to the parents of the forerunner, then spread to "many people [lit., 'sons'] of Israel" (v.16). Also "joy and gladness" stand in contrast to Zechariah's fear (v.12). The child will be "great" (μεγας) as the prophetic forerunner of the Messiah (v.15). "Great" also describes Jesus in v.32, though in the latter case it is absolute greatness without the qualifying "in the sight of the Lord." Later there would be those who found it hard to relinquish their devotion to John to follow Jesus. They would need to realize that while both were great, Jesus was the greater (3:16). Also John's greatness related to the pre-Messianic Age (7:28). "In the sight of the Lord" indicates divine choice and approval. This expression, or its equivalent, is used frequently in Luke and Acts (cf. Notes).

It is difficult to identify John with a particular religious group simply by this description or that in Mark 1:6. Abstinence from wine suggests the Nazirite vow (Num 6:1-12), but no mention is made of John's hair. Nazirites were to let their hair grow (Num 6:5). Danker (*Jesus*, p. 8) refers to the priests' abstinence from strong drink prior to entering the tabernacle and sees John as a priestly figure calling the people to repentance. On the other hand, the radical elements in John's appearance and behavior may exemplify his radical message of repentance. The Spirit's control is contrasted with the control wine can have over a person (cf. Eph 5:18). In the life of Jesus, the Spirit's ministry will be even more prominent than in John's life.

16-17 The OT prophets were repeatedly concerned with turning the erring people back to God, i.e., to repentance (v.16). In this work none was more prominent than Elijah on Mount Carmel (1 Kings 18:20-40). Luke does not here identify John as a reincarnated Elijah but qualifies his statement with the words "in the spirit and power of Elijah" (v.17). Moreover Luke uses the language of Malachi 4:5-6 (cf. Mal 3:1) to compare John's ministry with that of Elijah. (See comments on 9:30 for further discussion of Elijah.)

"To turn the hearts of the fathers to their children" must be interpreted with reference to both the expanded form in Malachi 4:6 and the next phrase in this context (v.17). If the words are parallel to the phrase "wisdom of the righteous," then "the fathers," previously disobedient, may be following the example of their children who are presumably listening to the message of John—"the wisdom of the righteous." Grammatically less likely but more probable, it might mean that when those who disobey heed wisdom, their Jewish ancestors would, if they knew of it, be pleased with them (Godet, pp. 79-80). In their OT context, the words "turn the hearts," etc., relate to averting divine wrath, a concept certainly basic in the ministry of John.

"People" (*laos*) is a significant word in Luke. Thirty-five of its forty-nine occurrences in the synoptic Gospels are in Luke (Gaston, p. 76; cf. Hawkins, pp. 20-21, 45). Minear ("Jesus' Audiences," pp. 81-109) holds that the term *laos* as used by Luke, in contrast to *ochlos* ("crowd"), "normally refers to Israel as the elect nation which forever retains the specific identity given to it by God." This suggestion accords with Luke's interest in Jewish origins of Christianity, though it may be too comprehensive. Minear (ibid.) also comments that "it is this specific entity ['people'] which Luke sees as the initial and ultimate audience for all God's messengers, whether John the Baptist (Acts 13:24) or the apostles ([Acts] 3:12f.)." The "people prepared for the Lord" ultimately includes not only these initial Jewish hearers but those who formerly were "not a people" (1 Peter 2:10), the Gentiles (see also Jervell).

33

18–20 Zechariah's question (v.18) seems innocent, but v.20 reveals that it was asked in doubt. In contrast Mary's question—"How can this be?" (v.34)—arises from faith (v.45). Mary simply inquired as to the way God would work; Zechariah questioned the truth of the revelation. "How can I be sure of this?" apparently was a request for a sign. Though we are told that Zechariah was devout (v.6), his quest for confirmation was perilously close to the attitude described in Luke 11:29. Since the gospel requires a response of faith, and since Zechariah, of all people, should have believed without question, the angel's reply (v.20) is not overly severe. The narrative gains solemnity by mentioning that Gabriel stood "in the presence of [*enōpion*] God" (v.19; cf. "in the sight of " [v.15] and "before"[v.17]). The "good news" will come to fulfillment in spite of human unbelief, but Zechariah must nevertheless bear the sign of his doubt. "Will come true" (*plērōthēsontai*) means "will be fulfilled" and forms part of Luke's presentation of the fulfilled word of God.

21–22 The element of suspense during the unusually long prayer-time contributes to the vividness of Luke's narrative (v.21; cf. v.10). The worshipers who had been praying outside now understood without anyone telling them that Zechariah had seen a vision. Verse 22 reinforces the extraordinary nature of his experience and his loss of speech.

23–25 As with the announcement to Mary, the word concerning Zechariah and Elizabeth's promised son was given before his conception (v.24; cf. Joseph's experience [Matt 1:18–25]). It is characteristic of Luke to mention Elizabeth's grateful acknowledgment of the Lord's grace in removing the stigma of her childlessness (v.25).

Notes

5–25 The literature on Luke 1 and 2 is extensive. The following are especially useful for the birth narratives: R.E. Brown, *Birth of the Messiah,* pp. 233–533; Marshall, *Luke: Historian and Theologian,* pp. 96–102; Paul S. Minear, "Luke's Use of the Birth Stories," in Keck and Martyn, pp. 111–30; and Oliver, "Lucan Birth Stories," pp. 202–26.

6 Ἄμεμπτοι (*amemptoi,* "blamelessly") does not imply sinlessness. Abraham was told to be "blameless" before the Lord (Gen 17:1 [LXX, *amemptoi*]). Paul, who affirms universal sinfulness (Rom 3:23), says he had been "faultless" (*amemptoi*) as regards "legalistic righteousness" (Phil 3:6).

8 Ἐγένετο δὲ (*egeneto de,* "once") reflects the Hebrew idiom וַיְהִי (*wayᵉhî,* "and it came to pass") in the narrative construction. This is a common expression in Luke, used in various combinations. In this form and in others, the verb γίνομαι (*ginomai,* "be") is used frequently in Luke, more than in Matthew and Mark together. Of the 107 occurrences, 31 in Luke are apparently editorial additions to his sources (Gastron, p. 70).

9 "According to the custom of the priesthood" could go with v.8, but NIV is probably right in taking it with "he was chosen by lot."

"Incense" was offered in connection with the morning and evening sacrifice (M *Tamid* 2.5; 5.2; 6.3). Marshall (*Luke: Historian and Theologian,* p. 54) connects the offering of incense, which symbolizes prayer in Scripture (Ps 141:2; Rev 5:8; 8:3–4), with Luke's particular interest in prayer.

13 "Prayer" here means, as noted above, a specific request. The more general word is προσευχή (*proseuchē,* cf. 6:12; 19:46; 22:45).

15 Luke is the only synoptic writer to use ἐνώπιον (enōpion, "in the sight of"). He does so twenty-two times.

19 Gabriel (cf. Dan 8:16; 9.21) is one of two angels named in Scripture, the other being Michael (Dan 10:13; 21; 21:1; Jude 9; Rev 12:7).

Εὐαγγελίζομαι (euangelizomai, "to tell ... good news") has a special significance in Luke. Of its eleven occurrences in the Synoptics, ten are in Luke (cf. 2:10; 3:18; 4:8, 43; 7:22; 8:1; 9:6; 16:16; 20:1). The noun εὐαγγέλιον (euangelion, "good news," "gospel") occurs in Mark but not in Luke. The words do not always denote news that is good (TDNT, 2:707–37; cf. Marshall, *Luke: Historian and Theologian*, pp. 123–24).

---

2. The birth of Jesus foretold

1:26–38

> [26]In the sixth month, God sent the angel Gabriel to Nazareth, a town in Galilee, [27]to a virgin pledged to be married to a man named Joseph, a descendant of David. The virgin's name was Mary. [28]The angel went to her and said, "Greetings, you who are highly favored! The Lord is with you."
>
> [29]Mary was greatly troubled at his words and wondered what kind of greeting this might be. [30]But the angel said to her, "Do not be afraid, Mary, you have found favor with God. [31]You will be with child and give birth to a son, and you are to give him the name Jesus. [32]He will be great and will be called the Son of the Most High. The Lord God will give him the throne of his father David, [33]and he will reign over the house of Jacob forever; his kingdom will never end."
>
> [34]"How will this be," Mary asked the angel, "since I am a virgin?"
>
> [35]The angel answered, "The Holy Spirit will come upon you, and the power of the Most High will overshadow you. So the holy one to be born, will be called the Son of God. [36]Even Elizabeth your relative is going to have a child in her old age, and she who was said to be barren is in her sixth month. [37]For nothing is impossible with God."
>
> [38]"I am the Lord's servant," Mary answered. "May it be to me as you have said." Then the angel left her.

Continuing in the same style in which he has described Zechariah's encounter with the angel of the Lord, Luke now weaves deep theological meaning into his simple and delicate narrative. This section is the highest of several summits of revelation in chapters 1 and 2. The account of Jesus' nativity, beautiful and essential as it is, rests theologically on the angel Gabriel's announcement to Mary. Luke presents the theology of the Incarnation in a way so holy and congruent with OT sacred history that any comparisons with pagan mythology seem utterly incongruous. Instead of the carnal union of a pagan god with a woman, producing some kind of semidivine offspring, Luke speaks of a spiritual overshadowing by God himself that will produce the "holy one" within Mary.

Several themes are intertwined in this passage: (1) the divine sonship of Jesus (vv.32, 35); (2) his messianic role and reign over the kingdom (vv.32–33); (3) God as the "Most High" (vv.32, 35; cf. v.76); (4) the power of the Holy Spirit (v.35); and (5) the grace of God (vv.29–30, 34–35, 38).

26 The mention of Elizabeth's "sixth month" (cf. v.24) points to the pattern of alternation and establishes a link with the prophet John the Baptist (cf. comments on vv.5–25). The same chronological device points in v.36 to God's power over human reproduction. This theme of the direct action of God is one of the basic ones in Luke-Acts. (See v.19 in reference to the angel Gabriel.) Luke calls Nazareth a *polis*, which can often be translated "city," but here describes a "town" (NIV) or "village." It was off, though not totally inaccessible from, the main trade routes. Its relatively insignificant size contrasts with Jerusalem, where Gabriel's previous appearance had taken place. John 1:46 records the contemporary Judean opinion of Nazareth.

Likewise, the region of Galilee contrasts with Judea. Surrounded as they were by Gentiles, the Galileans were not necessarily irreligious. They were, however, somewhat lax respecting such things as keeping a kosher kitchen (cf. Sean Freyne, *Galilee from Alexander the Great to Hadrian 323 B.C.E. to 135 C.E.* [Wilmington, Del.: Michael Glazier and Notre Dame: University of Notre Dame Press, 1980], pp. 259–97). Though the Galileans had a reputation for pugnacity, Galilee was not a hotbed of revolutionary activity, as some have thought (ibid., pp. 208–55).

27 The young virgin Mary contrasts with the old priest Zechariah, who was past the time for having children. The word "virgin" refers here to one who had not yet had sexual relations (cf. Notes). Mary's question in v.34 and the reference in v.27 to her being "pledged to be married" make this clear. Since betrothal often took place soon after puberty, Mary may have just entered her teens. This relationship was legally binding, but intercourse was not permitted until marriage. Only divorce or death could sever betrothal; and in the latter event the girl, though unmarried, would be considered a widow.

In v.27 Luke calls Joseph "a descendant of David." Even though the genealogy in 3:23–37 is often taken as showing Mary's line, this is never stated. Neither does Luke nor any other NT writer say that Mary was descended from David. Since Joseph is named here and in 3:23 and is explicitly linked with the royal line, we should probably assume that Luke considers Jesus a legitimate member of the royal line by what we today might call the right of adoption. This has an important bearing on the promise in v.32b.

28 Here Luke establishes another contrast with the preceding narrative—this time by relating Gabriel's greeting (vv.30–32) to Mary. But Zechariah had received no such greeting.

"Highly favored" renders *kecharitōmenē*, which has the same root as the words for "Greetings" (*chaire*), and "favor" (*charin*, v.30). Mary is "highly favored" because she is the recipient of God's grace. A similar combination of words occurs in Ephesians 1:6—"his glorious grace . . . which he has freely given [same Gr. word as for 'highly favored'] us." Some suggest that Luke implies that a certain grace has been found in Mary's character. While this could be so, the parallel in Ephesians (the only other occurrence of the verb in the NT) shows that the grace in view here is that which is given all believers apart from any merit of theirs. Mary has "found favor with God" (v.30); she is a recipient of his grace (v.28), and she can therefore say, "My spirit rejoices in God my Savior" (v.47).

"The Lord is with you" recalls the way the angel of the Lord addressed Gideon to assure him of God's help in the assignment he was about to receive (Judg 6:12).

29–30 Zechariah had been "gripped with fear" (v.12) at the very appearance of the angel, but it was the angel's words—viz., his greeting (v.28)—that "greatly troubled" Mary (v.29). He responded first by assuring her that she had indeed "found favor" with God (v.30; cf. Gen 6:8, where Noah is spoken of as having found favor with God). God's grace, like his love, banishes fear of judgment (1 John 4:17-18).

31 Gabriel now explains why his preliminary assurance of Mary's having found grace with God is so significant for her. The wording here is virtually identical to the "virgin" passage in Isaiah 7:14 (LXX) and to the assurance the angel of the Lord gave the fugitive Hagar (Gen 16:11 LXX). The word "virgin" is not, however, mentioned in the allusion to Isaiah, though Mary's question (v.34) shows she was a virgin, a fact Luke has mentioned in v.27.

The name Jesus (Joshua) had been common in OT times and continued to be a popular name through the first century A.D. (TDNT, 3:284-93). Matthew 1:21 provides an explanation for giving the child a name that contains, in its Hebrew form, the word "saves" (*yāša'*): "because he will save his people from their sins."

32-33 Some scholars consider it significant that whereas in v.15 Gabriel had qualified his prophecy of the greatness of John ("he will be great in the sight of the Lord"), here his statement of the greatness of Mary's Son has no qualification whatever. The striking term "Son of the Most High" (v.33; cf. vv.35, 76) leads to a clear messianic affirmation—the reference to the "throne of his father David." Jesus' divine sonship is thus linked to his messiahship in accord with 2 Samuel 7:12-14 and Psalm 2:7-9 (cf. Ps 89:26-29). The description of Jesus' messianic destiny follows the statement of his sonship, and that sonship is related in v.35 to his divine origin. Clearly Luke sees the messianic vocation as a function of God's Son, rather than seeing sonship as just an aspect of messiahship.

The OT concepts of "throne," Davidic line, "reign" (v.33), and "kingdom" are spoken of as eternal—i.e., "will never end." Though this idea is found in Micah 4:7, it is not common in Jewish thought.

34 Unlike Zechariah, Mary does not ask for a confirmatory sign (cf. comments on v.18) but only for light on how God will accomplish this wonder. As Luke has it, the question does not relate to the remarkable person and work of her promised Son but arises from the fact that she "does not know [*ou ginōskō*, i.e., has not had sexual relations with] a man" (NIV, "I am a virgin"). "While the tense is present, it describes a state resultant from a past pattern of behavior—Mary has not known *any* man and so is a virgin" (R.E. Brown, *Birth of the Messiah,* p. 289; emphasis his).

Because she was betrothed, we may assume that Mary fully expected to have normal marital relations later. It is difficult, therefore, to know why she saw a problem in Gabriel's prediction. The text does not say that Mary had Isaiah 7:14 in mind and wondered how she, still a virgin, could conceive. Perhaps Luke's condensed account is intended to suggest (1) that Mary assumed an immediate fulfillment before marriage and (2) that the informed reader should understand the issue in terms of Isaiah 7:14, already hinted at in v.31. Marshall (*Luke: Historian and Theologian,* pp. 69-70) lists several alternative explanations, none of which is satisfactory by itself (cf. also R.E. Brown, *Birth of the Messiah,* pp. 303-9).

35 Once again (cf. v.15) Luke mentions the Holy Spirit, as he does six more times in his first two chapters (1:41, 67, 80; 2:25, 26, 27). The word for "overshadow" (*episkiazō*) carries the sense of the holy, powerful presence of God, as in the description of the cloud that "covered" (Heb. *šākan;* NIV, "settled upon") the tabernacle when the tent was filled with the glory of God (Exod 40:35; cf. Ps 91:4). The word is used in all three accounts of the Transfiguration to describe the overshadowing of the cloud (Matt 17:5; Mark 9:7; Luke 9:34). Likewise, in each account the voice comes out of the cloud identifying Jesus as God's Son, a striking reminder of Luke 1:35 where the life that results from the enveloping cloud is identified as the Son of God.

The child whose life is thus engendered by the power of God, which power is identified as the Holy Spirit, is himself called by Gabriel "the holy one." Because of this connection with the Holy Spirit, and because of the ethical meaning of "holy" in v.49, that word probably relates here to the purity of Jesus instead of relating to separation for a divine vocation.

36–37 The angel cites the pregnancy of Elizabeth (v.36) as further evidence of God's marvelous power and concludes with the grand affirmation of v.37—surely one of the most reassuring statements in all Scripture.

38 Mary's exemplary attitude of servanthood recalls that of Hannah, when she was praying for a son (1 Sam 1:11, where the LXX also has *doulē,* "servant"). Nothing is said about the relation of Mary's submission to her consciousness of the shame a premarital pregnancy could bring her. Her servanthood is not a cringing slavery but a submission to God that in OT times characterized genuine believers and that should characterize believers today (cf. v.48). Understandably Mary doubtless felt an empathy with Hannah's sense of being at the Lord's disposal in part of life a woman before modern times had little or no control over. Mary's trusting submission at this point in her life may be compared with her attitude toward her Son later on (cf. John 2:5).

Notes

27 The meaning of παρθένος (*parthenos*) is not in doubt here since it is amplified in v.34 (where NIV introduces the term "virgin" to explain the text). Therefore, while it is alleged on the basis of some other literature that *parthenos* occasionally had a broader meaning under special circumstances (J. Massingbyrde Ford, "The Meaning of 'Virgin,' " NTS 12 [3, 1966]: 293–99), the meaning here is not affected. See commentary on 3:23. In addition to the works cited in the Bibliography, especially Machen, literature on the Virgin Birth includes James Orr, *The Virgin Birth of Christ* (New York: Scribner's, 1907); Thomas Boslooper, *The Virgin Birth* (Philadelphia: Westminster, 1962); R.E. Brown, *The Virginal Conception and Bodily Resurrection of Jesus* (New York: Paulist, 1973); Robert Gromacki, *The Virgin Birth: Doctrine of Deity* (Nashville: Nelson, 1974).

28 The meaning of "Greetings" (KJV, "Hail") for Χαῖρε (*chaire*) is debated. It is the simple Greek word for a greeting. In the LXX of Zeph 3:14, it means "Rejoice" (cf. Zech 9:9). Some have seen a connection—significant for Roman Catholic interpreters—between Mary and the "Daughter of Zion" addressed in Zephaniah. Although an allusion to Zeph 3:14 is dubious, the parallel between "mighty to save" in Zeph 3:17 and Mary's reference to God as "Savior" and "Mighty One" in Luke 1:47, 49 may make it a remote possibility. The Latin form of the greeting is preserved in the familiar words "Ave Maria."

'Ο κύριος μετὰ σοῦ (ho kyrios meta sou, "the Lord is with you") is followed, in many MSS, by the words εὐλογημένη σὺ ἐν γυναιξίν (eulogēmenē su en gynaixin, "blessed are you among women"). This clause, familiar from the Roman Catholic "Hail Mary," is in the later MSS represented in the KJV and is probably copied from v.42 (B. Metzger, *A Textual Commentary on the Greek New Testament* [New York: United Bible Societies, 1971], p. 129). Since it is hard to explain why Sinaiticus (ℵ) and Vaticanus (B) omitted it if it were authentic, and since its presence in other MSS can be explained as a transfer from v.42, it is best left out. It was included in the KJV and Douay Version.

28, 30 For studies on χάρις (charis, "grace," "favor"), see H. Conzelmann, TDNT, 9:372–402, and H.H. Esser, DNTT, 2:115–24.

32, 35 'Ο ὕψιστος (ho hypsistos, "Most High") is found seven times in Luke, twice in Acts, and only four times elsewhere in the NT. It is frequent in the LXX. See Marshall, *Luke: Historian and Theologian*, p. 67, for a defense of the Semitic rather than Hellenistic character of the term as used here. The issue affects the question of the Palestinian origin and, therefore, of the authenticity of the narrative.

35 Observe that the title υἱὸς θεοῦ (huios theou, "Son of God") occurs in a Jewish Palestinian setting here. Formerly its use in the NT was commonly attributed to Hellenistic influence. Recent scholarship has corrected this error. The literature on this subject is vast. For a summary of the data, see E. Schweizer, TDNT, 8:334–92, esp. pp. 376–82; cf. Martin Hengel, *The Son of God: The Origin of Christology and the History of the Jewish-Hellenistic Religion* (Philadelphia: Fortress, 1976). R.E. Brown, *Birth of the Messiah*, pp. 311–16, surveys the relevant data in this passage.

The syntax of τὸ γεννώμενον ἅγιον κληθήσεται υἱὸς θεοῦ (to gennōmenon hagion klēthēsetai huios theou, "the holy one to be born will be called the Son of God") is difficult. The alternate possibilities can be visualized as follows:

NIV: The holy one to be born
RSV: The   child to be born
NIV: . . . will be called   the Son of God
RSV: . . . will be called holy, the Son of God

The second possibility takes "holy" as a predicate adjective, rather than as a modifier of the subject. In supporting the second rendering, R.E. Brown (*Birth of the Messiah*, p. 291) cites Isa 4:3 and Luke 2:23 as parallels. (The parallel in Luke 2:23 is not clear in NIV, which substitutes "consecrated" for "called holy.") In both parallels, the verb καλέω (kaleō) follows the predicate, which is the normal order (Marshall, *Luke: Historian and Theologian*, p. 71). If v.35 follows this pattern, "holy," not "Son of God," is in the predicate position, with "Son of God" in apposition to "holy," as in RSV and RV. In either case, "will be called" is "tantamount to saying 'he will be'" (R.E. Brown, *Birth of the Messiah*, p. 291); so the virginal conception brings into human existence one who is the Son of God.

---

3. Mary's visit to Elizabeth

1:39–45

[39]At that time Mary got ready and hurried to a town in the hill country of Judea, [40]where she entered Zechariah's home and greeted Elizabeth. [41]When Elizabeth heard Mary's greeting, the baby leaped in her womb, and Elizabeth was filled with the Holy Spirit. [42]In a loud voice she exclaimed: "Blessed are you among women, and blessed is the child you will bear! [43]But why am I so favored, that the mother of my Lord should come to me? [44]As soon as the sound of your greeting reached my ears, the baby in my womb leaped for joy. [45]Blessed is she who has believed that what the Lord has said to her will be accomplished!"

At this point Luke deftly combines the two strands about Elizabeth and Mary. So far the narrative has not stressed Jesus' superiority to John. But now attention centers on Jesus and his mother (v.43). Even so, the pattern of alternation continues, giving John his own important place as the prophet who goes before the Lord.

39–40 Mary apparently started on her journey as soon as possible (v.39). Luke does not specify the town she went to, but we can assume that it was fifty to seventy miles from Nazareth to Zechariah's home (v.40), a major trip for Mary.

41–42 To speculate about how Mary's greeting caused the child to leap in Elizabeth's womb (v.41) would be to miss the unaffected beauty of this narrative in which the stirring of the unborn child becomes a joyful prelude to Elizabeth's being filled by the Holy Spirit, who enlightened her about the identity of the child Mary was carrying (v.42).

43 Nowhere in the NT is Mary called "Mother of God." Deity is not confined to the person of Jesus (we may say, "Jesus is God," but not [all of] "God is Jesus"). She was, however, the mother of Jesus the Messiah and Lord. In Luke "Lord" is a frequently used title (95 out of 166 occurrences in the Synoptics; so Gaston, p. 76). Jesus is called "Lord" two other times in the Lukan birth narratives (1:76; 2:11).

44–45 "Blessed" (v.45) describes the happy situation of those God favors. Elizabeth gave the blessing Zechariah's muteness prevented him from giving. See vv.68–79 for the blessing he later gave the infant Jesus. Luke uses the blessing Elizabeth gave Mary to call attention to Mary's faith.

4. Mary's song: The Magnificat

1:46–56

46And Mary said:

> "My soul glorifies the Lord
> 47 and my spirit rejoices in God my Savior,
> 48for he has been mindful
> of the humble state of his servant.
> From now on all generations will call me blessed,
> 49 for the Mighty One has done great things for me—
> holy is his name.
> 50His mercy extends to those who fear him,
> from generation to generation.
> 51He has performed mighty deeds with his arm;
> he has scattered those who are proud in their
> inmost thoughts.
> 52He has brought down rulers from their thrones
> but has lifted up the humble.
> 53He has filled the hungry with good things
> but has sent the rich away empty.
> 54He has helped his servant Israel,
> remembering to be merciful
> 55to Abraham and his descendants forever,
> even as he said to our fathers."

56Mary stayed with Elizabeth for about three months and then returned home.

This song, commonly known as the Magnificat, has several striking features. First, it is saturated with OT concepts and phrases. Plummer (pp. 30–31) cites twelve different OT passages it reflects line by line, in addition to Hannah's prayer in 1 Samuel 2:1–10, on which the song seems to have been modeled.

Second, assuming that the song is correctly attributed to Mary (see below), it shows her deep piety and knowledge of Scripture. Such familiarity with the OT was not at that time so unusual for a pious Jewess like Mary as to bar her from consideration as its author. Moreover, it reflects qualities suitable to the mother of the Lord.

Third, though it reveals a God who vindicates the downtrodden and ministers to the hungry (cf. 1 Sam 2:1–10), it also strikes a revolutionary note. If Hannah spoke of the poor being raised to sit with nobles (1 Sam 2:8), Mary sees the nobles toppled from their places of power (Luke 1:52). Yet Hannah's song is not without its elements of judgment in which the hungry and those who arrogantly oppose God are routed (1 Sam 2:3, 5, 10; cf. Luke 1:51, 53). Luke conveys a strong social message to us, one that is rooted in the OT and that, with cultural adaptations, is of continued meaning.

Fourth, Mary's Magnificat markedly transcends Hannah's song. It does this through its messianic element and implies Mary's consciousness of her own exalted role as the kingdom dawns (v.48).

This song can be divided into four strophes: (1) vv.46–48 praise God for what he has done for Mary, a theme that continues into the first part of the next strophe; (2) vv.49–50 mention certain attributes of God—power, holiness, and mercy; (3) vv.51–53 show God's sovereign action in reversing certain social conditions; and (4), finally, vv.54–55 recall God's mercy to Israel.

How much of the Magnificat was originally spoken by Mary rather than composed by Luke? Apart from basic matters of inspiration and literary or critical factors, several considerations ought to be kept in mind. One is the creative potential of even a poorly educated girl from a rural area. Another is the ability of people in ancient times to absorb and remember the spoken word, especially the biblical word. This applies both to Mary's knowledge of OT phraseology and to her repetition of these phrases.

Further, we are not told that Mary composed the song on the spot. Even a few days of meditation during her journey would have been sufficient time for her to produce the composition, especially since she was a girl who reflected deeply (cf. 2:51).

Finally, the song may be taken as prophecy in the broad biblical sense, in which case the Holy Spirit who instructed Elizabeth (v.41) may well have led both Mary and Luke in the composition and transmission of the song.

46–47 The excitement of Elizabeth, who actually shouted her benediction (v.42), gives way to a restraint that is no less joyful. A synonymous parallelism like that in the Psalms characterizes vv.46b–47.

This first major song in Luke derives its name Magnificat from the first word of the Latin version of the song, which translates *megalynei*. NEB's translation "Tell out . . . the greatness of the Lord" is a beautifully phrased expression of Mary's intent. The word *megalynei* literally means "enlarge." In this context it connotes the ascription of greatness to God.

Mary's song begins on the note of salvation, as she acknowledges her dependence on God (v.47). Her words are comparable to those of Habakkuk, who came through his trials rejoicing in God his Savior (Hab 3:18). Note that in beginning the Magnificat by praising "God my Savior," Mary answered the Roman Catholic dogma of the immaculate conception, which holds that from the moment of her conception Mary was by God's grace "kept free from all taint of Original Sin." Only sinners need a Savior.

48 Mary's "humble state" probably refers to her lowly social position. The word does not usually convey the idea of "humiliated." For the meaning of "servant," see comments on v.38; for that of "blessed," see v.45 and 6:20.

49 Mary is in awe of the "Mighty One," whose great power has been exercised in her life. The word "great" (*megala*) recalls "praises" (*megalynei*) in v.46. God's "name" is, according to the common ancient meaning, his whole reputation or character.

50 "Mercy" expresses an aspect of God's character sometimes overlooked when his power and holiness are stressed. A false dichotomy between holiness and mercy characterized some of the Pharisees (Matt 23:23). "Fear" means here, as often in Scripture, a pious reverence.

51–55 The main verbs in the next two strophes are in the past or aorist tense. The use of the aorist tense could be gnomic (somewhat like a proverb, e.g., v.53: "God always fills the hungry"). If not gnomic, the aorists could recall the specific times in the OT when God acted (vv.51–52). We must not, however, overlook the fact that Mary's references to the acts of God relate to the coming of the Messiah and indicate, as mentioned above, radical social reversals. Also, use of the past tenses here could actually be predictive (as in Isa 53:1–9), though general in content.

Mary recalls God's covenant (vv.54–55). The words translated "forever" (*eis ton aiōna*) occur emphatically as the final words in the original text of the song. To avoid the impression that "to Abraham and his descendants" are indirect objects of "as he said" (as though parallel with "to our fathers"), NIV reverses v.55a and 55b (cf. Notes).

56 Luke leaves us perplexed as to whether Mary's stay of "about three months" ended before or continued after the birth of John (cf. vv.26, 36, 39). His reticence should preclude rather than stimulate needless speculation.

Notes

46 There are several reasons—textual and contextual—for questioning the word "Mary" here. Some theorize that Elizabeth, not Mary, composed the Magnificat. Among the contextual reasons is the fact that the earlier social shame of Elizabeth's childless condition corresponds both to the situation of Hannah, whose prayer in 1 Samuel 2 is similar to this, and, possibly, to the description of the author of the Magnificat in v.48. The former parallel is significant, but the meaning of v.48 is equally or more appropriate to Mary. Of the contextual reasons, the strongest is the wording of v.56, which is, literally, "Mary stayed with her" (i.e., with Elizabeth; so NIV). If Mary had just sung the Magnificat, one might expect the verse to say, "She stayed with Elizabeth." Yet this is hardly conclusive.

Textually, there is only scant testimony to the reading "Elizabeth" in v.46 (Metzger, *Textual Commentary*, pp. 130–31). The editors of the UBS considered alternate possibilities but found the evidence for the originality of "Mary" in the text "overwhelming." (For a presentation of the argument that Elizabeth was the author of the Magnificat, see Creed, pp. 22–23.)

47 Ἠγαλλίασεν (*ēgalliasen*, "rejoices"), unlike μεγαλύνει (*megalynei*, "praises") in v.46, is in the aorist (past) tense. It may be a Semitism (*waw* conversive) or just an example of an aorist used with a perfective sense, i.e., describing a present state that is the continuation of a past event (cf. James Hope Moulton, *A Grammar of New Testament Greek*, vol. 3, *Syntax*, Nigel Turner [Edinburgh: T. & T. Clark, 1963], pp. 68–81).

49–55 A certain militant tone in the song calls to mind some extrabiblical phraseology as well as some of the ideals of the Zealots. For a significant, even if not entirely convincing, discussion of this, see J. Massingbyrde Ford, "Zealotism and the Lukan Infancy Narratives," *NovTest* 18 (1976): 281–92, especially pp. 284ff.

49 Ὁ δυνατός (*ho dynatos*, "the Mighty One") is a phrase that has no exact OT parallel, though God was often lauded for his power. Psalm 24 (23 LXX):8 does have the word *dynatos* ("mighty") twice, but the closest expression is in Zeph 3:17: "The LORD your God is in your midst, A victorious warrior" (lit. LXX; "mighty to save," NIV).

55 The words "to our fathers" clearly go with the verb "said." The second half of the verse, beginning with "to Abraham," probably completes "remembering to be merciful" in v.54.

B. Birth Narratives (1:57–2:20)

1. The birth of John the Baptist

1:57–66

[57]When it was time for Elizabeth to have her baby, she gave birth to a son. [58]Her neighbors and relatives heard that the Lord had shown her great mercy, and they shared her joy.

[59]On the eighth day they came to circumcise the child, and they were going to name him after his father Zechariah, [60]but his mother spoke up and said, "No! He is to be called John."

[61]They said to her, "There is no one among your relatives who has that name." [62]Then they made signs to his father, to find out what he would like to name the child. [63]He asked for a writing tablet, and to everyone's astonishment he wrote, "His name is John." [64]Immediately his mouth was opened and his tongue was loosed, and he began to speak, praising God. [65]The neighbors were all filled with awe, and throughout the hill country of Judea people were talking about all these things. [66]Everyone who heard this wondered about it, asking, "What then is this child going to be?" For the Lord's hand was with him.

This is a brief sequel to vv.5–25 and serves to introduce the Benedictus (vv.67–79). It pictures a rural, close-knit society where personal experiences are shared by the community.

57–61 These verses give the impression that no one in the neighborhood knew of Elizabeth's pregnancy (v.57). Perhaps a seclusion that would have prompted suspicion in the case of a younger woman seemed normal for an older one. On one level, the "joy" (v.58) is over Elizabeth's emergence from the shadow of childlessness; on another it accords with the messianic joy of vv.44, 46.

Circumcision on the eighth day (v.59) was in accord with Genesis 17:9–14. Luke offers no explanation as to why the child had not been publicly named at birth. Possibly the narrative reflects the Hellenistic custom of waiting a week or so to name a newborn child. In any event there was obviously a considerable audience for the naming at the circumcision. To choose a name after a baby's grandfather or father, especially if one of them was highly esteemed, was natural (v.61). The objection from Elizabeth (v.60) was against custom and was apparently discounted, probably because she was only a woman.

62–63 Zechariah may have been deaf as well as mute, though this has not been indicated. Luke says he was "unable to speak" (1:22), but the word used (*kōphos*) can also mean "deaf" (as in 7:22). In any case the relatives and neighbors made signs (v.62), to which he responded on a waxed writing tablet (v.63). The present tense in the statement "his name is John" has the ring of deliberate emphasis.

64–66 When the time of his disability (v.20) was over, Zechariah's first words were words of praise (v.64; cf. Acts 2:4, 11—"declaring the wonders of God"). Luke stresses the widespread response (v.65) to the events surrounding the birth of John, just as he later stresses the fame of Jesus (e.g., 2:52). A child whose birth was attended by such marvelous circumstances would surely have an unusual destiny (v.66).

Notes

58 The word "great" is actually a verb, ἐμεγάλυνεν (*emegalynen*), the same used in v.46, meaning to "magnify" or "make great." The idea of greatness is also repeated in v.49. For "mercy," see vv.50, 54.
59 The imperfect ἐκάλουν (*ekaloun*) could mean that they were already naming him John, or, as in NIV, that they were trying or "were going to name him."
66 The verb ἦν (*ēn*, "was") in the clause "for the Lord's hand was with him" probably indicates that the comment was not made by the people at the time but that it is Luke's own later reflection. A few Western texts omit the verb. The omission probably was a deliberate change to make the comment fit in as part of the dialogue (Metzger, *Textual Commentary*, p. 131).

2. *Zechariah's song: The Benedictus*

    1:67–80

       [67]His father Zechariah was filled with the Holy Spirit and prophesied:

          [68]"Praise be to the Lord, the God of Israel,
            because he has come and has redeemed his people.
          [69]He has raised up a horn of salvation for us
            in the house of his servant David
          [70](as he said through his holy prophets of long ago),
          [71]salvation from our enemies
            and from the hand of all who hate us—
          [72]to show mercy to our fathers
            and to remember his holy covenant,
          [73] the oath he swore to our father Abraham:

⁷⁴to rescue us from the hand of our enemies,
    and to enable us to serve him without fear
⁷⁵ in holiness and righteousness before him all our days.
⁷⁶And you, my child, will be called a prophet of the
        Most High;
    for you will go on before the Lord to prepare the way
        for him,
⁷⁷to give his people the knowledge of salvation
    through the forgiveness of their sins,
⁷⁸because of the tender mercy of our God,
    by which the rising sun will come to us from heaven
⁷⁹to shine on those living in darkness
    and in the shadow of death,
    to guide our feet into the path of peace."

⁸⁰And the child grew and became strong in spirit; and he lived in the desert until
he appeared publicly to Israel.

This second major song in Luke is called the Benedictus, the first word in the Latin version, which is a translation of the Greek *eulogētos* ("blessed"). The song has two main parts: (1) praise to God for messianic deliverance (vv.68–75), and (2) celebration of the significant role John the Baptist will have in this work of deliverance. In both sections there is a strong emphasis on salvation, national and personal, and on the covenant and preparation that are about to be realized in their fulfillment. There is striking use of chiasmus (a rhetorical device that entails inversion in parallel literary structures) in the first part of Zechariah's song. From the ends to the center, the following terms recur, usually in reverse order: "come" or "visit" (vv.68, 78 [some versions have "dawn" in v.78]); "his people" (vv.68, 77); "salvation" (vv.69, 77); prophet(s) (vv.70, 76); "hand of our enemies" (vv.71, 74); father(s) (vv.72–73); "covenant" and "oath" (vv.72–73). With the words "covenant" and "oath" in juxtaposition at the center, i.e., at the end of the first and the beginning of the second sequence of the chiasm (vv.72–73), God's faithfulness to his covenant occupies a central position theologically in the Benedictus. Once again Luke makes the connection between the Christian gospel and its OT roots. Plummer (p. 39) notes sixteen OT parallels in the Benedictus.

67 Zechariah the priest now prophesies. As the Holy Spirit had filled Elizabeth (v.41), he now fills Zechariah. Observe that Zechariah's previous doubt and his discipline through loss of speech did not mean the end of his spiritual ministry. So when a believer today has submitted to God's discipline, he may go on in Christ's service.

68 The NIV uses "praise" to translate both *eulogētos* in this verse and *megalynei* in v.46. The word *eulogētos* can refer both to a human being on whom God has showered his goodness (i.e., "blessed," as in vv.42, 45) and to God, to whom we return thanks for that goodness (i.e., "praise"). A form of the same word occurs in v.64. It is as though vv.68–79 provide the content of the blessing expressed in the earlier verse. "Israel" is paralleled by "his people" in vv.68, 77, carrying along the promise of v.17 (cf. comments there).

The action is centered in two verbs: "has come" and "has redeemed." The first, "has come," is from the verb *episkeptomai*. In secular Greek it means simply "to look at," "reflect on," or "visit" (often in a charitable way, such as a doctor visiting the sick; cf. Matt 25:36, 43; James 1:27). The element of special concern is deepened to the spiritual level in the LXX use of the word. A particular example is that of God "visiting" people in grace or in judgment (Exod 4:31; Zech 10:3; cf. TDNT, 2:599–605). The idea of God graciously "visiting" or "coming" to his people in the sense of vv.68, 78 appears also in 7:16. In these three verses, as well as in Acts 15:14, where *episkeptomai* is translated "showed his concern," the word "people" also occurs. Tragically, Jerusalem did not recognize the day of her "visitation" (19:44; NIV, "the time of God's coming").

The second verb, "redeemed," represents two Greek words: *epoiēsen lytrōsin* ("accomplished redemption"). The idea of redemption runs through Scripture, with the Exodus being the great OT example of rescue from enemies and captivity. Luke 24:21 shows the expectation Jesus' followers had that he would do a similar work of freeing God's people. Luke, though committed to the universal application of the gospel, includes these words of redemption that apply especially to Israel (see esp. v.69). Not only does this reflect his emphasis on the Jewish roots of Christianity, it also underlines the political aspects of redemption foremost in the minds of Zechariah's contemporaries.

69–70 "Horn" (v.69) is a common OT metaphor for power because of the great strength of the horned animals of the Near East. The word "salvation" describes the kind of strength Zechariah had in mind. The power of salvation resides in the Savior. Again, the messianic theme occurs—this time in an allusion to Psalm 132 (131 LXX): 17, where, in fulfilling the Davidic covenant, God "will make a horn grow for David." The verb "raised up" (*ēgeiren*) in v.69 is not used in the LXX of Psalm 132. Here it is appropriate for stressing God's sovereignty. Later in Luke's writing this verb will assume great importance in relation to the resurrection of Christ (24:6, 34; Acts 3:7, 15; 4:10).

The messianic motif is further emphasized by a reference to the "house of . . . David." The mention of the "holy prophets of long ago" (v.70), while placed in parenthesis in NIV for clarity, is not theologically parenthetical. Like a similar reference in Hebrews 1:1, it serves to confirm the OT origin of and support for the messianic role of Jesus.

71–73 Placing v.70 in a parenthesis clarifies the relationship of vv.71–75 to v.69. "Salvation" (v.71) is the link. It is the first of three aspects of God's redeeming work, the others being "mercy" (v.72) and the remembrance of God's "covenant." The salvation Zechariah is speaking of is at this stage clearly political. Mercy to the "fathers" seems to mean that God has not thwarted their hopes. This mercy may be related to v.17 and Malachi 4:6. The "oath" (v.73) to Abraham in view here is recorded in Genesis 22:16–18, where the Lord promised Abraham not only that his descendants' enemies would be subdued but also that universal blessing would result from his obedience. Therefore, the salvation in view here involves both political deliverance and spiritual blessing (cf. the next verses).

As noted earlier, the words "covenant" and "oath" form the central point of the chiasm (inverse repetition of terms). This has the effect of emphasizing the importance of God's covenant and his faithfulness to it. Not only does this serve an important theme in Luke, but it gives encouragement to us to trust the promises of God.

74–75 The fulfillment of God's promise does not mean passivity for Israel but a new opportunity for service—negatively, service "without fear" (v.74) and, positively, "in holiness and righteousness" (v.75, cf. Mal 3:3).

76–77 The second part of Zechariah's hymn begins with a direct word to his son (v.76). The role of John, like that of Paul and the Lord's servants throughout history, derives its significance and greatness from God's purpose and, even more, from the greatness of the Person served. Before addressing the theme of salvation, Zechariah speaks of the "Most High" and "the Lord" John represents.

The description of John in v.76, when compared with Isaiah 40:3; Malachi 3:1; 4:5, clearly links him with Elijah, dispelling any doubts about the recognition of this link in Luke. Such doubts have arisen largely from Luke's omission of the conversation (cf. Matt 17:10–13; Mark 9:11–13) about Elijah following the Transfiguration. There Jesus says that Elijah has "already come," i.e., the predictions about Elijah were fulfilled in John the Baptist. Also Luke's parallel to Matthew 11:12 (Luke 16:16) has seemed to some to detach John from the age of Jesus and the church. Thus some have considered it unlikely that Luke thought of John as the Elijah figure whose coming was to usher in the last days. We must keep in mind that as a physician Luke was strongly aware of corporeality. More than the other Gospel writers, he stressed the physical resurrection of Jesus ("they did not find the body of the Lord Jesus" [24:3]), the reality of Jesus' ascension, and the Spirit's descent in "bodily form" like a dove (3:22) at Jesus' baptism. It would, therefore, be understandable for Luke to hold that John had indeed come "in the spirit and power of Elijah" (1:17), yet for him to avoid saying anything that might imply the reincarnation of Elijah as John. If Elijah could still appear in recognizable form, as he did at the Transfiguration, Luke may have hesitated to include in his Gospel anything about his apparent identification with John. Verse 76, though consistent with the idea that John came in the "spirit and power of Elijah," avoids the kind of terminology Luke may still have had some hesitation about. See also Walter Wink, *John the Baptist in the Gospel Tradition* (London: Cambridge University Press, 1968), pp. 42–45.

The theme of "salvation" (v.77) for God's "people," expressed in political terms in v.71, now finds its spiritual identity through forgiveness. John will go on to preach "a baptism of repentance for the forgiveness of sins" (3:3).

78–79 NIV's "rising sun" (v.78; cf. Notes) has a dynamic quality that suits the word "come" or "visit" (cf. v.68). Verse 79 uses a beautiful quotation from Isaiah 60:1–3 to carry forward the imagery of light (the sun) and to offer hope of peace to those who were then outside the faithful remnant of Judaism (cf. Eph 2:12).

80 This brief description of John's boyhood reflects Luke's interest in human beings. Later he will comment more fully on Jesus' personal developments (2:40, 52). Since the discovery of the DSS near Qumran, there has been speculation about the possibility of contact between John and the Qumran community. If his elderly parents had been unable to care for him, or if they had died in his youth, it is conceivable that John might even have lived for a time at Qumran. Taking in young men was the only way the celibate community could reproduce itself. Nevertheless, such a connection lacks supporting evidence.

Notes

67 Both the unity and the literary history of the Benedictus are disputed. But its theology arises from the OT, the themes of the two parts (vv.68–75 and vv.76–79) are intertwined, and the concepts in each part are appropriate to Jesus and John respectively. For a discussion of the issues, see Marshall, *Luke: Historian and Theologian*, p. 87.

68–79 This passage is so thoroughly Jewish in its orientation and theology that it would be difficult to imagine that it originated in the Hellenistic church and was adapted back into this context. The distinction between "we" and "they" is ingrained throughout—e.g., "us" in vv.69, 74, which is parallel to "his people," over against the "enemies . . . all who hate us." Only at the end does a salvation seem to extend beyond Israel, and that promise is rooted in Isa 60.

68 The noun λύτρωσις (*lytrōsis*, "redemption") is found only twice in Luke—here (where the NIV renders the noun as a verb for smoother English) and in Anna's prophecy about the infant Jesus (2:38). The verbal form occurs in 24:21. Luke is the only Gospel to use the longer form ἀπολύτρωσις (*apolytrōsis*), which is of major importance in the Epistles. For a discussion of redemption in the NT, see Leon Morris, *The Apostolic Preaching of the Cross* (Grand Rapids: Eerdmans, 1955), pp. 9–59; cf. also David Hill, *Greek Words and Hebrew Meanings: Studies in the Semantics of Soteriological Terms*, SNTS 5 (London: Cambridge University Press, 1967). Significantly, despite Luke's stress on the concept of redemption, when λύτρον (*lytron*) occurs in Matt 20:28 and Mark 10:45, Luke omits it in his parallel of these verses. This may be because the concept is already inherent in the narrative of the Last Supper that, in the Lukan order, just precedes it. Luke 22:24–27 may not, however, be a true parallel.

69 Σωτηρία (*sōtēria* "salvation") is also mentioned in vv.71, 77; 2:30; 3:6, σωτήρ (*sōtēr*, "Savior" in 1:47; 2:11, and numerous occasions of σώζω (*sōzō*, "save"). See Marshall, *Luke: Historian and Theologian*, pp. 92–102.

71 The use of the accusative σωτηρίαν (*sōtērian*, "salvation") here is debatable. It seems to function as the object of ἐλάλησεν (*elalēsen*, "said") in v.70. Or it could stand in apposition to κέρας (*keras*, "horn"), which is already identified in v.69 with salvation.

78 Ἀνατολή (*anatolē*) is interestingly rendered "dayspring" in KJV, "day" in RSV, "sunrise" in NASB, and "rising sun" in NIV. These represent attempts to translate a word with a basically simple meaning, the rising of the sun or stars, yet one that the LXX used in translating the distinctive messianic term צֶמַח (*semah*, "sprout," "branch") in Jer 23:5; Zech 3:8; 6:12. However *anatolē* is translated, it is important to keep this messianic aspect in mind (see TDNT, 1:352–53).

80 Ἐκραταιοῦτο πνεύματι (*ekrataiouto pneumati*) probably means "became strong in spirit" in the sense of development of moral character, though somewhat similar wording in Eph 3:16 describes a strengthening by God's Spirit.

The plural form ἐν ταῖς ἐρήμοις (*en tais erēmois*, "in the desert") is idiomatic. John ministered near the Jordan River, but it is not certain that he grew up in the same area. While the desert had various popular connotations (e.g., the home of demons), here it simply implies relative isolation.

Ἀναδείξεως (*anadeixeōs*, "until he appeared publicly") is literally "until the day of his appearance" or "commissioning" (so BAG, s.v.).

3. The birth of Jesus
2:1–7

[1]In those days Caesar Augustus issued a decree that a census should be taken of the entire Roman world. [2](This was the first census that took place while Quirinius was governor of Syria.) [3]And everyone went to his own town to register.

⁴So Joseph also went up from the town of Nazareth in Galilee to Judea, to Bethlehem the town of David, because he belonged to the house and line of David. ⁵He went there to register with Mary, who was pledged to be married to him and was expecting a child. ⁶While they were there, the time came for the baby to be born, ⁷and she gave birth to her firstborn, a son. She wrapped him in cloths and placed him in a manger, because there was no room for them in the inn.

In comparison with the complex narrative in chapter 1, the actual birth narrative of Jesus is brief. In it Luke stresses three things: (1) the political situation (to explain why Jesus' birth took place in Bethlehem); (2) that Bethlehem was the town of David (to stress Jesus' messianic claim); (3) the humble circumstances of Jesus' birth.

The mention of Caesar Augustus may not only be for historical background but also to contrast the human with the divine decrees. A mere Galilean peasant travels to Bethlehem ostensibly at the decree of the Roman emperor. Actually, it is in fulfillment of the divine King's plan, which, as noted passim, is reflected in Luke's frequent reference to what "must" (*dei*) be done.

1–3 Luke clearly intends to secure the historical and chronological moorings of Jesus' birth. Ironically, it is precisely this that has led some to question Luke's accuracy.

The first census (i.e., enrollment prior to taxation) known to have occurred under the governorship of Quirinius took place later (i.e., A.D. 6) than usually reckoned as the time of Jesus' birth. Reference to this census is found in both Acts 5:37 and Josephus (Antiq. XVIII, 26 [ii.1]). Many have supposed that Luke confused this census of A.D. 6 with one he thinks was taken earlier, but which lacks historical support. The most satisfactory solutions that have been proposed follow.

1. Quirinius had a government assignment in Syria at this time and conducted a census in his official capacity. Details of this census may have been common knowledge in Luke's time but are now lost to us (cf. E.M. Blaiklock, "Quirinius," ZPEB, 5:5–6). An incomplete MS describes the career of an officer whose name is not preserved but whose actions sound as if he might have been Quirinius. He became imperial "legate of Syria" for the "second time." While this is ambiguous, it may be a clue that Quirinius served both at the time of Jesus' birth and a few years later (cf. F.F. Bruce, "Quirinius," NBD, p. 1069).

2. The word *prōtē* can be construed to mean not "first," as usually translated, but "former" or "prior." The meaning of v.2 is then "This census was *before* that made when Quirinius was governor" (N. Turner, *Grammatical Insights into the New Testament* [Edinburgh: T. & T. Clark, 1966], pp. 23–24; idem, *Syntax*, p. 32).

It was customary to return to one's original home for such a census. Also, powerful as he was, Herod was only a client king under Rome and, like others, was subject to orders for a census. Furthermore, it is scarcely conceivable that Luke, careful researcher that he was (1:1–4), would have stressed the census unless he had reasonable historical grounds for doing so. (See further F.F. Bruce, *Jesus and Christian Origins Outside the New Testament* [Grand Rapids: Eerdmans, 1974], pp. 192–94; Marshall, *Luke: Historian and Theologian*, pp. 98–104.)

Notes

1-3 For a negative judgment on the historicity of Luke's account of the census, see HJP, 1:399-427.

4-7 Luke does not say how long in advance of Jesus' birth Joseph left for Bethlehem (v.4) nor why he took Mary with him. It is possible that he used the emperor's order as a means of removing Mary from possible gossip and emotional stress in her own village. He had already accepted her as his wife (Matt 1:24), but apparently they continued in betrothal (v.5: "pledged to be married") till after the birth. The text neither affirms nor denies the popular image of the couple arriving in Bethlehem just as the baby was about to be born. Luke simply states that the birth took place "while they were there" (v.6). Since she had stayed three months with Elizabeth, Mary was at least three months pregnant. It is possible that they went down during her last trimester of pregnancy, when the social relationships in Nazareth would have grown more difficult. They may have stayed in a crowded room in the home of some poor relative till the birth of the baby necessitated their vacating it for privacy and more space. Any such reconstruction is, however, merely speculative.

The word *katalyma*, usually translated "inn" (v.7), may mean a room (e.g., the "guest room" used for the Last Supper [22:11], referred to as an "upper room" in 22:12), a billet for soldiers, or any place for lodging, which would include inns. It is not, however, the usual Greek word for an inn—*pandocheion,* to which the Good Samaritan took the robbery victim (10:34). As the etymology of the word—*pan* ("all") and *dechomai* ("receive")—suggests, inns accepted all kinds of people, often the worst. Stories were told of discomfort and even of robberies at inns.

Luke could have painted a sordid picture, had he so desired. Instead he uses the general word for a lodging place and states the simple fact that when Mary's time came, the only available place for the little family was one usually occupied by animals. It may have been a cave, as tradition suggests, or some part of a house or inn. Even today in many places around the world farm animals and their fodder are often kept in the same building as the family quarters. The eating trough, or "manger," was ideal for use as a crib. Luke does not seem to be portraying a dismal situation with an unfeeling innkeeper as villain. Rather, he is establishing a contrast between the proper rights of the Messiah in his own "town of David" and the very ordinary and humble circumstances of his birth. Whatever the reason, even in his birth Jesus was excluded from the normal shelter others enjoyed (cf. 9:58). This is consistent with Luke's realistic presentation of Jesus' humanity and servanthood. As to the "cloths," see comment on v.12.

4. The announcement to the shepherds

2:8-20

⁸And there were shepherds living out in the fields nearby, keeping watch over their flocks at night. ⁹An angel of the Lord appeared to them, and the glory of the Lord shone around them, and they were terrified. ¹⁰But the angel said to them, "Do not be afraid. I bring you good news of great joy that will be for all the people. ¹¹Today in the town of David a Savior has been born to you; he is Christ the Lord.

¹²This will be a sign to you: You will find a baby wrapped in cloths and lying in a manger."

¹³Suddenly a great company of the heavenly host appeared with the angel, praising God and saying

¹⁴"Glory to God in the highest,
and on earth peace to men on whom his favor rests."

¹⁵When the angels had left them and gone into heaven, the shepherds said to one another, "Let's go to Bethlehem and see this thing that has happened, which the Lord has told us about."

¹⁶So they hurried off and found Mary and Joseph, and the baby, who was lying in the manger. ¹⁷When they had seen him, they spread the word concerning what had been told them about this child, ¹⁸and all who heard it were amazed at what the shepherds said to them. ¹⁹But Mary treasured up all these things and pondered them in her heart. ²⁰The shepherds returned, glorifying and praising God for all the things they had heard and seen, which were just as they had been told.

The pastoral scene described in this section actually conveys more theological significance than is sometimes realized. Both the words of the angel and the symbolism of what happened have theological implications.

8 There may be several reasons for the special role of the shepherds in the events of this unique night. Among the occupations, shepherding had a lowly place (SBK, 2:114). Shepherds were considered untrustworthy and their work made them ceremonially unclean. Thus the most obvious implication is that the gospel first came to the social outcasts of Jesus' day. This would accord with a recurring emphasis in Luke. Moreover, it may be significant that in the Lord's instructions to Nathan about giving David the covenant the Lord reminds David, who was to become Messiah's ancestor, that he was called from the shepherd's life (2 Sam 7:8). Finally, in both testaments shepherds symbolize those who care for God's people, including the Lord himself (Ps 23:1; Isa 40:11; Jer 23:1–4; Heb 13:20; 1 Peter 2:25; 5:2). The shepherds of Luke 2 may, therefore, symbolize all the ordinary people who have joyfully received the gospel and have become in various ways pastors to others.

That the shepherds were out in the fields at night does not preclude a December date, as the winter in Judea was mild. But, of course, the text says nothing about the time of year. The traditional date for the Nativity was set, long after the event, to coincide with a pagan festival, thus demonstrating that the "Sol Invictus," the "Unconquerable Sun," had indeed been conquered. December 25 was widely celebrated as the date of Jesus' birth by the end of the fourth century. January 6 was also an important date in the early church, held by many as the occasion of the arrival of the wise men and known as Epiphany. (See Frank E. Gaebelein, "The Most Beautiful Story Ever Told," CT 23 [1979]: 1612–14 [18–20].) Morris (*Luke*, p. 84) suggests that, if the birth did take place in winter, the shepherds may have been raising sheep for sacrifice at Passover a few months later.

9 First a single angel (cf. 1:11, 26) appears; the multitude of angels does not appear till v.13. The shepherds' terror recalls that of Zechariah (1:12). It was not just the angel that terrified them but the visible manifestation of the glory of God—something neither Zechariah nor Mary had seen. Again, as in 1:13 and 1:30, the angel speaks reassuringly.

10-11 The angel's announcement (v.10) includes several of the most frequently used words in Luke's Gospel (cf. Notes)—a fact that shows the tremendous importance of the angelic pronouncement. It is a bold proclamation of the gospel at the very hour of Jesus' birth (v.11).

Thus in this whole section Luke shares his perception of major themes that support the declaration: the time has come ("today") for the fulfillment of the prophetic expectation of Messiah's coming.

12 The "cloths" (KJV, "swaddling clothes," from the verb *spargano*, "to swathe") would constitute a "sign." Babies were snugly wrapped in long strips of cloth, giving them warmth, protection of extremities, and a sense of security in their newborn existence. The combination of a newborn baby's wrappings and the use of the manger for a crib would be a distinctive "sign." Perhaps they also imply that in spite of seeming rejection, symbolized by the manger, the baby was the special object of his mother's care. In Ezekiel 16:1-5, Jerusalem is symbolically described as a heathen child who was neglected from birth till God rescued and cared for her. She had not been given the usual postnatal care and so was not wrapped with strips of cloth (Ezek 16:4). But Jesus was not so neglected. On the other hand, the "sign" might be only the strange circumstance of the newborn child being in the manger at all.

13 "Suddenly" (*exaiphnēs*), along with cognate words, often describes the unexpected nature of God's acts, especially the eschatological events. Malachi had predicted the sudden coming of the Lord to his temple (Mal 3:1). Now the angels suddenly announce his arrival at Bethlehem. The Spirit's coming at Pentecost was sudden (Acts 2:2), as was the appearance of the Lord to Saul on the road to Damascus (Acts 9:3). Mark 13:36 and 1 Thessalonians 5:3 describe the suddenness of future events.

The "heavenly host," which often meant heavenly bodies in the OT, refers here to an army or band of angels (cf. 1 Kings 22:19).

14 The doxology "Glory to God in the highest" is the climax of the story. Its two parts relate to heaven and to earth respectively. In Luke's account of the Triumphal Entry, the crowds say, "Peace in heaven and glory in the highest" (19:38). In Ephesians 3:21, Paul ascribes glory to God, not now in the heavens, but "in the church and in Christ Jesus." Verse 14b is best translated as in NIV: "and on earth peace to men on whom his favor rests." For reasons discussed in the Notes, "good will to men" (KJV) is inaccurate. Luke emphasizes the work of Christ on earth. (See also Jesus' own declaration that "the Son of Man has authority on earth to forgive sins"— Luke 5:24; Matt 9:6; Mark 2:10.)

The "peace" here is that which the Messiah brings (cf. 1:79). Those whom Jesus healed or forgave on the basis of their faith could "go in peace" (7:50; 8:48). Those on whom God's "favor" (*eudokia*) rests are the "little children" (10:21) to whom God graciously reveals truth according to his "good pleasure" (the only other use of *eudokia* in the Gospels, except for the parallel in Matt 11:26).

15-16 Luke does not say that the angels disappeared but that they went "into heaven" (v.15), an expression typical of his attention to spatial relationships (cf. comments on the Ascension at 24:51, where the same words appear in what is probably the original text; cf. Acts 1:11). The realization of God's promise ("this thing [*rhēma*] . . . which the Lord has told us") is expressed also in v.29: "as you have promised" (*kata to rhēma sou*, lit., "according to your word"). Luke combines the phenomena of ancient (v.15) and recent (v.29) prophetic words, thus emphasizing the connection between the old and new ages, the Jewish orientation of the gospel and the reality of the heavenly in the earthly.

Both the idiomatic particle *dē*, which conveys a note of urgency (BAG, s.v.), expressed in NIV's "Let's go" (v.15), and the words "hurried off" (*ēlthon speusantes*, v.16) heighten the sense of excitement and determination that propelled the shepherds to the baby's side.

17–18 Then they "spread the word" (v.17) and became the first evangelists of the Christian Era. Luke's observation (v.18) that those who heard them "were amazed" (*ethaumasan*) is the first of his many comments on the enthusiastic response to the messianic proclamation. The next occurrence is when Mary and Joseph "marvel" at what Simeon says about their child (v.33). In v.47 everyone is "amazed" (*existanto*) at Jesus' answers in the temple discussion. The initial reaction of the audience of Jesus' opening declaration in the synagogue of Nazareth that the prophecy of Isaiah 61 was at that moment fulfilled was amazement (4:22; cf. 8:25; 9:43; 11:14, 38; 20:26; 24:12, 41). There are also passages that use other words to describe a similar response (e.g., 4:15, 36; 5:26).

19–20 In contrast to the overreaction of the people, Mary (*hē de Mariam*, "Mary on the other hand") meditates on the meaning of it all (v.19; cf. v.51; cf. also Gen 37:11). Just as the seventy-two disciples returned (*hypestrepsan*) with joy after their preaching mission (10:17), so the shepherds returned (*hypestrepsan*) "glorifying and praising God" (v.20). It is clear that in Luke this spirit of doxology is the proper response to the mighty works of God (cf. 5:25–26; 7:16; 13:13; 17:15; 18:43; 23:47, along with similar occurrences in Acts).

Notes

9–11 The significant terms characteristic of Luke that occur in these verses include εὐαγγελ-ίζομαι (*euangelizomai*, "bring good news" [always in the verbal form in Luke], v.10); χαρά (*chara*, "joy"), which occurs more often in Luke than in Matthew and Mark combined; λαός (*laos*, "people"), used 35 times in Luke against 14 in Matthew and none in Mark (with Luke using it some 47 additional times in Acts); σήμερον (*sēmeron*, "today"), which occurs more in Luke than in Matthew and Mark together (see comment on 4:21 for its significance in Luke); σωτήρ (*sōtēr*, "Savior," v.11), used only by Luke among the Synoptics; and κύριος (*kyrios*, "Lord"), which occurs 95 times in Luke out of 166 in the Synoptics. The word δόξα (*doxa*, "glory"), which occurs in v.9 and reappears in v.14, is also distinctively Lukan. Along with the verb δοξάζω (*doxazō*, "glorify"), Luke uses it more than the two other Synoptics combined.

14 In KJV "good will" is the subject of the clause because KJV followed the TR, which has the nominative εὐδοκία (*eudokia*). However, the oldest MSS have an added sigma (ς), indicator of the genitive case (εὐδοκίας, *eudokias*). The inadvertant *omission* of the small elevated half-circle that was customarily used to indicate the genitive sigma is more likely than the *addition* of a sigma. On the principle that the harder reading is more likely the original one, the genitive should be assumed, since a nominative would read more smoothly. And since similar phrases, describing people "of [God's] good pleasure" are now known from hymns in the DSS (1QH 4.32–33; 8.6; 9.9), there is no difficulty in accepting this reading. More recently an Aramaic text from Cave 4 with a syntactical structure even closer to Luke's has confirmed the matter (Fitzmyer, *Semitic Background*, pp. 101–4). It is also more in accordance with the doctrine of grace than is the idea that those of "good will" are rewarded with peace (cf. also Metzger, *Textual Commentary*, p. 133).

C. *Jesus' Early Years* (2:21–52)

1. *Presentation of Jesus in the temple*

2:21–40

21On the eighth day, when it was time to circumcise him, he was named Jesus, the name the angel had given him before he had been conceived.

22When the time of their purification according to the Law of Moses had been completed, Joseph and Mary took him to Jerusalem to present him to the Lord 23(as it is written in the Law of the Lord, "Every firstborn male is to be consecrated to the Lord"), 24and to offer a sacrifice in keeping with what is said in the Law of the Lord: "a pair of doves or two young pigeons."

25Now there was a man in Jerusalem called Simeon, who was righteous and devout. He was waiting for the consolation of Israel, and the Holy Spirit was upon him. 26It had been revealed to him by the Holy Spirit that he would not die before he had seen the Lord's Christ. 27Moved by the Spirit, he went into the temple courts. When the parents brought in the child Jesus to do for him what the custom of the Law required, 28Simeon took him in his arms and praised God, saying:

29"Sovereign Lord, as you have promised,
you now dismiss your servant in peace.
30For my eyes have seen your salvation,
31 which you have prepared in the sight of all people,
32a light for revelation to the Gentiles
and for glory to your people Israel."

33The child's father and mother marveled at what was said about him. 34Then Simeon blessed them and said to Mary, his mother: "This child is destined to cause the falling and rising of many in Israel, and to be a sign that will be spoken against, 35so that the thoughts of many hearts will be revealed. And a sword will pierce your own soul too."

36There was also a prophetess, Anna, the daughter of Phanuel, of the tribe of Asher. She was very old; she had lived with her husband seven years after her marriage, 37and then was a widow until she was eighty-four. She never left the temple but worshiped night and day, fasting and praying. 38Coming up to them at that very moment, she gave thanks to God and spoke about the child to all who were looking forward to the redemption of Jerusalem.

39When Joseph and Mary had done everything required by the Law of the Lord, they returned to Galilee to their own town of Nazareth. 40And the child grew and became strong; he was filled with wisdom, and the grace of God was upon him.

21–24 It is important to understand the sequence and background of these events. According to Jewish law a woman became ceremonially unclean on the birth of a child. On the eighth day the child was circumcised (cf. 1:59; Gen 17:12), after which the mother was unclean an additional thirty-three days—sixty-six if the child was female (Lev 12:1–5). At the conclusion of this period, the mother offered a sacrifice, either a lamb or, if she was poor, two doves or two young pigeons (Lev 12:6–8). In addition, the first son was to be presented to the Lord and then, so to speak, bought back with an offering (Num 18:15; cf. 1 Sam 1:24-28, where Hannah actually gives up Samuel to the Lord).

Luke, conflating the performance of these OT obligations into this single narrative, shows how Jesus was reared in conformity with them. His parents obeyed the Lord (1:31) in naming him. The offering of birds instead of a lamb shows that he was born into a poor family. Perhaps this helped him identify with the poor of the land (cf. 6:20).

25 In vv.25-38 Luke presents two pious figures who, under divine inspiration, testify to the significance of Jesus. Once again Luke assures us of the credentials of Jesus as Messiah, taking care to show that each witness is an authentic representative of Judaism.

"Now" represents the attention-getting word *idou* ("behold"). Luke neither associates Simeon with a leading sect or party nor calls him a priest. The important thing is that he is "righteous and devout" (cf. Zechariah and Elizabeth, 1:6). He could be described as one of the believing remnant of Judaism, looking forward to the Messianic Age in its spiritual aspect. It is appropriate that the Spirit who is the Consoler (cf. Notes) was upon one who awaited the consolation.

26-28 The same Spirit had revealed to Simeon (v.26) that the Messiah ("the Lord's Christ") would come before Simeon died. This may, but need not necessarily, imply that he was an old man.

Mary and Joseph are referred to as Jesus' "parents" (v.27) and as "the child's father and mother" (v.33). Jesus would have been considered Joseph's own son; so Luke's terminology is not inconsistent. In the genealogy, however, the particulars of the relationship had to be made more explicit (3:23). Here, as in v.38, Luke notes the providential timing, as the Spirit brings Simeon to the temple courts to be ready for the family's arrival. In this touching scene, Luke again shows the presence of Jesus, now in Simeon's arms (v.28), as an occasion of praise (*eulogeō*) to God. Actually, the word is "blessed," the same as in v.34.

29-32 Simeon's psalm begins with the word *nun* ("now"), emphasizing the fact that the Messiah has indeed come (hence the Latin title Nunc Dimittis ["Now Dismiss"]). "Dismiss" (*apolyō*) here means "allow to die" (BAG, s.v.; cf. Num 20:29 LXX). NIV loses the emphasis of the Greek word order because it reverses the phrases. Nevertheless it does retain the words "in peace" in their place of final emphasis (cf. 1:79; 2:14). On "as you promised," see comment on v.15. Note the contrast between "Sovereign Lord" and "servant." God's servant is now ready for his final order—to depart in death (cf. Gen 15:15 LXX; Num 20:29)—because he has indeed seen the "Lord's Christ" (v.26).

Simeon does not say, however, that he has seen the Messiah but rather that his eyes have seen God's salvation (v.30). To see Jesus is to see salvation embodied in him, a theme already noted as prominent in Luke (cf. 1:69, 71, 77; 19:9, and comments). Luke's concern for the universal application of the gospel finds support in the words "in the sight of all people" (v.31). Verse 31 echoes Isaiah 52:10 and Psalm 98:3. The parallel structure in v.32 may involve a detailed contrast as well as a larger one. That is, not only are Gentiles and Jews put in contrast, but the same light (Isa 49:6) that brings "revelation" to pagans (cf. 1:78-79) brings "glory" to Israel (cf. 1:77). Note also "all people" (v.31) and "your people" (v.32; cf. comments on 1:77).

33–35 In spite of what they already know, Joseph and Mary are amazed (v.33; cf. comment on v.17) at Simeon's song. Moreover, in it a somber note is sounded. In vivid language Simeon predicts that because of the child "many in Israel" (v.34) would be brought to moral decision, some to a point of collapse (*ptōsis;* NIV, "falling") and others to what can well be called a resurrection (*anastasis;* NIV, "rising"). Some think there is but one group that falls and then rises (Marshall, *Luke, Historian and Theologian,* p. 122). But there will be a cost to Jesus. As the one who himself is the ultimate "sign," the visible affirmation of God's declared intentions, he will be vulnerable to the hostility of unbelievers. A negative attitude toward him, however, serves to brand the unbeliever as one who has rejected not only him but the whole of God's revelation (v.35; cf. John 5:45–47). This clash will inevitably wound Jesus' mother.

36–38 Luke's attention to the renewal of prophecy at the coming of the Messianic Age continues with the introduction of Anna as a "prophetess" (v.36). Zechariah had been "filled with the Holy Spirit and prophesied" (1:67). Simeon, though not called a prophet, was filled with the Spirit and also prophesied. Prophetesses functioned in both OT and NT times (Exod 15:20; Judg 4:4; 2 Kings 22:14; Neh 6:14; Isa 8:3; Acts 2:17; 21:9; 1 Cor 11:5). Apparently Anna could trace her genealogy; and, though the tribe of Asher was not outstanding (Gen 30:12–13; 35:26), Luke considered it important to show her true Jewishness. She was a familiar figure at the temple. Possibly she lived in one of the rooms surrounding the temple precinct; or she may have, like the disciples in 24:53, centered her life there. She was the ideal widow (v.37) described in 1 Timothy 5:5. Once more Luke points out the providential timing (v.38; cf. v.27). He may be underlining the desire for the messianic deliverance of Jerusalem (cf. Isa 52:9) by describing Anna's thanksgiving with a rare verb (*anthōmologeomai*), which ocurs in a psalm lamenting the defilement of the Jerusalem temple (Ps 79 [78 LXX]:13). Later Luke will mention another pious Jew who had been expecting the messianic kingdom, Joseph of Arimathea (23:51).

39–40 Luke takes another opportunity to mention the fidelity of Jesus' parents to the Jewish law as he continues the narrative (v.39). He omits mention of the flight to Egypt. It is important to Matthew, providing another example of fulfilled prophecy (Matt 2:13–15); but this is not so significant at this point in Luke. What is significant is that Jesus' parents were faithful to the Jewish law and that the child grew normally, the object of God's grace (v.40; cf. v.52).

Notes

25 The "consolation [παράκλησις, *paraklēsis*] of Israel" refers to the time when, according to Isa 40:1–2, God would end Israel's time of alienation and suffering through the advent of the Messiah (cf. Isa 49:13; 57:18; 61:2; and contrast the promise of 5:4 with Luke 6:24). Notice also the theme of encouragement in Acts 4:36; 9:31; 13:15; 15:31. The time of the "consolation" would also be the age of the promised Holy Spirit, who himself is the one who consoles and encourages—παράκλητος (*paraklētos,* "Counselor," John 14:16; 15:26; 16:7).

33 Understandably, the designation ὁ πατὴρ αὐτοῦ καὶ μήτηρ (*ho patēr autou kai mētēr*, "his father and mother") for Joseph and Mary raises questions in the minds of believers in the Virgin Birth. Some early scribes doubtless felt the need for making it clear that Joseph was not Jesus' biological father. As a result there are far too many readings and sources to cite here (see UBS apparatus in loc. and Metzger, *Textual Commentary*, p. 134). NIV's rendering has strong MS support and is the natural way the family would be described.

37 "Until she was eighty-four" is the most natural way to understand ἕως ἐτῶν ὀγδοήκοντα τεσσάρων (*heōs etōn ogdoēkonta tessarōn*). Goodspeed's conclusion is that if Luke meant "for eighty-four years" (which would make her 105 years old), he would have omitted *heōs* ("until") and used the accusative instead of the genitive, or used *heōs* with an ordinal, rather than cardinal, numeral in the genitive (E.J. Goodspeed, *Problems of New Testament Translation* [Chicago: University of Chicago Press, 1945], pp. 79–81). If Anna were 105 years old, she would have been the same age as Judith in the Apocrypha (Jud 16:23).

---

2. The boy Jesus at the temple

2:41–52

41Every year his parents went to Jerusalem for the Feast of the Passover. 42When he was twelve years old, they went up to the Feast, according to the custom. 43After the Feast was over, while his parents were returning home, the boy Jesus stayed behind in Jerusalem, but they were unaware of it. 44Thinking he was in their company, they traveled on for a day. Then they began looking for him among their relatives and friends. 45When they did not find him, they went back to Jerusalem to look for him. 46After three days they found him in the temple courts, sitting among the teachers, listening to them and asking them questions. 47Everyone who heard him was amazed at his understanding and his answers. 48When his parents saw him, they were astonished. His mother said to him, "Son, why have you treated us like this? Your father and I have been anxiously searching for you."

49"Why were you searching for me?" he asked. "Didn't you know I had to be in my Father's house?" 50But they did not understand what he was saying to them.

51Then he went down to Nazareth with them and was obedient to them. But his mother treasured all these things in her heart. 52And Jesus grew in wisdom and stature, and in favor with God and men.

This section provides the only account of Jesus' boyhood we possess apart from apocryphal legends. The focal point is not his precocious wisdom, noteworthy as that was. Rather, Luke leads us to the real climax, Jesus' reference to God as "my Father" (v.49). This is the first instance of Jesus' "filial consciousness," his awareness that in a unique way he was the Son of God.

41–42 Luke takes yet another opportunity to emphasize the fidelity of Jesus' family to Judaism. Adults were supposed to attend the three major feasts in Jerusalem annually—Passover, Pentecost, and Tabernacles. For many this was impossible, but an effort was made to go at least to Passover. With puberty, a boy became a "son of the covenant," a custom continued in the present bar-mitzvah ceremony. It was considered helpful for a boy to attend the Jerusalem festivals for a year or two before becoming a son of the covenant so that he would realize what his new relationship involved. Luke calls Jesus a "boy" (*pais*, a term also used for servanthood, v.43) in contrast to "child" (*paidion*, v.40).

43–47 At this intermediate age, Jesus might have been either with the women and children or with the men and older boys, if the families were grouped this way in the caravan. Each parent might have supposed he was with the other (v.43). We need not assume that his parents neglected him. It was after a day of travel that they missed Jesus (v.44); another day would have been required for the trip back (v.45), and on the next day ("after three days," v.46) the successful search was made.

The questions Jesus put to the teachers (v.46) were probably not merely boyish inquiries but the kind of probing questions used in ancient academies and similar discussions. He also gave answers (v.47). J.W. Doeve suggests that Jesus engaged in a midrashic discussion of biblical texts: "Their amazement must relate to his deducing things from Scripture which they had never found before" (*Jewish Hermeneutics in the Synoptic Gospels and Acts* [Assen: Van Gorcum, 1954], p. 105).

48 Luke vividly describes the parents' emotions. The first is astonishment (cf. v.33). There is no inconsistency or lapse in Luke's attributing surprise to those who should have known best the uniqueness of Jesus' person and mission. It is one of the characteristics of Luke to observe the various responses of awe at the words and deeds of Jesus, which is also consistent with ancient narratives touching on the observation of wonders. His mother's natural concern then issues very humanly in a hint of scolding. Next she uses the word "anxiously" (the participle *odynōmenoi*) to describe her and Joseph's feelings as they hunted for him. The word is unusually strong, often indicating pain or suffering (16:24–25; Acts 20:38; cf. TDNT, 5:115).

49–50 Jesus' answer, "Why were you searching for me?" (v.49), pointedly prepares the hearer for a significant statement that is then understood as being theologically inevitable. The same pattern occurs in 24:5: "Why do you look for the living among the dead?" followed by "He is not here; he has risen!" (24:6). In the present instance, the second part of the statement is of extraordinary significance. The importance of Jesus' use of the phrase "my Father," with its implied designation of himself as the unique Son of the Father, is heightened not only by the preceding question but by the subsequent statement of v.50. By saying that Mary and Joseph did not understand, Luke underlines the awesome mystery of Jesus' statement of filial consciousness. There may also be, though it is doubtful, a subtle contrast between the words "your father" (v.48) and "my Father" (v.49).

51 Immediately following this intimation of Jesus' divinity, Luke assures us also of his perfect humanity by noting his obedience to his parents. Once more Mary reflects inwardly on the significance of it all (cf. Gen 37:11). Like the boy Samuel (1 Sam 2:26) and the responsible son in Proverbs 3:4, Jesus matures into a person both God and men approve.

52 Jesus' growth was normal. Unlike some stories in the apocryphal gospels, Luke does not try to portray Jesus as exhibiting unusual powers. To say Jesus "grew in wisdom" does not detract from his deity. Even if wisdom means innate knowledge, Philippians 2:7 suggests that as a servant Jesus was willing to forgo the full use of his divine powers; so a normal development of knowledge is not ruled out. "Stature" (*hēlikia*) is ambiguous, referring either to physical growth or, more likely, personal development, i.e., maturity. The good reputation Jesus enjoyed "with men" was continued in the church (Acts 2:47).

Notes

49 The tendency in recent versions has been to understand the Greek idiom ἐν τοῖς τοῦ πατρός μου (en tois tou patros mou, "in the [noun omitted] of my Father") to refer to the temple rather than to affairs or "business" of God. The latter is not impossible (cf. 1 Cor 7:33; 1 Tim 4:15), but the former is more appropriate to the context (cf. Gen 41:51 LXX; cf. also Creed, p. 46).

III. Preparation for Jesus' Ministry (3:1–4:13)

A. *The Ministry of John the Baptist*

3:1–20

[1]In the fifteenth year of the reign of Tiberius Caesar—when Pontius Pilate was governor of Judea, Herod tetrarch of Galilee, his brother Philip tetrarch of Iturea and Traconitis, and Lysanias tetrarch of Abilene—[2]during the high priesthood of Annas and Caiaphas, the word of God came to John son of Zechariah in the desert. [3]He went into all the country around the Jordan, preaching a baptism of repentance for the forgiveness of sins. [4]As is written in the book of the words of Isaiah the prophet:

"A voice of one calling in the desert,
'Prepare the way for the Lord,
    make straight paths for him.
[5]Every valley shall be filled in,
    every mountain and hill made low.
The crooked roads shall become straight,
    the rough ways smooth.
[6]And all mankind will see God's salvation.'"

[7]John said to the crowds coming out to be baptized by him, "You brood of vipers! Who warned you to flee from the coming wrath? [8]Produce fruit in keeping with repentance. And do not begin to say to yourselves, 'We have Abraham as our father.' For I tell you that out of these stones God can raise up children for Abraham. [9]The ax is already at the root of the trees, and every tree that does not produce good fruit will be cut down and thrown into the fire."

[10]"What should we do then?" the crowd asked.

[11]John answered, "The man with two tunics should share with him who has none, and the one who has food should do the same."

[12]Tax collectors also came to be baptized. "Teacher," they asked, "what should we do?"

[13]"Don't collect any more than you are required to," he told them.

[14]Then some soldiers asked him, "And what should we do?"

He replied, "Don't extort money and don't accuse people falsely—be content with your pay."

[15]The people were waiting expectantly and were all wondering in their hearts if John might possibly be the Christ. [16]John answered them all, "I baptize you with water. But one more powerful than I will come, the thongs of whose sandals I am not worthy to untie. He will baptize you with the Holy Spirit and with fire. [17]His winnowing fork is in his hand to clear his threshing floor and to gather the wheat into his barn, but he will burn up the chaff with unquenchable fire." [18]And with many other words John exhorted the people and preached the good news to them.

¹⁹But when John rebuked Herod the tetrarch because of Herodias, his brother's wife, and all the other evil things he had done, ²⁰Herod added this to them all: He locked John up in prison.

This narrative, like the foregoing, bears Palestinian Jewish characteristics in its language, themes, and setting. An example of this is vv.1–2. Here Luke not only shows classical historical precision in the dates he provides but also reflects the opening words of the OT prophets (e.g., Isa 1:1; Jer 1:1–3; Hos 1:1; Amos 1:1). God's word is not simply the vehicle for timeless truth; it is a word in and to specific human circumstances. At this point in history, after a long silence, the prophetic word was again being heard.

1 The dating provided in this verse was more immediately useful to Luke's first-century readers than to the average reader today who does not know the period when Luke was writing. If the reign of Tiberius was dated from the occasion of his predecessor's death (Augustus died on 19 August A.D. 14), his "fifteenth year" would be from August, A.D. 28, to August, A.D. 29, according to the normal Roman method of reckoning. If Luke was following the Syrian method as a native of Antioch, Tiberius's "fifteenth year" would have been from the fall of A.D. 27 to the fall of A.D. 28 (cf. discussion in Notes). For Luke to use the Roman method would have been in keeping with his cultural environment and appropriate for his readers.

"Herod" is Herod Antipas, son of Herod the Great who ruled Galilee and Perea 4 B.C.–A.D. 39 (cf. Luke 3:19–20; 13:31; 23:7). Philip, like Herod Antipas, was a son of Herod the Great. He ruled a group of territories to the northeast of Palestine, Iturea and Traconitis (4 B.C.–A.D. 33/34). Lysanias, unlike an earlier ruler of the same name, is unknown except through inscriptions (see Creed, pp. 307–9). Pontius Pilate was governor (Luke uses the general term *hēgemoneuontos*, not the disputed "procurator") from A.D. 26–36 (cf. F.F. Bruce, "Procurator," NBD, 2d ed., pp. 973–74).

2 The official high priesthood of Annas had ended in A.D. 15, but his influence was so great, especially during the high priesthood of his son-in-law Caiaphas (A.D. 18–36) (cf. John 18:13), that his name is naturally mentioned along with that of Caiaphas. With the reference to the high priests, we move from the secular world to the religious and are ready for the introduction of the prophet John. He is in the desert, where he had gone (1:80). The desert held memories for the Jews as the locale of the post-Exodus wanderings of Israel. It also had eschatological associations (cf. not only Isa 40:3 but also Hos 2:14). Some thought demons inhabited the desert, and it was later alleged that John had a demon (Matt 11:18). Luke's interest is not only in the coming of John (Matt 3:1; Mark 1:4: "John came") but in the message "the word of God came" (cf. Notes).

3 The impression Luke, more than the other Gospels, gives is that John had an itinerant ministry. Apparently he not only preached in the wilderness but followed the Dead Sea coast to the Jordan River and then away a distance from there. The "desert" is a barren rocky area that covers a large territory. Naturally he went where there was enough water to perform baptisms (see John 3:23).

John's baptism was "of repentance" (*metanoias*), that is, its chief characteristic was that it indicated sorrow for sin and a moral change on the part of those he baptized (vv.8–14). The noun *metanoia* ("repentance") appears also in 3:8; 5:32; 15:7; and 24:47. The verb *metanoeō* ("repent") occurs in Luke 10:13; 11:32; 13:3, 5; 15:7, 10; 16:30; and 17:3–4. The basic idea comes from the Hebrew *šûb* ("turn," i.e., from sin to God; cf. TDNT, 4:975–1008). Repentance is an ancient prophetic theme (e.g., Ezek 18:21, 30). "For [*eis*, or 'with a view to'] forgiveness of sins" expresses the result of the repentance shown in baptism.

4–6 Isaiah 40:3 was used by the community at Qumran as a rationale for leading a separated life in the desert, where they believed they were preparing the way of the Lord by means of a constant reading of the Law (1QS 8.12–16; 9.19–20). For Luke, as for Matthew and Mark, the Isaiah passage was a clear prophecy of the ministry of John the Baptist. Luke includes more of the quotation than Matthew and Mark do. First he cites the extraordinary way in which, on the analogy of preparations made for a royal visitor, even the seemingly immovable must be removed to make way for the Lord (vv.4–5). What needs removal is the sin of the people.

Luke concludes the Isaiah quotation with words that aptly describe his own evangelistic and theological conviction: "And all mankind will see God's salvation" (v.6). Luke finds here, following the LXX, a biblical basis for his own universal concern and his central theme of salvation (Morris, *Luke*, p. 95). The words concerning the appearance of God's glory (Isa 40:5) are omitted. Luke does stress the glory of God often elsewhere, beginning with 2:14; but for some reason he apparently does not think it appropriate to stress it here.

7 The word "crowds" represents *ochlos*, an assorted group of people, rather than *laos* (cf. v.18). Luke does not specify who was in this group (Matt 3:7 says that they were Pharisees and Sadducees; cf. John 1:19, 24). Perhaps Luke wants to leave the first narration of a specific confrontation with the Pharisees till they have one with Jesus himself (5:17). Similarly, no mention is made of people coming from Jerusalem (cf. Mark 1:5).

John's language is strong, as was that of OT prophets who preceded him. His words (vv.7–9) are virtually identical with those in Matthew 3:7–10. Luke has, however, omitted one element and added another. Matthew's reference to John's words "Repent, for the kingdom is near" (Matt 3:2) is not found anywhere in Luke's account. Although Luke does emphasize the kingdom, he reserves its introduction for Jesus (4:43). What he adds here is a list of specific instances in which his audience ought to exhibit behavioral changes consistent with repentance.

Later on Jesus himself used the epithet "brood of vipers" against the Pharisees (Matt 23:33). Here John uses it as a prophet of judgment under the direction of God's Spirit. OT prophets had spoken strongly also and made similar allusions to reptiles (Isa 59:5). The question "Who warned you to flee from the coming wrath?" suggests that while their "coming out to be baptized by him" was the proper thing to do, their motives were in question.

8–9 The language is picturesque. Two images are presented. First, a tree that does not produce fruit should be chopped down and removed to make way for one that will. Jesus speaks later about appropriate fruit (6:43–45) and also tells a parable about cutting down a barren fruit tree (13:6–9). The imagery may be intended to call to mind the figure of Israel as a fig tree or vine (cf. Isa 5:1–7). Black, p. 145, suggests a possible word-play in the original Aramaic that would have included *raq* and *qar* (twice) in the words for "flee," "root," and "cut down." The second image, the axe "at the root," symbolizes an impending radical action, the destruction of the whole tree. The theme of Abraham's children (v.8) is found in John 8:31–41, Romans 4:12–17, and Galatians 3:6–9.

Mere physical descent from Abraham is not important; God can create his own children out of stones just as he can cause inanimate stones to praise his Son, if humans remain silent (19:40). The threat of judgment is heightened through the imagery of fire, a theme reintroduced in the reference to Jesus' ministry (vv.16–17).

10–11 This prophetic word of judgment elicits a response, first from the crowd in general (v.10), then from the unpopular and greedy tax collectors (v.12), and finally from the soldiers (v.14). The conversations, which are unique to Luke, provide opportunity for some clear statements about social justice and responsibility.

The crowd, which is mixed, in contrast to the groups of tax collectors and soldiers (vv.12, 14), is told to share clothing and food with the needy (v.11). John is not requiring a strict communal life like that at Qumran but "fruit in keeping with repentance" (v.8; cf. Gal 5:22–23). The "tunic" was the short garment (*chitōn*) worn under the longer robe (*himation*). One might have an extra tunic, for warmth or a change of clothes (cf. 9:3: "Take . . . no extra tunic"). Those who had broken the biblical law of love needed to demonstrate their repentance in this kind of sharing.

12–13 The "tax collectors" (v.12) were part of a despised system (cf. 5:27; 15:1). Of the three groups, they would have been considered most in need of repentance. The chief tax collectors (*architelōnēs*), such as Zacchaeus (19:2), bid money for their position. Their profit came from collecting more than they paid the Romans. The chief tax collectors hired other tax collectors to work for them. Because their work and associations rendered them ritually unclean and because they regularly extorted money, they were alienated from Jewish society and linked with "sinners." While John shows social concern, he does not advocate overthrow of the system but rather advocates a reform of the abuses. Since these abuses arose out of individual greed, a radical change in the practice of the collectors themselves was required (v.13).

14 The "soldiers" (*strateuomenoi*) were probably not Roman but Jewish, assigned to internal affairs (cf. comment on "officers" at 22:4). The very nature of their work gave them opportunity to commit the sins specified. Soldiers could use threats of reprisal to extort money from the people. The soldiers' question suggests the seriousness of their moral need, by means of the added words *kai hemeis* ("even we")— "What about us?" as JB puts it. Here again the need of others is set over against personal greed. The second great commandment (cf. 10:27b) needs to be applied.

15–17 The question naturally came to the minds of "the people" (v.15; cf. v.18) whether such a radical prophet as John might be the Messiah. In John 1:19–25 popular opinion about him is reported in greater detail. Here John answers the unexpressed question in several ways. The Messiah is "more powerful" than he is (v.16). The Messiah is worthy of such reverence that even the task of tying his sandals is more than John feels worthy of (cf. John 3:30).

The Messiah will baptize, not with water in a preparatory way, as John had done, but actually "with the Holy Spirit and with fire" (v.16). These are not two separate categories of baptism. The single word "with" (*en*) combines the two (cf. Matt 3:11; Mark 1:8). The coming of the Spirit is to have the effect of fire. John uses an agricultural image to explain this. The grain is tossed in the air with a "winnowing fork" (v.17). The lighter and heavier elements are thus separated, the heavier grain falling on the "threshing floor." The "chaff," which is not the true grain, is burned up and the wheat stored in the barn.

Interpreters have discussed whether the fiery work of the Spirit is judgment or purification also. Modern readers find it difficult to understand how the concepts of the Spirit, baptism (usually associated with water), and fire relate to one another. The biblical background (e.g., Isa 44:3; Ezek 36:25–27; Joel 2:28–29) and also 1QS 4.20–21 show that the concept of washing and refreshing was associated with the Spirit. Fire is an ancient symbol of judgment, refinement, and purification (cf. Notes). We may conclude that John and his contemporaries were already acquainted with all these nuances. The Holy Spirit was understood as being active in saving, purifying, and judging. The Spirit had definitely, but not frequently, been associated with the Messiah (Isa 11:1–2), whose coming would mean also the availability of the Spirit's ministry.

18 That John not only "exhorted" the people but "preached the good news" shows that grace accompanies the warning to flee from judgment. It is noteworthy that here and in v.21 Luke uses the word *laos* ("people"; cf. v.21)—the term he specifically employs to describe not just a "crowd" (*ochlos;* v.7) but a potentially responsive group (see comments on 1:68, 77). It is this "people," who apparently stayed on to hear more of John's message, who heard the further proclamation of "good news."

19–20 "Herod" (v.19) is Herod Antipas, mentioned in v.1. His brother is Philip, whose wife, Herodias, left him for Herod. His marriage to her was one of many sins, and the climactic sin "added" (v.20) to this sordid series was his imprisonment of John. For John's death, see 9:7–9 and the fuller account in Mark 6:17–29. By his brief anticipation here of John's imprisonment, Luke underscores both the boldness of John and the sickness of the society he called to account. Verse 20 also indicates that John's ministry was completed before that of Jesus began. The same point is made in Peter's sermon to Cornelius (Acts 10:37–38). (C. Talbert, "The Lukan Presentation of Jesus' Ministry in Galilee," *Review and Expositor* 64 [1967]: 490, presents this relationship between John's and Jesus' ministry as part of a comprehensive theological scheme in Luke.)

Notes

1 Several alternate methods of chronological reckoning have been applied to the data in this verse. Some have proposed that Luke followed a chronology used at that time in the Near East by which the reign would have been counted, not from the actual date, but by a regnal year scheme. According to the Julian calendar, 19 August to 31 December A.D. 14 would have been the accession year, with the first full year beginning 1 January A.D. 15. The fifteenth year would have been 1 January to 31 December A.D. 29. This calculation and that cited in the commentary above allow for an A.D. 33 crucifixion date, which many now think likely.

It is also possible that a Syrian system was used, by which Tiberius's fifteenth year was 21 September A.D. 27 to 8 October A.D. 28. Still other possibilities exist (see Harold W.

Hoehner, *Chronological Aspects of the Life of Christ*, pp. 29–37; cf. G. Ogg, "Chronology of the New Testament," NBD, pp. 222–25). These dates must be correlated with those of Luke 3:23; John 2:20; 8:57, and other passages relating to the Crucifixion, as well as those pertaining to Jesus' birth. For further information about Herod Antipas, see Harold W. Hoehner, *Herod Antipas* (Grand Rapids: Zondervan, 1972).

2 'Ρῆμα (*rhēma*, "word") emphasizes the actual words spoken, whereas λόγος (*logos*, "word") looks more at the expression of thought (cf. A–B, s.v.). Seventeen of *rhēma*'s twenty-three occurrences in the Synoptics are in Luke.

3 Dipping and washing ritually in water was becoming increasingly common in the first century A.D. (cf. J. Thomas, *Le mouvement baptiste en Paletine et Syrie* [Gembloux: J. Duculot, 1935]). Such lustrations were used at Qumran, both as one confessed his sins and entered the community (1QS 5.7–20) and on subsequent occasions (1QS 2.25ff.; 3.4–5). John's probable knowledge of the Qumran community, which was in the Judean desert, has led some to see a connection between his baptism and theirs. His baptism was not, however, intended for frequent repetition, nor did it link the participants with a community like theirs. Probably as early as John's day, baptism along with circumcision (for males) and the offering of a sacrifice marked the full conversion of a proselyte to Judaism. The striking difference between Jewish proselyte baptism and that which John practiced is that John's subjects were already Jews. For them to be baptized carried negative implications as to the sufficiency of Judaism. Josephus (Antiq. XVIII, 117 [v.2]) has a different understanding of John's baptism, perhaps seeing it only as a lustration such as he knew was practiced at Qumran. In Josephus's view, John wanted people to do righteous deeds and then be baptized. But Luke shows John baptizing repentant sinners, who then go on to live righteous lives.

4 Αὐτοῦ (*autou*, "for him") is parallel with κυρίου (*kyriou*, "for the Lord") and has the pronoun *autou* whereas Isa 40:3 LXX has τοῦ θεοῦ ἡμῶν (*tou theou hēmōn*, "our God"). In this way, Luke makes it easier to understand that the words "the Lord" here refer to Christ (cf. Matt 3:3; Mark 1:3).

7 On ἀπὸ τῆς μελλούσης ὀργῆς (*apo tēs mellousēs orgēs*, "from the coming wrath"), see also Rom 2:5; 1 Thess 1:10; Rev 6:15–17. John will allude to this in Luke 3:9 (cf. TDNT, 5:422–47).

16 In the clause "with the Holy Spirit and with fire," the second "with" (ἐν, *en*) was omitted in the 1973 edition of NIV. That was technically correct, as the Greek does not repeat the word. The 1978 edition added the second "with" possibly for stylistic reasons.

17 Among the relevant passages in OT, intertestamental, and NT literature on the Spirit, water, fire, purification, and judgment are Gen 19:24 (cf. Luke 17:29); Amos 7:4; Mal 3:2; Enoch 90:24–27; Pss Sol 15:6; 1QS 2.8; 1QpHab 2.11ff.; Matt 5:22; 13:40; 25:41; 1 Peter 1:7; Rev 20:14. For the association of fire with fluidity, see Dan 7:9–10 and 1QH 3.29–32. See also J.D.G. Dunn, *Baptism in the Holy Spirit*, Studies in Biblical Theology, 2d series, 15 (Naperville, Ill.: A.R. Allenson, 1970), pp. 8–22.

B. *The Baptism of Jesus*

3:21–22

21When all the people were being baptized, Jesus was baptized too. And as he was praying, heaven was opened 22and the Holy Spirit descended on him in bodily form like a dove. And a voice came from heaven: "You are my Son, whom I love; with you I am well pleased."

21 For a comprehensive study of the events contained in vv.21–22, the parallels in Matthew 3:13–17; Mark 1:9–11; and John 1:32–34 should be consulted. As in the

birth narratives, there is at Jesus' baptism a supernatural attestation. Many see in the event his "call" to his mission. His baptism comes as the climax of the baptism of "all the people" (cf. Notes).

Jesus was baptized, not because he was a sinner in need of repentance, but as a way of identifying himself with those he came to save. His reasons are expressed in Matthew 3:15. This is the first of several important events in Luke that took place when Jesus prayed (cf. esp. 6:12; 9:18, 29; 22:41). Though Luke's description of the opening of the heavens is not so dramatic as Mark's (1:10), it does make clear that Jesus had a true vision of the Deity (cf. Ezekiel's vision, Ezek 1:1; Stephen's, Acts 7:56; and Peter's, Acts 10:11). In contrast, the disciples on the Mount of Transfiguration were enveloped by a cloud. Although they heard God speaking, their vision was of Christ and the heavenly visitors rather than of God in heaven.

22 God had appeared in OT times through theophanies. Now the Spirit appears as a dove. Only Luke has the expression "in bodily form," giving more substance to the experience of the Spirit's presence. Luke does not say that anyone other than Jesus was aware of the Holy Spirit. Perhaps others present saw only a dove without realizing its significance. The descent of the Spirit is reminiscent of Genesis 1:2, but no specific parallel is drawn (cf. Notes).

"You are my Son, whom I love" designates Jesus as the unique Son of God. The words, like those heard at the Transfiguration (9:35; cf. Matt 17:5; Mark 9:7), effect a blend of OT christological passages: Psalm 2:7 and Isaiah 42:1. Present scholarly opinion holds that the concept of divine sonship in Jewish thought was not only applicable to angels (Job 1:6; 2:1) and to the nation of Israel and her kings (Exod 4:22; 2 Sam 7:14; Hos 11:1) but was coming into use, at least at Qumran, as a designation for the Messiah (4QFlor 10–14). At the Annunciation Jesus was designated the "Son of the Most High" (1:32). On his sonship and OT passages, see the comments on the Transfiguration (9:35) for a full discussion of the wording common to both passages. Here we may simply observe that the words "love" and "well pleased" convey the idea of choice and special relationship. Jesus has now received his commission. He is ready (following the Temptation, 4:1–12) to begin his ministry.

Notes

21 The infinitive phrase βαπτισθῆναι (*baptisthēnai*, "were baptized"; NIV, "were being baptized") could, because the verb is an aorist, imply antecedent action. In this case it would indicate that the baptism of the people had ended, thus distinguishing Jesus' baptism from theirs. The construction does not necessarily imply this, however.

Luke also uses an aorist, this time in participial form, βαπτισθέντος (*baptisthentos*, "was baptized") to describe Jesus' own baptism, perhaps in contrast to the durative idea of the present participle προσευχομένου (*proseuchomenou*, "was praying"). Jesus' baptism, like that of the people, was a single event in time; but his praying continued for his lifetime. The most striking aspect of Luke's use of grammar in vv:21–22 is his use of dependent clauses leading up to the affirmation "You are my Son. . . ."

22 The significance of the dove's descent has been much discussed (cf. L.E. Keck, "The Spirit and the Dove," NTS 17 [1970–71]: 41–67; Marshall, *Luke: Historian and Theolo-*

gian, pp. 151–52. While it may be impossible to determine the symbolism with certainty, its basic significance relates to God's presence, call, and approval.

Scholars have debated the relationship of the "voice . . . from heaven" to the בַּת קוֹל (*bat qôl*, lit., "daughter of a voice," i.e., the voice of God heard not directly but as an echo). The rabbis thought that God, having ceased speaking through prophets as in the OT, now spoke indirectly. O. Betz (TDNT, 9:288–90, esp. 298) shows that the voice was still considered a shared communication from God. The heavenly voice to Jesus was not identical to the *bat qôl*, being directed to one person and involving a first-person address: "*You* are *my* Son, whom *I* love" (emphasis mine).

Against the view that the word υἱός (*huios*, "son") is a later substitute for an original παῖς (*pais*, "servant") under Hellenistic influence, see I.H. Marshall, "Son of God or Servant of Jehovah?—A Reconsideration of Mark I.11," NTS 15 (1968–69): 326–36.

An early variant in the Western text, "This day I have begotten you," echoing Ps 2:7 and the synoptic parallels, is not supported by the best MSS (Metzger, *Textual Commentary*, p. 136).

C. Jesus' Genealogy

3:23–38

23Now Jesus himself was about thirty years old when he began his ministry. He was the son, so it was thought, of Joseph,

the son of Heli, 24the son of Matthat,
the son of Levi, the son of Melki,
the son of Jannai, the son of Joseph,
25the son of Mattathias, the son of Amos,
the son of Nahum, the son of Esli,
the son of Naggai, 26the son of Maath,
the son of Mattathias, the son of Semein,
the son of Josech, the son of Joda,
27the son of Joanan, the son of Rhesa,
the son of Zerubbabel, the son of Shealtiel,
the son of Neri, 28the son of Melki,
the son of Addi, the son of Cosam,
the son of Elmadam, the son of Er,
29the son of Joshua, the son of Eliezer,
the son of Jorim, the son of Matthat,
the son of Levi, 30the son of Simeon,
the son of Judah, the son of Joseph,
the son of Jonam, the son of Eliakim,
31the son of Melea, the son of Menna,
the son of Mattatha, the son of Nathan,
the son of David, 32the son of Jesse,
the son of Obed, the son of Boaz,
the son of Salmon, the son of Nahshon,
33the son of Amminadab, the son of Ram,
the son of Hezron, the son of Perez,
the son of Judah, 34the son of Jacob,
the son of Isaac, the son of Abraham,
the son of Terah, the son of Nahor,
35the son of Serug, the son of Reu,
the son of Peleg, the son of Eber,
the son of Shelah, 36the son of Cainan,
the son of Arphaxad, the son of Shem,
the son of Noah, the son of Lamech,
37the son of Methuselah, the son of Enoch,

the son of Jared, the son of Mahalalel,
the son of Kenan. [38]the son of Enosh,
the son of Seth, the son of Adam,
the son of God.

23-38 The age of Jesus is given in very approximate terms. He might have been in his mid-thirties. "Thirty" is a round number and might also indicate that, like the priests who began their service at that age, he was ready to devote himself to God's work. Compare the extreme comment recorded in John 8:57. Both Matthew and Luke recognize the importance of establishing a genealogy for Jesus, in accordance with the care given such matters in ancient Israel.

In their handling of Jesus' genealogy, Matthew and Luke differ in several ways.

1. Matthew begins his Gospel with the genealogy, thereby establishing an immediate connection with the OT and with Israel. Luke waits till the significant part of the ministry of John the Baptist is completed and Jesus stands alone as the designated Son of God.

2. Matthew begins with Abraham, stressing Jesus' Jewish ancestry; Luke, in reverse order, goes back to Adam, probably with the intention of stressing the identification of Jesus with the entire human race.

3. Matthew groups his names symmetrically; Luke simply lists them.

4. Both trace the lineage back through ancestral lines that diverge for a number of generations from Luke's, though both meet at the generation of David.

5. Matthew includes the names of several women (a feature one might have expected in Luke because of his understanding and respect for women).

The significance of the genealogy in Luke probably lies in the emphasis on Jesus as a member of the human race, a son of Adam; in the contrast of Jesus, the obedient Second Adam (a theme implicit but not explicit in Luke), with the disobedient first Adam; and in Jesus as the true Son of God (cf. "Adam," v.38).

The differences outlined above, as well as some problems of detail, have been explained in part by one or more of the following assumptions: (1) Joseph's lineage is given in Matthew, Mary's in Luke; (2) the legal line is traced in Matthew, the actual line of descent in Luke; and (3) there was a levirate marriage at one or more points in the line.

The first assumption is without solid foundation and does not seem to accord with the emphasis on Joseph in 1:27. Nevertheless, Luke's narrative seems to be from Mary's point of view, whereas Matthew's is from that of Joseph (cf. Machen, pp. 202-9; 229-32). The second assumption is possible; it allows for breaks in Matthew's line, with heirship still retained. The levirate marriage assumption has been a popular option since ancient times (proposed by Africanus, third century, as cited in Eusebius, *Ecclesiastical History* 1.7). The widow of a childless man could marry his brother so that a child of the second marriage could legally be considered as the son of the deceased man in order to perpetuate his name. In a genealogy the child could be listed under his natural or his legal father.

Joseph is listed as the son of Heli in Luke but as the son of Jacob in Matthew. On the levirate marriage theory, Heli and Jacob may have been half-brothers, with the same mother but fathers of different names. Perhaps Heli died and Jacob married his widow.

To all this it must be added that we possess not a poverty but a plethora of possibilities. Therefore the lack of certainty due to incomplete information need not imply error in either genealogy. Morris (*Luke*, p. 100) observes that it is not possible to know how Luke would have handled a genealogy involving a virgin birth and so "the case is unique."

Recent studies include M.D. Johnson, *The Purpose of the Biblical Genealogies* (Cambridge: University Press, 1969); E.L. Abel, "The Genealogies of Jesus HO CHRISTOS," NTS 20 (1974): 203–10; and H.C. Waetjen, JBL 95 (1976): 205–30. M.D. Johnson summarizes the data (and his viewpoint that the genealogies are "probably examples of the tendency to historicize traditional motifs in the Gospel material") in his article "Genealogy," ISBE (rev. ed.), 2:424–31. For a conservative approach to this complex subject, see the concise summary in Marshall, *Luke: Historian and Theologian*, pp. 157–66.

D. The Temptation of Jesus

4:1–13

[1]Jesus, full of the Holy Spirit, returned from the Jordan and was led by the Spirit in the desert, [2]where for forty days he was tempted by the devil. He ate nothing during those days, and at the end of them he was hungry.

[3]The devil said to him, "If you are the Son of God, tell this stone to become bread."

[4]Jesus answered, "It is written: 'Man does not live on bread alone.' "

[5]The devil led him up to a high place and showed him in an instant all the kingdoms of the world. [6]And he said to him, "I will give you all their authority and splendor, for it has been given to me, and I can give it to anyone I want to. [7]So if you worship me, it will all be yours."

[8]Jesus answered, "It is written: 'Worship the Lord your God and serve him only.' "

[9]The devil led him to Jerusalem and had him stand on the highest point of the temple. "If you are the Son of God," he said, "throw yourself down from here. [10]For it is written:

> " 'He will command his angels concerning you
>   to guard you carefully;
> [11]they will lift you up in their hands,
>   so that you will not strike your foot against a stone.' "

[12]Jesus answered, "It says: 'Do not put the Lord your God to the test.' "
[13]When the devil had finished all this tempting, he left him until an opportune time.

This vivid narrative (vv.1–13) contains an important blend of theological themes— the divine sonship and messiahship of Jesus, the warfare between Christ and Satan, OT theology, and principles of obedience to the divine Word.

1–2 These two verses shed light on the significance of the episode. Jesus is in the "desert" (v.1) for a period of "forty days" (v.2). This probably relates to Israel's experience in the desert after the Exodus. It may also allude to Moses' forty days without food on the mountain (Deut 9:9). The parallel with Israel becomes stronger if it is meant as a comparison between Israel as God's "son" (Exod 4:22–23; Hos 11:1) who failed when tested and Jesus as his unique Son who conquered temptation. God led Israel into the desert; likewise the Spirit led Jesus. In the former case, God tested his people. Now God allows the devil to tempt his Son.

It is important here to distinguish between three kinds of tempting (*peirasmos*, "testing").

1. Satan tempts people, i.e., lures them to do evil. God never does this nor can he himself be tempted in this way (James 1:13). Further, not all temptation comes directly from Satan; often it comes from our own lower nature (James 1:14-15).

2. People may tempt (test) God in the sense of provoking him through unreasonable demands contrary to faith. This is what Israel did in the desert and what is probably referred to in Jesus' quotation of Deuteronomy 6:16 (cf. v.12).

3. God tests (but does not tempt) his people, as he did in the desert (Deut 8:2). All three kinds of testing are involved in the parallels between the desert experiences of Israel and Jesus. (On this theme, see B. Gerhardsson, *The Testing of God's Son*, Coniectanea Biblica NT Series 2:1 [Lund: C.W.K. Gleerup, 1966].)

Although God already knows all about us, he reveals the thoughts and intents of our hearts through our response to him in times of trial. Thus he tested Israel in the desert to "see" whether the people would obey (Exod 16:4).

In this temptation by the devil, the Lord Jesus shows the validity of what God had just said of him: "With you I am well pleased" (3:22).

In this section we see several contrasts. One—between Israel and Jesus—has just been discussed. Another is the absolute contrast between Jesus, who is both filled and led by the Spirit (note Luke's emphasis on the Spirit), and the devil, who opposes both Christ and the Spirit. (The unpardonable sin is called blasphemy against the Spirit [12:10; cf. Matt 12:31-32].) Another contrast is the one implied between Jesus as "hungry," i.e., physically empty, and yet as "full of the Spirit." Our own experience is usually the reverse.

3-4 The "devil" (*diabolos*, v.3) has several names in biblical and other Jewish literature, notably the OT name "Satan," which is used often in the NT (*Satanas*; cf., e.g., 4:8; 10:18; 11:18). He opposes God and God's servants (1 Chron 21:1; Job 1:6-12; 2:1-7; Zech 3:1-2). He may seem to be ubiquitous but is not omnipresent. Sometimes he works indirectly through the evil spirits who form his domain (cf. 11:14-20). Here the devil's statement "If you are the Son of God" picks up the declaration of Jesus' sonship in 3:22. The conditional construction does not imply doubt but is a logical assumption in the dialogue.

The reference to bread is conceivably an allusion to God's provision of manna for Israel during the Exodus. Apparently some of Jesus' contemporaries expected that the coming Messiah would perform some such miracle of provision for them (cf. John 6:30). Consequently this temptation may have been an appeal for Jesus to do a work of messianic significance. Alternately, and more probably, his temptation may have been to satisfy his own need and gratify himself. Bread, however, is necessary, not evil, and hardly an object of "the cravings of sinful man" (1 John 2:16). Further, Jesus' temptation is not the same as the self-engendered lusting described in James 1:14-15—a fact to keep in mind when we question how Jesus could have been perfect and yet truly tempted. The issue, therefore, is not one of allurement to perverted self-gratification but a challenge to act apart from faithful dependence on God.

Jesus' reply is brief, a partial quotation of Deuteronomy 8:3 (found more fully in Matt 4:4). In Deuteronomy Moses was reminding Israel that during the forty years in the desert God had led them "to humble you [i.e., Israel] and to test you in order to know what was in your heart, whether or not you would keep his commandments" (Deut 8:2). The next verse (Deut 8:3) specifically refers to hunger and the provision of manna, which the Lord gave Israel so that the people might know that man needs not merely bread but the sustaining word of God.

Thus while he is being "tempted" by the devil, Jesus is also proving faithful to God in contrast to Israel's response when "tested" by him. Jesus proves by his response that his heart is not divided but that he is dependent on God and obedient to his word (v.4). So he becomes our example in temptation (Heb 4:14–16; 5:8).

5–8 The second temptation, though of a different nature, involves similar issues. The devil takes Jesus to a "high place" (v.5; cf. "mountain" in Matt 4:8, where a parallel with Moses on Mount Nebo may be implied [Deut 32:49; 34:1–3]). "In an instant" probably shows that this part of the Temptation involved a vision. It was not necessary for Jesus to see every part of the world physically for this to be an actual temptation. Once again, what the devil offered was legitimate in itself. The Messiah would one day rule all the world, possessing all "authority and splendor" (v.6). In this temptation the devil claims to possess the world. Jesus does not challenge the claim (cf. John 12:31); neither does he acknowledge it. To worship the devil in order to recapture the world, even for its good, would have meant "casting out devils by Beelzebub" (Morris, *Luke*, p. 103).

Had Jesus accepted the devil's offer, our salvation would have been impossible. First, Jesus would have sinned by giving worship to the devil and thus could not have offered himself a perfect sacrifice for our sins. (The same thing applies to all three temptations.) Second, Scripture teaches that the Messiah should first suffer and only then "enter his glory" (24:26). Third, since the devil tried to prevent Christ's voluntary death for our sins, the implication of this second temptation was that accepting an immediate kingdom would avoid the Cross.

The temptations deal with both the divine sonship and messiahship of Jesus—related concepts in biblical thought. But the temptations also tested his perfect manhood. This aspect of them especially interested Luke. Moreover, they show us Jesus as our example. By quoting Deuteronomy 6:16, he responded as the perfect man—the obedient last Adam (Rom 5:19)—should respond, worshiping and serving his only God (v.8). Both the OT texts Jesus quoted so far (vv.4, 8) are more than weapons against the devil; they apply to Jesus himself.

9–12 Luke records this temptation in the last rather than second place (cf. Matt 4:5–7). It may be that Matthew preferred to conclude with a kingdom reference. Possibly Luke wants to center on the city of Jerusalem (v.9), which Matthew does not mention by name, because of his theme of the progression of the gospel from Jerusalem to the Gentile nations. The essence of this temptation is that of presuming on God (v.12) and displaying before others one's special favor with him. In this instance the devil quotes a passage of Scripture (Ps 91:11–12) out of context—notice that the mere use of Bible words does not necessarily convey the will of God (v.10). Further, Satan omits the words "in all your ways" (Ps 91:11), possibly to facilitate application to an act inconsistent with the normal "ways" of the godly person. Gerhardsson ("Testing God's Son," pp. 54ff.) sees here a theme of protection (cf. Deut 1:31 with the context of Ps 91, from which the devil quotes). He sees the temple as a place of protection and finds a play on words between "wings" (Ps 91 [90 LXX]:4, *pterygas*) and "highest point" or "pinnacle" (*pterygion*). But it is doubtful whether Luke intended this parallel. The rabbinic tradition that the Messiah would appear on top of the temple (SBK, 1:151) may provide a background that accounts for the form of this temptation, even though the idea of jumping down is absent.

Again Jesus responds with Scripture (v.12), this time by quoting Deuteronomy 6:16. This quotation could be understood as applying to the devil, who "tempted" Jesus in the first sense of the word (cf. comments on temptation, v.2). More probably it is applied to Jesus, who thus refuses to "tempt" God in the second sense of the word. That is, he will not repeat the sin that Israel committed in the desert by putting God to the test. To do that would be to provoke God by making inappropriate demands for a divine sign to be used for display. This request for a sign would actually be an act of unbelief, masquerading as extraordinary faith.

13 This verse may be considered the conclusion of this section rather than the beginning of the next (so NIV 1978 ed.). The devil leaves only temporarily—"until an opportune time."

Notes

9 Tò πτερύγιον (*to pterygion*, "the highest point") may be the corner of the walls that encompassed the temple area. The southeastern corner was directly above a cliff, making a terrifying drop down to the Kidron Valley possible.

13 Conzelmann's view (*Theology of Luke*, p. 38) that Luke thought Satan was inactive during Jesus' ministry imposes an artificial scheme on this Gospel. Conzelmann reads too much into the first half of this verse and holds that the "opportune time" does not come till Luke 22:3 Schuyler Brown (*Apostasy and Perseverance*, in loc.) counters this concept. He maintains that Satan is active throughout Luke's Gospel, a conclusion based on a view of the nature of temptation in Luke that differs from Conzelmann's.

IV. The Galilean Ministry (4:14–9:50)

A. *Initial Phase* (4:14–6:16)

1. *First approach and rejection at Nazareth*

4:14–30

¹⁴Jesus returned to Galilee in the power of the Spirit, and news about him spread through the whole countryside. ¹⁵He taught in their synagogues and everyone praised him.

¹⁶He went to Nazareth, where he had been brought up, and on the Sabbath day he went into the synagogue, as was his custom. And he stood up to read. ¹⁷The scroll of the prophet Isaiah was handed to him. Unrolling it, he found the place where it is written:

¹⁸"The Spirit of the Lord is on me,
   because he has anointed me
   to preach good news to the poor.
He has sent me to proclaim freedom for the prisoners
   and recovery of sight for the blind,
   to release the oppressed,
¹⁹ to proclaim the year of the Lord's favor."

²⁰Then he rolled up the scroll, gave it back to the attendant and sat down. The eyes of everyone in the synagogue were fastened on him, ²¹and he began by saying to them, "Today this scripture is fulfilled in your hearing."

²²All spoke well of him and were amazed at the gracious words that came from his lips. "Isn't this Joseph's son?" they asked.

²³Jesus said to them, "Surely you will quote this proverb to me: 'Physician, heal yourself! Do here in your hometown what we have heard that you did in Capernaum.' "

²⁴"I tell you the truth," he continued, "no prophet is accepted in his hometown. ²⁵I assure you that there were many widows in Israel in Elijah's time, when the sky was shut for three and a half years and there was a severe famine throughout the land. ²⁶Yet Elijah was not sent to any of them, but to a widow in Zarephath in the region of Sidon. ²⁷And there were many in Israel with leprosy in the time of Elisha the prophet, yet not one of them was cleansed—only Naaman the Syrian."

²⁸All the people in the synagogue were furious when they heard this. ²⁹They got up, drove him out of the town, and took him to the brow of the hill on which the town was built, in order to throw him down the cliff. ³⁰But he walked right through the crowd and went on his way.

14–15 Once again, as Jesus enters a new phase of his experience, Luke mentions the special activity of the Holy Spirit (v.14; cf. 4:1). Shortly Jesus will make a significant declaration about the meaning of the Spirit's ministry in his life (v.18). So far we have seen the Spirit's activity at Jesus' conception (1:35), baptism (3:22), and temptation (4:1). The "news" that spread about Jesus and the fact that "everyone praised him" (v.15) are the first of several observations Luke makes about public response to Jesus' ministry (cf. vv.22, 28, 32, 36–37).

This passage (vv.16–30) has an important place in the Lukan presentation. It not only marks the beginning of Jesus' ministry; it is also the first major narrative about his ministry that is not largely paralleled in Matthew or Mark. The setting is Nazareth, the place of Jesus' childhood. A lengthy quotation from Isaiah (vv.18–19) issues in a proclamation of immediate fulfillment. Jesus also implies, at the very outset of his ministry, the selection of Gentiles for divine favor (vv.24–27). Observe that this event occurs in Luke much earlier than what appears to be the same occurrence later in presentations of Matthew and Mark. Whatever the literary and historical relationship may be between this passage and Mark 6:1–6, its placement here shows that Luke considers it of prime importance and a bold introductory statement as Jesus begins his ministry in Galilee. Also a pattern appears here that is unveiled more clearly later on in Luke-Acts: (1) the presentation of the gospel to Jews in their synagogues, (2) rejection, and (3) turning to the wider Gentile world (cf. Acts 13:46; cf. also commentary on Acts, R.L. Longenecker, EBC, vol. 9).

16–17 Luke emphasizes that Jesus was in his hometown by the words "where he had been brought up." Luke stresses Jesus' Jewish piety with a reference to his custom of synagogue attendance. This strengthens the contrast with his rejection. Luke does not say whether Jesus had publicly read from the Scriptures before; nor does Luke say whether Jesus chose Isaiah 61 himself (v.17), or whether the passage was assigned for that Sabbath (cf. Notes). The passage was Isaiah 61:1–2, with the words "to release the oppressed" taken from Isaiah 58:6. The variation from the usual wording may simply reflect the interpretive translation in use at that time.

18–19 The quotation has significance both as our Lord's statement of his call to his saving ministry and as Luke's affirmation of this ministry as thematic in his Gospel. In saying "Today this scripture is fulfilled in your hearing" (v.21), Jesus identifies himself as the subject of Isaiah's prophetic word. As such he is (1) the bearer of the Spirit (v.18); (2) the eschatological prophet, proclaimer of the "good news"; and (3) the one who brings release to the oppressed (a messianic function). His role as Suffering Servant is not specified here, but an association may be assumed on the basis of the place of Isaiah 61 among the Servant passages.

1. We have already observed Luke's frequent mention of the Holy Spirit in Jesus' life (cf. comment on 4:14). Now we see that Jesus' ministry will be uniquely marked by the presence of the Spirit as prophetically foretold.

2. His role as eschatological prophet is intertwined with that of John the Baptist as prophetic forerunner. For the sense in which John was a prophet and was characterized by the spirit of Elijah, see comments on 1:17 and 7:24–28. However Jesus, not John, was *the* prophet predicted in Deuteronomy 18:18 (cf. John 1:19–24, esp. v.21). Luke gives special attention to Jesus as a prophet in a number of ways. Among them are sayings of Jesus not found in other Gospels (v.24 in this chapter; 13:33) and comments by others (7:16, 39; 24:19, only in Luke, and 9:8, 19; see also Acts 3:22; 7:37, 52). In the present passage, the prophetic mission described by Isaiah, a mission of proclamation, is accepted by Jesus.

3. The prophetic role of Jesus overlaps his role as Messiah (cf. discussion in Marshall, *Luke: Historian and Theologian*, pp. 124–28). His ministry of deliverance is messianic in character. This assumption probably lay behind the doubts in John's mind when release from prison was not forthcoming (7:18–19).

The "good news" (v.18) Jesus was to proclaim recalls both the joyful announcement in 1:19 and the frequent use of the term elsewhere in Luke. It also builds on Isaiah 40:9; 41:27; and especially 52:7. The "poor," like the "prisoners," the "blind," and the "oppressed," are not only the unfortunate of this world but those who have special need of dependence on God (cf. comment on 1:53; 6:20). The words "to release the oppressed" fill out the meaning of the previous words. Luke 7:22 cites some ways Jesus fulfilled this mission.

The "year of the Lord's favor" (v.19) is reminiscent of the Jubilee (one year in every fifty) when debts were forgiven and slaves set free (Lev 25:8–17). It means not so much a time that is "acceptable" to people but the time in history when God in sovereign grace brings freedom from the guilt and effects of sin. The inclusion of this quotation is consistent with Luke's stress on the dawning of the new age of salvation.

The omission of the next phrase in Isaiah 61:2—"the day of vengeance of our God"—is also significant. Jesus' audience would suppose that the day of their own salvation would be the day of judgment on their pagan enemies. But the delay of judgment means that this time of the Lord's favor benefits the Gentiles also. Jesus affirms (vv.24–27) that Gentiles are also recipients of God's grace, even when Jews were not so blessed. It has been suggested that the omission of the vengeance phrase is the cause of the hostility in v.28. But while the two may be related, Luke does not say so.

In summary, Luke presents the quotation and Jesus' ensuing comments as a programmatic statement of Jesus' ministry. As prophet and Messiah, he will minister to the social outcasts and needy, including Gentiles, in the power of the Spirit.

20 We now have a description of the synagogue procedure. Jesus hands back the scroll to the "attendant." In addition to other services rendered to the synagogue (including at times the teaching of children), the attendant had the sacred duty of handling the revered scroll. After this was replaced in its cabinet or ark, the reader took the customary sitting position for instructive comments on the passage. Luke now makes the first of several comments on the response of the congregation, which is at first intense attention and ultimately hostility.

21 Jesus' comment is short but of the highest importance. We do not know whether he said more than Luke recorded. But that is not important, for the single sentence recorded is of profound significance. It announces the fulfillment of the reading from Isaiah concerning the subject of the prophecy (Jesus) and the time of God's gracious work ("today"). Since the Isaiah quotation lacks the phrase about the day of God's wrath, it must be understood that "today" refers only to the part about God's grace.

The term "fulfilled" (*peplērōtai*) is not as prominent in Luke as in Matthew. Usually it occurs with a unique Lukan meaning (cf. comment on 7:1). Only here and in the Emmaus conversation (24:44) does Luke use the word in relation to the fulfillment of OT prophecy, and in both cases the Matthean formula "to fulfill what was spoken" is lacking. These two lone references to fulfillment stand out then at the beginning and end of Jesus' public appearances, emphasizing the fulfillment of God's eternal purpose in the ministry of Christ.

22 The response of the audience to Jesus' comment on Isaiah's words has been variously interpreted. Most expositors take the words "bore him witness" (*emartyroun autō*) as implying a positive attitude toward what he had said; hence NIV translates them "spoke well of him." The same verb is used in Acts 22:12 of Ananias, where NIV translates it "was . . . highly respected." But J. Jeremias (*Jesus' Promise to the Nations. Studies in Biblical Theology* [London: SCM, 1958], pp. 44–45) takes it in a negative sense, as he does the statement in v.20b, assuming that hostility against Jesus began when he did not refer to the day of God's judgment. The ambiguous nature of the passage continues with *ethaumazon* ("were amazed"), which does not indicate clearly either favor or disfavor. The cause of their amazement was Jesus' "gracious words" (*hoi logoi tēs charitos*)—i.e., the kind and wise manner of his speech or of what he said about the grace of God. A near parallel in Acts 14:3 suggests the latter, but there it is "word" (*ho logos*, singular, i.e., "message") of grace, which is closer to the phrase "the gospel of God's grace" in Acts 20:24.

Certainly Luke appreciates and conveys the gracious nature of Jesus' ministry. But at some point, here or shortly after, the hostility of the audience begins. Does the question "Isn't this Joseph's son?" indicate hostility? The question does seem to express perplexity and irritation at this man who grew up in the home of a fellow Nazarene and is now making such impressive claims. The question could be colloquially rendered "He's Joseph's son, this one, isn't he?"

23 Jesus' response is not intended to reassure his audience but rather to draw out their subconscious attitudes. The future tense in "you will quote" (*ereite*) might refer to another occasion, especially if we assume that Jesus has not yet preached in Capernaum. Yet this incident might be the same as that recorded in Matthew 13:53–58 and Mark 6:1–6. Both Gospels have made prior references to Jesus' preaching in Capernaum. Matthew 4:13 says Jesus lived there and Mark 1:21–28 tells of his teaching and his popularity there. It is not necessary, however, to go to the other Gospels for support; Luke himself records an apparently extensive and popular ministry in Galilee prior to this time (4:14–15). It would be strange if this had not included Capernaum. It is, therefore, more likely that Jesus is expressing the reply he would expect the people to make in response to his message in the synagogue— namely, that they would challenge him to fulfill Isaiah's prophecy by doing miracles in the presence of those who heard him. Throughout his ministry Jesus would be challenged to do miraculous signs (e.g., 11:16, 29) to prove his claims.

24 "I tell you the truth" (*amēn legō hymin*) is used six times in Luke to introduce a solemn assertion. This expression shows the authority with which Jesus spoke and is clearly an authentic word of Jesus. This introductory formula with the Greek word for "amen" appears often in Mark and even more frequently in Matthew, especially in the material unique to that Gospel. Luke includes a few other quotations in which he changes the "amen" to its equivalent in idiomatic Greek, most notably in 9:27: *legō de hymin alēthōs* ("I tell you the truth").

Here the statement so solemnly introduced anticipates Jesus' rejection. It sees him as a prophet and may be a variation of the saying found in Matthew 13:57 and Mark 6:4. The difference is in the sentence structure and in Luke's use of the word "accepted," the same adjective (*dektos*) used in v.19 to describe the year of the Lord. The double use of this word in this context may be intended to show that, though God desires to accept the people, they do not respond by accepting the prophet who tells them of God's grace. The "proverb" (*parabolē*, v.23) itself is apparently a version of a common adage making the point that whoever achieves greatness is never fully trusted back home. But here its meaning is the deeper one that Jesus stands in the line of the prophets who were rejected by their own people.

25–27 These verses are introduced by Jesus saying, "I assure you" (v.25), a phrase very like the "amen" formula in v.24. Observe that Jesus does not state here that the prophets Elijah (v.26) and Elisha (v.27) went to Gentiles because they were rejected by the Jews; rather, they went because they were sent there by God. Jesus' audience is becoming more and more enraged as they realize that they will receive no special favors from him and that he considers himself above home ties and traditions.

28–30 Nazareth lay among the ridges of the southern slopes of the Galilean hills. Jesus allowed the crowds to drive him (v.29) out of the town (as he later did on going to the place of crucifixion). But it was not yet his time to die, and by some unexplained means he made his way out (v.30).

Notes

16–30 The location of this narrative in Luke has been a major problem of critical scholarship. If the similar incident recorded in Matthew 13:53–58 and Mark 6:1–6 is actually a different and later occurrence, several questions arise. Did the same sort of event take place twice? In that case it would seem strange that Jesus would return a second time and meet a similar incredulous response, as though no such incident had occurred before. Yet even though this may seem improbable, it is not for us to judge it impossible. Also the wording in Matthew and Mark, including most of the dialogue portion, is almost totally different from that in Luke. (Note another variation in John 6:42.)

Nevertheless, a case may be made for the same incidents being described in all three Synoptics. If so, Luke has simply placed it earlier in his narrative. It may be, as often suggested, that he had theological reasons for placing it early, in order to show the progression of the gospel from Jewish environs to the Gentile world and Rome (at the end of Acts). Luke emphasizes this progression by featuring here the statements about the extent of God's grace to the Gentiles. On the other hand, the order may reflect Luke's care in following a source or combination of sources in which this incident did in fact stand at the beginning of Jesus' ministry. This explanation is congruous with the remarkable fact that not only Mark but even Matthew, who is so interested in the fulfillment theme, does not include the quotation from Isaiah. If Luke has used a different source than those known to Matthew, the whole matter is clarified and Luke has written an "orderly account" (1:3).

At any event, this is a crucial passage in Luke. Recent significant studies include H. Anderson, "Broadening Horizons: The Rejection at Nazareth Pericope of Lk 4, 16–30 in Light of Recent Critical Trends," Int 18 (1964): 259–75; D. Hill, "The Rejection of Jesus at Nazareth," NovTest 13 (1971): 161–80; Robert Sloan, *Favorable Year* (cf. n. 29); and the discussion in Marshall, *Gospel of Luke*, pp. 175–90; cf. the treatment of the text by J. Jeremias, *Jesus' Promise to the Nations*, pp. 44–46. On the Isaiah quotation itself and its use by Jesus, see J.A. Sanders, "From Isaiah 61 to Luke 4," in *Christianity, Judaism and other Graeco-Roman Cults: Studies for Morton Smith at Sixty*, Part One (Leiden: E.J. Brill, 1975), pp. 75–106.

16 Ἀνέστη ἀναγνῶναι (*anestē anagnōnai*, "he stood up to read") shows the synagogue custom of standing to read Scripture and sitting to preach. The first reading, following the shema—"Hear, O Israel . . ." (Deut 6:4)—and prayers, was of the passage for the day from the lectionary (selected verses of Bible readings) of the Pentateuch. The second reading was from the Prophets. The choice of the passage may have still been up to the reader in Jesus' day.

18 Ἔχρισεν (*echrisen*, "anointed") designates appointment to the messianic mission, possibly referring to Jesus' baptism (3:22–23). Εὐαγγελίσασθαι (*euangelisasthai*, "to preach") is a significant word in Luke, already found in 1:19; 2:10; 3:18. Ἀπέσταλκεν (*apestalken*, "sent") is from ἀποστέλλω (*apostellō*), commonly used in relation to sending someone on a mission. It could refer, as in John 3:17 and elsewhere in John, to the Father's sending Jesus into the world.

19 Ἐνιαυτὸν κυρίου δεκτόν (*eniauton kyriou dekton*) is literally the "acceptable" (RSV) or "favorable" (NASB) "year of the Lord." NIV both expresses the meaning here and follows the Hebrew text (cf. Isa 61:2 NIV). Luke's text follows the LXX.

20 The verb ἀτενίζω (*atenizō*, "to fasten on"), in the phrase οἱ ὀφθαλμοὶ ἦσαν ἀτενίζοντες αὐτῷ (*hoi ophthalmoi ēsan atenizontes autō*, "the eyes . . . were fastened on him"), is used once more in Luke (22:56) and ten times in Acts. It is usually found in situations of extreme emotion, e.g., of those watching the ascension of Christ (Acts 1:10), and of Stephen looking into heaven just before his martyrdom (Acts 7:55). It can connote hostility (Acts 13:9). In a somewhat parallel situation, the Sanhedrin "looked intently" at Stephen at the beginning of his trial, "and they saw that his face was like the face of an angel." Here (v.20), since no hostility to Jesus has yet been expressed, we cannot take *atenizontes* as meaning more than intense anticipation of how Jesus will interpret the Isaiah passage.

21 Ἤρξατο λέγειν (*ērxato legein*, "began to say") is omitted by NIV. It may be "simply a case of redundant usage," but more likely "what follows is the arresting opening of a sermon, so that the use of the verb is justified" (Marshall, *Gospel of Luke*, pp. 184–85).

Σήμερον (*sēmeron*, "today") occurs relatively often in Luke (2:11; 5:26; 12:28; 13:32–33;

19:5, 9, 22:34, 61; 23:43) and nine times in Acts. Its use is consistent with Luke's interest in the presence of the kingdom and of the time of salvation.

---

2. Driving out an evil spirit

4:31–37

³¹Then he went down to Capernaum, a town in Galilee, and on the Sabbath began to teach the people. ³²They were amazed at his teaching, because his message had authority.

³³In the synagogue there was a man possessed by a demon, an evil spirit. He cried out at the top of his voice, ³⁴"Ha! What do you want with us, Jesus of Nazareth? Have you come to destroy us? I know who you are—the Holy One of God!"

³⁵"Be quiet!" Jesus said sternly. "Come out of him!" Then the demon threw the man down before them all and came out without injuring him.

³⁶All the people were amazed and said to each other, "What is this teaching? With authority and power he gives orders to evil spirits and they come out!" ³⁷And the news about him spread throughout the surrounding area.

31–32 Luke has already mentioned Capernaum (v.23) as a center of miraculous activity in the ministry of Jesus. Capernaum was on the northwest shore of the Sea of Galilee. Luke adds a geographical note for Gentile readers. The ruins of a later (probably third-century) synagogue may be seen today in that vicinity. The expression "went down" reflects the descent necessary from the elevated situation of Nazareth to the coastal plain.

The implication of the imperfect periphrastic ēn didaskōn ("was teaching") may be that it was Jesus' custom to attend the synagogue (v.33) and to teach there. Though the plural tois sabbasin can have a singular meaning (NIV, "on the Sabbath") as it does in the Markan parallel (Mark 1:21), if it has a plural meaning here in Luke, it would support the possibility that the imperfect implies repeated action. This would be true to the pattern Jesus had established. It is more likely, however, that the imperfect means he was "just in the process of teaching" (NIV, "began to teach") when the demon-possessed man interrupted him.

The incident Luke next gives is perhaps more striking than the parallel in Mark (1:21–34) because it exemplifies the liberating work described in the preceding Isaiah quotation (vv.18–19). The reaction of the people, though comparable to that in the preceding incident (vv.20–22), differs from it in one important aspect. Now they are astonished that this teacher, who in their eyes was not even a rabbi, taught with authority (v.32). The contrast is sharpened in Mark 1:22 by the additional words "not as the teachers of the law." The majority of rabbis would base their teaching on the chain of tradition, citing the opinions of their predecessors. By omitting this specific comparison, Luke may simply be deferring to his Gentile readership, who would perhaps not be as aware as Jewish readers of rabbinical custom. But it may also be that Luke is emphasizing the absolute authority of Jesus. In support of this is Luke's use of the word "message" (logos, lit., "word"). For the importance of the "word" in Luke, see comment on 1:1–4. Keeping in mind that the parallel passage in Mark does not use "word" but says "he taught them," Luke would seem to be emphasizing the "authority" of Jesus' "word" (cf. v.36).

33–35 Demon possession is too frequent and integral to the Gospel narratives to minimize or, worse, to discard it as Hellenistic superstition. This is only the first mention of it in Luke, the climax of such incidents coming in 11:14–22. Significantly, Jesus is confronted by demonic activity during his first public ministry Luke describes following the introductory sermon at Nazareth. The "good news of the kingdom of God" (v.43) Jesus was proclaiming signaled an attack on the forces of evil. Luke wants us to understand the centrality of the kingdom in Jesus' ministry and in that of his disciples. (See his unique use of the expression "kingdom of God" in such passages as 9:27, 60, 62.) A holy war is being launched and, as v.34 suggests, the demons know it. This war will be carried on by Jesus' disciples (9:1–2; 10:8–9, 17).

The man is possessed by a spirit (v.33) that is "evil" (*akathartou*, "unclean," so NIV mg.). Though some would see in the terms "evil" and "unclean" evidence for different kinds of demons, there is little biblical support for this. In 8:2 "evil" spirits are mentioned; several verses later we read simply of a "demon" (8:27), which is said to be "unclean" (8:29, NIV mg.). There seems to be no difference and NIV uses the same term "evil" in both cases. An evil spirit is unclean in contrast to the holiness of God and may well cause both moral and physical filth in a possessed human (cf. R.K. Harrison, "Demon, Demoniac, Demonology," ZPEB, 2:92–101).

The possessed man shrieks and utters an expression of "indignant surprise" (Creed, p. 70). The word "Ha" (v.34) is followed by an idiomatic rhetorical question (*ti hēmin kai soi*, "What do you want with us?") that may be rendered "What do we have to do with each other?" or, loosely, "Why this interference?" (Danker, *Jesus*, p. 61). The demon, perhaps exemplifying James's comment that "the demons believe and shudder" (James 2:19), senses the purpose of Jesus' presence. In keeping with the pattern in the Gospels, testimony to the truth about Christ comes from a number of different and unexpected sources. The term "the Holy One of God" (*ho hagios tou theou*) contrasts strongly with the remark that this was an unclean demon.

Jesus responded sternly (cf. Notes) with a command to be silent (v.35). In Jesus' action we may see the beginning of a pattern of prohibiting the premature proclamation of his identity. Throughout the Gospels Jesus guards the fact of his messiahship, probably (1) to prevent a misinterpretation that would draw to him revolutionary minded dissidents seeking a leader against Rome; (2) to allow his messianic works themselves to establish his authority among true believers (cf. 7:18–23); and (3) to avoid an inappropriate self-proclamation as Messiah, especially if there was, as it now appears (cf. R.N. Longenecker, *The Christology of Early Jewish Christianity*, Studies in Biblical Theology, Second Series 17 [London: SCM, 1970], pp. 71–74), an understanding that the true Messiah would allow others to proclaim him as such, rather than doing so himself. If none of these is the reason here, Jesus is at least maintaining his authority by silencing the enemy.

What follows is not technically an exorcism, because Jesus does not use an incantation or invoke the authority of another. Instead he speaks a simple word of command on his own authority. Luke, always interested in the physical condition of people, observes that the demon came out violently but without hurting the man.

36–37 Once again Luke notes the amazement of the people (v.36). The astonishment this time is not only at his teaching and authority (*logos*, cf. above on v.32) but at his power. Luke's theme of the spread of the gospel finds expression in the conclusion of the narrative (v.37).

Notes

35 Ἐπετίμησεν (*epetimēsen*, "said sternly") is a strong word of rebuke or warning (cf. v.39; 8:24; 9:42, and note on v.39).

3. *Healing many*

4:38-44

> 38Jesus left the synagogue and went to the home of Simon. Now Simon's mother-in-law was suffering from a high fever, and they asked Jesus to help her. 39So he bent over her and rebuked the fever, and it left her. She got up at once and began to wait on them.
> 40When the sun was setting, the people brought to Jesus all who had various kinds of sickness, and laying his hands on each one, he healed them. 41Moreover, demons came out of many people, shouting, "You are the Son of God!" But he rebuked them and would not allow them to speak, because they knew he was the Christ.
> 42At daybreak Jesus went out to a solitary place. The people were looking for him and when they came to where he was, they tried to keep from leaving them. 43But he said, "I must preach the good news of the kingdom of God to the other towns also, because that is why I was sent." 44And he kept on preaching in the synagogues of Judea.

38-39 Jesus' healing ministry continues in a more private setting (v.38). This account lacks the vivid detail of Mark's, but Luke stresses the miraculous by adding the word "immediately" (*parachrēma*, v.39; NIV, "at once"). Luke mentions Simon Peter here without special introduction, though he has not yet described Peter's call. Probably Peter was so well known by Luke's readership that this did not seem abrupt, and the call does follow immediately. Both this passage and 1 Corinthians 9:5 inform us that Peter was married. A crisis of serious illness in the family gives occasion for Jesus to help. The fact that Jesus "rebukes" (cf. Notes) an impersonal fever, as he had earlier rebuked the demon, has led some to assume that a personal evil force had caused the fever. If so, one might also suspect this in 8:24. Otherwise either the fever is simply personified in effect, through the use of a vivid verb, or Luke is emphasizing the active force of Jesus' word. The vividness of the scene continues as Jesus bends over the woman; she immediately rises; and, doubtless in keeping with her character, she begins to serve the group.

40 One of the most beautiful scenes in Scripture now follows. The crowds have apparently waited till evening, after the Sabbath was over. In the remaining hours of diminishing light, they perform the labor of love they could not do on the Sabbath, carrying the sick to Jesus. It is noteworthy that Jesus himself has not yet ventured out on the Sabbath to perform healings publicly. This bold action will take

79

place later (6:1–11). Luke carefully distinguishes between those who were just sick (v.40) and those who were demon-possessed (v.41). This warns us not to assume that the Gospel writers thought all disease was caused by demons. Luke mentions that Jesus laid his hands on the people who came to him, a detail not found in the parallel accounts (Matt 8:16; Mark 1:34). Though laying on hands was a common practice in ancient religious acts, here it shows that Jesus is the source of the healing power and that he had a personal concern.

41 Luke is also the only synoptic writer who says at this point that the demons called Jesus the Son of God. As already mentioned (cf. comment on v.34), the Gospel writers show various people testifying to the identity of Christ, including even unbelievers and demons. This provides a broad base for the case the Gospels are establishing. The injunction to silence (v.35) is here amplified. This knowledge of the demons is in ironic contrast to the unbelief of the crowds.

42–44 Shifting quickly from dusk to dawn, Luke portrays Jesus in a sharply contrasted setting. He is alone (v.42). Surprisingly, in view of his special attention to prayer (cf. 5:16), Luke does not tell us, as Mark does (1:35), that Jesus is praying. Luke, however, does express with greater force than Mark the reason for Jesus' refusal to linger at Capernaum. The difference gives us a clue to one of the dominant themes in Luke. The words "must," "kingdom of God," and "sent" (v.43) are unique to Luke's narrative at this point (cf. Notes). Along with "preach," these words constitute a programmatic statement of Jesus' mission and also of Luke's understanding of it. Verse 44 emphasizes the continuation of the misson, as Jesus preaches in the synagogues throughout the "land of the Jews" (NIV mg.; cf. Notes).

Here, then, Luke has provided representative incidents from the ministry of Jesus. It is the kind of activity summarized in Acts 10:38 as "doing good and healing all who were under the power of the devil."

Notes

38 Mark (1:29) connects this incident more closely with the synagogue incident than Luke by using the word εὐθύς (*euthys*, "immediately"; NIV, "as soon as"), but the implication in Luke is also that it occurs on the same Sabbath day.

Luke's use of πυρετῷ μεγάλῳ (*pyretō megalō*, "high fever") shows that he follows the ancient medical custom in distinguishing levels of fever.

39 "In NT ἐπιτιμάω [*epitimaō*] has no other meaning than 'rebuke'" (Plummer, p. 134; cf. note on v.35 above). It is a "prerogative of Jesus in the Gospels. . . . which declares His position as the Lord. . . . He is also Lord over the demons and bends them to do His will" (E. Stauffer, TDNT, 2:625–26). This being the case, some think that here and in Luke 8:24 (cf. Matt 8:26; Mark 4:39) there must be demonic influence behind fever and storm. However, this is not the case in God's shaking of the heavens or the Red Sea (Job 26:11; Ps 106 [105 LXX]:9) and need not be assumed here.

Παραχρῆμα (*parachrēma*, "at once") is one of Luke's favorite words, though he does not use it as frequently as Mark does εὐθύς (*euthys*, "at once," "without delay"; cf. note above on v.38). *Parachrēma* contributes to the sense of urgency in Luke (see below).

43 Δεῖ (*dei*, "must") conveys a strong sense of urgency. Two thirds of its occurrences in the Synoptics are in Luke, most of these in the material unique to this Gospel and the others added by Luke as he edited his work. While the number of occurrences is not great, the proportion is statistically significant and the particular applications striking. Among the significant examples of its use are 2:19; 13:33, 22:37; 24:7, 26, 44.

Luke's distinctive stress on the sovereign purpose of God and the relationship of that to Jesus' mission appears also in Luke's use of the word ἀποστέλλω (apostellō, "send"). Luke uses it only slightly more times than Mark, but it has greater significance in Luke because of the way he introduces it into the narratives. The present passage is an example of this, because where Mark 1:38 has ἐξῆλθον (exēlthon, "have come"), Luke has the stronger ἀπεστάλην (apestalēn, "was sent").

Τὴν βασιλείαν τοῦ θεοῦ (tēn basileian tou theou, "the kingdom of God") is a major topic in Jesus' teaching and in Luke's presentation of that teaching. Several passages that summarize Jesus' ministry and that of his disciples specify that the kingdom is the core of Jesus' message (e.g., 8:1; 9:2; cf. 9:62; 10:9; 16:16). The occurrences of the term in Matthew and the proportion of occurrences in Matthew's work are even greater than in Luke. For a full study of the kingdom in Jesus' teaching, see G.E. Ladd, *The Presence of the Future* (Grand Rapids: Eerdmans, 1974).

44 Τῆς Ἰουδαίας (tēs Ioudaias, "of Judea") is a difficult reading since Luke is clearly describing Jesus' Galilean ministry. For that very reason early copyists of the NT seem to have welcomed alternative possibilities: τῆς Γαλιλαίας (tēs Galilaias, "of Galilee"), in conformity with Mark 1:39 and Matt 4:23, and τῶν Ἰουδαίων (tōn Ioudaiōn, "of the Jews"). By using a slight paraphrase, "the land of the Jews," the NIV margin has conveyed what is probably Luke's intention. The word "land" is the traditional word for all of Palestine, the home of the Jews. In Luke's mind Judea may have had the same significance. Marshall notes that it is not correct to draw a sharp distinction between "the two parts of Jesus' ministry" (i.e., Galilee and Judea), for "v.43 indicates that Jesus' ministry is directed to the Jews as a whole; the point is theological rather than geographical" (*Gospel of Luke*, p. 199).

---

4. Calling the first disciples

5:1–11

[1]One day as Jesus was standing by the Lake of Gennesaret, with the people crowding around him and listening to the word of God, [2]he saw at the water's edge two boats, left there by the fishermen, who were washing their nets. [3]He got into one of the boats, the one belonging to Simon, and asked him to put out a little from shore. Then he sat down and taught the people from the boat.
[4]When he had finished speaking, he said to Simon, "Put out into deep water, and let down the nets for a catch."
[5]Simon answered, "Master, we've worked hard all night and haven't caught anything. But because you say so, I will let down the nets."
[6]When they had done so, they caught such a large number of fish that their nets began to break. [7]So they signaled their partners in the other boat to come and help them, and they came and filled both boats so full that they began to sink.
[8]When Simon Peter saw this, he fell at Jesus' knees and said, "Go away from me, Lord; I am a sinful man!" [9]For he and all his companions were astonished at the catch of fish they had taken, [10]and so were James and John, the sons of Zebedee, Simon's partners.
Then Jesus said to Simon, "Don't be afraid; from now on you will catch men."
[11]So they pulled their boats up on shore, left everything and followed him.

This narrative (vv.1–11) is similar in certain details to Matthew 4:18–22 and Mark 1:16–20. Luke's account is much fuller, containing the unique encounter between

Jesus and Peter. The climax of each account is a call to "catch men" and the obedience of the disciples. Luke lacks the specific command "Follow me." The sequence in which this account occurs in Luke is different from that in Mark, who records the call in 1:16–20, before the Capernaum incidents (1:21–28), which Luke put just prior to the present narrative (4:31–41). Naturally these similarities and differences have led scholars to different conclusions about the relationship of the two accounts and the history of the tradition behind them. In the light of Luke's method of focusing on individuals as a means of them drawing attention to Jesus, we can understand the placement and character of the narrative (cf. G.N. Stanton, *Jesus of Nazareth in NT Preaching*, pp. 20, 59). Although Jesus might have called the disciples several times (one such calling has already taken place according to John 1:35–51), to attempt a harmonization by defining the Lukan narrative and that in Matthew and Mark as separate incidents is unnecessary. Luke focuses on Peter, shows the sovereignty and holiness of Jesus in a way Matthew and Mark do not, and alone mentions the total abandonment of the disciples' possessions as an act of discipleship (cf. 14:33).

The difference in placement is likewise understandable. None of the Synoptics ties the incident into a strict chronological sequence; so the placement is flexible. Luke first establishes the program of Jesus' ministry (4:16–30, 43). Now he is ready to establish the sovereign lordship of Christ in his relationship first with Peter as representative of the disciples and then with the social outcasts and "sinners" whom he has come to save (5:32; 19:10), such as the man with leprosy (5:12–15) and Levi also (5:27–32).

Elements of this narrative also resemble the postresurrection story in John 21:1–14. Scholars are not agreed as to the relation between the traditions represented in the two passages (see discussions in Creed, pp. 73–74; Marshall, *Gospel of Luke*, pp. 199–200; R.E. Brown, *The Gospel According to John*, II, AB [Garden City: Doubleday, 1970], pp. 1089–92). The Johannine issues aside, the Lukan narrative is coherent and natural in its context. Arguments for an original postresurrection setting for Luke's tradition are unconvincing.

1–3 "One day" (v.1) represents the simple *egeneto* ("it happened [that]"; KJV, "it came to pass"). It does not indicate a specific chronological sequence. The geographical description is more precise: "lake" is used instead of the more general word "sea." Luke mentions the pressure of the crowds, as he occasionally does elsewhere (8:42, 45; 19:3). Their attention is on the "word of God," another instance of Luke's focus on the "word" (cf. 4:32, 36). The shore of the lake provided an excellent, acoustically serviceable amphitheater. Luke, being observant of detail, draws our attention to two boats (v.2). Next he singles out Simon as the owner of one of them (v.3). The description in v.2 along with the comment in v.5 serve to emphasize the futility of the night's work. Luke is careful to mention that Jesus again teaches—now from the boat, from which his voice would carry across the water to the crowd. Not even the next event, miraculous as it is, may, in Luke's narrative, be allowed to direct attention away from Jesus' teaching ministry.

4–5 The sharp contrast between the expert but unsuccessful fisherman and Jesus needs no comment. Jesus' command (v.4) must have seemed unreasonable to them after their failure during the night (v.5). Peter, here called by his old name, Simon, demurs; but he does what Jesus says.

6–10a Luke now moves quickly to three focal points in his narrative. First, he describes the gathering of the fish (v.6). This extraordinary happening is similar to that in John 21 (cf. also Jesus' uncanny ability to direct Peter to a fish with a coin in its mouth [Matt 17:24–27]). The details of the breaking nets and loaded boats (v.7) help give the narrative the ring of truth. Second, the miracle moves Peter (Luke now uses his full name, Simon Peter), who is overcome by awe (v.9), to abase himself before Jesus (v.8). He now calls Jesus "Lord" (*kyrios*), with a greater depth of meaning than the common "Sir." Peter is gripped not merely by a sense of his inferiority but of his own sinfulness. The experience of Isaiah 6:5 comes to mind, but Peter needs no such vision; he is face to face with Jesus. Luke's reason for including this incident may be not only to portray the confrontation of human sinfulness with Jesus but also to show that to receive the saving grace of Christ a "sinful" (*hamartōlos*, cf. Notes) man must repent. Long before Luke speaks of the Gentiles with their gross sins and their being included in saving grace, we are faced with the realization that even Peter, who in Luke's time was known for his obedience to the Jewish laws, must take his place as a sinner (Danker, *Jesus*, p. 65). Luke (v.10a) mentions James and John, but only in passing; the central figures are Jesus and Peter.

10b–11 The third focal point in the narrative following Peter's obedience to Jesus in letting down the net is Jesus' declaration that he will "catch men" from then on (v.10b). Here interpretations vary. But in view of Luke's emphasis on the kindness of God reaching out to embrace all mankind, it is more likely to signify a beneficent rather than judgmental ingathering. It presages the widening horizons of both Luke and Acts, culminating, in a sense, in Peter's vision symbolizing the reception of Gentiles into the church and his subsequent witness to the Gentile Cornelius (Acts 10:9–48, esp. vv.34–35).

After the declaration about catching men, the disciples followed Jesus (v.11). Luke's observation that they left everything, which is not stated in Matthew and Mark, underscores the condition of discipleship Jesus taught later on (14:33). Compare also his words to the rich ruler (18:22).

Notes

5 All seven synoptic occurrences of ἐπιστάτα (*epistata*, "Master") are in Luke. In all but one of these (17:13), it is the disciples who use the title. It is used instead of διδάσκαλος (*didaskalos*, "teacher") in 8:24 (cf. Mark 4:38), 9:49 (cf. Mark 9:38), and instead of "rabbi" in 9:33 (cf. Mark 9:5). It was a term Luke's readers understood, and it often referred to officers.

8 Ἁμαρτωλός (*hamartōlos*, "sinner") is one of Luke's characteristic words. Of twenty-two occurrences in the Synoptics, fifteen are in Luke, mainly in material unique to his Gospel and usually assigned to the "L" source. Luke does not use the term pejoratively but compassionately, as a common term applied to those who were isolated from Jewish religious circles because of their open sin, their unacceptable occupation or lifestyle, or their paganism. Luke shows that these sinners are the objects of God's grace through the ministry of Jesus.

10 Ἀπὸ τοῦ νῦν (*apo tou nyn*, "from now on") is an important indicator of transition in Luke (cf. 22:18, 69; Acts 18:6). Ἔση ζωγρῶν (*esē zōgrōn*, "you will catch") is a future periphrastic suggesting continuity of action.

5. *The man with leprosy*

5:12–16

12While Jesus was in one of the towns, a man came along who was covered with leprosy. When he saw Jesus, he fell with his face to the ground and begged him, "Lord, if you are willing, you can make me clean."
13Jesus reached out his hand and touched the man. "I am willing," he said. "Be clean!" And immediately the leprosy left him.
14Then Jesus ordered him, "Don't tell anyone, but go, show yourself to the priest and offer the sacrifices that Moses commanded for your cleansing, as a testimony to them."
15Yet the news about him spread all the more, so that crowds of people came to hear him and to be healed of their sicknesses. 16But Jesus often withdrew to lonely places and prayed.

Luke not only presents the gospel of salvation but supports it with signs and witnesses (though not as prominently as John does). In this section Jesus performs a miracle that is to be a "testimony" (v. 14).

12 Leprosy is a general term in Scripture for certain skin diseases. They were not necessarily equivalent to what we know as Hansen's disease. While their interpretation as a type of sin may have been overdrawn by some commentators, such an application is consistent with the nature of such diseases. They were repulsive and resulted in physical, social, and psychological isolation of their victims (cf. Lev 13, esp. v. 45). Luke is once again careful to note the nature and extent of a disease ("covered with leprosy"). The assumption is that the man has some knowledge of Jesus' prior miracles. Just as Peter fell at Jesus' feet for shame at his sinfulness, this man falls face downward for shame at his uncleanness. The disease was of such nature as to give the impression of filth, and the appeal for cleansing was appropriate to the condition. The appellation "Lord" doubtless has less meaning than on Peter's lips (v. 8), meaning here no more than "Sir." The condition "if you are willing" may express a sense of unworthiness rather than doubt as to Jesus' ability or kindness.

13 The very act of touching is significant, especially since lepers were always kept at a distance. Later, Jesus touched a coffin (7:14), an act ritually prohibited. Perhaps our contemporary society, having rediscovered the significance of touching as a means of communicating concern, can identify to an extent with Jesus' kindness in touching the leper. Such contact also symbolized the transfer of healing power (cf. being touched by a suppliant, 8:44). Jesus' "I am willing" meets the man's need of reassurance, just as his "Don't be afraid" reassured Peter (v. 10). Luke notes that the healing was accomplished "immediately" (*eutheōs*, more common in Mark).

14 The command to silence follows the pattern noted above in 4:41. Jesus wanted first to do the works of the Messiah and to fulfill his basic mission of sacrificial suffering before being publicly proclaimed as Messiah. The healing of lepers is one of the messianic signs that John the Baptist in prison was reminded of (7:22). Also, as has often been observed, the crowds could all too easily apply to Jesus their commonly held view of the Messiah as a military or political liberator.

For the cleansed leper to show himself to the priest was essential. One reason often suggested for this is that Jesus wanted to observe the ritual prescribed in Leviticus 14, (In 17:14 he gives the same command.) Here, however, something further is involved: the messianic act of healing was to be "as a testimony to them" (see comments on 7:21-23).

15-16 If the command to silence is part of a pattern in the Gospels, so is the failure to obey it. The immediate effect of the healing is Jesus' increased popularity. Though this popularity leads others to come and be healed (v.15), Jesus is forced to withdraw in order to seek quiet (v.16). Once again Luke speaks of Jesus' habit of prayer (cf. note on 3:21). In contrast to his earlier freedom to minister in "the towns" (v.12), Jesus must now make a practice of finding solitude in deserted areas.

Notes

12 Ἀνήρ (*anēr*, "man") occurs far more often in Luke than in all the other synoptic Gospels. On leprosy, see R.H. Pousma, "Diseases of the Bible," ZPEB, 2:138.
16 "Often" represents an imperfect periphrastic, ἦν ὑποχωρῶν (*ēn hypochōrōn*, lit., "was withdrawing"), suggesting repeated action.

6. *Healing a paralytic*

5:17-26

17One day as he was teaching, Pharisees and teachers of the law, who had come from every village of Galilee and from Judea and Jerusalem, were sitting there. And the power of the Lord was present for him to heal the sick. 18Some men came carrying a paralytic on a mat and tried to take him into the house to lay him before Jesus. 19When they could not find a way to do this because of the crowd, they went up on the roof and lowered him on his mat through the tiles into the middle of the crowd, right in front of Jesus.
20When Jesus saw their faith, he said, "Friend, your sins are forgiven."
21The Pharisees and the teachers of the law began thinking to themselves, "Who is this fellow who speaks blasphemy? Who can forgive sins but God alone?"
22Jesus knew what they were thinking and asked, "Why are you thinking these things in your hearts? 23Which is easier: to say, 'Your sins are forgiven,' or to say, 'Get up and walk'? 24But that you may know that the Son of Man has authority on earth to forgive sins...." He said to the paralyzed man, "I tell you, get up, take your mat and go home." 25Immediately he stood up in front of them, took what he had been lying on and went home praising God. 26Everyone was amazed and gave praise to God. They were filled with awe and said, "We have seen remarkable things today."

Jesus' activities inevitably brought him into confrontation with the religious authorities. Far from minimizing this, the Gospels actually focus on several such occasions. (See, for example, the Sabbath controversies in ch. 6 and the encounters in ch. 20.) Luke is especially concerned in his Gospel and in Acts to clarify the original relationship beween Christianity and Judaism and to show the reasons why the gospel had to break out of the confines of Judaism. Here he stresses the authority of

Jesus once more. In 4:32 Jesus' teaching was authoritative; 4:36 shows his authority over demons; 5:24 shows his authority to forgive sins.

17 The opening words, "one day," loosely connect this narrative with the preceding ones. The implication is that Jesus was teaching over a period of some time. Luke mentions, as often, the teaching ministry of Jesus. The word "teach" does not occur in this context in Matthew or Mark. While this is not specifically stated, it seems that Jesus' reputation had aroused the attention of the Jewish religious authorities, who considered it important to hear what he was teaching. Whereas Mark (2:6) introduces the scribes (NIV, "teachers of the law," *grammateis*) almost casually later in the narrative, Luke centers attention on them immediately, even specifying that they had come from as far away as Jerusalem. By doing this he lays stress on the crucial nature of the religious issues to be raised. This is also Luke's first introduction of the Pharisees and "teachers of the law."

The Pharisees had, earlier in their history, helped the Jews maintain the purity of their religion by teaching how the Mosaic Law and the traditions that grew up along side it ought to be applied in daily life. Many of them became rigid, imbalanced, and hypocritical (cf. comments on 11:37–54). Here Luke introduces them without any comment.

The "teachers of the law" were not a religious party, like the Pharisees, though most of them were also Pharisees. They were respected as having expert knowledge of the details of the Jewish legal tradition and so would be expected to form an opinion about the correctness of Jesus' teaching.

Luke now turns from Jesus' teaching ministry to that of healing, a subject of great interest to him. These two elements, doctrine and healing power, climax this narrative. The presence of the Lord's power to heal means that God himself was there.

18–19 Attention now focuses on a different group motivated by earnestness and faith (v.18). The typical flat roof could be reached by an outside stairway (v.19). Roofing materials, whether tiles (as in Luke) or mud thatch (as implied, though not stated, in Mark 2:4; cf. Notes) were separable without being damaged.

20 Two declarations form the focal point of this narrative, which, because it appears in the Gospel in order to provide a context for a pronouncement, may be called a "pronouncement story" (without prejudice to its historicity). The first is a declaration of forgiveness, the second an affirmation of Jesus' authority to make that declaration (v.24). The plural reference in the term "their faith" is to the four who brought the man, though we may assume from his subsequent forgiveness that he also believed. Jesus' attention to the faith of the man's helpers demonstrates the important fact that God responds to the intercession of others regarding a person in need. This does not imply, of course, that faith that trusts Jesus for salvation can ever be by proxy. Those who brought the paralytic to Jesus believed that Jesus would save him. But the paralytic's salvation was an intensely personal matter between him and Jesus. Indeed, we are not even told that he had faith. Jesus chose to heal him; and, out of the totality of his need, the paralytic looked in faith to Jesus. Perhaps when he did what Jesus asked him to do, *that* was his declaration of faith in Jesus.

Jesus' declaration of the forgiveness of the paralytic's sin does not imply that sin was the immediate cause of his disease. To be sure, this was commonly assumed, even by Jesus' own disciples (John 9:2). Although correct theology sees sickness and death as part of the deterioration mankind has suffered because of universal sin, and though some specific ills may be connected with a particular sin (1 Cor 11:29-30), no such connection appears in this context.

21 In Jewish law conviction of blasphemy, which was a capital crime penalized by stoning, had to be based on unmistakable and overt defilement of the divine name. Luke shows that with his divine insight, Jesus probed the unvoiced thoughts of the Pharisees and teachers of the law, who were convinced that he had arrogated to himself the divine prerogative.

22-23 Without making a point of it, Luke indicates that Jesus exercises extraordinary knowledge (v.22). In a typical dialogue form of question and counterquestion, the challengers are impaled on the horns of a hypothetical dilemma (v.23; cf. 6:9; 20:3-4, 44). Obviously while the two sentences are in one sense equally easy to say (and equally impossible to do), in another sense it is easier to say that which cannot be disproved: "Your sins are forgiven."

24 The structure of this sentence is broken by the redirecting of Jesus' comments from the leaders to the man. This presents no problem. The form of the sentence is virtually identical in all three Synoptics, which deliberately retain its irregular structure. Thus a focus is maintained both on Jesus' running controversy with the religious leaders and on his ministry to the paralytic.

Here (v.24) is the first appearance of the term "Son of Man" in Luke (cf. Notes). It occurs earlier in the Gospel than we might have expected, certainly before the issues of Jesus' identity and titles have been spelled out. Further, it occurs in connection with the right to pronounce forgiveness rather than with the themes of suffering and glory that characterize its specific use in the other passages where it is used.

25-26 The healing validates the declaration of forgiveness. The command to the paralyzed man is impossible of fulfillment—except for the power of God. To respond took an act of obedience based on faith. He stood up "immediately" (*parachrēma*, which appears ten times in Luke out of twelve in the Synoptics). The result is the glorification of God (v.25), both by the man and by the crowd (v.26). As we have already observed (cf. comment on 2:20), to glorify God is one of Luke's important objectives. This praise is offered by the one who is the object of God's power and by the witnesses of that power. The onlookers were "amazed" (v.26); Luke uses the same word to describe the response of the crowds to the events at Pentecost, when by God's power the disciples told of his great works (Acts 2:11-12). In this case the people say that what they have observed is contrary to expectation (*paradoxa*, from which our word "paradox" is derived; NIV, "remarkable"). The final word in both the Greek and the NIV is "today." Its use in this particular position, at the very end of the passage, strikingly recalls its occurrence as the first word said by Jesus after reading the Isaiah passage in Nazareth (4:21). The other Gospels do not have the word in this final sentence. By including it here Luke assures the reader that this indeed is the awaited eschatological "today."

Notes

17 Literature on the Pharisees is vast. Among recent significant studies are W.D. Davies, *Introduction to Pharisaism* (Philadelphia: Fortress, 1954, 1967); A. Finkel, *The Pharisees and the Teacher of Nazareth* (Leiden: Brill, 1964). See also J. Jeremias, *Time of Jesus*, and the summary article "Pharisees" by D.A. Hagner, ZPEB, 4:745–52.

Luke thoughtfully avoids the Jewish word γραμματεύς (*grammateus*, "scribes"), using instead νομοδιδάσκαλοι (*nomodidaskaloi*, "legal experts"; NIV, "teachers of the law") for the benefit of his largely Gentile readership (see J. Jeremias, TDNT, 1:740–42; and K. Rengstorf, TDNT, 2:159).

19 Much discussion has centered around what is alleged to be a contradiction between Mark, who describes an action suitable to a roof made of thatch held together with mud, and Luke, who uses the word κέραμος (*keramos*, cf. "ceramic"). But it is wrong to call it a contradiction, for at most Luke is adapting the terminology in order to communicate the scene vividly to those used to tile roofs. Even so, tile was not unknown in Palestine; and Luke's terminology may be even more suitable to the specific nature of the roof than we realize.

20 "Friend" translates Ἄνθρωπε (*Anthrōpe*, "[O] Man"), a surprising use by Luke of a less tender term than that used by Matthew and Mark: τέκνον (*teknon*, "son," Matt 9:2; Mark 2:5). For the sake of theological precision, it should be noted that Jesus does not say here that *he* forgives sins but that they *are forgiven*. The passive ἀφέωνται (*apheōntai*, "are forgiven") probably suggests that God is the source of forgiveness (cf. 7:48, where, in the only other similar pronouncement, the passive is also used). The premise was correct: only God can forgive sins, but the leaders failed to recognize who stood before them.

24 Ὁ υἱὸς τοῦ ἀνθρώπου (*ho huios tou anthrōpou*, "the Son of Man") is common in the Synoptics and was certainly used often by Jesus. However, many think that its inclusion in this narrative is redactional or due to the influence of the early church during the history of its tradition. This conclusion is partly based on the assumption that Jesus did not attach to the OT figure of the Son of Man (e.g., Dan 7:13), or to himself, the authority to forgive sins. The immense concentration of study on the development of concepts about the Son of Man still leaves enough questions to prevent dogmatizing here. But to forgive sins is certainly a legitimate function of an eschatological figure who is concerned with righteous judgment.

There is no textual evidence against the genuineness of this saying, nor does the literary structure of the passage in Luke or Mark require a negative judgment against its appropriation in the passage. Nor does Son of Man here mean man in general. It is inconsistent with the rest of the Gospels and NT literature to allow mankind the authority implied in this statement. For a survey that incorporates much of the extensive discussion and conclusions of work during the 1960s, see C. Colpe, TDNT, 8:400–477; for conservative approaches, see I.H. Marshall, "The Synoptic Son of Man Sayings in Recent Discussion, NTS 12 (1965–66):327–51. Two more recent and very fine surveys of the topic, including citation of the significant literature, will be found in D. Guthrie, *New Testament Theology* (Downers Grove, Ill.: Inter-Varsity, 1981), pp. 270–91; G.E. Ladd, *A Theology of the New Testament* (Grand Rapids: Eerdmans, 1974), pp. 145–58. Another significant work is A.J.B. Higgins, *The Son of Man in the Teaching of Jesus*. SNTS Monograph Series, 39 (New York: Cambridge, 1980). On the passage in question, see Marshall, *Gospel of Luke*, pp. 214–16.

7. Calling Levi

5.27-02

27After this, Jesus went out and saw a tax collector by the name of Levi sitting at his tax booth. "Follow me," Jesus said to him, 28and Levi got up, left everything and followed him.

29Then Levi held a great banquet for Jesus at his house, and a large crowd of tax collectors and others were eating with them. 30But the Pharisees and the teachers of the law who belonged to their sect complained to his disciples, "Why do you eat and drink with tax collectors and 'sinners'?"

31Jesus answered them, "It is not the healthy who need a doctor, but the sick. 32I have not come to call the righteous, but sinners to repentance."

The succession of people on whom the Lord bestows his favor continues. We have seen his grace to a demoniac, a leper, and a paralytic; and now we see it given to a tax collector. So Jesus liberates those suffering from malign spirits, physical handicap, and social disfavor. The antagonists, Pharisees and teachers of the law, who were merely named in the preceding narrative, are again on the scene. D. Daube has discerned a pattern here (cf. 4:15-30; 5:17-26; 6:1-11; 11:14-54; 13:10-17; 20:1-8): "(1) Jesus and his disciples perform a revolutionary action, (2) the Pharisees remonstrate with him—or, on occasion, merely 'marvel'—and (3) he makes a pronouncement by which they are silenced" (*The New Testament and Rabbinic Judaism* [New York: Arno, 1973], p. 170).

27-28 Levi (v.27) is identified as Matthew in Matthew 9:9. He was a tax collector (cf. Notes); as such he had incurred the dislike of those who looked on such officials as crooked and serving an unpopular government (see comments on 15:1; 19:2). Levi himself was not a "chief" tax collector, as Zacchaeus was (cf. Notes; cf. also comments on 3:12); nor is it said that he, like Zacchaeus, was wealthy, but he obviously was treated by the Pharisees as a religious outcast.

The direct command of Jesus to follow him results in Levi's immediate and total obedience, a paradigm of the kind of discipleship Jesus will later specify in detail. Luke notes both the negative aspect (leaving everyting) and the positive one (following Jesus) of what Levi did (v.28; cf. also 9:23-25).

29-30 A banquet (v.29) in the NT symbolizes joy and often hints at the eschatological banquet, the future celebration of God's people with the patriarchs in the presence of God. Jesus is the guest of honor; but Levi does not, as might be expected, limit the guest list to his new Christian friends, the disciples of Jesus. Instead of immediately cutting off his old associates, Levi invites them into his home, probably to bring them also into contact with Jesus. Luke mentions "others," who turn out (v.30) to be "sinners," as far as the Pharisees are concerned. The joy of the participants is now opposed by the dour criticism of the religious leaders, a contrast we can see running throughout the Gospels.

The complaint of the Pharisees, and particularly of those among them who were also scribes, is more than a superficial attempt to find fault. To join in table fellowship with irreligious "sinners" is to cast doubt on one of the essential assumptions of Pharisaic teaching. This sect was dedicated to upholding the purity of Jewish faith and life. Implicit in their teachings was strict adherence to both law and tradition, including necessary rites of purification and separation from all whose moral or ritual purity might be in question. The Galilean people had a reputation (not always deserved) for disdaining such scruples and disregarding the traditions.

The Pharisees' complaint is specifically directed to the act of eating and drinking because in their society table fellowship implied mutual acceptance. No act, apart from participation in the actual sinful deeds of the guests, could have broken the wall of separation more dramatically. Yet the Pharisees are not yet ready to argue with Jesus himself. In the previous incident they did not even express their thoughts openly (v.21). They direct their question to Jesus' disciples and also (in Luke only) charge the disciples themselves, not just Jesus, with this unacceptable conduct.

31-32 It is important to recognize that Jesus not only originated proverbs and parables but also made wise use of current ones. So, citing a self-evident proverb of his day (v.31), he described his mission in terms that he would go on to amplify in the parables in chapter 15. Since none are truly "righteous" (v.32; cf. 18:19; Rom 3:23), Jesus used the word here either in a relative sense or with a touch of sarcasm. The Prodigal Son's older brother, for example, could rightly claim that he had not deserted his father as the Prodigal had. If, therefore, Jesus meant by "righteous" those who are generally loyal or devout, v.32 means that he gave more help to those in greater need. But if, as is more likely, Jesus implied that the Pharisees only *thought* that they were righteous, the point is that one must first acknowledge himself to be a sinner before he can truly respond to the call to repentance. Luke allows the proverb Jesus quoted to come full circle theologically by including the word "repentance," omitted in Matthew 9:13 and Mark 2:17. With this word, Luke introduces a topic of major importance. While the gospel of grace and forgiveness is for everyone (2:10), repentance is a prerequisite to its reception. The tax collector in 18:13-14 met this prerequisite, but not the Pharisee (18:11-12). The Lukan theme of joy is linked with that of repentance in 15:7, 10, 22-27, 32. Repentance was previously mentioned in Luke 3:3, 8, but only in the context of John the Baptist's ministry.

Notes

27 "Tax collector" is the proper translation for τελώνης (*telōnēs*), not "publican" (KJV). The latter comes from the Latin *publicanus*, which was normally applied to chief tax collectors (Gr. ἀρχιτελώνης, *architelōnēs*), like Zacchaeus (19:2). Levi is not further mentioned by that name in Luke but is called "Matthew" in 6:15.

30 On the connotation of the word ἁμαρτωλόι (*hamartōloi*, "sinners") in Jesus' day, see Rengstorf, TDNT, 1:327-33.

8. The question about fasting

5:33-39

> 33They said to him, "John's disciples often fast and pray, and so do the disciples of the Pharisees, but yours go on eating and drinking."
> 34Jesus answered, "Can you make the guests of the bridegroom fast while he

is with them? 35But the time will come when the bridegroom will be taken from them; in those days they will fast."

36He told them this parable: "No one tears a patch from a new garment and sews it on an old one. If he does, he will have torn the new garment, and the patch from the new will not match the old. 37And no one pours new wine into old wineskins. If he does, the new wine will burst the skins, the wine will run out and the wineskins will be ruined. 38No, new wine must be poured into new wineskins. 39And no one after drinking old wine wants the new, for he says, 'The old is better.' "

In all three Synoptics the issues related to Levi's banquet lead to further questions about religious practices. From Jesus' mention of fasting and prayer along with almsgiving as "acts of righteousness" in the Sermon on the Mount (Matt 6:1–18), we know that these practices were considered significant indications of religious devotion. In contrast to the two previous incidents (vv.21, 30), this time the leaders challenge Jesus directly.

33 The question, which is stated as a fact, not a query, is cleverly expressed. First, the Pharisees and the disciples of John the Baptist, who were assumed to be particularly sympathetic to Jesus, are lined up against Jesus' disciples, who are thus made to appear out of step. Second, there is a hint that Jesus' disciples were neglecting the important duty of prayer. Again Jesus himself is not criticized directly but through his disciples. Fasting was actually only prescribed for one day in the year (cf. Notes) but was practiced as a religious exercise more often—viz., twice a week by the Pharisees (cf. 18:12). The disciples are now criticized, not only for eating with sinners, but for having a lifestyle that seems to be in contrast to proper religious decorum.

34–35 Jesus' answer is so remarkable that many have assumed that the saying in v.35 must not be an authentic prophecy but is a reflection of the church after Jesus' death. The first part of the saying is clear (v.34). Jesus compares the situation to a wedding, which naturally calls for joy. (The image of the bridegroom is most fully treated in Eph 5:25–33; Rev 19:6–9.) But to think at a wedding of the possibility of the groom's death is highly unusual. The allusion is so abrupt that we cannot ignore it. Neither can we ignore the fact that Jesus anticipated his rejection and his death at the hands of his enemies.

36 The context provides opportunity for Jesus to state a basic principle in a series of parabolic figures. His mission involved a radical break with common religious practices. Jesus neither affirms nor denies the value of fasting, and he does not mention prayer here at all. He teaches rather that he has not come merely to add devotional routines to those already practiced, for what he brings is not a patch but a whole new garment. Merely to "patch things up"—i.e., to have a dinner celebration in place of fasting—would fail for two reasons. First, it would ruin the rest of the new garment from which it is taken. Second, just one new patch will not help preserve the old garment but will in fact be conspicuously incongruous. The form of the saying in Luke carries the image beyond the way Matthew and Mark state it.

37–38 The second illustration has a slightly different connotation—viz., Jesus' teaching is like fermenting wine that seems to almost have inherent vigor and cannot be contained within an old rigid system. Later on Jesus will speak of a new covenant (22:20), which is indeed new and not merely an improved extension of the old.

39 Jesus is not reversing himself and saying that his new teaching is not as good as the old it replaces. The point emphasized is that people tend to want the old and reject the new, assuming (wrongly in this case) that the old is better.

9. Sabbath controversies

6:1-11

> ¹One Sabbath Jesus was going through the grainfields, and his disciples began to pick some heads of grain, rub them in their hands and eat the kernels. ²Some of the Pharisees asked, "Why are you doing what is unlawful on the Sabbath?"
> ³Jesus answered them, "Have you never read what David did when he and his companions were hungry? ⁴He entered the house of God, and taking the consecrated bread, he ate what is lawful only for priests to eat. And he also gave some to his companions." ⁵Then Jesus said to them, "The Son of Man is Lord of the Sabbath."
> ⁶On another Sabbath he went into the synagogue and was teaching, and a man was there whose right hand was shriveled. ⁷The Pharisees and the teachers of the law were looking for a reason to accuse Jesus, so they watched him closely to see if he would heal on the Sabbath. ⁸But Jesus knew what they were thinking and said to the man with the shriveled hand, "Get up and stand in front of everyone." So he got up and stood there.
> ⁹Then Jesus said to them, "I ask you, which is lawful on the Sabbath: to do good or to do evil, to save life or to destroy it?"
> ¹⁰He looked around at them all, and then said to the man, "Stretch out your hand." He did so, and his hand was completely restored. ¹¹But they were furious and began to discuss with one another what they might do to Jesus.

The uneasy tension between Jesus and the Pharisees described in chapter 5 hardens into controversy over one of the main institutions of Judaism, the Sabbath. The Gospels list three Sabbath controversies. Two occur in the Synoptics and one in John 5. In each instance Jesus allows or even stimulates the controversy, providing several types of response: (1) the Sabbath is for man's benefit (Mark 2:27); (2) the Son of Man is "Lord of the Sabbath" (v.5); (3) the Sabbath is for helpful deeds, the omission of which would be evil (v.9); and (4) the Father works even on the Sabbath and so may the Son (John 5:17).

Keeping the Sabbath provided an appropriate issue for debate because it (1) had roots both in the creation account and in the Ten Commandments, (2) involved every seventh day and consequently called for many decisions about what was permitted or forbidden on that day, (3) consequently became the subject of two tractates in the Mishna (*Shabbath* and *Erubin*), and (4) afforded a public disclosure of one's observance or nonobservance of the day.

1-2 Luke centers attention on the disciples (v.1), though in accordance with custom their teacher was held responsible. To glean by hand (not using a sickle) in someone's field was permitted by law (Deut 23:25). But to do this and to rub the heads of grain (a detail Luke alone has) was considered to be threshing. The Mishnah forbids threshing (v 2) on the Sabbath (*Shabbath* 7.2).

3–4 Jesus' response (v.3) centers in an analogy from Scripture (1 Sam 21:1–6). He is not providing a specific teaching, such as would be necessary to establish a rabbinical rule (W. Lane, *The Gospel According to Mark* [Grand Rapids: Eerdmans, 1974], p. 117). Instead he simply calls to mind an instance in which the infringement of a rule to meet human need received no condemnation (v.4). His illustration is apt because the general principle then and in his time continues to be the same and because a leader (David and David's messianic descendant) is involved along with his companions. The point is that ceremonial rites (being only means to an end) must give way to a higher moral law.

5 Following this analogy, on which the Pharisees offer no comment, Jesus makes a statement in which for the second time in Luke he uses the phrase "Son of Man" (cf. 5:24). While some have argued that "Son of Man" simply means "man" here (cf. Creed, pp. 84–85), Morris (*Luke*, p. 122) objects that "Jesus never taught that man is Lord over a divine institution." Therefore what Jesus says at this point is a claim to unique authority and takes the argument of vv.3–4 a step further.

6–8 The second Sabbath controversy involves basically the same issue as the first— human need versus ceremonial law. Luke presents some specific details, lacking in the parallels in the other Synoptics, that show this event occurred on a different Sabbath, and that it was the man's right hand Jesus healed (v.6). As in 4:15–16, 31–33, Jesus is teaching in the synagogue. Luke does not say that the man actually asked for healing; Jesus simply took the initiative. The hand was "shriveled," i.e., atrophied and useless. As in 5:17, the "Pharisees and teachers of the law" (v.7) are present, scrutinizing Jesus' every action to find fault. Now, after the first Sabbath controversy, they think they have a case against him. Man's reasonings tend to be evil (Gen 6:5; 8:21; Eph 5:17–18); Jesus is aware of their thoughts (v.8) and in the light of that knowledge performs the healing. He has the man stand in front of the people so that all will see what follows.

9 Jesus' question goes beyond the fact that the healing could have been postponed a day. After all, it was not a critical illness that might take a turn for the worse if not treated immediately. Were that the case, rabbinical law would have permitted healing on a Sabbath. But Jesus implies in his double question that if any illness is left unattended when healing can be provided, evil is done by default. Jesus is not breaking the Sabbath; he is using it to do good to a human being in need.

10 Here Jesus commanded the impossible. Presumably the man exercised obedience born of faith, though Luke has not said that the man had faith or asked to be healed. Jesus healed the withered hand completely.

11 The response is violent; the opposition to Jesus mounts in a crescendo of fury more intense than that after the previous miracle. So now, near the very start of Jesus' ministry, a plot against him was beginning to form.

Notes

1 Σαββάτῳ δευτεροπώτῳ (sabbatō deuteropōtō, "second-first Sabbath"), an alternative reading to σαββάτῳ (sabbatō, "a Sabbath"), has puzzled textual critics. First, the meaning of the variant is uncertain. There is an attractive speculation that Luke keeps a careful chronological record and that this is the second Sabbath after Jesus' major sermon (4:16, followed by 4:31 and 6:1). Marshall (*Gospel of Luke*, p. 230) calls this "a solution born of despair." This reading could refer to a sequence of Sabbaths beginning with the one occurring after Passover, during the week-long Feast of Unleavened Bread. The Sabbath in 6:1 would be the first after that feast, the second after Passover. But this also seems a strained solution, except that Lev 23:15–16 shows that this period, leading up to Pentecost, is carefully numbered by weeks (cf. TDNT, 7:23, n. 183). Also Luke seems to be interested in the Sabbath along with the Jubilee (cf. comments on 4:19) as symbols of God's work of salvation and freedom. However, this variant reading seems to have little support (cf. UBS apparatus). While it is the more difficult reading, and on that ground more likely to be the original, it may not be original. Instead, it may have arisen if the word πρώτῳ (prōtō, "first") had been (1) written in, (2) crossed out, with δευτέρῳ (deuterō, "second") substituted, and then (3) through scribal confusion reinstated along with deuterō (Metzger, *Textual Commentary*, p. 139). This, too, seems strained; but at least it might balance the claim that as the more difficult reading it should be accepted, by showing how it might have arisen. The MS evidence is the least problematic factor in the decision and should probably lead to a rejection of the extra word.

10. *Choosing the twelve apostles*

6:12–16

12One of those days Jesus went out to a mountainside to pray, and spent the night praying to God. 13When morning came, he called his disciples to him and chose twelve of them, whom he also designated apostles: 14Simon (whom he named Peter), his brother Andrew, James, John, Philip, Bartholomew, 15Matthew, Thomas, James son of Alphaeus, Simon who was called the Zealot, 16Judas son of James, and Judas Iscariot, who became a traitor.

At this point in the narrative sequence, Mark (3:7–12) summarizes Jesus' ministry of healing. Luke postpones that summary to 6:17–19 as his introduction to the Sermon on the Plain. He puts the call of the disciples first, though not necessarily "in order to gain an audience for the sermon" (Marshall, *Gospel of Luke*, p. 237), since a statement about a crowd of disciples and others already stood available in the Markan summary (Mark 3:7).

12 Jesus spent an entire night in prayer, a sure indication that the circumstances were pressing: the preceding controversy, the resultant threatening atmosphere, and the selection to be made of the twelve apostles. The second clause indicates that the first was not a routine devotional exercise.

How many of us Christians today have ever spent a whole night in prayer? In his prayer life, as in all else, the Lord Jesus stands far above even the best of us whose words about prayer need to be matched by the consistent practice of it.

13–16 The "disciples" (v.13) up to this time were a group of followers interested in attaching themselves to Jesus the teacher. (See further on discipleship in the comments on 9:23–27; 14:25–33.) From among these followers, Jesus chose the Twelve. Luke alone tells us that Jesus gave them the designation "apostles" (cf. Notes). That Luke does this accords with his regard for apostolic authority.

Most interpreters assume that Jesus intended the number of apostles to correspond with the number of the tribes of Israel, thereby indicating that a new people of God was coming into existence. The apostles' names appear several other times in the Gospels and Acts (Matt 10:2–4; Mark 3:16–19; Acts 1:13), with the same grouping, differing only in the form of a few names.

"Judas son of James" (v.16) apparently had, like many people, two names and is to be identified with Thaddaeus in Mark and Matthew. One of the two Simons was a "Zealot," i.e., one who had advocated revolutionary opposition to Rome. The other Simon, Peter, is at the head of every list. Judas Iscariot (cf. Notes) is always last. From a promising beginning he "became a traitor." The group is not distinguished by particular abilities or position in life (cf. the principle in 1 Cor 1:26–29).

Notes

12 Conzelmann (*Theology of Luke*, p. 44) thinks that Luke has enlarged Mark's concept of the mountain as "the place of revelation," and that "there is no question of locating 'the' mountain." It is a mythical place, to which the people "cannot come." Mountains did provide an environment that seemed very near to heaven, but it is unnecessary to assume that Luke uses mountains (NIV, "hills") or any other topographical or geographical site merely as a symbol (cf. comment and Note on 9:28).

13 From later Jewish literature we learn that an "apostle" was a messenger who, during his particular mission, acted with the full authority of the one who sent him (jHag. 1.8). It may be anachronistic to see that particular meaning here, but there is no reason why the basic concept cannot be attributed to Jesus' situation (cf. TDNT, 1:398–447).

16 Ellis (*Gospel of Luke*, p. 110) and Marshall (*Gospel of Luke*, p. 240) support the option that the name Ἰσκαριώθ (*Iskariōth*, "Iscariot") means the "false one," a derivation from the Aramaic שקר (*šeqar*, "falsehood"). Other suggestions are an unlikely derivation from *sicarius* (lit., "dagger man" or "assassin") and the traditional "man of Kerioth" (cf. Josh 15:25), which still remains a possibility.

B. *Jesus' Great Sermon* (6:17–49)

1. *Blessings and woes*

6:17–26

[17]He went down with them and stood on a level place. A large crowd of his disciples was there and a great number of people from all over Judea, from Jerusalem, and from the coast of Tyre and Sidon, [18]who had come to hear him and to be healed of their diseases. Those troubled by evil spirits were cured, [19]and the people all tried to touch him, because power was coming from him and healing them all.

[20]Looking at his disciples, he said:

"Blessed are you who are poor,
for yours is the kingdom of God.

> 21Blessed are you who hunger now,
>   for you will be satisfied.
> Blessed are you who weep now,
>   for you will laugh.
> 22Blessed are you when men hate you,
>   when they exclude you and insult you
>   and reject your name as evil,
>   because of the Son of Man.

> 23"Rejoice in that day and leap for joy, because great is your reward in heaven.
> For that is how their fathers treated the prophets.

> 24"But woe to you who are rich,
>   for you have already received your comfort.
> 25Woe to you who are well fed now,
>   for you will go hungry.
> Woe to you who laugh now,
>   for you will mourn and weep.
> 26Woe to you when all men speak well of you,
>   for that is how their fathers treated the false prophets.

The settings of this passage and of the Sermon on the Mount in Matthew 5–7 are not indisputably the same, and there is considerable difference in content. Therefore many scholars call the Lukan material the "Sermon on the Plain," with the implication that it is, in Luke's opinion, an entirely different sermon. The probability is that there was one sermon among many that Jesus preached on similar themes that was something like a "keynote" address. This was a basic affirmation of the kingdom message, beginning with beatitudes and ending with a parable about builders. Within this framework Matthew and Luke present samples or selections of Jesus' teachings that differ at points; Luke (Matthew also to a lesser extent) distributes some of the sermon's teachings, which Jesus probably repeated frequently, in other contexts in the Gospel narrative. One clear example is the Lord's Prayer in Luke 11:2–4 (cf. Matt 6:9–13).

The sermon as presented in this chapter includes the "Blessings and Woes" (vv. 20–26), "Love for Enemies" (vv.27–36), "Judging Others" (vv.37–42), and a final section on the test of genuineness in two parts: "A Tree and its Fruit" and "The Wise and Foolish Builders" (following the divisions in the NIV text). However, vv.39–49 may be viewed as a unified section from a literary perspective, as this part is marked by a parabolic style.

17–19 The "level place" (*epi topou pedinou*, v.17) is apparently an area on the "mountainside" mentioned in Matthew 5:1. If it were a plain, such as Jesus often used for his teaching near the sea, just the words *epi pedinou* would probably have been used (Godet, p. 295). Luke mentions a "large crowd" of Jesus' disciples plus "a great number of people" (cf. 4:14–15 and Luke's stress on Jesus' popularity). Matthew mentions disciples in 5:1, speaking of "crowds" only at the end of the sermon (7:28).

Although Jesus directs his comments to the disciples (v.20), he is surely conscious of his larger audience. His teachings in the sermon, especially those in Matthew 5:17–20, keep a balance between two extreme viewpoints that would have been familiar to any crowd. One is the strong legalistic "righteousness" often characteristic of the Pharisees; the other is the attitude attributed to many of the "people of the land," who knew little of the rabbinic tradition and were thought to disregard many religious practices. The emphasis in vv 18 19 on "power" and "healing" is characteristic of Luke. (For another instance of Jesus' power being drawn on by a "touch," see 8:43–46.) Luke clearly distinguishes here between those affected by demons and those whose illness was basically physical.

20–23 Luke's version of the blessings (or "Beatitudes") is shorter than Matthew's and is different in some particulars. Also the Beatitudes appear in negative form in the woes. Both blessings and woes are familiar forms in the OT (e.g., Ps 1, which also carries an implication of woes; Isa 5:8–23). The entire theme of reversal of fortune has already been encountered in the Magnificat (1:51–55). It is also implicit in the attention Luke gives to social and religious outcasts throughout his Gospel.

"Blessed" (vv.20–22), as elsewhere in the NT, "refers to the distinctive religious joy which accrues to man from his share in the salvation of the Kingdom of God" (Hauck, TDNT, 4:367). "Poor" (*ptōchoi*) in Luke implies those who are utterly dependent on God (v.20). They are the special recipients of the "good news" Jesus came to preach (4:18). Often the economically destitute sense their need of God more than others. Whether voluntary poverty such as that practiced at Qumran is in view is not clear (cf. Ellis, *Gospel of Luke*, p. 113). Marshall (*Gospel of Luke*, p. 249) shows that nonviolence is implied. Matthew 5:3 specifies the spiritual poverty —i.e., recognition of one's spiritual need. To inherit the kingdom of God is the antithesis of poverty. Note the emphatic sense of assurance the present tense gives: "yours *is*" (emphasis mine). There may also be an element of "inaugurated eschatology" in the present tense—i.e., the presence of some aspects of the coming kingdom of God. In this case, the poor can rejoice even in the midst of their destitution because they are already able to partake of some of the kingdom blessings.

"Hunger" (*peinōntes*) is presented in its reality without spiritualization (v.21). It may well carry the connotation of hungering for righteousness (Matt 5:6). Those who "weep" (*klaiontes*) may be those who carry the burden not only of personal grief but of a hurting society. (The passage Jesus quoted in his synagogue sermon [4:18–19] goes on to speak of mourning giving way to gladness [Isa 61:2b–3a].) Both parts of v.21 stress the contrast between the situation "now" and the future blessing. Notice the difference in tone between Luke's "laugh" (*gelasete*) and Matthew's "be comforted" (*paraklēthēsontai*, 5:4).

The idea of laughter is vividly carried forward in the next section on persecution (vv.23–26). Persecution is described in some detail and the contrasting "rejoice" (*charēte*) and "leap for joy" (*skirtēsate*) stand out all the more (v.23). Note the progression from hate (v.22) to exclusion (which later took the form of being banned from the synagogue) to insult (cf. 1 Peter 4:14) to defamation of their name (cf. Matt 5:11). Those who share the rejection of the "Son of Man" relive the experience of the prophets (cf. comments on 20:9–12).

The promise of "reward in heaven" (v.23) does not suggest that the disciples are to work for some future gain but that there will be personal vindication and appropriate recognition and blessing from the Lord. Luke emphasizes the vindication of God's people who patiently wait for him (cf. 18:1–8 and comments). He also presents Jesus' teaching on reward for faithful servants (12:37, 42–44).

24–26 The woes in both structure and content form a direct contrast to the blessings. This again is after the Magnificat. "He has filled the hungry with good things but has sent the rich away empty" (1:53).

Woe comes to the "rich" (*tois plousiois*), not simply because they are wealthy, but (1) because the implication is that they have chosen present gratification over future blessing (v.24); (2) because rich people criticized in Luke disregard spiritual realities (e.g., 12:15–21); and (3) perhaps because, as was generally assumed, the wealthy became so at the expense of others (cf. James 2:6–7). The same thought runs through v.25—"well fed"—and probably v.26—where those who "laugh now" presumably do so at the expense of others.

The word "all" in the clause "when all men speak well of you" (v.26) should be carefully noted, lest we distort the basic concepts of honor and praise. False prophets plagued God's people in OT times; they were a threat in Jesus' day (Matt 7:15–23), in Paul's day (Acts 13:6; cf. 20:29–30), and on into the church age (cf. *Didache* 11:5–6; 12:5).

Notes

22 In its parallel to ἕνεκα τοῦ υἱοῦ τοῦ ἀνθρώπου (*heneka tou huiou tou anthrōpou*, "because of the Son of Man"), Matt 5:11 lacks *tou huiou tou anthrōpou* ("Son of Man"), having only ἕνεκεν ἐμοῦ (*heneken emou*, "because of me"). Since Luke does not add the title "Son of Man" where it does not appear in the tradition as he received it, its appearance here is authentic, contrary to some critical opinion (cf. Marshall, *Gospel of Luke*, p. 253).

24 Ἀπέχετε (*apechete*) means "you have received your full payment," hence NIV's "you have already received." This is in contrast to the blessed ones whose full reward lies ahead (v.23).

2. Love for enemies

6:27–36

27"But I tell you who hear me: Love your enemies, do good to those who hate you, 28bless those who curse you, pray for those who mistreat you. 29If someone strikes you on one cheek, turn to him the other also. If someone takes your cloak, do not stop him from taking your tunic. 30Give to everyone who asks you, and if anyone takes what belongs to you, do not demand it back. 31Do to others as you would have them do to you.

32"If you love those who love you, what credit is that to you? Even 'sinners' love those who love them. 33And if you do good to those who are good to you, what credit is that to you? Even 'sinners' do that. 34And if you lend to those from whom you expect repayment, what credit is that to you? Even 'sinners' lend to 'sinners,' expecting to be repaid in full. 35But love your enemies, do good to them, and lend to them without expecting to get anything back. Then your reward will be great, and you will be sons of the Most High, because he is kind to the ungrateful and wicked. 36Be merciful, just as your Father is merciful.

In place of the five antitheses of Matthew 5:21–48, Luke selects one theme (contained in two of the antitheses, Matt 5:38–42, 43–48) and enlarges on it. As might be expected from his basic concern for people, he chooses the theme of love. He does not present the teaching of Jesus over against the prevalent distortion of the OT (cf. Matt 5:43–44). Instead he conveys only the positive command The Golden Rule, which Matthew apparently postpones to use as a summary statement later in the sermon (7:12), occurs in Luke in what seems to be a natural context. Also, the conclusion in v.36 is significantly different from Matthew 5:48, each expression being eminently appropriate to its context (see below).

27–31 "You who hear me" (v.27) are probably those who are taking in what Jesus is saying, not casual listeners. The word "love" (*agapē* in the noun form) must be understood in its classic Christian sense of having a genuine concern for someone irrespective of his or her attractiveness or of the likelihood of any reciprocation in kind. The spirit of Jesus' words finds expression in Romans 12:14–21. Here in Luke the specifics are spelled out. In the first instance (v.28), apparently no physical harm has been done; so the response also is not physical but to "bless" (*eulogeite*) and to "pray" (*proseuchesthe*). The next situations involve action that must be met by some physical response. Opinions differ as to whether when "someone strikes you on the cheek" (v.29), it is (1) a mere insult (in Matt 5:39 it is the right cheek, indicating a backhanded slap, (2) the "ritual slap on the cheek given a Christian 'heretic' in the synagogue" (Ellis, *Gospel of Luke*, p. 115), or (3) "a punch to the side of the jaw," on the basis that *siagōn* means jaw, not cheek (Morris, *Luke*, p. 129, but cf. Notes). In any case, the injunction is directed to individuals (the form of the Greek imperatives and pronouns here is singular, not plural) who desire to live as "sons of the Most High" (v.35). Jesus is not advocating the suspension of normal civil judicial procedures. If pagan governments abandoned the protection of civil rights, the result would be an unbiblical anarchy (Rom 13:4).

"If someone takes your cloak" (v.29) may refer to a street robbery (since the clothing seized is the immediately accessible outer robe [*himation*]). In Matthew (5:40) the short tunic (*chitōn*), which is worn underneath, is taken first, possibly in court action. Nevertheless the implication seems to be that the person has a need or thinks he does. The teaching of the passage as a whole relates not so much to passivity in the face of evil as to concern for the other person. Inevitably, as ancient Greek philosophers recognized, to refrain from doing evil often means suffering evil. This was the path of the Lord Jesus (cf. 1 Peter 2:20–24), who prayed for his enemies (Luke 23:34) and died for them (Rom 5:10).

The same spirit is expressed in v.30, where the practical application of this hyperbolic command would be to refuse to demand that which would genuinely be to the good of the other person, even at our expense. The Golden Rule is now cited (v.31), not with theological comment, as in Matthew 7:12, but as a practical governing principle (cf. Notes).

32–36 At this point we have a remarkable series of comparisons between the courtesies of believers and those of worldly people. Even "sinners" act decently to others when kindnesses are reciprocated. In the sermon in Matthew, three basic comparisons are made with unbelievers regarding the quality of their relationship (1) to God (Matt 6:7–8), (2) to people (Matt 5:46–47; cf. the present passage), and (3) to material possessions (Matt 6:32; cf. Luke 12:30).

Loving (v.32) is augmented by doing good (v.33), which, in turn, is expressed in lending (v.34). Marshall (*Gospel of Luke,* p. 263) argues that *hina apolabōsin ta isa* ("expecting to be repaid in full," v.34) means "the reception of loans in return." One hardly makes a loan "expecting to" receive back the principal; that is assumed. Nor would a good Jew normally charge interest. Therefore some kind of equal treatment in return seems to be implied. One should benefit the helpless as well as one's friends.

Believers are to be like what they really are, "sons of the Most High" (v.35), and as such will have recognition. Jesus is not teaching that one earns sonship (cf. John 1:12–13). Rather, the day will come when the world will recognize God's children (Rom 8:19, 23).

"Be merciful" (*ginesthe oiktirmones,* v.36) singles out that area of life in which, given the preceding examples, one is very likely to come short. The Pharisees tithed spices but neglected "justice, mercy and faithfulness" (Matt 23:23). The believer's righteousness must exceed theirs (Matt 5:20). It should be measured against the perfection of God himself (Matt 5:48). Since Luke omits a discussion of law and Pharisees that would not be appropriate for his readership, he omits the imperative about being perfect and replaces it with one about being merciful. This accords with his emphasis on kindness to others in need (cf. 10:25–37).

Notes

29 Although σιαγών (*siagōn*) meant "jaw" in earlier classical literature, it came to mean "cheek" (so NIV) in the Hellenistic period. With the omission of Matthew's δεξιὰν (*dexian,* "right") (5:39), any allusion to a ritual slap is gone (it would have been meaningless to his Gentile audience anyway); so the idea of outright violence is stressed here in Luke. This is heightened by his statement about yielding the cloak, which he presents as a robbery rather than a court action.

31 No claim to originality is inherent in Jesus' use of the Golden Rule. It existed in a negative form, attributed to Rabbi Hillel, to the effect that one should not do to others what he does not want to happen to himself (*Shabbath* 31a; Tobit 4:15). Jesus uses and strengthens the "rule." There is a change from the singular verb form in the preceding injunctions to the plural in this general command καθὼς θέλετε . . . ποιεῖτε (*kathōs thelete . . . poieite,* "As you desire . . . do").

32–34 Χάρις (*charis*) here means "favor" or "credit" (cf. μισθὸς [*misthos,* "reward"] in v.35 and Matt 5:46). God will not overlook what is done for him at personal sacrifice.

35 On υἱοὶ ὑψίστου (*huioi hypsistou,* "sons of the Most High"), cf. 1:32 and comments.

3. Judging others

6:37–42

[37]"Do not judge, and you will not be judged. Do not condemn, and you will not be condemned. Forgive, and you will be forgiven. [38]Give, and it will be given to you. A good measure, pressed down, shaken together and running over, will be poured into your lap. For with the measure you use, it will be measured to you."

[39]He also told them this parable: "Can a blind man lead a blind man? Will they not both fall into a pit? [40]A student is not above his teacher, but everyone who is fully trained will be like his teacher.

[41]"Why do you look at the speck of sawdust in your brother's eye and pay no

attention to the plank in your own eye? [42]How can you say to your brother, 'Brother, let me take the speck out of your eye,' when you yourself fail to see the plank in your own eye? You hypocrite, first take the plank out of your eye, and then you will see clearly to remove the speck from your brother's eye.

37-38 These verses deal with the kind of mercy expected of the Lord's disciples. If the preceding imperative about being merciful refers indirectly to the lack of mercy among the Pharisees, then this one may refer to the kind of judgmental attitude religious people like the Pharisees often have. Since "do not judge" (v.37) could be misunderstood as ruling out any ethical evaluation at all, it is important to note the further definition provided by the parallel "Do not condemn" (*mē katadikazete*). In Matthew (7:6) the injunction not to "give dogs what is sacred," which obviously requires some discernment, provides the balance. Just as God will give a suitable reward to the merciful (vv.32-36), so v.37 implies that he will bring appropriate judgment on the unmerciful. The idea of suitable reward carries over in the next illustration of an overflowing measuring cup (v.38). Those who are generous (both materially [vv.27-36] and in their estimation of others [v.37]) will be abundantly repaid.

39-40 Some have found vv.39-40 difficult to relate to the context. If Jesus still has the Pharisees in mind (cf. Schürmann, *Das Lukasevangelium*, 1:365-79), it is not necessary to assume that he is directly accusing them. Rather his thought in addressing the disciples runs like this: The disciple of a rabbi dedicates himself to his master's teachings and way of life. Thus he cannot be expected to be different from, or better than, his master (v.40). If the rabbi lacks a proper view of life, his student will be also misled (v.39). The criticism and hostility already apparent in the Pharisees may unfortunately crop up in their disciples, but it must never find a place among Jesus' disciples.

This interpretation assumes that v.40 carries on the thought of v.39, in which both teacher and follower are blind—not a description of Jesus and his disciples. If, however, v.40 introduces a new comparison, it might mean that Jesus' disciples ought not to go beyond what they have learned from him—viz., a merciful uncensorious spirit. In that instance v.39 could refer to the Pharisees or others.

41-42 The humorous illustration (v.41) of the "speck" (*karphos*) and the "plank" (*dokon*) hits the mark with force when the person who casually calls the person he is criticizing "brother" (v.42) suddenly hears himself called "hypocrite" by the Lord. Danker (*Jesus*, p. 89) observes, "What is criticized by Jesus is the moralist's patronizing attitude." He cites Democritus (fifth century B.C.): "Better it is to correct one's own faults than those of others." Jesus' humor makes the point vividly.

Notes

38 Εἰς τὸν κόλπον ὑμῶν (*eis ton kolpon hymōn*, "into your lap") refers to the fold of one's robe used as a pocket.

4. *A tree and its fruit*

6:43–45

> ⁴³"No good tree bears bad fruit, nor does a bad tree bear good fruit. ⁴⁴Each tree is recognized by its own fruit. People do not pick figs from thornbushes, or grapes from briers. ⁴⁵The good man brings good things out of the good stored up in his heart, and the evil man brings evil things out of the evil stored up in his heart. For out of the overflow of his heart his mouth speaks.

43–45 The thought of v.40 continues—like teacher, like student; like tree, like fruit. The parallel passage in Matthew 7:15–20 refers to false prophets—a fact that supports a link between this verse (43) and v.39 about a blind leader. Throughout the preceding section and this one, the idea is that of consistency between source and product (cf. the teaching of John the Baptist [3:7–9 and comments]).

Notes

45 Ἐκ τοῦ ἀγαθοῦ θησαυροῦ τῆς καρδιάς (*ek tou agathou thēsaurou tēs kardias*) is literally "out of the good treasure of the heart." The heart is a treasury in which good or evil is "stored up" (NIV). See also Matt 15:19 and Mark 7:21, both of which are in contexts criticizing the Pharisees.

46 "Already . . . during his [Jesus'] ministry, the address of Κύριε [*kyrie*, 'Lord'] was taking on a deeper significance than a mere honorific 'Sir' " (Marshall, *Gospel of Luke*, p. 274).

5. *The wise and foolish builders*

6:46–49

> ⁴⁶"Why do you call me, 'Lord, Lord,' and do not do what I say? ⁴⁷I will show you what he is like who comes to me and hears my words and puts them into practice. ⁴⁸He is like a man building a house, who dug down deep and laid the foundation on rock. When a flood came, the torrent struck that house but could not shake it, because it was well built. ⁴⁹But the one who hears my words and does not put them into practice is like a man who built a house on the ground without a foundation. The moment the torrent struck that house, it collapsed and its destruction was complete."

46–49 If Jesus' audience was relaxing in the assumption that the preceding teachings were directed only at the Pharisees and their followers, they could not dodge the direct force of this challenge. It is specifically directed to those who profess to follow Jesus (v.46). In Matthew the statement is amplified with a description of self deception, probably at first deliberate and then habitual. Here only the basic point is made: It is not mere words, nor even generally ethical behavior or religious practice, that mark true believers but whether they "do" (*poieite*) what Jesus says (cf. James 1:22–25). The thrust of the parable is clear. Luke includes reference to the foundation (v.48), but he omits some of the graphic detail found in Matthew 7:24–27. Luke also omits the response of the people (cf. Matt 7:28–29).

C. Ministry to Various Human Needs (7:1–9:17)

1. The faith of the centurion

7:1–10

> ¹When Jesus had finished saying all this in the hearing of the people, he entered Capernaum. ²There a centurion's servant, whom his master valued highly, was sick and about to die. ³The centurion heard of Jesus and sent some elders of the Jews to him, asking him to come and heal his servant. ⁴When they came to Jesus, they pleaded earnestly with him, "This man deserves to have you do this, ⁵because he loves our nation and has built our synagogue." ⁶So Jesus went with them.
>
> He was not far from the house when the centurion sent friends to say to him: "Lord, don't trouble yourself, for I do not deserve to have you come under my roof. ⁷That is why I did not even consider myself worthy to come to you. But say the word, and my servant will be healed. ⁸For I myself am a man under authority, with soldiers under me. I tell this one, 'Go,' and he goes; and that one, 'Come,' and he comes. I say to my servant, 'Do this,' and he does it."
>
> ⁹When Jesus heard this, he was amazed at him, and turning to the crowd following him, he said, "I tell you, I have not found such great faith even in Israel." ¹⁰Then the men who had been sent returned to the house and found the servant well.

This incident has an important place in Luke's narrative. First, it marks a pivotal point in the progress of the word of the Lord from its original Jewish context to the Gentile world. The Jews' appreciation of a pious Gentile (the centurion) is an important theme in Luke, which was written partly to show the compatibility of early Christianity with Judaism. At the same time, Jesus compares the Gentile's faith more than favorably with that of the Jews, which serves Luke's desire to justify the prominence of Gentiles in the church.

Second, the incident is paralleled by the conversion of Cornelius (Acts 10), which itself marks a historic transition from a purely Jewish church to one including Gentiles. Luke is careful to speak well of each centurion and his religious concern. Third, Luke has been careful to note those who had "faith" (*pistis*), beginning with Mary (1:45) and then the four men who brought the paralyzed man to Jesus (5:20). Further, the authority of Jesus is stressed, and his "word" (v.7) is believed to have power (cf. 4:32, 36).

1–5 The introductory words "When Jesus had finished saying all this" (v.1) provide more than just a transition from the preceding sermon. They suggest another step in the mission Jesus came to fulfill (1:1) because the word "finished" translates *eplērōsen* ("fulfilled"). Matthew's formula following a collection of sayings uses *etelesen* ("finished," e.g., 7:28). "In the hearing of the people" (*eis tas akoas tou laou*) echoes "you who hear me" (6:27) and establishes the reliability of the witnesses from Galilee who would later bear testimony to the truth about Jesus' words and deeds.

On behalf of his seriously ill "servant" (*doulos*, v.2; cf. below on v.7), the centurion "sent some elders [*presbyterous*] of the Jews" (i.e., the leaders of the community) to Jesus (v.3). At this point a comparison with Matthew 8:5–13 shows a significant difference of detail. Luke, with his great interest in the character and importance of the centurion, gives us a fuller narrative than Matthew. Two groups come from the centurion to talk with Jesus on his behalf. Matthew provides a more condensed version, as is his custom, relating the words of the centurion to Jesus as though he had been there in person.

In v.4 we learn why the village elders were willing to intercede for the centurion. They were genuinely indebted to him for his generosity (v.5).

6-8 It seems strange that at this point, having invited Jesus to come, the centurion now sends another group of "friends" (*philous*) to stop him short of entering (v.6). They express the centurion's sense of unworthiness (v.7). Indeed, one wonders why at this point the centurion did not simply come out and speak for himself. Luke, however, apparently wishes to stress the humility of the man and possibly also his concern, on second thought, that Jesus might be criticized for entering a Gentile's house.

The focal point of the section is the centurion's concept of Jesus' authority (v.8). The wording is significant: "For I myself am a man under authority" (*gar egō anthrōpos eimi hypo exousian tassomenos*). He compares Jesus' relationship to God with his own to his superiors. The position of responsibility implies "authority" (*exousia*) to command others. Therefore he has faith that Jesus' authoritative "word" (*logos*) will accomplish the healing.

9-10 Jesus is not criticizing the faith he has found among Jews but rather says that "not even" (*oude*) in Israel has he found such faith (v.9). The Jews would be expected to have faith, considering their possession of God's revelation in their Scriptures (cf. Rom 3:1-2). "But not all the Israelites accepted the good news" (Rom 10:16), missing the element of personal faith (Rom 10:6-13). This failure to respond to their privileges was ending in Jesus' day, and the response of the centurion stood out in welcome contrast.

Notes

2, 6 Ὁ ἑκατοντάρχης (*ho hekatontarchēs*, "the centurion") is presumably a Roman, though stationed not over Roman but Jewish soldiers, hired by the Herodian rulers to maintain their position. A centurion was comparable to an army lieutenant, though a noncommissioned officer, and was responsible for about a hundred men.

2. Raising a widow's son

7:11-17

[11]Soon afterward, Jesus went to a town called Nain, and his disciples and a large crowd went along with him. [12]As he approached the town gate, a dead person was being carried out—the only son of his mother, and she was a widow. And a large crowd from the town was with her. [13]When the Lord saw her, his heart went out to her and he said, "Don't cry."

[14]Then he went up and touched the coffin, and those carrying it stood still. He said, "Young man, I say to you, get up!" [15]The dead man sat up and began to talk, and Jesus gave him back to his mother.

[16]They were all filled with awe and praised God. "A great prophet has appeared among us," they said. "God has come to help his people." [17]This news about Jesus spread throughout Judea and the surrounding country.

Jesus is now about to perform the ultimate kind of miracle that will certify him as the Messiah and will be reported to John the Baptist ("the dead are raised," v.22). Luke also wants his readers to understand that while John the Baptist came in the spirit and power of Elijah, it is Jesus himself who is the great prophet of the end time. This miracle bears significant resemblance, as we shall note, to one performed by Elijah. Luke has already included a reference to the widow Elijah ministered to (4:25–26).

11 The time reference is vague. The trip to Nain would not have taken more than a day; it lay a few miles to the southeast of Jesus' hometown, Nazareth. Nain lay on the other side of the Hill of Moreh from Shunem, where Elisha raised the son of the Shunammite woman. Perhaps the local people recalled this. Luke typically notes the "large crowd" (e.g., 5:15, 29; 6:17, 8:4).

12–13 The cortege has already gone through the town and is on the way to the place of burial, which was customarily outside the town (v.12). The deceased was the "only son" (*monogenēs*) of his mother (cf. Notes). The compassion of the Lord Jesus, and of Luke as well, goes out to the woman. She is a widow (*chēra*) who, without a man in her family, would probably become destitute, unable in that society to earn a living. Our Lord's words are deeply human: "Don't cry" (*mē klaie*, v.13), but only he could say that and at the same time remove the cause of the tears. Otherwise such words would be hollow, though well meant.

14–15 Jesus risked ritual defilement by touching the "coffin" (*sorou*, a litter on which the shrouded body was laid, v.14). One can only imagine the thoughts of the pallbearers as they stopped. Jesus did what would seem useless—he spoke to a dead person. On the young man's return to life, Jesus "gave him back to his mother" (v.15), words similar to those in 1 Kings 17:23 regarding Elijah and the widow.

16–17 Once more Luke records the response of the people, noting that they "praised" (*edoksazon*, lit., "glorified") God (v.16; cf. 5:26; 18:43; 23:47). The similarities we have noted with Elijah and Elisha would naturally cause the people to use the word "prophet" to describe Jesus. They also echo an OT expression: "God has come to help his people" (e.g., Ruth 1:6). For the significance of "come" (*epeskepsato*), see comment on Luke 1:68. Once again Luke emphasizes the spread of the "news" (*logos*) about Jesus (v.17).

Notes

---

12 Whenever μονογενὴς υἱός (*monogenēs huios*, "the only son") is used in Scripture, it is of an only son who is either in mortal danger or already dead (cf. 8:42; 9:38; cf. also Judg 11:34–35, Zech 12:10; John 3:16; Th.C. de Kruif, "The Glory of the Only Son, John 1:14," *Studies in John*, Presented to J.N. Sevenster [Leiden: Brill, 1970], pp. 111–23). Luke shows his compassion and the beauty of God's saving grace by showing that these were precious only children even where Matthew and Mark do not have the term.

---

3. *Jesus and John the Baptist*

7:18–35

18John's disciples told him about all these things. Calling two of them, 19he sent them to the Lord to ask, "Are you the one who was to come, or should we expect someone else?"

20When the men came to Jesus, they said, "John the Baptist sent us to you to ask, 'Are you the one who was to come, or should we expect someone else?' "

21At that very time Jesus cured many who had diseases, sicknesses and evil spirits, and gave sight to many who were blind. 22So he replied to the messengers, "Go back and report to John what you have seen and heard: The blind receive sight, the lame walk, those who have leprosy are cured, the deaf hear, the dead are raised, and the good news is preached to the poor. 23Blessed is the man who does not fall away on account of me."

24After John's messengers left, Jesus began to speak to the crowd about John: "What did you go out into the desert to see? A reed swayed by the wind? 25If not, what did you go out to see? A man dressed in fine clothes? No, those who wear expensive clothes and indulge in luxury are in palaces. 26But what did you go out to see? A prophet? Yes, I tell you, and more than a prophet. 27This is the one about whom it is written:

> " 'I will send my messenger ahead of you,
>   who will prepare your way before you.'

28I tell you, among those born of women there is no one greater than John; yet the one who is least in the kingdom of God is greater than he."

29(All the people, even the tax collectors, when they heard Jesus' words, acknowledged that God's way was right, because they had been baptized by John. 30But the Pharisees and experts in the law rejected God's purpose for themselves, because they had not been baptized by John.)

31"To what, then, can I compare the people of this generation? What are they like? 32They are like children sitting in the marketplace and calling out to each other:

> " 'We played the flute for you,
>   and you did not dance;
> we sang a dirge,
>   and you did not cry.'

33For John the Baptist came neither eating bread nor drinking wine, and you say, 'He has a demon.' 34The Son of Man came eating and drinking, and you say, 'Here is a glutton and a drunkard, a friend of tax collectors and "sinners." ' 35But wisdom is proved right by all her children."

In Luke 3:16–17, John had described the one who would come baptizing with the Holy Spirit and with fire. Then Jesus was baptized, receiving divine approval and anointing for his work. In 4:16–21 Jesus assumed the task prophesied in Isaiah 61:1–2. Now, after a cycle of teachings and healings, the validity of his messianic calling is once more under consideration; and John the Baptist is the other central figure.

18–20 "These things" (v.18), i.e., the healings and presumably also the raising of the widow's son, apparently have not sufficed to convince John of Jesus' messiahship. This reluctance seems strange, considering John's role in announcing the Coming One and in baptizing Jesus. There are several reasons why John needed further confirmation (v.19). He was in prison (Matt 11:2). This could lead to depression and, in turn, doubt. Further, he might wonder why, if the Messiah was to release prisoners (Isa 61:1), and if Jesus was the object of that prediction (Luke 4:18), he had not freed John. Also, though he had received reports of Jesus' ministry, John himself had apparently not witnessed spectacular messianic miracles such as he might have expected; nor had he heard Jesus claim outright that he was the Messiah. The fact that John still had "disciples" (vv.18, 20) does not necessarily mean he had been continuing a separate movement because of uncertainty about the Messiah. A number continued with John even after he had pointed them to Jesus.

21–23 Jesus responds by listing the messianic works (some of them just described in Luke) that he has accomplished (v.21). It was understood in those days that the true Messiah would not proclaim himself such but would first do appropriate messianic works that would lead to public acknowledgment of his identity (R. Longenecker, *The Christology of Early Jewish Christianity*, Studies in Biblical Theology, Second Series 17 [London: SCM, 1970], pp. 71–74). The works of Jesus echo not only Isaiah 61, quoted at Nazareth, but other passages from Isaiah (e.g., 42:7). Isaiah 35:5–6 declares that in the Messianic Age those who could not see, hear, walk, or speak would be healed. Jesus pronounces a blessing (v.23) on the person who accepts his credentials rather than being trapped (*skandalisthē*, NIV, "fall away") because of a false evaluation of Jesus.

24–28 The topic now changes from the role of Jesus to that of John (v.24). Jesus asks a couple of gently ironic questions that, through obviously negative answers, stress the inflexibility and austerity of John. Jesus uses the term "prophet" (v.26) and adds the role of "messenger" (v.27) from Malachi 3:1. If John is the messenger, obviously this forcefully implies the significance of Jesus' own role.

Jesus now puts John into historical perspective. John came in advance of the kingdom, which has now become a reality (16:16). Great as John was (v.28), it is greater to participate in the kingdom than to announce it. We are not to conclude from this, however, that John himself is excluded. Luke 13:28 says that all the prophets will be in the kingdom.

29–35 Attention now turns to the response of the people and of their leaders to John and Jesus also. Observe the contrast between the "people" (*laos*, v.29; see comment on 1:17) and the hostile religious leaders. In v.24 the neutral word "crowd" is used. The "tax collectors" (*telōnai*) are mentioned along with the "people" as those who stood ready to believe Jesus and thereby to "acknowledge that God's way was right." Notice that the issue is not only the role of Jesus and John but the entire counsel of God, whose "purpose [*boulēn*] for themselves" (v.30) was rejected by the "Pharisees and experts in the law [*nomikou*]." John's baptism was a symbol they chose to reject. The obdurate opposition to each of God's messengers is described as childish fickleness (v.32; cf. their earlier attempt to play John against Jesus, 5:33). The children's words are those of annoyed leaders who want their friends to play "grownup" and, when the leaders play cheerful or sad music, pretend that they are at a celebration, like a wedding, or at a funeral. They become petulant when their friends refuse to play. Jesus and John, when in confrontation with the Jewish leaders, refused to "play their game" and so are the object of their taunts. The people not only criticize but exaggerate the habits both of John (v.33), calling his asceticism demonic (demons were said to inhabit the desert where John was), and Jesus (v.34), calling his normal habits of food and drink gluttony and drunkenness. The concluding saying (v.35) probably means that those who respond to wisdom prove its rightness (cf. Notes).

Notes

19 Κύριον (*kyrion*, "Lord") does not have convincing MS support, but UBS chose it because "it is not likely that copyists would have deleted the name Ἰησοῦν [*Iēsoun*, 'Jesus'], and since κύριος is in accord with Lukan style" (Metzger, *Textual Commentary*, p. 143).

Ὁ ἐρχόμενος (*ho erchomenos*, "he who is coming"; NIV, "the one who was to come") alludes to the coming Messiah or prophet (John 6:14; 11:27; cf. Dan 7:13; Hab 2:3 and Heb 10:37; Mal 3:1).

27 Danker (*Jesus*, p. 97) sees a reminder here to the angel who went before the people of Israel in the desert (Exod 23:20).

30 Οἱ νομικοί (*hoi nomikoi*, "experts in the law") is a term used almost exclusively by Luke. It was more readily understood by his Gentile readers than γραμματεύς (*grammateus*, "scribe"; cf. Note on 5:17).

4. *Anointed by a sinful woman*

7:36–50

36Now one of the Pharisees invited Jesus to have dinner with him, so he went to the Pharisee's house and reclined at the table. 37When a woman who had lived a sinful life in that town learned that Jesus was eating at the Pharisee's house, she brought an alabaster jar of perfume, 38and as she stood behind him at his feet weeping, she began to wet his feet with her tears. Then she wiped them with her hair, kissed them and poured perfume on them.

39When the Pharisee who had invited him saw this, he said to himself, "If this man were a prophet, he would know who is touching him and what kind of woman she is—that she is a sinner."

40Jesus answered him, "Simon, I have something to tell you."

"Tell me, teacher," he said.

41"Two men owed money to a certain moneylender. One owed him five hundred denarii, and the other fifty. 42Neither of them had the money to pay him back, so he canceled the debts of both. Now which of them will love him more?"

43Simon replied, "I suppose the one who had the bigger debt canceled."

"You have judged correctly," Jesus said.

44Then he turned toward the woman and said to Simon, "Do you see this woman? I came into your house. You did not give me any water for my feet, but she wet my feet with her tears and wiped them with her hair. 45You did not give me a kiss, but this woman, from the time I entered, has not stopped kissing my feet. 46You did not put oil on my head, but she has poured perfume on my feet. 47Therefore, I tell you, her many sins have been forgiven—for she loved much. But he who has been forgiven little loves little."

48Then Jesus said to her, "Your sins are forgiven."

49The other guests began to say among themselves, "Who is this who even forgives sins?"

50Jesus said to the woman, "Your faith has saved you; go in peace."

The criticism Jesus has received (v.34) does not preclude Luke from setting down another example of Jesus' concern for sinners. The story contrasts a sinner and a

Pharisee. It is similar to another incident (cf. Matt 26:6–13; Mark 14:3–9; John 12:1–8). A woman brings perfume to Jesus while he is at a banquet hosted by a Pharisee named Simon (anonymous in John). There are several differences: the other incident occurs immediately before Jesus' crucifixion, the host is a leper (Matt and Mark), the woman pours the perfume on Jesus' head (Matt and Mark), and the controversy centers in the cost of the perfume, not the character of the woman.

The differences are sufficient to require two traditions. Some of the similarities may be coincidental (e.g., Simon was a common name); others may be due to cross influence.

36–38 Since he accepted an invitation from a Pharisee (v.36), Jesus cannot be accused of spurning the Pharisees socially. The woman (v.37) took advantage of the social customs that permitted needy people to visit such a banquet to receive some of the leftovers. She came specifically to see Jesus, bringing a jar or little bottle of perfume. Since Jesus was reclining (*kateklithē*) at the table according to custom (v.36), she prepared to pour the perfume on his feet (v.38), a humble act (cf. 3:16). A flow of tears preceded the outpouring of the perfume; so she wiped his feet lovingly with her hair and, perhaps impulsively, kissed them before using the perfume.

39–43 In this masterly narrative, Luke now directs attention to the Pharisee (v.39). He mulls over the matter and reaches three conclusions: (1) if Jesus were a prophet, he would know what kind of woman was anointing his feet; (2) if he knew what kind of a woman she was, he would not let her do it; and (3) since he does let her anoint his feet, he is no prophet and should not be acknowledged as such. But Jesus does let her expend the perfume on him and does not shun her. He shows that he does have unique insight into the human heart, for he knows what the Pharisee is thinking. When Jesus tells Simon his host that he has something to say to him (v.40), Simon, perhaps expecting some stock word of wisdom from his teacher-guest, replies perfunctorily, "Tell me, teacher."

The point of the incident (vv.41–42) is clear, and Simon is made to give the conclusion that will condemn him. His "I suppose" (v.43) probably implies an uneasy reluctance.

44–50 Again the woman is the focal point of the narrative. Surprisingly, Jesus first contrasts her acts of devotion with a lack of special attention on Simon's part as host (vv.44–46; cf. Notes). The main point is reached swiftly. Jesus can declare that her sins (which he does not hesitate to say were "many") have been forgiven (v.47). He can affirm this (v.48) because her act of love shows her realization of forgiveness. Her love is not the basis of forgiveness; her faith is (v.50). As in the event itself, the forgiveness was unearned; and it is this fact that elicits her love (cf. note on v.47).

As the episode ends, attention rapidly shifts from one person to the other. Simon obviously knows little of either forgiveness or love (v.47). Jesus pronounces the woman forgiven. Then he becomes the object of another discussion because he presumes to absolve her from her sins (v.49; cf. 5:21). The woman receives his pronouncement of salvation—"saved" (*sesōken*) is in the perfect tense, expressing an accomplished fact—and his benediction "go in peace" (v.50), traditional and common words that have true meaning only for those who have been saved by faith

(8:48; 17:19; 18:42; cf. Judg 18:6; 1 Sam 1:17; 2 Sam 15:9; 1 Kings 22:17; Acts 16:36; James 2:16).

Notes

37 Ἁμαρτωλός (*hamartōlos*, "sinner"; NIV, "who lived a sinful life") is the word Luke often uses to identify a person who has a reputation for gross immorality. The woman's unbound hair (v.38) might indicate that she was a prostitute.

41 A δηνάριον (*dēnarion*, "denarius") was the approximate daily wage of a laborer.

44-46 Schürmann (*Das Lukasevangelium*, 1:435-36), followed by Marshall (*Gospel of Luke*, pp. 312-13), holds that Simon was not actually at fault as a host, because the amenities mentioned, while customs of the day, were not necessary acts of hospitality. Bailey (*Peasant Eyes*, p. 5), on the other hand, says, "The formal greetings were clearly of crucial significance in first-century times." The contrast remains strong in either case because of the extraordinary nature of what the woman did.

47 NIV (so UBS) has a comma before and after "I tell you," making the phrase οὖ χάριν λέγω σοι (*hou charin legō soi*, "Therefore, I tell you") parenthetical, which links "therefore" with "her many sins have been forgiven." While this is grammatically possible, KJV, RSV, NASB, and JB are probably correct in linking the deeds of the woman (described in vv.44-46) with Jesus' response rather than with her forgiveness (e.g., JB: "For this reason I tell you"). The use of ὅτι (*hoti*, "for") here is not to show causality but evidence (see discussions in C.F.D. Moule, *An Idiom-Book of New Testament Greek*, 2d ed. [Cambridge: University Press, 1959], p. 147; M. Zerwick, *Biblical Greek* [Rome: Pontifical Biblical Institute, 1963], par. 422). TEV has "the great love she has shown proves that her many sins have been forgiven."

5. Parable of the sower

8:1-15

[1]After this, Jesus traveled about from one town and village to another, proclaiming the good news of the kingdom of God. The Twelve were with him, [2]and also some women who had been cured of evil spirits and diseases: Mary (called Magdalene) from whom seven demons had come out; [3]Joanna the wife of Cuza, the manager of Herod's household; Susanna; and many others. These women were helping to support them out of their own means.

[4]While a large crowd was gathering and people were coming to Jesus from town after town, he told this parable: [5]"A farmer went out to sow his seed. As he was scattering the seed, some fell along the path; it was trampled on, and the birds of the air ate it up. [6]Some fell on rock, and when it came up, the plants withered because they had no moisture. [7]Other seed fell among thorns, which grew up with it and choked the plants. [8]Still other seed fell on good soil. It came up and yielded a crop, a hundred times more than was sown."

When he said this, he called out, "He who has ears to hear, let him hear."

[9]His disciples asked him what this parable meant. [10]He said, "The knowledge of the secrets of the kingdom of God has been given to you, but to others I speak in parables, so that,

" 'though seeing, they may not see;
though hearing, they may not understand.'

[11]"This is the meaning of the parable: The seed is the word of God. [12]Those along the path are the ones who hear, and then the devil comes and takes away

the word from their hearts, so that they may not believe and be saved. ¹³Those on
the rock are the ones who receive the word with joy when they hear it, but they
have no root. They believe for a while, but in the time of testing they fall away.
¹⁴The seed that fell among thorns stands for those who hear, but as they go on
their way they are choked by life's worries, riches and pleasures, and they do not
mature. ¹⁵But the seed on good soil stands for those with a noble and good heart,
who hear the word, retain it, and by persevering produce a crop.

1–3 The opening verses provide a summary of yet another preaching tour (cf. the
previous circuit described in 4:44). Luke states Jesus' mission both in that passage
and here as announcing the "good news of the kingdom of God." During this time,
Jesus has chosen the "Twelve." Luke is careful to mention them here, as they will
serve as witnesses and authorities in the days following Jesus' ascension.

What is new is the mention of several women who not only accompany Jesus but
share in his support (vv.2–3). It was not uncommon for ancient itinerant cult leaders, fortune tellers, and their kind to solicit the financial support of wealthy women
(Lucian, *Alexander the False Prophet* 6; cf. 2 Tim 3:6–7). In this case, however, it is
in a Jewish, not a pagan, culture; and the relationship is morally pure. Some of these
women, at least, had a great debt of love to Jesus, as did the woman in the preceding incident (7:36–50). Luke does not say that Mary Magdalene, as often thought,
had been a prostitute; she is not identified with the woman of 7:36–50. He does
refer to her as an object of the grace and power of God in being released from seven
demons. "Joanna the wife of Chuza" is otherwise unknown, but her presence at the
Crucifixion (in contrast to the flight of most of the disciples) shows her faithfulness.
She is the first person connected with the Herodian household to be mentioned in
this Gospel. Later on, the gospel often reached into distinguished and royal homes
through the witness of Christian servants. It is noteworthy that these women were
industrious, in their time truly "liberated," and helped in the support not only of
Jesus but of the Twelve, to whom the word "them" (*autois*) in v.3 refers.

As in Matthew 13:1–23 and Mark 4:1–20, the sequence in vv.4–15, is (1) the
parable of the sower, (2) Jesus' reason for using parables, and (3) the interpretation
of the parable of the sower. Each part deals with the mixed response Jesus was
receiving from his audiences, a response also basic in the next two pericopes (vv.16–
18; 19–21). Jesus' realism regarding the failure of people to believe his message also
appears elsewhere in Luke, notably in the saying about the persistent widow and
others who cry for vindication. They will receive justice quickly, but "when the Son
of Man comes, will he find faith on the earth?" (18:8). Jesus explains the present
parable and his reasons for using the parabolic form—both to warn those who neglect the word they hear and to encourage his disciples when that word is not fully
accepted.

4 Luke begins with an observation on the size of the crowds (so also Matt 13:2;
Mark 4:1). But whereas Matthew and Mark specify a location by the lake, Luke
omits this. Instead, he adds to the comment on the crowd by speaking of those who
were coming to Jesus from "town after town." The effect is to help the reader
visualize a large mixed group of people who represent the various types of "soil" in
the parable.

5–8 This particular parable reflects a situation well known to the audience, and the
details of the parable would have immediately been grasped by the hearers. The

111

very fact that circumstances so familiar need still further comment before the spiritual meaning is clear underlines the paradox presented in v.10—namely, that those who see and hear do not understand.

The focal point of the parable has been variously interpreted. In none of the Gospels is the sower (v.5; NIV, "farmer") the center of attention (not even in Mark, though some have taken Mark 4:14 as directing attention to the sower). Nor is particular stress laid on the seed—certainly not as in the parable of the secretly growing seed (Mark 4:26–29). This is not to say that the seed is unimportant. On the contrary, it represents the word of God (v.11); and the whole act of sowing the seed is proclaiming the gospel of the kingdom (cf. Mark 4:14).

What does catch attention is the variety of soils. Contrary to what a modern Western perspective might lead us to expect, the sower is not immediately concerned about the kind of soil. Since plowing followed sowing in Jesus' culture, the trampled ground where people crossed the field might later be plowed under with seed; so it is not excluded from the sowing. The same could be true of young thorn bushes (v.7). Furthermore, the rocky subsoil (v.6) might not be visible at the time of sowing. The low yield from the poor soil is overshadowed by the very large yield from the good soil (v.8)—an encouragement for Jesus' disciples to realize that the ultimate greatness of the kingdom will make all their efforts worthwhile.

9–10 Here in Luke the disciples' question (v.9) refers only to this parable, not to Jesus' larger ministry as in Matthew 13:10 and Mark 4:10. The reference to the "secrets" (*mystēria*, v.10) occurs in this context in all three Synoptics. Mark 4:11 uses the singular form *mystērion*; and Matthew (13:11), like Luke, includes the word "knowledge" (*gnōnai*, lit., "to know"). Only in this situation does *mystērion* occur in the teachings of Jesus. A word of immense significance in biblical literature, *mystērion* is found also in extrabiblical Jewish literature. Biblical scholars, now freed from the earlier idea that NT references to a "mystery" derived from the Hellenistic mystery religions, have been finding a rich meaning in the word. While it occurs in the LXX only in Daniel 2, where God is praised as the one who reveals secrets (Dan 2:20–23, 28–30), it appears in varied frames of reference in the NT. The basic concept of *mystērion* is that of the purpose and plan of God, which he works out phase by phase in human history and through the church. The issues of the problem of evil, suffering, and the delay of vindication will be resolved when God finally reveals his "secret," which is "accomplished" (*etelesthē*) after the "delay" (*chronos*) has ended in Revelation 10:6–7. The "mystery" or "secret" is only revealed by God's sovereign grace to his people. As Luke says here, "The knowledge of the secrets of the kingdom of God has been given to you."

"To others" (*tois loipois*, lit., "to the rest") is not as specific as Mark's "those on the outside" (*tois exō*, 4:11). The quotation from Isaiah 6:9 in v.10—"though seeing . . . not understand"—shows that Jesus' teaching is in accord with the consistent principle in Scripture that those who fail to respond to a saving word from God will find that they are not only under judgment for rejecting what they have heard but that they are unable to understand further truth (cf. John 3:17–19 with John 9:39–41, which contains words similar to Isa 6:9; Exod 8:32, regarding Pharaoh, with Exod 9:12 and Rom 9:17–18; and see Acts 28:26–27, another quotation from the Isaiah passage; Matt 7:6; Luke 20:1–8; Rev 22:11). For such, the very parable that reveals truth to some hides it from them. Given this sober reality, it is all the more important that the interpretation of the present passage be in full accord both with

112

the Greek syntax of this sentence and with the whole biblical revelation of God's character and the way he deals with unbelief (see also B. Lindars, *New Testament Apologetic* [Philadelphia: Westminster, 1961], pp. 159–67).

While "so that" (*hina*, v.10) may be understood as indicating result, it more normally indicates purpose. The thought may be that the principle of Isaiah 6:9 may be fulfilled. Luke does not include the additional difficult words from Isaiah that are found in Mark 4:12—"otherwise they might turn and be forgiven" (see commentary on this verse in this vol.)—but instead hastens on to the interpretation of the parable in question.

11–12 Having shown the danger of unbelief in v.10, Jesus now returns to the parable, explaining why the proclaimed "word of God" (v.11) fails to bring a uniform response of faith. Luke's inclusion of the clause "so that they may not believe and be saved" (v.12; lacking in Matthew and Mark) reflects his intense concern regarding salvation. The clause is introduced by *hina* ("so that"); and here, unlike its use in v.10, there is no doubt that it expresses deliberate purpose. Note the contrast between the devil's purpose and God's purpose (2 Peter 3:9).

13–14 In the next two instances (seed fallen on the rock, v.13; seed fallen among thorns, v.14), there is an initial response. The superficial reception given the word may be compared to those who "believed" Jesus (John 8:31), only to be called children of the devil (John 8:44). Obviously they did not go on to true liberating faith (vv.31–32). Luke alone among the synoptic writers says these people actually "believe for a time" (*pros kairon pisteuousin*, v.13; cf. Matt 13:21 and Mark 4:17—"last only a short time"). It is "in the time of testing" (*en kairō peirasmou*; cf. *thlipseōs ē diōgmou* ["trouble or persecution"], Matt 13:21; Mark 4:17) that they "fall away" (*aphistantai*; cf. the use of *skandalizo* ["stumble"], Matt 13:21; Mark 4:17). In all three Synoptics the response is superficial and cannot endure adversity. Schuyler Brown (*Apostasy and Perseverance*, p. 14) would see this as characteristic of Luke's concern for apostasy under external testing.

The third example (v.14) has to do, not with adversity, but with distractions, like those Jesus warned against in Matthew 6:19–34; Luke 11:34–36; 12:22–32; 16:13. The comment that the hearers in this example "do not mature" (*ou telesphorousin*, often used of fruit; cf. *akarpos* ["unfruitful"], Matt 13:22; Mark 4:19) is comparable to the statements in James 2:14–26 on a "dead" (*nekra*, v.17) and "useless" (*argē*, v.20) faith and in 2 Peter 1:8 on those who are "ineffective" (*argous*) and "unfruitful" (*akarpous*; NIV, "unproductive"). That this matter of being fruitful is not simply a matter of the quality of one's Christian life but of whether one has life at all is suggested by Jesus' parallel teaching on wealth in Matthew 6:19–34. There the "single ['good'] eye" (see on Luke 11:34) is opposed to the total darkness that envelops a divided heart (Matt 6:22–24; cf. Hos 10:1–2: "Israel was a spreading vine . . . their heart is deceitful"). The unresponsive people described here (v.14) apparently lack the following essentials to true saving faith: understanding (Matt 13:23; cf. v.19), accepting the word (Mark 4:20), and retaining it (Luke 8:15).

15 Luke's stress on the character of the individual is in contrast to Matthew's reference (13:23) to "understanding" (*synieis*) the word. This is in accord with Matthew's interest in comprehending the secrets of the kingdom (cf. Matt 13:11, 14–15, 19, 25). The description "noble and good" (*kalē kai agathē*) is a Christian adaptation of an ancient Greek phrase. The word "heart" (*kardia*) means the spiritual, intellectual, volitional center of a person's being, i.e., the whole person. This person is marked by singleness of purpose, unlike those of divided heart mentioned in Hosea 10:1–2 (cf. Ps 101[100 LXX]:2—*en akakia kardias mou* ["with blameless heart"] and 1 Chron 29:17–19). Jesus' emphasis here is not so much on whether a person perseveres but on the kind of person who does persevere. RSV's "bring forth fruit with patience" (*en hypomonē*) is more literal and perhaps more accurate than NIV's "by persevering produce a crop."

Notes

4 Teaching in παραβολαί (*parabolai*, "parables," i.e., placing things alongside of others for comparison) was common among the rabbis of Jesus' day.

The ancient Greeks used the literary form of parable. In the Hebrew tradition, there were a variety of figures of speech all subsumed under the word מָשָׁל (*māšāl*), usually translated *parabolē* in the LXX. Contemporary NT scholars generally recognize that while the parable is distinct from allegory, in that the various features in the parable do not each convey a particular meaning, neither does the parable convey a simplistic ethical truth. Rather the parable is an art form offering various possibilities of expression to the speaker or writer. In the NT it usually conveys a message about the kingdom of God, which, in its very telling by Jesus, involved the hearer in a crisis of personal response. Among the useful works on parables are K.E. Bailey, *Poet and Peasant;* id., *Peasant Eyes;* A.M. Hunter, *The Parables Then and Now* (Philadelphia: Westminster, 1971); J. Jeremias, *Parables of Jesus;* R.H. Stein, *An Introduction to the Parables of Jesus* (Philadelphia: Westminster, 1981). Recent critical and literary studies include John Dominic Crossan, *In Parables* (New York: Harper and Row, 1975); Geraint Vaughn Jones, *The Art and Truth of the Parables* (London: SPCK, 1964); Eta Linneman, *Parables of Jesus* (London: SPCK, 1966); R.W. Funk, ed., "A Structuralist Approach to the Parables," *Semeia* 1; Mary Ann Tolbert, *Perspectives on the Parables* (Philadelphia: Fortress, 1979); Dan O. Via, *The Parables: Their Literary and Existential Dimension* (Philadelphia: Fortress, 1967). On the parables and Luke 8:4–15, see P.B. Payne, "Metaphor as a Model for Interpretation of the Parables of Jesus with Special Reference to the Parable of the Sower" (Ph.D. dissertation, Cambridge University, 1975).

5 Τὸν σπόρον αὐτοῦ (*ton sporon autou*, "his seed") is found only in Luke and is probably merely a stylistic addition, not a theological emphasis on "seed."

6–8 Φυὲν (*phuen*, "when it came up") occurs only in Luke; so also συμφυεῖσαι (*symphueisai*, "grew up with") in v.7. *Phuen* again occurs in v.8.

6 Διὰ τὸ μὴ ἔχειν ἰκμάδα (*dia to mē echein ikmada*, "because they had no moisture") replaces διὰ τὸ μὴ ἔχειν ῥίζαν (*dia to mē echein rhizan*, "because they had no root") in Mark 4:6. The statement is less vivid than in Mark and Matthew because Luke does not refer to the scorching heat of the sun.

8 Ἐφώνει (*ephōnei*, "called out") is unique to Luke here and perhaps emphasizes the opportunity of the crowds, to whom Jesus has given special attention (v.4), to receive the teaching. The call to "hear" (ἀκουέτω, *akouetō*) prepares for the saying in v.10 (cf. a similar exhortation in 14:35; Matt 11:15; Rev 2:7 [and in each letter to the seven churches]; 13:9).

10 Ἵνα (*hina*, "so that") can be causal, but grammarians are reluctant to acknowledge it as such in this passage or Mark 4:12 (cf. Zerwick, *Biblical Greek,* p. 413; BDF, par. 369 [2]). Moule (*Idiom Book,* pp. 142–43) notes this reluctance but hesitates to see this as a final (purpose) clause because of the apparent incongruity of a purpose sense here with the rest

of NT thought. Zerwick notes that after the parallel verse in Mark 4:12, Mark (4:33) says that Jesus spoke in parables "according as they were able to hear."

11–15 The interpretation of the parable often has been attributed to the early church rather than to Jesus. Jeremias acceded to this view on the basis of the vocabulary and theology, which he thought were more characteristic of the primitive church than of Jesus (*Parables of Jesus*, pp. 77–79; 149–50). Gerhardsson concluded that it is not possible to identify here a later hortatory application by the early church distinct from the original eschatological teaching given by Jesus (B. Gerhardsson, "The Parable of the Sower and its Interpretation," NTS 14 [1968]: 165–93). The supposition that Jesus could not have employed a multiple form of interpretation such as we have in this passage can no longer be sustained in view of the allegorical methods used by rabbis in the first century. Luke's own modifications of the tradition expand but do not alter the theological teaching in Mark (cf. I.H. Marshall, "Tradition and Theology in Luke. Luke 8:5–15," *Tyndale Bulletin* 20 [1969]: 56–75). We can conclude that the interpretation in vv.11–15 belongs to Jesus' authentic teaching.

13 Ἀφίστανται (*aphistantai*, "fall away") is related to ἀποστασία (*apostasia*), from which our word "apostasy" is derived (cf. 1 Tim 4:1 and Heb 3:12, where the verbal form clearly means to depart from a biblical faith in God).

---

6. *Parable of the lamp*

8:16–18

> [16]"No one lights a lamp and hides it in a jar or puts it under a bed. Instead, he puts it on a stand, so that those who come in can see the light. [17]For there is nothing hidden that will not be disclosed, and nothing concealed that will not be known or brought out into the open. [18]Therefore consider carefully how you listen. Whoever has will be given more; whoever does not have, even what he thinks he has will be taken from him."

This section contains three distinct sayings. The order of the sayings is the same in Mark and Luke, but Matthew places the first two in entirely different contexts. The considerable dissimilarities in wording between the Gospels suggest that the sayings were repeated on many occasions and written down separately.

16–17 Here the theme is the same as that of vv.11–15—viz., that what is genuine can and will be tested for its authenticity. If what is "hidden" (v.17) is evil, this saying affirms that God's judgment on those referred to in v.10 and in vv.12–15 will be just. If what is "hidden" is good, the saying may refer to the truth of Jesus' private teachings to his disciples, which they are exhorted to proclaim publicly. More likely it indicates that God's truth, now partially hidden from those who reject it, will one day be publicly vindicated. The absurdity of lighting a lamp (v.16) only to hide it reinforces the point.

18 In Matthew 13:11 this saying relates to personal response to the proclamation of the kingdom of heaven. There the meaning is that those who accept the message of the kingdom will also be given the knowledge of the "secret," but those who reject it will lose even the opportunity of hearing more teaching. Here Luke has the verse in a different setting, though its meaning may well be the same as in Matthew. Notice the additional word "think" in Luke: "even what he thinks he has."

7. *Jesus' true family*

8:19–21

> ¹⁹Now Jesus' mother and brothers came to see him, but they were not able to get near him because of the crowd. ²⁰Someone told him, "Your mother and brothers are standing outside, wanting to see you."
> ²¹He replied, "My mother and brothers are those who hear God's word and put it into practice."

19–21 Matthew and Mark continue with parabolic teaching at this point, but Luke turns to an incident Matthew and Mark locate at the conclusion of the Beelzebub controversy. When he comes to this controversy (11:14–28), Luke inserts something different, though on the same theme of obedience to God's word. Here the theme of obedience appropriately continues vv.5–15.

Jesus is not, of course, dishonoring his family (vv.19–20) but honoring those who obey God (v.21). The incident Luke now gives us teaches a profound lesson about how believers may be near to the Lord Jesus. Most Christians would probably say that we come closest to him through prayer and reading the Bible. But with searching practicality Jesus says that the way to be close to him—even as close as his own family—is through being receptive to ("hearing") God's word and then doing it. Hours of praying and reading the Bible will not bring disobedient Christians as close to the Lord as doing his truth brings even the simplest believer. Elsewhere Luke shows the place family must take in the life of one who desires to be Jesus' disciple (14:25–26).

Notes

---

20 Οἱ αδελφοί (*hoi adelphoi*) is most naturally translated "brothers." To render it "cousins" or "step-brothers" on the theory that Mary remained a virgin is to strain the meaning.
21 Τὸν λόγον τοῦ θεοῦ (*ton logon tou theou*, "God's word") may be an alternate term Luke uses to express the idea behind "the will of God" in the parallels (Matt 12:50; Mark 3:35) in order to stress again God's "word" (cf. v.11), which is the expression of his will.

---

8. *Calming the storm*

8:22–25

> ²²One day Jesus said to his disciples, "Let's go over to the other side of the lake." So they got into a boat and set out. ²³As they sailed, he fell asleep. A squall came down on the lake, so that the boat was being swamped, and they were in great danger.
> ²⁴The disciples went and woke him, saying, "Master, Master, we're going to drown!"
> He got up and rebuked the wind and the raging waters; the storm subsided, and all was calm. ²⁵"Where is your faith?" he asked his disciples.
> In fear and amazement they asked one another, "Who is this? He commands even the winds and the water, and they obey him."

Luke resumes the sequence of narratives illustrating the powerful, authoritative word of Jesus (notice esp. 8:25, 29, 32, 54; cf. 4:36). Jesus exercises his power against natural forces, demons, illness, and death. Then he delegates this power to his disciples (9:1–2). Schürmann (*Das Lukasevangelium*, 1:472–73) groups the incidents in 8:22–56 as a trilogy of "*Grosswunder*" ("great miracles") that are "*fast johanneische σημεῖα* ("almost Johannine signs").

The story itself is noteworthy for its vividness and for its portrayal of the Lord Jesus in complete control of himself and his environment. The climax comes not with the miracle itself but with the question of the disciples (v.25) concerning the identity of the Master. It is a nature miracle, marking the first time in Luke that Jesus applied his power to a nonliving object rather than to a person. Jesus is affirming sovereignty over storm and sea as God did in the Exodus.

22–23 Luke omits some of the detail found in Mark, including a specific reference to the time of day. His words "Let us go over to the other side of the lake" (v.22) should have assured the disciples that they would indeed complete their trip across the water (as the Jews did in the Exodus). Luke uses vivid language, as Mark does, to describe the fury of the storm. Luke mentions the wind three times (vv.23, 24, 25). This was an intense squall (*lailaps anemou*, lit., "windstorm of wind"), such as characteristically swept down on the Sea of Galilee, which lies in a shallow basin rimmed by hills. Luke mentions earlier in the narrative than do Matthew and Mark that Jesus was asleep. This placement heightens the contrast between the turmoil of the storm and Jesus' peaceful rest.

24–25 The fear and unbelief of the disciples is in contrast not only to the calm of their Master but also to the endurance they themselves should have had in "the time of testing" (cf. v.13). Even so, in Luke's account Jesus does not say, "Do you still have no faith?" as in Mark 4:40, but only, "Where is your faith?" (v.25). The double "Master, Master" (v.24) expresses both respect and terror (contrast the less respectful question in Mark 4:38). The fear of being lost at sea is a common human fear and typical of helplessness in the immensity of life (cf. Ps 107:23–31). Also the Christian church has thought of herself as a boat navigating treacherous waters. Jesus' miracle would have had special meaning during the unsettling and threatening conditions the church encountered through persecutions during its early period.

The question of the disciples, "Who is this?" serves to show not only their amazement but also the slowness of their apprehension of the "Master's" true identity. This question not only marks the climax of this story but is a key question in Luke. In fact, because Luke omits a large amount of material found in Mark (6:45–8:26, which otherwise would come between v.17 and v.18 of Luke 9), he can move quickly from the next occurrence of this question (9:9) to the question at Caesarea Philippi: "Who do you say I am?" (9:20).

Notes

24 Ἐπετίμησεν (*epetimēsen*, "rebuked") suggests to some interpreters that there is a demonic presence behind the storm (cf. comments on 4:39). On the other hand, the word

may simply reflect the tendency of Semitic and other peoples to personify natural forces. In the LXX the word ἐπιτιμάω (epitimaō, "to blame, reprove") often expresses the "creative or destructive" work of God (TDNT, 2:624). It would be natural for the disciples to say that these forces "obey" (ὑπακούω hypakouō, lit., "hearken to") him (v.25).

---

9. Healing a demon-possessed man

8:26–39

26They sailed to the region of the Gerasenes, which is across the lake from Galilee. 27When Jesus stepped ashore, he was met by a demon-possessed man from the town. For a long time this man had not worn clothes or lived in a house, but had lived in the tombs. 28When he saw Jesus, he cried out and fell at his feet, shouting at the top of his voice, "What do you want with me, Jesus, Son of the Most High God? I beg you, don't torture me!" 29For Jesus had commanded the evil spirit to come out of the man. Many times it had seized him, and though he was chained hand and foot and kept under guard, he had broken his chains and had been driven by the demon into solitary places.

30Jesus asked him, "What is your name?"

"Legion," he replied, because many demons had gone into him. 31And they begged him repeatedly not to order them to go into the Abyss.

32A large herd of pigs was feeding there on the hillside. The demons begged Jesus to let them go into them, and he gave them permission. 33When the demons came out of the man, they went into the pigs, and the herd rushed down the steep bank into the lake and was drowned.

34When those tending the pigs saw what had happened, they ran off and reported this in the town and countryside, 35and the people went out to see what had happened. When they came to Jesus, they found the man from whom the demons had gone out, sitting at Jesus' feet, dressed and in his right mind; and they were afraid. 36Those who had seen it told the people how the demon-possessed man had been cured. 37Then all the people of the region of the Gerasenes asked Jesus to leave them, because they were overcome with fear. So he got into the boat and left.

38The man from whom the demons had gone out begged to go with him, but Jesus sent him away, saying, 39"Return home and tell how much God has done for you." So the man went away and told all over town how much Jesus had done for him.

This narrative provides the strongest expression yet of the power of Jesus against the forces of evil. (A previous instance of Jesus' casting out demons [4:33–35] offered little descriptive comment.) Luke gives us far more detail than Matthew, though not quite as much as Mark, and provides a lively, forceful picture of the destructive effects of demon possession. If a raging sea is a threat, demonic force is much worse. Not only the power of the kingdom (11:20), but also the power of the Messiah to release the captives of the kingdom of darkness move against this demonic force. The very narrative that describes this power of Jesus grips the reader. First, there are several progressive levels of action (in both Luke and Mark) involving the demoniac, the demons, the swine, the townspeople, and finally the demoniac after his healing. Second, Luke by his literary skill has inserted part of the description of the demoniac's past life in between the lines of dialogue to heighten the readers' awareness of the man's helplessness under demonic control.

26–29 "They sailed" (v.26) connects this episode with the previous one, suggesting the accomplishment of the goal stated in v.22. If the purpose of the trip across the lake was to liberate the demoniac (no other activity is recorded in the region of the Gerasenes), we are probably to understand the storm at sea as the deliberate attempt of evil forces to prevent Jesus' arrival, though biblical teaching is not clear on this point. Also, the connection between the calming of the sea and the healing of the demoniac is more likely to underscore the sequence of Jesus' mighty works rather than suggest a continuum of demonic activity (cf. v.40).

The NIV has adopted the reading "Gerasenes" (cf. Notes). Luke may have added the clause at the end of v.26 simply as a geographical explanation. Yet the fact that the locale was in Gentile territory is especially important to Luke as validating the Christian mission to Gentiles. Verse 27 implies that the man was right by the shore when Jesus arrived.

In vv.27 and 29 we have a classic description of demon possession. The symptoms of such possession are like those of certain psychic illnesses known today, but Luke does not confuse illness with demon possession (cf. 4:40–41), though he does link the two when appropriate. Certain effects of demon possession cited in this passage are (1) disregard for personal dignity (nakedness), (2) social isolation, (3) retreat to the simplest kind of shelter (caves, often containing tombs, were also used for shelter by the very poor), (4) demons' recognition of Jesus' deity, (5) demonic control of speech, (6) shouting, and (7) extraordinary strength. The basic tragedy of the demoniac lay not in mental or physical symptoms; in his case a human being was controlled by powers totally antithetical to God, his kingdom, and the kingdom blessings of "righteousness, peace and joy in the Holy Spirit" (Rom 14:17).

The term "Most High God" (v.28) appears in the NT in an orthodox sense, as in the OT (Gen 14:18–22; Num 24:16; Isa 14:14; Dan 3:26; 4:2), and also as a general term for deity apart from worship (contrast Luke 1:32, 35, 76, with Acts 16:17). Here it is used in the latter sense. The words "fell at his feet" do not indicate worship: the plea "I beg you, don't torture me!" (v.28) along with the dialogue in vv.30–31 make it clear that the man's words and actions are not his own. The "torture" (from *basanizō*, which can indicate either physical or mental torture) is presumably that of being cast into the "Abyss" (cf. v.31), or else the advance threat of that fate. Matthew 8:29 adds "before the appointed time," i.e., the eventual judgment of Satan and his followers after his incarceration in the Abyss (Rev 20:1–3, 10; cf. the intertestamental literature: 1 Enoch 15–16; Jub 10:8–9; T Levi 18:12).

30–31 Jesus was not actually an exorcist, because he did not need formulas nor invoke the authority of another in driving out demons. Therefore his asking the demoniac's name (v.30) should not be interpreted as an attempt to control the demons through knowing their host's name. That was pagan magical procedure. Moreover, it is not clear whether Jesus asked the name of the man or of the demons, though the response comes from the latter. "Legion" was not normally used as a proper name. It refers to a Roman military unit consisting of thousands of soldiers (the precise number varied). Thus "Legion" implies that there were many demons. As for "Abyss" (*abyssos*, v.31), the word has a long history and varied meanings ranging from the idea of primeval chaos to the abode and prison of evil beings (cf. Notes).

32–39 When the demons entered them, the swine were carried into the lake (v.33). In ancient thought, waters of the sea or a large lake was one form of the Abyss. The cosmology behind this, however, is not clear; nor is it clear that the demons, intent

119

on carrying out their destructive work even on animals, met the fate they wanted to avoid.

The episode of the pigs, often considered a legendary accretion, is integral to the present narrative in two ways. Theologically, it completes the cycle just described. Psychologically, it is essential for understanding the complex response of the towns-people. The report of what happened to the swine (vv.34, 36) first triggered the people's fear, which merged into overwhelming awe on seeing the former demoniac "dressed and in his right mind" (vv.35, 37).

But what about the ethical aspect of the pigs' destruction? Obviously the good of the man was more important than that of the pigs. Moreover, the demons them-selves insisted on entering the pigs; Jesus permitted them to do this but did not actively send them there. Inevitably the discussion moves from exegesis to theology and the problem of evil—why it exists and why God in his wisdom, power, and love permits evil in this world.

The narrative does not say that the demons were destroyed so that they could never again be at large. The biblical references to the Abyss connote that God may allow evil beings to go abroad from there, just as Satan, though defeated, still roams the earth (1 Peter 5:8). In any event, once the demons are off the scene, attention centers on the man and Jesus (vv.38–39). Now healed and a new man (observe the contrast between vv.27–29 and 35), the former demoniac is commissioned by Jesus, not to go with him as a disciple, but to be a witness where he lived. Jesus has different ways for different believers to serve him (cf. John 21:21–22).

Notes

26 Γερασηνῶν (Gerasēnōn, "of the Gerasenes") is the preferred reading (UBS, 3d ed.) over Γεργεσηνῶν (Gergesēnōn, "of the Gergesenes") and Γαδαρηνῶν (Gadarēnōn, "of the Gadarenes"). The appearance of several names at this point in the various MSS results not only from possible phonetic confusion but also from the existence of several towns with similar names east and south of the Sea of Galilee. "Gerasenes" seems original in Luke, as in Mark, having good MS support (see Metzger, Textual Commentary, p. 145). Perhaps Mark had reasons unknown to us for assuming that the territory of Gerasa extended some thirty miles from the town of that name (southeast of the sea) to the place on the shore of Galilee, which, with its steep slopes and modern city of Kursi (or Kersa) may have been the scene of the incident (cf. V. Taylor, The Gospel According to St. Mark [London: MacMillan, 1963], p. 278).

Another suggestion is that there may have been another town with the name Gerasa, or a phonetically similar name, on the sea coast near modern Kursi (Kersa) and near the steep slopes (C.E.B. Cranfield, The Gospel According to St. Mark, An Introduction and Commentary [Cambridge: University Press, 1960], p. 176; Marshall, Gospel of Luke, p. 337). But it is also possible that Kursi marks the site of Gergesa rather than a second Gerasa. Origen, writing on John 6, suggested that the town was Gergesa, a suggestion reflected in some MSS.

The claim of Gadara (the modern Umm Qeis) to be the site of the miracle lies in the importance of that name in MSS of Matthew, in its location six miles from the shore of the lake, and from the possibility that the territory named after the town might have extended to the shore of Galilee. It is possible that people in the area were identified by the name of the more important city of Gerasa rather than by that of the smaller Gadara (cf.

E. Smick, *Archaeology of the Jordan Valley* [Grand Rapids: Baker, 1973], pp. 135–37). However, Smick did not deal with M. Avi-Yonah's evidence against Cadara (*The Holy Land* [Grand Rapids: Baker, 1966], p. 174). Without more certain knowledge, the textual reading *Gerasēnōn* should tentatively be considered correct. Also we must keep in mind that all three Synoptics use a general expression, εἰς τὴν χώραν (*eis tēn chōran*, "into the region"), leaving the precise location unspecified.

29 παρήγγειλεν (*parēngeilen*, "had commanded") is aorist. The twenty-fifth edition of the Nestle text had the imperfect παρήγγελλεν (*parēngellen*, "was commanding"), a reading assumed by Turner (*Syntax*, p. 65) and by Marshall (*Gospel of Luke*, p. 338). However, the UBS text has the aorist, following B and P75, among other MSS, but with no footnote, and consequently no comment in Metzger, *Textual Commentary*.

31 Ἄβυσσος (*abyssos*, "abyss") is used only here in Luke (cf. Rom 10:7; Rev 9:1–3; 11:7; 17:8; 20:1–3; cf. ZPEB, 1:30–31).

---

10. Jesus' power to heal and restore life

8:40–56

40Now when Jesus returned, a crowd welcomed him, for they were all expecting him. 41Then a man named Jairus, a ruler of the synagogue, came and fell at Jesus' feet, pleading with him to come to his house 42because his only daughter, a girl of about twelve, was dying.

As Jesus was on his way, the crowds almost crushed him. 43And a woman was there who had been subject to bleeding for twelve years, but no one could heal her. 44She came up behind him and touched the edge of his cloak, and immediately her bleeding stopped.

45"Who touched me?" Jesus asked.

When they all denied it, Peter said, "Master, the people are crowding and pressing against you."

46But Jesus said, "Someone touched me; I know that power has gone out from me."

47Then the woman, seeing that she could not go unnoticed, came trembling and fell at his feet. In the presence of all the people, she told why she had touched him and how she had been instantly healed. 48Then he said to her, "Daughter, your faith has healed you. Go in peace."

49While Jesus was still speaking, someone came from the house of Jairus, the synagogue ruler. "Your daughter is dead," he said. "Don't bother the teacher any more."

50Hearing this, Jesus said to Jairus, "Don't be afraid; just believe, and she will be healed."

51When he arrived at the house of Jairus, he did not let anyone go in with him except Peter, John and James, and the child's father and mother. 52Meanwhile, all the people were wailing and mourning for her. "Stop wailing," Jesus said. "She is not dead but asleep."

53They laughed at him, knowing that she was dead. 54But he took her by the hand and said, "My child, get up!" 55Her spirit returned, and at once she stood up. Then Jesus told them to give her something to eat. 56Her parents were astonished, but he ordered them not to tell anyone what had happened.

The third part of the section on Jesus' power is composed of two intertwined stories—a pattern of alternation common to all the synoptic accounts and apparently one that goes back to the tradition (see Introduction: Method of Composition). We must ask why the two events are so closely connected. In both, the power and compassion of Jesus are notably displayed. Also, in both we see the importance of faith. Another point of comparison may be that Jairus's daughter was about twelve years old, while the woman (vv. 43–48) had suffered a hemorrhage the same period of time. Perhaps we ought also to reflect on the tension created for Jesus and his disciples by the two pressing needs: prevention of impending death, and helping a pathetic woman whose illness had isolated her from normal life and relationships.

40–42a The words "Now when Jesus returned" (v. 40) establish a continuity with the preceding episodes and alert the reader to this sequence of Jesus' mighty works. Once again Luke shows us the popularity of Jesus. The only recent event to have caused such expectation was the episode in Gerasene territory, word of which must have spread immediately. The present section now before us ends, by contrast, with Jesus' command not to speak of the girl's healing (v. 56). As a leader of the synagogue, Jairus was locally prominent (v. 41; cf. Notes). In the extremity of his need, he humbled himself as a suppliant. Luke describes the girl as Jairus's "only" (*monogenēs*) daughter (v. 42a). The term "only" (or "one and only," as in John 3:16 NIV) adds to the pathos, as it is used in Scripture to designate an only child who has died or is in mortal danger (cf. note on 7:12). The further detail "about twelve" points out that in Jewish society she was about to become a young lady of marriageable age. This intensifies the poignancy.

42b–46 The "crowds" (*ochloi*), now an integral part of the narrative, cover the woman's furtive approach to Jesus (42b). The verbs "almost crushed" (*synepnigon*), "crowding" (*synechousin*, v. 45), and "pressing against" (*apothlibousin*) bring the scene to life. Luke does not specify the nature of the "bleeding" (v. 43), which is usually taken to have been a gynecological problem. The restrictions imposed by Leviticus 15:25–33 and by Jewish custom (codified in M *Zabim*) would have radically affected the woman's life. But her primary problem was the discomfort and embarrassment of her prolonged malady. If Luke did not mention the failure of the physicians to help the woman (v. 43; cf. Mark 5:26) because he was one himself, that would be understandable. Yet the omission may be of no more significance than others (as in v. 42; cf. Mark 5:23).

More serious questions are raised by (1) the woman's touching his cloak (v. 44), as though magical power could be transferred, and (2) by Jesus' awareness of the transfer of power apparently without knowledge of who had done this (vv. 45–46). As to the first, the intrusion of Hellenistic ideas and superstitions may indeed have influenced her action; but Jesus did not quench the "smoldering wick" (Matt 12:20) of her faith; instead, he fanned it into flame (v. 48). Elsewhere it is implied that God honored even stranger expressions of faith, presumably because imperfect knowledge did not hinder confidence in the Lord himself (cf. Acts 5:14; 19:11–12).

Regarding Jesus' awareness of the transfer of some of his power, his question (v. 45) need not imply ignorance of the woman's identity but only his intention of singling her out. The dialogue (vv. 45b–46) suggests that he knew only the fact that power had been transferred. (Just as Jesus was the bearer of the Spirit [see comment on 3:22], so he was the bearer of the power of God.) While at times he chose to heal people who had not expressed any faith, the reverse seems to be true here—viz., that someone with faith in him drew on his power without his conscious selection of that person. Since he bore the very power of God, and since God the Father had not assumed the voluntary human limitations the incarnate Son had, God could have extended his healing power through his Son even though Jesus may not yet have been aware of the woman's identity. "Power has gone out from me" (v.46) does not mean that Jesus' power was thereby diminished, as though it were a consumable commodity.

47–48 The woman had desired to go unnoticed (v.47), possibly because of the embarrassment of her illness or because of her audacity in breaking her ritual isolation to touch Jesus' cloak. Her public confession of faith may constitute the purpose for which Jesus asked, "Who touched me?" (v.45). Jesus prefaced his traditional words of benediction (v.48) by words of grace (see comment on 7:50).

49–50 The episode of the sick woman delayed Jesus until word of the death of Jairus's daughter reached him (v.49). Yet the woman's healing also paved the way for Jesus' words in v.50.

51–56 It was only on particular occasions that Jesus selected Peter, James, and John alone (v.51) to be with him—e.g., at the Transfiguration (Matt 17:1; Mark 9:2; Luke 9:28) and in Gethsemane (Matt 26:37; Mark 14:33). The secrecy involved and the command to silence (v.56) may seem incomprehensible to some apart from the awkward theory of the "messianic secret" (see comments on 7:20–23; 9:21 and on Mark 9:9 in this volume). In actuality Jesus often tried to avoid publicity to prevent premature or misguided declarations of his messiahship from being made. Of course, it would be hard to keep silent about the girl's restoration to active life; but the use of the word "asleep" (v.52) might have diverted the attention of the mourners and others from Jesus to the girl. While Jesus' statement "she is . . . asleep" (*katheudei*) meant that her death was not forever but only till the Resurrection (cf. John 11:11; 1 Thess 4:13–14), the others probably assumed that she had, after all, only been in a coma. If they thought she was only revived, not raised from death, Jesus could thus reserve the public acknowledgment of his messiahship till the proper time. But the words "her spirit returned" (v.55) plainly imply that the child actually was dead. Because of these words, Marshall (*Gospel of Luke*, p. 348) suggests that the miracle is not to be described as a resuscitation of a body but as the calling back of the girl's spirit. The secrecy of this miracle is in contrast with the public nature of the raising of the young man from Nain (7:16–17).

11. *Sending out the Twelve*

9:1–6

> ¹When Jesus had called the Twelve together, he gave them power and authority to drive out all demons and to cure diseases, ²and he sent them out to preach the kingdom of God and to heal the sick. ³He told them: "Take nothing for the journey—no staff, no bag, no bread, no money, no extra tunic. ⁴Whatever house you enter, stay there until you leave that town. ⁵If people do not welcome you, shake the dust off your feet when you leave their town, as a testimony against them." ⁶So they set out and went from village to village, preaching the gospel and healing people everywhere.

Luke describes the mission of the Twelve in less detail than does Matthew, who presents it as one of his five major discourses. Some of the instructions that appear in Matthew 10:1–10 (as well as the saying about the harvest in Matt 9:37–38) are not found here in Luke 9 but rather among the instructions to the group of seventy-two Jesus sent out (Luke 10:1–12). There are a large number of verbal similarities between the accounts in Matthew 10, Mark 6, Luke 9, and Luke 10, along with some apparent discrepancies (see comments on each passage in this volume of EBC). The usual approach to these textual phenomena is to postulate an intertwining of traditions. There is also the possibility that Jesus gave approximately similar instructions on different occasions, and that parts of these instructions were also repeated in the early church as normative guidelines. (For example, the teaching in Matt 10:10 about the worker being worth his keep is repeated in Luke 10:7; 1 Cor 9:14; 1 Tim 5:18; and in *Didache* 13:1.) What is described in these "sending" passages in the Gospels is not appointment to a permanent office but commissioning for an immediate task. The practice of sending a man on a mission empowered to act with full authority on behalf of the sender is known from the Talmud (j Hagigah 1.8). Such an appointment could therefore be repeated using words essentially similar though varying in detail. The common theme that is found in the biblical passages cited above, and in others such as 3 John 5–7, is that the servants of Christ should go forth, not seeking support from unbelievers, but trusting God completely to supply their needs through his people.

1–2 The "Twelve" (*dōdeka*) receive both the "power" (*dynamis*) and the "authority" (*exousia*) to do works of the sort Jesus has performed in the episodes Luke has thus far reported. Luke includes the word *dynamis*, which does not occur in either Matthew 10 or Mark 6. While the word *dynamis* itself is not usually prominent in Luke's vocabulary (it is absent in 9:27, but the parallel in Mark 9:1 has it), nevertheless signs and wonders are important in his books, especially in Acts. This is because Luke stresses the validation of the Gospel by, among other means, the apostles' miraculous power as God's messengers. Others were claiming supernatural powers (cf. the Jewish sorcerer Bar-Jesus, or Elymas, and the itinerant Jewish exorcists, Acts 13:6–10; 19:13); so it was necessary for Jesus' disciples to have both "authority" (*exousia*) and "power" (*dynamis*). This principle appears in a different context in Luke 5:24. The connection between casting out demons and the coming of the kingdom is not as clear there as in 11:20; but the double mention of the ministry of healing here in 9:1–2 suggests that relationship. The authority of the Twelve extends over "all" (*panta*) demons. None is too powerful for them.

3 The instructions indicate the urgency of the task. The severely limited provisions Jesus allows the Twelve to take with them may be intended to express their dependence on God alone. Without bread or money they would need to be given daily food. The forbidden "bag" (*pēra*) may be the kind frequently used by itinerant philosophers and religious mendicants for begging (cf. Notes). The disciples are learning to trust God for food, protection, and shelter. (See comment on the apparent reverse of these instructions in Luke 22:3.)

4 The disciples should receive hospitality graciously. Hospitality was important as well as necessary in days of difficult travel conditions and poor accommodations at inns. The disciples are not to move about from house to house, a practice that might gain them more support but would insult their hosts.

In "The Passing of Peregrinus," the satirist Lucian described a Cynic preacher, Peregrinus, who for a time pretended to be a Christian and lived off the generosity of Christian hosts. The *Didache* (chs. 11–12) also warns of wandering false prophets and contains careful instructions about receiving prophets.

5 The disciples will also encounter those who refuse them a welcome. As a solemn symbol of judgment, the disciples are to shake the dust of an unresponsive town off their feet, just as Jewish travelers might do on returning from pagan territory (SBK, 1:571). This action expressed symbolically what Jesus would say about Korazin and Bethsaida in 10:13–15. Jesus himself later wept over Jerusalem's unresponsiveness (19:41).

Elsewhere, Jesus specifies the kind of person who is to have the privilege of supporting the disciples. He must be a "worthy [*axios*] person" (Matt 10:11), a "man of peace" (*huios eirēnēs*, lit., "son of peace," Luke 10:16). Such a person is clearly in sympathy with the message brought by Jesus' disciples.

6 Luke concludes this section with a summary of the mission of the Twelve, including another reference to preaching and healing. Their instructions had not included any limitation of scope such as in Matthew 10:5. "Everywhere" (*pantachou*) may even indicate the opposite.

Notes

1, 2, 6 Luke uses two words for healing without a difference in meaning: θεραπεύω (*therapeuō*) and ἰάομαι (*iaomai*). See DNTT, 2:164–69.

3 The problem of Luke's "no staff" (μήτε ῥάβδον, *mēte rhabdon*, lit., "neither a staff"; cf. Matt 10:10—μηδὲ ῥάβδον [*mēde rhabdon*, "nor a staff"]) over against the apparently contradictory words in Mark 6:8—μηδὲν . . . εἰ μὴ ῥάβδον μόνον (*mēden . . . ei mē rhabdon monon*, "nothing . . . except a staff") has several possible explanations.

1. Luke follows Q, which contains the original wording; he is not intentionally changing Mark (Marshall, *Luke: Historian and Theologian*, p. 352). This may well be so, but the difference remains.

2. The authors had different types of staves in mind, one for walking and the other, a club, for protection (E. Power, "The Staff of the Apostles, a Problem in Gospel Harmony," *Biblica* 4 [1923]: 241–66). But only one Greek word is used for "staff."

3. Mark adapts his wording so as to parallel the instructions to Israel (Exod 12:11). But the difference remains.

4. Two similar sounding Aramaic words are used, meaning "except" and "and not" respectively (M. Black, *An Aramaic Approach to the Gospels and Acts*, 3d ed. [Oxford: Clarendon, 1967], pp. 216ff.). This is attractive but improbable; it does not solve the problem for those who hold to the inerrancy of the canonical Greek text.

5. Jesus taught that the disciples were not to procure a staff if they lacked one. But this fits Matt 10:10 better than Luke, for Matt 10:9 uses κτάομαι (*ktaomai*, "acquire"), whereas Luke uses αἴρω (*airō*, "take").

6. Jesus meant that they were not to take an *extra* staff. This would fit the wording of each Gospel, but it leaves the question of whether anyone would normally carry two staffs.

The answer probably lies near the approaches of 1, 5, and 6. Whether or not one chooses some such explanation or does not attempt a harmonization of detail, the intent in all three Synoptics is the same: travel light, trust God, accept the gracious help of pious people, and do not let a mere staff interfere with these principles.

Πήρα (*pēra*, "bag") was commonly used to designate both a leather pouch in which provisions could be carried and a wallet for collecting alms (cf. LSJ, s.v.; BAG, s.v.; Deiss LAE, pp. 108–10). The latter use was so well known and such a symbol of itinerant, begging preachers that it probably has that sense here.

---

12. Herod's perplexity

9:7-9

> [7]Now, Herod the tetrarch heard about all that was going on. And he was perplexed, because some were saying that John had been raised from the dead, [8]others that Elijah had appeared, and still others that one of the prophets of long ago had come back to life. [9]But Herod said, "I beheaded John. Who, then, is this I hear such things about?" And he tried to see him.

Jesus has come to the end of his great Galilean ministry. The subsequent events take place to the north and east of Galilee and culminate in the confession of Jesus' messiahship, followed by the first passion prediction (vv.19–27). These events are related more fully in Mark 6:30–8:26 along with other episodes Luke chose not to include, perhaps (1) because of their similarity with the other examples of Jesus' ministry he includes elsewhere, (2) because of the limitations of space, and (3) in order to move quickly to Peter's confession in 9:18–21. It is also possible that Luke used an earlier draft of Mark that lacked these parts, but this cannot be proved. Luke does include the event that is most important for his purpose, the feeding of the five thousand (9:10–17). And here, prior to that narrative, he states that Herod "was perplexed" (*dieporei*) about Jesus. This is of great importance in the sequence of Luke's Gospel because it introduces the question "Who then is this . . .?" (v.9; cf. Mark 6:16, where Herod answers his own question). This all-important question is picked up again in vv.18–20.

7-9 "All that was going on" (*ta ginomena panta*, v.7) probably refers to the activities of both Jesus (cf. Matt 14:1) and the disciples on their mission. In Matthew 14:2 and Mark 6:14, Herod is interested in the "powers" (*dynameis*) Jesus was reputed to have. (On the identity of Herod the tetrarch, see comments on 3:1. Luke uses the proper official title.) The questions of Jesus' identity and also of the reappearance of a dead prophet (v.8) are reintroduced in vv.18–19 and parallels (cf. John 1:19–22). John the Baptist is naturally on Herod's mind (and doubtless also on his conscience). Luke makes only a brief reference to John's execution (cf. 3:19–20, described more fully in Matt 14:3–12; Mark 6:17–29). Herod was not able to see Jesus (v.9) but had his curiosity satisfied when Pilate sent Jesus to him (23:8–11).

13. Feeding the five thousand

9:10-17

> [10]When the apostles returned, they reported to Jesus what they had done. Then he took them with him and they withdrew by themselves to a town called Bethsaida, [11]but the crowds learned about it and followed him. He welcomed them and spoke to them about the kingdom of God, and healed those who needed healing.
> [12]Late in the afternoon the Twelve came to him and said, "Send the crowd

away so they can go to the surrounding villages and countryside and find food and lodging, because we are in a remote place here."

[13]He replied, "You give them something to eat."

They answered, "We have only five loaves of bread and two fish—unless we go and buy food for all this crowd." [14](About five thousand men were there.)

But he said to his disciples, "Have them sit down in groups of about fifty each." [15]The disciples did so, and everybody sat down. [16]Taking the five loaves and the two fish and looking up to heaven, he gave thanks and broke them. Then he gave them to the disciples to set before the people. [17]They all ate and were satisfied, and the disciples picked up twelve basketfuls of broken pieces that were left over.

The fact that this miracle is in all four Gospels indicates its importance. Luke's account is sparse and straightforward, a little shorter than Mark's, though including some additional words (e.g., on the kingdom, v.11).

10 The return of the disciples is the occasion for Jesus' withdrawal to Bethsaida (for the purpose of resting, according to Mark 6:31). This town was on the northeast side of the lake outside Herod's territory. Only Luke mentions its name.

11 The image of the shepherd in the parallels (Mark 6:34; cf. Matt 14:14) is here replaced by that of the Savior who "welcomed" (apodexamenos) all who came and told them about the kingdom. Thus even a time set aside for rest becomes an opportunity to fulfill the purpose expressed in Luke 4:43. As in Matthew 14:14, Luke mentions healings. He presents Jesus as having ministered to the total needs of people as he taught, healed, and fed those who came to him.

12–13 Each of the Synoptics records the disciples' unimaginative suggestion that the crowds be sent away to find their own food (v.12; Matt 14:15; Mark 6:36) and Jesus' response, "You give them something to eat" (v.13; Matt 14:16; Mark 6:37), putting the responsibility back on the disciples. The loaves (artoi) were a basic food, often eaten stuffed with fish (ichthys) from the Sea of Galilee.

14–17 The crowd was much greater than five thousand, since there were that many men (andres, v.14), plus women and children (Matt 14:21). Luke briefly summarizes the miracle, showing the orderliness of the distribution, Jesus' thanks (v.16, providing a lasting example for Christian table fellowship in the presence of God), and the adequacy of the food (v.17). Luke's description of the miracle does not direct attention to the Lord's Supper, though there are some common factors.

Notes

16 Εὐλόγησεν αὐτούς (eulogēsen autous) could mean "he blessed them," i.e., the fish, as an act of consecration (KJV, NASB), or "he gave thanks for them," which is the sense of NIV. The latter meaning is supported by Marshall, who takes autous to be an accusative of respect rather than a direct object; so "Jesus' prayer of thanks will here be one of thanks for what God is able to do to the bread" (Gospel of Luke, p. 362).

D. *Climax of Jesus' Galilean Ministry* (9:18–50)

1. *Peter's confession of Christ*

9:18–21

18Once when Jesus was praying in private and his disciples were with him, he asked them, "Who do the crowds say I am?"
19They replied, "Some say John the Baptist; others say Elijah; and still others, that one of the prophets of long ago has come back to life."
20"But what about you?" he asked. "Who do you say I am?"
Peter answered, "The Christ of God."
21Jesus strictly warned them not to tell this to anyone.

Luke moves directly from the miracle of multiplying the loaves and fishes, which pointed to Jesus' messiahship, to Peter's confession of that messiahship. To do this, Luke omits, or includes elsewhere, the material in Mark 6:45–8:26 (cf. comments on 9:7–9).

If the priority of Mark (or Matthew) is assumed, questions regarding the genuineness and literary history of this narrative properly belong to the study of those Gospels (cf. comments on Matt 16:13–20; Mark 8:27–30 in this volume.) However, it is important to recognize the contextual integrity of its position at this point in Luke, following Herod's question about Jesus' identity (v.9) and the feeding of the five thousand, with its messianic implications. It leads directly to the transfiguration narrative through the natural transition of v.28.

Theologically, this is the most important statement thus far in Luke. It is the first time a disciple refers to Jesus as Messiah (cf. 2:11, 26; 3:15; 4:41). Observe that immediately after Peter's great declaration, Jesus predicts his rejection, death, and resurrection (v.22), thus shedding light on the implications of his messiahship.

18–19 Luke's introduction to the dialogue between Jesus and his disciples is unique in two respects: he omits reference to Caesarea Philippi and inserts a reference to Jesus at prayer (v.18; cf. Matt 17:13; Mark 8:27). The omission is surprising because one might have expected Luke, with his interest in the Gentile world, to show Jesus' penetration of the area of Caesarea, where extant inscriptions still show the influence of Hellenistic religion. On the contrary, Luke apparently disconnects Peter's confession from time and space in order to emphasize the link between the miraculous feeding and also Jesus' intimate fellowship with God, as exemplified in his praying. This is one of the insights Luke gives us into Jesus' prayer life (cf. 3:21; 6:12; 11:1). Jesus asks for the opinion of the "crowds" (*ochloi*, in place of *anthrōpoi* ["men"], Matt 16:13; Mark 8:27), a word Luke frequently uses to draw attention to the uncommitted masses of people who heard Jesus. The responses (v.19) echo the rumors expressed in vv.7–8.

20 "Christ" (*Christos*) represents the Hebrew word for "anointed" and was first an adjective before it came to be used as a proper name. Its OT occurrences with the idea of a coming anointed King include Psalm 2:2 and Daniel 9:26. The idea, without the title, appears in such passages as Isaiah 9:6–7; 11:1–16. The additional words "of God" in Luke do not explicitly express sonship as does the longer phrase in the parallel in Matthew 16:17, but they do emphasize Jesus' divine commission.

21 The command not to tell others (cf. comments on 8:51–56) probably stems from two circumstances: (1) the Jewish people, chafing under the domination of Rome, were all too ready to join a messianic revolutionary; and (2) there was apparently an understanding that one should not claim messiahship for himself but should first do the works of the Messiah and then be acclaimed as such by others (see Longenecker, *Early Jewish Christianity*, pp. 71ff.). The idea that Mark had imposed a motif of secrecy (the so-called messianic secret) on the tradition of Jesus' teachings is neither a necessary nor a provable hypothesis for explaining Jesus' commands to silence in Mark and the other Gospels (cf. comments on 7:20–23; 8:56).

2. The suffering and glory of the Son of Man

9:22–27

> 22And he said, "The Son of Man must suffer many things and be rejected by the elders, chief priests and teachers of the law, and he must be killed and on the third day be raised to life."
> 23Then he said to them all: "If anyone would come after me, he must deny himself and take up his cross daily and follow me. 24For whoever wants to save his life will lose it, but whoever loses his life for me will save it. 25What good is it for a man to gain the whole world, and yet lose or forfeit his very self? 26If anyone is ashamed of me and my words, the Son of Man will be ashamed of him when he comes in his glory and in the glory of the Father and of the holy angels. 27I tell you the truth, some who are standing here will not taste death before they see the kingdom of God."

22 This statement is known as the first passion prediction. Although there had been foreshadowings of a dark fate for Jesus—Simeon's prediction (2:35) and Jesus' statement about the bridegroom (5:35)—here in Jesus' words is the first explicit recitation in Luke of the sequence of events at the close of his life. Some scholars find it difficult to accept the authenticity of such a prediction. Arguments pro and con tend to revolve around subjective judgments as to what Jesus might or might not have foreseen at this point in his ministry and what may or may not have been added editorially. The entire following teaching on discipleship requires some basic understanding of the Passion and, indeed, of the Crucifixion, since Jesus mentions the Cross (v.23). The use of the term "Son of Man" in vv.22, 26 is understandable, assuming that (1) Jesus used it frequently, (2) that he used it especially in connection with his passion, and (3) that the occurrence of the term in Matthew 16:14 is not editorial but reflects Jesus' actual use of it in his initial question to the disciples.

23 The person who wants to be Jesus' disciple—viz., "come after me" (*opisō mou erchesthai*)—can only truly be said to "follow" (*akoloutheitō*) him when he has made and implemented a radical decision to "deny" (*arnēsasthō*) himself. This verb functions as a polar opposite to the verb "confess" (*homologeō*), which has the sense of acknowledging a thing or a person. We should therefore on the one hand "confess" Christ, i.e., acknowledge him and identify ourselves with him, but on the other hand "deny" ourselves. This means that as Christians we will not set our desires and our will against the right Christ has to our lives. It does not mean cultivating a weak, nonassertive personality or merely denying ourselves certain pleasures. Furthermore, we are to recognize that we now live for the sake of Christ, not for our own sake. The next words about the daily cross explain and intensify this principle. A condemned criminal was forced to carry one bar of his cross to the place of execution. He was "on a one-way journey. He'd not be back" (Morris, *Luke*, p. 170). To take up the cross daily is to live each day, not for self, but for Christ.

24–26 These two statements (vv. 24–25) show the futility of clinging to one's "life" (*psyche*), because that, paradoxically, would result in losing the very self one wants to preserve. In contrast, the person who invests his life for God finds that, like the kernel of wheat planted in the ground (John 12:24), the "buried" life is not lost after all. Jesus next uses a "magnificent hyperbole" (Morris, *Luke*, p. 170) to emphasize his point. The world the disciple is willing to forfeit rather than lose his "very self" is, after all, to be succeeded by the new order when the Son of Man comes in glory (v. 26). If one seeks gain by letting the world's view of Christ make him ashamed of the Lord, he rightly draws a corresponding response from the glorified Son of Man. Mention of the fact that the glory is Christ's own, along with that of the Father and of the angels, heightens the contrast with the shame Christ experienced in the world.

27 This is a perplexing verse. "Some who are standing here" (*tines tōn autou hestekotōn*) may refer to the disciples as a group as opposed to the crowd, or to some of the disciples as opposed to the rest of the disciples. Marshall (*Gospel of Luke*, in loc.) argues well for the former. But both are possible. Even if the larger group from whom the "some" are selected is broader than the Twelve, that does not mean that the select group includes all or even most of the Twelve.

There have been a number of different proposals as to what specific experience Jesus had in mind when he said these words. If he meant the future consummation of a literal kingdom, he would have been mistaken, as that has not yet occurred. He may have meant Pentecost, for the coming of the Spirit brought the dynamic of the kingdom (Mark 9:1 has the word "power" [*dynamis*]), but the imagery is not obvious. The resurrection of Christ declared him "with power to be the Son of God" (Rom 1:4), but that event does not seem to be understood in Scripture as an expression of the kingdom as such. It is true that Pentecost and the Resurrection are expressions of the same power, by which the kingdom of God proved itself over the kingdom of Satan and his demons in Jesus' casting out of demons.

There is, however, another event, the Transfiguration (vv. 28–36), which Luke is about to describe, that may suit the saying better. It focuses even more sharply on the kingdom. The Transfiguration is, among other things, a preview of the Parousia, which event is clearly connected with the reign of Christ (see comment below on vv. 28–36). Moreover, the specific reference to the brief interval of time between this saying and the Transfiguration, which is made even more specific by Luke— "about eight days after Jesus said this" (v. 28)—tightens the connection between the saying and that event. In 2 Peter 1:16–18, Peter mentions in connection with the Transfiguration the elements of power and the coming of Jesus that are associated with the kingdom. If Jesus was referring to the Transfiguration in this saying, then the "some" who would not die before seeing the kingdom were Peter, James, and John, who saw Jesus transfigured. Why Jesus said they would "not taste death" before participating in an event only days away is perplexing. But he may have chosen those words because most people despaired of seeing the glory of the kingdom in their lifetime.

3. The Transfiguration

9:28–36

²⁸About eight days after Jesus said this, he took Peter, John and James with him and went up onto a mountain to pray. ²⁹As he was praying, the appearance of his face changed, and his clothes became as bright as a flash of lightning. ³⁰Two men, Moses and Elijah, ³¹appeared in glorious splendor, talking with Jesus. They spoke about his departure, which he was about to bring to fulfillment at Jerusalem. ³²Peter and his companions were very sleepy, but when they became fully awake, they saw his glory and the two men standing with him. ³³As the men were leaving Jesus, Peter said to him, "Master, it is good for us to be here. Let us put up three shelters—one for you, one for Moses and one for Elijah." (He did not know what he was saying.)

³⁴While he was speaking, a cloud appeared and enveloped them, and they were afraid as they entered the cloud. ³⁵A voice came from the cloud, saying, "This is my Son, whom I have chosen; listen to him." ³⁶When the voice had spoken, they found that Jesus was alone. The disciples kept this to themselves, and told no one at that time what they had seen.

This glorious transformation of the appearance of Christ is the most significant event between his birth and passion. In each of the synoptic Gospels, it stands as a magnificent christological statement. Both the transformation itself and the divine commentary expressed in the Voice from heaven declare Jesus Christ to be the beloved Son of God. Luke emphasizes a further dimension of the event—the suffering that lay ahead of God's chosen Servant. Luke does this both through the conversation of Moses and Elijah (vv.30–31) and through a slightly different wording of the message of the Voice. In addition to the main elements of the Transfiguration itself and the words from heaven, the narrative contains several motifs of deep significance: the eight day interlude (v.28), the mountain, Moses and Elijah (v.30), Jesus' impending "departure" (*exodos*, v.31), the shelters (v.33), and the cloud (v.34).

Two frames of reference will help us understand these motifs. One is the Exodus of the people of Israel from Egypt with the events at Mount Sinai, especially Moses' experience on the mount (Exod 24). The other is the second coming of Christ, the "Parousia" (cf. reference in v.26). These two frames of reference—one past, the other future—will help us understand the biblical imagery the events of the transfiguration episode would have brought to the minds of the disciples and all later readers familiar with Scripture.

There seems to be a pattern involving the two adjoining sections—vv.18–27 and vv.28–36. Three themes are stated and then repeated in reverse (chiastic) order. The first theme is the affirmation of Jesus' identity as the Messiah (v.20); the second is the prediction of his passion (v.22); and the third is the promise of his glory (v.26). In the transfiguration narratives the order is reversed (not only in Luke, but also, except for the words about his "departure," in Matthew and Mark), and the three themes are portrayed dramatically. The third theme, that of Jesus' glory, is first portrayed (v.29). The prediction of his passion is confirmed by the conversation between Moses and Elijah (v.30). The identity of Jesus is the subject of the heavenly proclamation (v.35).

28 Luke's note on the passage of time—"about eight days after Jesus said this" (*meta tous logous toutous hōsei hēmerai oktō*, lit., "after these words about eight days")—is less precise than "after six days" in Matthew and Luke. It is obviously an alternative way of indicating the passage of approximately one week. However, commentators have not agreed as to any specific reason for the different wording. Luke is, as pointed out above, more precise than the other Synoptics in linking the Transfiguration with Jesus' preceding sayings by a specific reference to Jesus' "words." There may be an allusion here to the time Moses waited on Mount Sinai for the revelation of God (Exod 24:15–16). This is even more likely in Matthew and Mark, where the phrase "after six days" corresponds directly to the period Moses waited.

Peter, James, and John had been taken into Jesus' confidence elsewhere, e.g., at 8:51 and in the Garden of Gethsemane (Mark 14:33). Luke uses the definite article *to* ("the") with "mountain," from which we may infer that the original readers knew what location he had in mind. On the other hand, the construction might indicate that Luke uses "mountain" symbolically. Symbolism is not infrequent in references to mountains, in Matthew especially; but this does not rule out a specific geographical location. The locale of the Transfiguration could have been any high mountain (Mark 9:2; cf. Notes). The article with *oros* ("mountain") is normal in similar grammatical constructions in the Gospels (except for Matt 5:14). If we think of the Exodus as a frame of reference, then Sinai is symbolically in mind; if the Parousia, then the Mount of Olives may be symbolized (Zech 14:4; Acts 1:10–12).

Once again Luke mentions that Jesus is at prayer, an observation repeated in v.29 but absent from the account in Matthew 17:1–2; Mark 9:2.

29 Luke omits the actual word "transfigured" (*metemorphōthē*, used in Matt 17:2, Mark 9:2), possibly to avoid a term that might have suggested Hellenistic ideas of an epiphany, the appearance of a god. Instead he describes the remarkable alteration of Jesus' face and the dazzling whiteness of his clothing, "bright as a flash of lightning" (*exastraptōn*).

30–31 Moses and Elijah also appear in this scene of supernatural glory (NIV, "glorious splendor," *en doxē*, lit., "in glory," only in Luke). Nevertheless, Luke still describes them in ordinary human terminology (*andres*, "men"; cf. 24:4 and comments). Scholars debate the significance of Moses' and Elijah's presence. The old view that they represent the Law and the Prophets respectively does not do justice to the rich associations each name has in Jewish thought. Moses had a mountaintop experience at Sinai; his face shone (Exod 34:30; 2 Cor 3:7); he was not only a lawgiver but also a prophet—indeed the prototype of Jesus (Deut 18:18). Elijah was not only a prophet but was also related to the law of Moses as symbolizing the one who would one day turn people's hearts back to the covenant (Mal 4:4–6). In Jewish thought, Elijah was an eschatological figure, that is, one associated with the end times. So one may say that in the transfiguration scene Moses is a typological figure who reminds us of the past (the Exodus), Moses being a predecessor of the Messiah, while Elijah is an eschatological figure pointing to the future as a precursor of the Messiah. Each man was among the most highly respected OT figures; both had one distinctive thing in common—their strange departure from this world. Elijah was taken up to heaven in a whirlwind (2 Kings 2:11), and Moses was buried by the Lord (Deut 34:6). (The disposition of Moses' body was a matter of speculation in ancient Judaism, cf. Jude 9.) In summary, it seems that the presence of Moses and Elijah on the Mount of Transfiguration draws attention, first, to the place of Jesus in continuing the redemptive work of God from the Exodus to the future eschatological consummation; second, to the appropriateness of Jesus' association with heavenly figures, and, third, to the superiority of Jesus over even these great and divinely favored heroes of Israel's past.

The conversation (v.31) is about Jesus' "departure" (*exodos*, lit., his "exodus"). In 2 Peter 1:15 the term means death. But here in Luke it also recalls the redemptive work of God in the Exodus from Egypt. Jesus' coming death was one that he would deliberately accomplish (*hēn ēmellen plēroun*, "which he was about to bring to fulfillment"). Luke portrays Jesus as moving unhurriedly toward the accomplishment of his goals (e.g., 4:43; see comments there). He specifies Jerusalem as the city of destiny for Jesus (v.31; see esp. comments on 13:31–35; cf. 9:51; 18:31). Thus Luke, having knowledge of this saying, which perhaps Matthew and Mark did not, included it to reinforce Jesus' passion prediction in v.22.

32 The writers of the Gospels use fear and sleepiness to indicate the slowness of the disciples to understand and believe. On this point see the explanation of Peter's words in v.33 in Mark 9:6 and the way Mark and Luke handle the sleepiness of the disciples at Gethsemane in different ways [Mark 14:40; Luke 22:45].) It is not clear from the Greek whether they were only drowsy but managed to keep awake or whether they actually fell asleep and woke up. At the least they were far from alert during the conversation about Jesus' approaching passion; and the spectacular scene aroused them thoroughly.

33 Only Luke mentions that it was as Moses and Elijah "were leaving" (*diachōrizesthai*, present tense) that Peter made the suggestion to make three shelters. This may imply that Peter did this to keep them from going. Both Luke's parenthesis here and Mark's in 9:6 show that Peter's suggestion was highly inappropriate. His use of "Master" (*epistata*, cf. 5:5) is itself appropriate (cf. "Lord" in Matt 17:4; "Rabbi" in Mark 9:5). His comment "It is good," though banal given the grandeur of the occasion, is not entirely out of order. The idea of three shelters is the main problem. These would have been temporary shelters, such as were used at Sukkoth, the Feast of Tabernacles. Peter's proposal of three, presumably equal, shelters may have implied a leveling perspective, putting Jesus on a par with the others. More than that, it connotes an intention to perpetuate the situation as though there were no "departure" (v.31) for Jesus to accomplish. Whether the shelters symbolize a future or present rest is not completely clear (cf. TDNT, 7:380; Marshall, *Gospel of Luke*, pp. 386–87; W. Liefeld, "Theological Motifs in the Transfiguration Narrative," in Longenecker and Tenney, *New Dimensions*, pp. 174–75). What does seem clear is that Peter wanted to prolong the stay of the heavenly visitors because he still failed to grasp the significance of the passion prediction of v.22 and its confirmation in v.31.

34 The cloud, like other elements in this narrative, can symbolize more than one thing, among them the cloud in the wilderness after the Exodus (Exod 13:21–22; 16:10; 24:16; 40:34–38). But clouds are also associated with the future coming of the Son of Man (Dan 7:13; cf. Mark 14:62), of the Messiah in intertestamental literature (2 Baruch 53:1–12; 4 Ezra 13:3), and with the two prophets in Revelation 11:12.

G.H. Boobyer (*St. Mark and the Transfiguration Story* [Edinburgh: T. & T. Clark, 1942]) sees in this symbolism a possible reference to the Parousia. H. Riesenfeld (*Jésus transfiguré. L'arrière-plan du récit évangélique de la Transfiguration de Notre-Seigneur*. Acta Seminarii Neotestamentici Upsaliensis 16 [Copenhagen: Ejnar Munksgaard, 1947], p.296) thinks it relates to Jewish concepts of eschatology, especially a future enthronement of the Messiah. Isaiah 4:5 describes a cloud, reminiscent of that which showed God's "shekinah" glory in the wilderness, which will appear during a future time of rest under the Messiah. The word "shekinah" is from the Hebrew *šāḵan*, which is translated by the Greek *episkiazō* ("overshadow") in Exodus 40:35 LXX. The same Greek verb is used here in v.34 ("enveloped"). But above all the cloud symbolizes the glorious presence of God (cf. Exod 19:16). This is notably true in the passage so clearly recalled by the Transfiguration (Exod 24:15–18). Matthew's use (17:5) of *phōteinē* ("bright") also suggests the shekinah glory. Though the disciples enter the cloud (v.34), a sense of the transcendence of God is retained as the Voice comes "from" (*ek*) the cloud (v.35).

35 The Voice speaking from the cloud is that of God the Father himself. No indirect or mediated message, no mere echo or "daughter of a voice," as Jewish writings put it, was sufficient to unmistakably identify Jesus. The awesome voice of God himself must be heard. The message expressed by the Voice is so clear that any uncertainty about the meaning of some of the other aspects of this great scene become comparatively unimportant. Whether seen in relation to the Exodus or to the second coming of the Son of Man, the focus throughout the Transfiguration is on the supreme person and glory of the Lord Jesus Christ. And now he is expressly declared to be God's Son—a declaration similar to that spoken by the Voice at Jesus' baptism (cf. 3:22; cf. also Matt 3:17; Mark 1:11). In Mark the Voice addresses Jesus directly; here it addresses the three disciples. In John 12:28–30, just preceding Jesus' passion, the Voice from heaven speaks for the "benefit" (v.30) of a whole crowd. In each case the Voice from heaven affirms that Jesus is the one who is sent by God and who has God's authority. These words spoken by the Voice on these three occasions affirm that Jesus is the Son of God, is obedient to him, and possesses divine authority for his mission. The words "this is my Son" (*houtos estin ho huios mou*), also in Matthew and Mark, recall Psalm 2:7. "Chosen" (*eklelegmenos*) for "whom I love" (Matt 17:5; Mark 9:7; KJV, "beloved") points us to Isaiah 42:1 ("my servant . . . my chosen one") and the concept of the Suffering Servant found in the broader context of Isaiah, especially 52:13–53:12.

"Listen to him" is not only a command; it is a correction of the human tendency to substitute human opinion for divine revelation (e.g., Peter after his confession in Matt 16:22, also implied here in the Transfiguration [v.33]). The words also fulfill Deuteronomy 18:15, which predicts the coming of the prophet God would raise up and commands, "You must listen to him." Jesus alone is the True Prophet, the Chosen Servant, and the Son of God.

36 All three synoptic Gospels note that at the end of the Transfiguration only Jesus was there with the disciples. So the scene ends with Jesus as the center of their attention. Luke's statement is concise and ends emphatically with the word "alone" (*monos*). Luke's comment on the silence of the disciples is shorter than Mark's very significant treatment of this (cf. Wessel's commentary on Mark, this vol., at Mark 9:9–10).

Notes

28 Τὸ ὄρος (*to oros*, "the mountain") has usually been identified as either Tabor, in Galilee, or Hermon, north of Caesarea Philippi. The former is doubtful, not only because of its distance from Caesarea Philippi, where Jesus had been about a week earlier, but because shortly after that time Josephus mentions that a Roman fortress was there (War II, 572–73 [xx.6]; IV, 54–61 [i.8]). Furthermore, though Tabor does stand out as the only mountain in its immediate area, it is not really "high" (Mark 9:2) but only 1,929 feet. Hermon, on the other hand, is high—9,232 feet. If Jesus went all the way to the summit, that would have required an exhausting climb of about six hours. Also, considering Hermon's remoteness, it is difficult to imagine such a large crowd (v.37), including scribes (cf. Mark 9:14), at its base. Moreover, the return trip from Hermon would not have been in the main "through Galilee" (Mark 9:30). A more likely place, not mentioned in tradition, is Meron, the highest mountain within Israel itself, 3,926 feet. It is just to the northwest of the Sea of Galilee. The distance from Caesarea Philippi is moderate; privacy would have been possible in the higher levels above the city of Safed (which, at 2,790 feet, is possibly the "city on a hill" of Matt 5:14); crowds, including scribes, would be normal on the lower slopes of the mountainside; and the subsequent short trip to Capernaum would have literally been "through Galilee" (Mark 9:30).

Literature on the Transfiguration includes H. Baltensweiler, *Die Verklärung Jesu* (Zurich: Zwingli-Verlag, 1959); Boobyer, *St. Mark and the Transfiguration*; H.C. Kee, "The Transfiguration in Mark: Epiphany or Apocalyptic Vision?" *Understanding the Sacred Text: Essays in Honor of Morton S. Enslin*, ed. J. Reumann (Valley Forge, Pa.: Judson, 1972); W. Liefeld, "Theological Motifs in the Transfiguration Narrative," Longenecker and Tenney, *New Dimensions*, pp. 162–79; H.-P. Müller, "Die Verklärung Jesu," ZNW 51 (1960): 56–64; A.M. Ramsay, *The Glory of God and the Transfiguration of Christ* (London: Darton, Longman and Todd, 1967); Riesenfeld, *Jésus transfiguré*; M. Thrall, "Elijah and Moses in Mark's Account of the Transfiguration," NTS 16 (1970): 305–17.

4. *Healing a boy with an evil spirit*

9:37–45

[37]The next day, when they came down from the mountain, a large crowd met him. [38]A man in the crowd called out, "Teacher, I beg you to look at my son, for he is my only child. [39]A spirit seizes him and he suddenly screams; it throws him into convulsions so that he foams at the mouth. It scarcely ever leaves him and is destroying him. [40]I begged your disciples to drive it out, but they could not."

[41]"O unbelieving and perverse generation," Jesus replied, "how long shall I stay with you and put up with you? Bring your son here."

[42]Even while the boy was coming, the demon threw him to the ground in a convulsion. But Jesus rebuked the evil spirit, healed the boy and gave him back to his father. [43]And they were all amazed at the greatness of God.

While everyone was marveling at all that Jesus did, he said to his disciples, [44]"Listen carefully to what I am about to tell you: The Son of Man is going to be betrayed into the hands of men." [45]But they did not understand what this meant. It was hidden from them, so that they did not grasp it, and they were afraid to ask him about it.

This healing is another significant example of the power of God over demons. It also implies Jesus' strong censure of the disciples for not performing the exorcism. But it is much shorter than the account in Mark and lacks the specific comment on prayer that concludes Mark's account. Moreover, Luke omits the intervening discussion on the coming of Elijah (Matt 17:10–13; Mark 9:11–13).

37–42 "The next day" (*tē hexēs hēmera,* v.37) may imply that the Transfiguration happened at night. If so, then that great event would have been even more striking, were that possible. The descent of Jesus and the disciples "from the mountain" meant a descent into the earthly world of illness, evil, and unbelief. The "large crowd" would be surprising if the location of the Transfiguration were Mount Hermon (cf. note on v.28). Since Luke was a physician, it is interesting that he does not identify the boy's condition as epilepsy, as Matthew 17:15 does. Clearly Luke is more concerned with the demonic aspect of the boy's affliction (v.42). The physical manifestations were similar to those of epilepsy—a fact that has contributed to the unfortunate misunderstanding of epilepsy down through the ages. Luke alone notes the continual debilitating oppression the boy endured (v.39). While three of the disciples were witnessing the Transfiguration, the others were helpless in the face of demonic power (v.40).

43a Instead of centering attention on the efficacy of prayer in exorcism, as Matthew and Mark do, Luke concludes his account of the boy's healing by speaking of the greatness of God. We might have expected Luke to dwell on the role of prayer, given his interest in it. He does have a saying similar to the one Matthew includes in his parallel to this narrative (Matt 17:21 mg.), but that is in another context (Luke 17:6). Actually the climax in the present story is typical of Luke, for it records the reaction of those who observe a healing by Jesus. They were "amazed" (*exeplēsonto;* cf. 4:32) at the "greatness" of God. Elsewhere Luke speaks similarly of people giving God glory (5:25; 7:16).

43b–45 This repetition of the prediction of Jesus' passion (cf. 9:22 and comments) might be considered as a separate section, had not Luke connected it closely with the preceding incident. This is not the case in Matthew 17:22 or Mark 9:30. Luke uses another word, *thaumazontōn* ("marveling," v.43b; cf. 43a), to describe the amazed reaction of the people to the healing. The passion prediction (v.44) serves to emphasize that Jesus' ultimate purpose went beyond such miracles. This time Jesus includes a reference to his betrayal. The failure of the people to understand (v.45), even at the very time they are marveling at the greatness of God's work through Jesus, is comparable to Peter's resistance to the first passion prediction immediately after his great confession (Matt 16:22). The people were not granted understanding of the meaning of Jesus' words. See the comparable situation in Luke 8:10 and its parallels (cf. commentary there). Here, however, the implication is that had they asked Jesus for help in understanding his words, they might have been given it.

5. Two cases of rivalry

9:46–50

46An argument started among the disciples as to which of them would be the greatest. 47Jesus, knowing their thoughts, took a little child and had him stand beside him. 48Then he said to them, "Whoever welcomes this little child in my name welcomes me; and whoever welcomes me welcomes the one who sent me. For he who is least among you all—he is the greatest.

49"Master," said John, "we saw a man driving out demons in your name and we tried to stop him, because he is not one of us." 50"Do not stop him," Jesus said, "for whoever is not against you is for you."

46–48 This passage naturally follows the preceding two verses. The disciples did not understand Jesus' role as the Suffering Servant and so could not grasp its implications for them as his disciples. They were still thinking of the Messiah only in terms of triumph, assuming, quite naturally, that their position was important. The issue was not whether there would be rank in the kingdom but the nature and qualifications of such rank (v.46) The point of Jesus' reference to the "little child" (*paidion*, v.47) does not illustrate simple faith (as in Matt 18:2–4). Nor does it refer to receiving a disciple who comes in the name of Jesus, as in Matthew 10:40–42. Rather, it refers to receiving for the sake of Christ a person who has no status (v.48; cf. Matt 18:5). This is consistent with Jesus' (and Luke's) concern for neglected people. The meaning, then, is that instead of seeking status for ourselves (out of pride as an associate of the Messiah) we Christians should, as Jesus did, identify ourselves with those who have no status at all, welcoming them to join us in the kingdom. To put it another way, in Matthew 10 one receives a Christian apostle as consciously receiving Christ himself, whereas here in Luke 9 by ministering to a child one ministers, without realizing it, to Christ himself.

49 The next episode reveals the apostles' attitude of rivalry. The issue is not orthodoxy but association. Far from merely invoking the name of Jesus in a formula and without genuine faith (as did the seven sons of the Jewish priest Sceva, to whose formula the demon refused to respond, Acts 19:13–16), the man referred to here had actually been "driving out demons" through Jesus' name.

50 This verse is proverbial in form. The man was not against Jesus. Apparently he had not yet joined the group of Jesus' disciples. Perhaps he represents those who are "on the way" to joining the body of believers and who should be welcomed rather than repulsed. In a different situation (Matt 12:30), Jesus used a reverse form of this proverb and did so without contradicting the truth set forth here in Luke.

V. Teaching and Travels Toward Jerusalem (9:51–19:44)

This extensive section has no counterpart in Matthew or Mark, though much of its material is found in other contexts in those Gospels. Luke 9:51 implies that Jesus was setting out on a journey one would expect to be described in the succeeding chapters. Yet these chapters say comparatively little about Jesus' traveling from one place to another.

To be sure, we do find some clues showing that Jesus is moving toward Jerusalem: e.g., 9:52—approaching Samaria; 10:38—"on their way . . . to a village where . . . Martha opened her home" (presumably Bethany, near Jerusalem); 13:22—"Jesus went through towns and villages . . . as he made his way to Jerusalem"; 13:32–33—"I will reach my goal. . . . no prophet can die outside Jerusalem"; 17:11—"Now on his way to Jerusalem, Jesus traveled along the border between Samaria and Galilee."

137

Following this section, Luke further notes Jesus' words "We are going up to Jerusalem" (18:31). Then he mentions Jesus' approach to Jericho (18:35; 19:1) and finally his arrival near Jerusalem (19:28–29). It is clear from all this that Jesus is now heading toward Jerusalem, not Galilee. However, he did not make one continuous journey from Galilee to Jerusalem. (See 10:38 and the subsequent note on 17:11, which poses a notorious problem [see comments, in loc.].)

To assume that Luke intends to describe a single continuous journey involves difficult problems, including the question of Luke's knowledge of geography raised by Conzelmann (*Theology of Luke*, pp. 60–73). To see the travel motif in this section as a mere literary or theological device entails some wrong preconceptions about what certainly appears to be a straightforward narrative. It is more reasonable and more consistent with the data to understand this section as showing that Jesus' ministry has entered a new phase and has taken on some new characteristics. Jesus follows routes that bring him away from Galilee and nearer to Jerusalem than his former itineraries did (except for visits for the feasts, as in John 2:13; 5:1 et al.). During this period Jesus is no longer committed to the locale of his former ministry but is looking toward Jerusalem and the Cross. Much of his teaching at this time is directed to the disciples. Warnings to the rich and complacent are prominent, as well as words aimed at the Pharisees. On several occasions he actually visits Jerusalem, where he proclaims the truth about himself and enters into controversy with those who oppose his claims.

If there is a travel motif in this section, it is not an artificial scheme but one that is (1) consistent with the nature of Jesus' ministry, which has been itinerant all along; (2) consistent with the emphasis on travel in both Luke and Acts, possibly to maintain the reader's interest; and (3) consistent with the fact that, while Jesus did not go directly from Galilee to Jerusalem, his mind was definitely set on the impending events he faced in that city. Even at times when he may have traveled north again, his ultimate goal was Jerusalem. This also accords with the prominence of Jerusalem in the Gospel of Luke (see comments especially on 13:33–34; 19:28, 41). (For bibliography on the characteristics of Luke 9:51–19:44, cf. Notes.)

Notes

9:51–19:44 There are many approaches to the characteristics of this large section of Luke. Some, such as the search for chiasms by Bailey and by Talbert and the comparison with Deuteronomy most recently by Drury, are suggestive and useful, even if overdone. The following is a partial bibliography of significant contributions to the subject: Bailey, *Poet and Peasant*, pp. 79–85; Drury, *Tradition and Design in Luke's Gospel*, pp. 138–64; C.F. Evans, "The Central Section of St. Luke's Gospel," in D.E. Nineham, ed., *Studies in the Gospels*, 1955), pp. 37–53; C.C. McCown, "The Geography of Luke's Central Section," JBL 57 (1938): 51–66; G. Ogg, "The Central Section of the Gospel According to St. Luke," NTS 18 (1971–72): 39–53; W.C. Robinson, Jr., "The Theological Context for Interpreting Luke's Travel Narrative (9:51ff.)," JBL 79 (1960): 20–31; Talbert, *Literary Patterns*, pp. 51–56.

A. The New Direction of Jesus' Ministry (9:51–10:24)

1. Travel south through Samaria

9:51–56

[51]As the time approached for him to be taken up to heaven, Jesus resolutely set out for Jerusalem. [52]And he sent messengers on ahead, who went into a Samaritan village to get things ready for him, [53]but the people there did not welcome him, because he was heading for Jerusalem. [54]When the disciples James and John saw this, they asked, "Lord, do you want us to call fire down from heaven to destroy them?" [55]But Jesus turned and rebuked them, [56]and they went to another village.

51 Luke uses the transitional *egeneto de* (the Semitic "and it came to pass"), omitted by NIV for stylistic reasons. As observed above, there is now a major change in Jesus' orientation. At this significant turning point, Luke once again uses a word expressing fulfillment, *symplēroō*, translated "approached" in NIV (cf. Notes). God's plan is another step nearer fulfillment. The approaching goal is not only the death and resurrection but especially the ascension of Christ (cf. note on *analēmpsis*). In the account of the Transfiguration, Luke has a reference to Jesus' "exodus" (v.31; cf. v.22). But now that Jesus faces the Cross, Luke mentions the exaltation that would follow his "exodus." He "resolutely set out" (NIV's contemporary idiom for the Semitic is "set his face towards") for Jerusalem, the designated place of his passion. We shall be reminded again of this destination as Jesus draws nearer Jerusalem (19:28, 41).

52 Jesus "sent messengers on ahead." This custom is described further in the particular mission of the seventy-two disciples (10:1–16). In this instance they were not told to preach but simply to "get things ready for him," a fact that makes the attitude of James and John (v.54) even less appropriate.

53–54 The residents of the Samaritan village (v.52) reciprocated the hostile attitude of the Jews (v.53; cf. John 4:9). They were especially negative because Jesus was going to Jerusalem, which they refused to acknowledge as a valid center of worship (cf. John 4:20).

The history of the Samaritans is uncertain. Many hold that they were a mixed race since the fall of the northern kingdom of Israel. The king of Assyria deported the leaders of Israel, among them the religious teachers, replacing them with foreigners (2 Kings 17:6; 24–26). From that time on, the northern kingdom inhabitants received no further prophetic instruction and refused to acknowledge the continuing revelation received by the Jews in the southern kingdom. Some think that the Samaritans known in the NT arose in the early Hellenistic period (cf. H.G.M. Williamson, "Samaritans," NBD, rev. ed., 1062–63). Being semipagan, the Samaritans were a fringe segment of the Jewish world for which Jesus, and Luke following him, had a concern. They are not mentioned unfavorably elsewhere in Luke; on the contrary, he mentions them favorably in 10:30–37 and 17:11–19. James and John may have thought that Jesus would respond as Elijah had (v.54; 2 Kings 1:9–12).

55 Jesus' strong disapproval of James and John's suggestion is seen in his use of the word "rebuked" (*epetimēsen;* cf. 4:35, 41; 8:24). If the Samaritans were consciously rejecting Christ by rejecting his disciples, one would have expected that v.5 would apply—a mild reaction compared to that of James and John. But Jesus' messengers were rejected merely because they were Jews going to Jerusalem, as v.53 indicates.

Notes

51 Ἐν τῷ συμπληροῦσθαι τὰς ἡμέρας (en tō symplērousthai tas hēmeras) literally means "as the days were [or 'time was'] being fulfilled" rather than "as the time approached" (NIV; cf. RSV, NASB). It is true that συμπληρόω (symplēroō) can mean "approach," and the NIV translation does convey a sense of destiny. But in view of Luke's significant use of words of fulfillment and accomplishment (e.g., in 1:1; 4:21; 9:31; 22:16; 24:44), symplēroō probably continues that theme here. It would be awkward, in an English translation, to describe days as being "fulfilled"; but from the perspective of God's plan, that is the meaning (cf. TDNT, 6: 308–9). See also Jer 25:12, where the LXX ἐν τῷ πληρωθῆναι τὰ ἑβδομήκοντα ἔτη (en tō plērōthēnoi ta hebdomēkonta etē) is translated "when the seventy years are fulfilled" (NIV).

Ἀναλήμψεως (analēmpseōs, "of his ascension"; NIV, "for him to be taken up to heaven") can refer to Jesus' death, since the word can be so used (BAG, s.v.). However, not only is there evidence in extracanonical literature for its use with reference to ascension, but also that is clearly the meaning of the verb form (ἀναλαμβάνω, analambanō) Luke used to describe the ascension of Jesus in Acts 1:2, 11.

54 The parallel between the disciples' suggestion and Elijah's action probably gave rise to the gloss "even as Elijah did" (see NIV mg.). The words were included in KJV but are absent from such important early texts as P 45,75 ℵ B.

55 Some ancient texts add "And he said, 'You do not know what kind of spirit you are of, for the Son of Man did not come to destroy men's lives but to save them.'" The first part of the sentence, up to "you are of," is in the Western text D and a couple of versions. The rest is, with varying details, found in a number of texts generally lacking the stature of those MSS that omit them. Those that lack the questionable reading are P45,75 ℵ A B C L W, among many others. The longer reading is in KJV, is bracketed in NASB, and is placed in a footnote in RSV and NIV. Marshall, after weighing arguments pro and con, including (pro) the appropriateness of the saying in the context and (con) the weak MS evidence and likelihood that a scribe would add words that seemed appropriate, concludes that in view of the "considerable doubt" the words should be either omitted or bracketed (*Gospel of Luke*, p. 408). Metzger (*Textual Commentary*, p. 148) also considers the claim to genuineness weak.

2. *The cost of following Jesus*

9:57–62

57As they were walking along the road, a man said to him, "I will follow you wherever you go."
58Jesus replied,"Foxes have holes and birds of the air have nests, but the Son of Man has no place to lay his head."
59He said to another man, "Follow me."
But the man replied, "Lord, first let me go and bury my father."
60Jesus said to him, "Let the dead bury their own dead, but you go and proclaim the kingdom of God."
61Still another said, "I will follow you, Lord; but first let me go back and say good-by to my family."

62Jesus replied, "No one who puts his hand to the plow and looks back is fit for service in the kingdom of God."

This is the second major treatment of discipleship in Luke (cf. v.23). The first two conversations (vv.57–60 through the words "bury their own dead") are found in Matthew 8:18–22. It is difficult to tell whether Matthew has omitted part of the material they had in common or whether Luke has used a combination of sources. There are some differences. The order of the dialogue in v.59 is the reverse of that in Matthew 8:21–22. Also, while a saying about the kingdom would have been equally at home in Matthew or Luke, the words "you go and proclaim the kingdom of God" are lacking in Matthew but made the central statement in Luke's section. The "man" of v.57 is a "teacher of the law" in Matthew 8:19.

The structure of this passage is noteworthy. The familiar "rule of three" is employed by Luke in recording three conversations. There is an interchange of order: in the first conversation the inquirer initiates the conversation and Jesus states the objection; in the second this is reversed; in the third the man both initiates the dialogue and raises the objection, with Jesus adding a comment. (On this structure, see Johannes P. Louw, "Discourse Analysis and the Greek New Testament," *Bible Translator* 24 [1973]: 104–8.) Each dialogue contains some theological language: "Son of man" (v.58), "proclaim the kingdom of God" (v.60), "service in the kingdom of God" (v.62). This shows that discipleship is not simply following Jesus in one's lifestyle but is involvement in the important work of the kingdom.

57–58 The man uses the terminology of discipleship, "follow" (v.57), and amplifies it with a sweeping promise. Jesus' reply is in accord with his prior definition of discipleship in v.23 and constitutes a comment on the man's "wherever you go." Since most men do have homes, "Son of Man" (v.58) must refer specifically to Jesus. The idea of the rejection—if not his actual suffering—of the Son of Man is implied in Jesus' words.

59–60 Since it was a religious, social, and family obligation to provide a suitable funeral for one's father, Jesus' refusal to permit this is a striking example of the radical transfer of loyalty he demanded in 14:25–27. To conjecture that the length of time required for mourning was the reason Jesus did not accept the excuse of the second man he asked to follow him, or that the man's father was not yet dead, misses the point. "The dead" who are to perform the burial are usually thought to be the spiritually dead who do not follow Jesus but remain at home. Manson's understanding (*Sayings of Jesus,* p. 73) of this as a paradoxical saying, meaning, "That business must look after itself," is appealing; but it loses the sharp thrust of the saying.

61–62 Although to "say good-by" (*apotaxesthai,* v.61) is not at all the emotional equivalent of a funeral (cf. vv.59–60), it still represents family duty that must be forsaken for service to Jesus. Danker (*Jesus,* p. 125) sees here (v.62) an allusion to the call of Elisha while plowing and his request to say good-by to his family (1 Kings 19:19–21; cf. Marshall, *Gospel of Luke,* p. 412). A further illustration of discipleship is keeping the hand on the plow. Jeremias (*Parables of Jesus,* p. 195, drawing on E.E. Bishop, *Jesus of Palestine* [London: Lutterworth, 1955], pp. 93–94) describes the plowman concentrating on the furrow before him, guiding the light plow with his left hand while goading the oxen with the right. Looking away would result in a crooked furrow.

Notes

62 The word "service" is not in the Greek text but is implied by the word εὔθετος (*euthetos*, "fit") and by the context.

3. *Sending out the seventy-two*

10:1–24

¹After this the Lord appointed seventy-two others and sent them two by two ahead of him to every town and place where he was about to go. ²He told them, "The harvest is plentiful, but the workers are few. Ask the Lord of the harvest, therefore, to send out workers into his harvest field. ³Go! I am sending you out like lambs among wolves. ⁴Do not take a purse or bag or sandals; and do not greet anyone on the road.

⁵"When you enter a house, first say, 'Peace to this house.' ⁶If a man of peace is there, your peace will rest on him; if not, it will return to you. ⁷Stay in that house, eating and drinking whatever they give you, for the worker deserves his wages. Do not move around from house to house.

⁸"When you enter a town and are welcomed, eat what is set before you. ⁹Heal the sick who are there and tell them, 'The kingdom of God is near you.' ¹⁰But when you enter a town and are not welcomed, go into its streets and say, ¹¹'Even the dust of your town that sticks to our feet we wipe off against you. Yet be sure of this: The kingdom of God is near.' ¹²I tell you, it will be more bearable on that day for Sodom than for that town.

¹³"Woe to you, Korazin! Woe to you, Bethsaida! For if the miracles that were performed in you had been performed in Tyre and Sidon, they would have repented long ago, sitting in sackcloth and ashes. ¹⁴But it will be more bearable for Tyre and Sidon at the judgment than for you. ¹⁵And you, Capernaum, will you be lifted up to the skies? No, you will go down to the depths.

¹⁶"He who listens to you listens to me; he who rejects you rejects me; but he who rejects me rejects him who sent me."

¹⁷The seventy-two returned with joy and said, "Lord, even the demons submit to us in your name."

¹⁸He replied, "I saw Satan fall like lightning from heaven. ¹⁹I have given you authority to trample on snakes and scorpions, and to overcome all the power of the enemy; nothing will harm you. ²⁰However, do not rejoice that the spirits submit to you; but rejoice that your names are written in heaven."

²¹At that time Jesus, full of joy through the Holy Spirit, said, "I praise you, Father, Lord of heaven and earth, because you have hidden these things from the wise and learned, and revealed them to little children. Yes, Father, for this was your good pleasure.

²²"All things have been committed to me by my Father. No one knows who the Son is except the Father, and no one knows who the Father is except the Son and those to whom the Son chooses to reveal him."

²³Then he turned to his disciples and said privately, "Blessed are the eyes that see what you see. ²⁴For I tell you that many prophets and kings wanted to see what you see but did not see it, and to hear what you hear but did not hear it."

Luke's account of Jesus' commissioning of the seventy-two, while in some points similar to that of the Twelve (9:1–6) but differing from it, fits well its immediate context; and in several respects it resembles Matthew's account of the commissioning of the Twelve. It continues the procedure of sending messengers ahead during Jesus' journey (9:52). At the same time, the obedient response of the seventy-two provides a contrast to the three men (9:57–62) whose excuse disqualified them from discipleship. The mere repetition of some travel instructions given the Twelve does not constitute a doublet. While the question of sources is complex (see comments at introduction to 9:1–6), the material here seems to be drawn from Q (cf. Matt 9:37–38; 10:7–16) and is properly included in this place. As noted in the introduction to 9:1–6, the instructions prescribed by Jesus were undoubtedly repeated frequently by Jesus and in the early church.

1 "After this" (meta de tauta) establishes the connection we have just observed with the context. The title "Lord" (ho kyrios) occurs only here among the various accounts of commissioning, possibly to emphasize the serious dominical aspect of the instructions—namely, that they came from the Lord Jesus himself. Not only does the commissioning of the seventy-two lack any restriction to Jewish hearers (Matt 10:5–6), but the number of missionaries sent out (cf. Notes) parallels the number of nations thought to exist in the world and so suggests the deliberate inclusion of Gentiles.

Sending messengers "two by two" (ana duo) was common not only among the early Christians (Mark 6:7; Luke 7:18–19; Acts 13:2; 15:27, 39–40; 17:14; 19:22) but also among the Jews. It provided companionship, protection, and the double witness prescribed in Deuteronomy 17:6; 19:15 (cf. Joachim Jeremias, New Testament Theology. The Proclamation of Jesus [New York: Scribners, 1971], p. 235). The seventy-two were to go everywhere Jesus was going. The extent of this mission underscores that of the church: to reach the "plentiful harvest." It may also look toward the conclusion of the church's mission at Jesus' return (cf. Matt 10:23).

2 Although the harvest imagery in Scripture usually refers to God's intervention in history through gathering his people together (cf. Matt 13:37–43), here it applies to the urgent missionary task of the present age (cf. Matt 9:37–38; John 4:35).

3 The imperative "go" (hypagete) and the untranslated exclamation idou ("behold") anticipate the difficulties of the journey. Wolves are natural enemies of sheep. No specific enemies are pointed out; the warning is a general one. The disciples are like "lambs" (arnas)—defenseless and dependent on God alone.

4 The limitations on what the seventy-two may take with them increases their vulnerability (see comment and note on 9:3). They must also be single-minded even to the extent of not becoming involved in time-consuming greetings (cf. 2 Kings 4:29).

5–6 Greetings (cf. v.4), which go beyond mere formality, are to be reserved for the hosts of the seventy-two. "Peace" (eirēnē), so familiar in Jewish salutations, has a rich connotation here (v.5). If the host has a proper attitude toward God (v.6), he will receive the blessing of the kingdom (v.9). "Man of peace" is literally "son of peace" (huios eirēnēs)—an idiomatic way of expressing not only a person's character

143

but also the destiny he is worthy of. Such a person would be open to the kingdom message.

7 Like the Twelve (9:4), the seventy-two are to remain with their original hosts. As the Lord's servants, they are deserving of support by the Lord's people (cf. 1 Tim 5:18). For the definitive discussion of this principle of support for Christian workers, see 1 Corinthians 9:3–18, where Paul speaks (v.14) of what the Lord "commanded." Likewise John says that Christians are obligated to support the Lord's messengers who, unlike the other itinerant preachers of the first century, sought no help from unbelievers but trusted in God alone (3 John 5–8).

8 It is not clear whether the messengers feared being offered food prohibited to Jews. This would have been less likely in Samaria and central Judea than elsewhere. The words may have been preserved because of their appropriateness to later situations (cf. Acts 10:9–16; 1 Cor 10:27).

9 Healing and the proclamation of the kingdom are linked together. This accords both with the mission of the Twelve and with the ministry of Jesus (Luke 9:1–2, 11).

10–11 These verses introduce a transition to the consequences of rejecting the kingdom message. In 4:18–19, Jesus' quotation of Isaiah 61:1–2 stopped short of the words "and the day of vengeance of our God." Nevertheless that day is coming, and Luke includes such warnings of it as 6:24–26; 12:46–48; 16:23–24; 21:22.

12 Sodom, destroyed along with Gomorrah (Gen 19:24–29), represents the consequences of ignoring God's warning to repent (cf. Matt 10:15; 11:20–24 [almost verbally identical with the present text]; Rom 9:29 [quoting Isa 1:9]; 2 Peter 2:6; Jude 7). "More bearable" (*anektoteron*) probably relates not so much to the degree of punishment as to the degree of culpability. If Sodom cannot escape judgment, what hope does a city that rejects the Lord Jesus have?

13–14 The probable site of Korazin along with that of Bethsaida is near Capernaum, at the north end of the Sea of Galilee, where Jesus concentrated his ministry. The comparison with the pagan Phoenician towns of Tyre and Sidon suggests utter rebellion against the Lord. Those ancient towns suffered drastic judgment for their proud opposition to God and his people (Isa 23:1–18; Jer 25:22; 47:4; Ezek 26:1–28:23; Joel 3:4–8; Amos 1:9–10).

"Sackcloth" was a coarse, black material worn as a sign of mourning or repentance (cf. 1 Kings 21:27 for an example). "Ashes" could also symbolize repentance or contrition (e.g., Job 42:6). "Sitting" (or lying) on these was one custom; another was wearing the sackcloth and putting ashes on the head (cf. Esth 4:2–3, where both customs are followed).

15 Capernaum had the high privilege of hearing Jesus preach there frequently, but this privilege guaranteed neither its fame nor its survival. On the contrary, in language like that of Isaiah 14:12–15, Jesus graphically portrays Capernaum's fall to the "depths" (*heōs tou hadou*, lit., "to Hades"; cf. the fall of Satan in v.18; cf. also Rev 12:10).

16 Reception or rejection of Christ's messengers shows one's attitude to the Lord himself (cf. Christ's identification of himself with the "least" of his "brothers" in Matt 25:31 46). In the parable of the vineyard, both son and servants were rejected (Luke 20:9–17). Moreover, whoever rejects Christ also rejects Moses (John 5: 45–47).

17 Whatever their experiences may have been, the messengers returned to Jesus filled with joy. The power of the kingdom was effective against demons just as it was in the ministry of Christ (11:20). Exorcism must be done in the name of Christ; it is not an incantation but signifies his authority (contrast Acts 19:13–16).

18 The taunt-song describing the fall of the king of Babylon (Isa 14:4–11) and the fall of the "morning star" ("Lucifer," KJV, vv. 12–21), to which Luke 10:15 alludes, also relates to Revelation 12:9. When the disciples exorcise demons, the forces of evil are shaken, symbolizing the defeat of Satan himself.

19 To have authority "to trample on snakes and scorpions" relates to the victorious work of Christ, who, according to the first promise of the gospel in Genesis 3:15, was to bruise (NIV, "crush") the head of the Serpent, the devil. The ultimate implication of overcoming "all the power of the enemy" is to be victorious over the chief enemy, i.e., through whose temptation Adam and Eve fell and sin entered into humanity. Therefore, Jesus' saying is far from an invitation to snake handling (cf. the instructions and context in vv. 17–18 of the questionable ending of Mark 16).

20 This verse with its call to rejoicing in the supreme blessing of assurance of heaven is one of Jesus' great sayings. "Do not rejoice" does not exclude the disciples' taking joy in spiritual victories but rather introduces a strong and typically Semitic comparison. The idea of the names of God's faithful people being written down in heaven is common in biblical and extrabiblical Jewish writings. In those days it was natural to refer to this through the metaphor of a book or scroll (e.g., Exod 32:32–33; Ps 69:28; Dan 12:1; Mal 3:16; Rev 20:12–15).

21–22 The emphasis on joy combines with another subject of Luke's special interest —the Holy Spirit in the life of Christ. The apparent parallel to this passage (Matt 11:25–27) lacks the reference to joy and the Holy Spirit. Correspondingly, Luke omits the words that follow in Matthew—the invitation to those who are weary and burdened. With their allusion to the "yoke" (Matt 11:29–30) of the Jewish law, these words are not as appropriate for Luke's audience as for Matthew's.

Verses 21–22 are of great doctrinal importance because they show (1) God's sovereignty in imparting revelation, (2) the relationship between the Father and the Son, and (3) the privilege the disciples had of participating in this instance of messianic revelation and salvation.

Jesus' words relate to the time (*hōra*, lit., "hour"; cf. *kairos*, "time" or "season," in Matt 11:25) in which the power of the kingdom is revealed. Jesus himself participates in the joy that characterizes the day of God's salvation, a theme established at the beginning of Luke's Gospel (e.g., 1:44). Like Mary (in the Magnificat, 1:46–47), he combines joy with thanksgiving on the occasion of God's mighty saving work. Jesus had already spoken about God's sovereignty in hiding and revealing divine mysteries in explaining his use of parables (8:10 and synoptic parallels; cf. 1 Cor

1:18–25). A remarkable thing—and one that Jesus' thanksgiving stresses—is not that the wise do not understand but that the simple do. This has to do with revelation and does not negate what Scripture teaches (e.g., in Proverbs) about the importance of study and pious wisdom. The "children" (*nēpiois*) are those whose open, trusting attitude makes them receptive to God's word. The theme of revelation appears in both v.21 and here, in v.22, first the revelation of "things" and now of God himself. The knowledge God gives is "committed" (*paredothē*, lit., "delivered," "handed over") directly to the Son. This explains why Jesus spoke with authority (4:32) in contrast to the scribes (Matt 7:29, Mark 1:22, cf. Matt 28:18), who received their ideas through tradition, passed on from rabbi to rabbi. Jesus' sayings confirm other teachings in the Synoptics and in John about the fatherhood of God and the unique sonship of Christ. While some aspects of his sonship relate to his role as the Messiah, who was designated God's Son, the relationship expressed here is clearly personal rather than functional. The same truth is one of the major themes in John's Gospel (see also Matt 24:36; Mark 13:32).

23–24 Here Jesus congratulates the disciples privately on participating in this revelation (v.23). The woes (vv.13–15) on those whose pride will be broken are balanced by the blessings of those granted salvation. This pattern has already appeared in the Magnificat (1:52–55) and in Jesus' beatitudes and woes (6:20–26). See also 1 Corinthians 2:9–10.

Notes

1 Ἑβδομήκοντα [δύο] (*hebdomēkonta* [*duo*], "seventy [-two]") has strong MS support, including P⁷⁵ B D, but the number "seventy" has a stronger precedence in the OT. There were seventy descendants of Jacob according to the MT of Exod 1:5, seventy elders in the Sanhedrin (Sanh 1.6), seventy nations in the world and so on (cf. TDNT, 2:634). There are fewer significant instances of the number seventy-two, if one is looking for possible precedents, though S. Jellicoe ("St. Luke and the Seventy-two," NTS 6 [1960]: 319–21) suggests that the seventy-two translators of the LXX, mentioned in L Aristeas, may have relevance. Marshall (*Gospel of Luke*, p. 415) suspects that Luke wrote that number thinking of the table of nations in the LXX of Gen 10, which lists seventy-two rather than seventy nations. Copyists, who were more familiar with the number seventy, may have changed the text in that direction. This is a reasonable proposal, which fits both the MS evidence and the background situation.

2 Τοῦ κυρίου τοῦ θερισμοῦ (*tou kyriou tou therismou*, "the Lord of the harvest") is presumably God the Father. Although Jesus is called "Lord" in v.1, his reference to the Lord of the harvest as the hearer of prayer is clearly in the third person in meaning as well as form.

4 Ὑποδήματα (*hypodēmata*, "sandals") are not mentioned in 9:3. The summary in 22:35 mentions them among prohibited equipment. See note on 9:3 regarding the differences between the Synoptics as to what was or was not allowed.

6 Ἐπαναπαήσεται ἐπ᾽ αὐτὸν ἡ εἰρήνη ὑμῶν (*epanapaēsetai ep' auton hē eirēnē hymōn*, "your peace will rest on him") portrays peace almost as an objective, personal power. God's spoken word had this characteristic in Semitic thought. It was to leave the host if he was not the kind of person who would be receptive to the kingdom message.

9 Ἤγγικεν ἐφ᾽ ὑμᾶς ἡ βασιλεία τοῦ θεοῦ (*engiken eph' hymas hē basileia tou theou*, "the kingdom of God is near you") is one of many statements of Jesus that teach the nearness

of the kingdom. It is not so clear in this passage that the kingdom has actually arrived as it is in 11:20, where the verb ἔφθασεν (ephthasen) means "has come." In the latter case, Jesus' casting out demons was an act of kingdom power. Here (v.9) it is not clear whether the disciples actually embodied or brought the kingdom, or whether they just announced it. The prepositional phrase eph hymas occurs both here and in 11:20, giving rise to the question of whether a common Aramaic saying underlies both, even though the Greek verbs are difficult. While this is improbable (Marshall, *Gospel of Luke*, p. 422), the potential of ἐγγίζω (engizō, "draw near," "approach") to indicate actual arrival plus the idea of proximity in the prepositional phrase are sufficient to establish the point: the hearers had adequate assurance of the coming of the kingdom to them in time and space through the arrival and ministry of Jesus' representatives.

11 On καὶ τὸν κονιορτὸν (kai ton koniorton, "even the dust"), cf. comment on, 9:5.

21 Ἠγαλλιάσατο [ἐν] τῷ πνεύματι τῷ ἁγίῳ (ēgalliasato [en] tō pneumati tō hagiō) presents a textual and a theological problem. In turn (as often) the theological problem may have produced the textual. The wording here (UBS text) may be translated "rejoiced [or 'exulted'] in the Holy Spirit." Metzger (*Textual Commentary*, p. 152) says, "The strangeness of the expression . . . (for which there is no parallel in the Scriptures) may have led to the omission of τῷ ἁγίῳ [tō hagiō, "the holy"] from P45 A W Δ Ψ f13 itq goth Clement *al*." The more important MSS have *hagiō*; and it is most likely that it is in the Spirit of God, not his own human spirit, that Jesus exulted. The use of square brackets around *en* in the UBS text acknowledges that some significant MSS omit that word. NIV interprets the word *en* as instrumental and has "full of joy through the Holy Spirit." In the theology of Luke this clause is especially significant because of his stress both on Jesus and the Holy Spirit and on joy.

B. *Teachings* (10:25–11:13)

1. *Parable of the Good Samaritan*

10:25–37

25On one occasion an expert in the law stood up to test Jesus. "Teacher," he asked, "what must I do to inherit eternal life?"

26"What is written in the Law?" he replied. "How do you read it?"

27He answered: " 'Love the Lord your God with all your heart and with all your soul and with all your strength and with all your mind'; and, 'Love your neighbor as yourself.' "

28"You have answered correctly," Jesus replied. "Do this and you will live."

29But he wanted to justify himself, so he asked Jesus, "And who is my neighbor?"

30In reply Jesus said: "A man was going down from Jerusalem to Jericho, when he fell into the hands of robbers. They stripped him of his clothes, beat him and went away, leaving him half dead. 31A priest happened to be going down the same road, and when he saw the man, he passed by on the other side. 32So too, a Levite, when he came to the place and saw him, passed by on the other side. 33But a Samaritan, as he traveled, came where the man was; and when he saw him, he took pity on him. 34He went to him and bandaged his wounds, pouring on oil and wine. Then he put the man on his own donkey, took him to an inn and took care of him. 35The next day he took out two silver coins and gave them to the innkeeper. 'Look after him,' he said, 'and when I return, I will reimburse you for any extra expense you may have.'

36"Which of these three do you think was a neighbor to the man who fell into the hands of robbers?"

37The expert in the law replied, "The one who had mercy on him."
Jesus told him, "Go and do likewise."

This parable, unique to Luke, requires the utmost care in its interpretation. It must neither be overallegorized, as it was by the early church fathers, nor reduced to a simplistic meaning hardly worthy of Jesus' teaching. Above all, it must be understood in its context, with attention to the questions of v.25 and v.29 and to Jesus' application in vv.36-37.

The dialogue that precedes the parable in Luke is similar to the one Matthew and Mark locate in Jerusalem (Matt 22:34-40; Mark 12:28-34). It is possible that Luke incorporates the same conversation in this section of Jesus' sayings; but it is equally possible, if not more likely, that the somewhat different wording indicates a different conversation. Questions about achieving eternal life and about the essence of the law were common in Judaism. Totally different conversations follow the recitation of the two commandments in Mark and in Luke.

25 The man's expertise lay in details of the Jewish religion. The fact that he wanted to "test" (*ekpeirazōn*) Jesus may, but does not necessarily, indicate hostility. He addressed Jesus as "teacher" (*didaskalē*). Note his assumption of human responsibility in the attainment of eternal life, and see the similar assumption on the part of the rich ruler in 18:18. "Eternal life" (*zoēn aiōnion*) here means the life of the kingdom (18:18, 24-25, 29; cf. John 3:3, 5, 15-16, 36). This concern regarding life is seen in two stories found in later Jewish tradition in which a rabbi and a merchant respectively ask who desires life. They then quote Psalm 34:12-14 as the means of achieving it (*Abodah Zara* 19b; R Lev 16).

26 Jesus' counterquestion does not constitute an affirmation of the assumption behind the question but directs the questioner back to the law, the commandments of the OT, which are not only his special field but also the ultimate source of religious knowledge. "How do you read it?" invites the expert's personal interpretation.

27 In Luke it is the interlocutor, not Jesus, who quotes the commandment (cf. Matt 22:37-40; Mark 12:29-31). The answer is satisfactory so far as it goes. It is based on the OT (Deut 6:5; Lev 19:18; cf. Rom 13:9). The words "as yourself" will provide the crucial means of evaluating one's love of neighbor. The ultimate evaluation will have to be based on deeds, not words, as the parable shows. It is noteworthy that the command to love one's neighbor is not subordinated to the first commandment as strongly in Luke (where it is joined by the coordinate conjunction "and," *kai*) as it is in Matthew 22:39 and Mark 12:31, where the word "second" (*deutera*) is used. (On the command itself, see V.P. Furnish, *The Love Command in the New Testament* [Nashville and New York: Abingdon, 1972].)

28 Jesus affirms that the man has answered correctly (*orthōs*, "right," "properly," from which our word "orthodox" is derived). This does not mean that the inquirer has grasped the full meaning of the law, nor does it support the idea held by many Pharisees that by keeping the law, as some kind of contract with God, a person can earn eternal life.

29 The only way he (or any person) can "justify himself" is to limit the extent of the law's demand and consequently limit his own responsibility. This maneuver not only fails but has an opposite effect. Jesus will change the man's very words "who is my neighbor?" from a passive to an active sense (v.36).

30 The overallegorization of the parable (vv.30–35) that saw the Samaritan as Christ, the inn as the church, etc., must be rejected. The characters of the story must have the same significance they had to the original hearers. The religious persons act contrary to love, though not contrary to expectation. It is made clear that the priest, at least, is pursuing his religious duty, going "down," i.e., back from Jerusalem (v.31). To an extent, the "Law" (vv.26–27) was being observed, but studious readers will recognize the neglect of mercy (cf. Matt 23:23 and especially the occurrence of "merciful" in Luke 6:36 in place of "perfect" in Matt 5:48). The "rule of three" is fulfilled by the appearance of a third character, but unexpectedly he is not just a layman (in contrast to the clerical characters) but a Samaritan (in contrast to the Jewish victim).

The distance from Jerusalem to Jericho is about seventeen miles, descending sharply toward the Jordan River just north of the Dead Sea. The old road, even more than the present one, curved through rugged, bleak, rocky terrain where robbers could easily hide. It was considered especially dangerous, even in a day when travel was normally full of hazards.

31–32 Priests served in the temple; their highest duty was to offer sacrifices. Levites assisted in the maintenance of the temple services and order. It has been suggested that the priest (v.31) and the Levite (v.32) refrained from helping the man because he appeared to be dead and they feared ritual defilement. Jeremias rejects this explanation on the grounds that (1) ritual purity was only significant when carrying out cultic activities; (2) the priest was going "down" (v.31), i.e., away from Jerusalem, presumably having finished with those duties; (3) the Levite by implication (v.32) was probably also going away from Jerusalem; and (4) when priests and Levites were on their way to serve in the temple, they traveled in groups; but these two were alone and therefore not on their way to Jerusalem (*Parables of Jesus*, pp. 203–4). Also, the point of the story seems to require that the priest and the Levite be without excuse.

33–36 "Took pity" (*esplanchnisthē*) implies a deep feeling of sympathy (v.33), a striking response that stands in contrast, not only to the attitude of the priest and the Levite, but also to the usual feelings of hostility between Jew and Samaritan. This pity is translated into sacrificial action. The Samaritan probably used pieces of his own clothing to make the bandages (v.34); he used his own wine as a disinfectant and his own oil as a soothing lotion (Jeremias, *Parables of Jesus*, p. 204). He put the man on "his own donkey" and paid the innkeeper out of his own pocket (v.35), with a promise to pay more if needed.

The NT parables aim to lead one to a decision; Jesus' second counterquestion (v.36) forces the "expert in the law" to voice his decision. In his question, Jesus does not focus on the object of neighborly love, the Jewish victim, but on the subject, the Samaritan who made himself a neighbor. This reversal of the "expert's" question (v.29) provides in itself the key to the meaning of the parable and to Jesus' teaching on love. Love should not be limited by its object; its extent and quality are in the control of its subject. Furthermore, love is demonstrated in action, in this case in an act of mercy. It may be costly: cloth, wine, oil, transportation, money, and sacrifice of time. There is a striking reversal of roles here. The Jewish "expert" would have thought of the Jewish victim as a good person and the Samaritan as an evil one. To a Jew there was no such person as a "good" Samaritan. Jesus could have told the story with a Samaritan victim and a Jewish helper, but the role reversal drives the story home by shaking the hearer loose from his preconceptions.

37 The "expert" cannot avoid the thrust of the parable, though he apparently finds it impossible to say the word "Samaritan" in his reply. Jesus now refers back to the original question, "What must I do?" by saying, "Go and do likewise." Both this man and the rich ruler of 18:18–25 needed to learn that God does not bestow the life of the kingdom on those who reject the command to love. Such rejection shows that they have not truly recognized how much they need the love of God themselves. In this respect they are identified with Simon the Pharisee rather than with the woman who was forgiven much and therefore loved much (7:36–50).

Notes

30–37 The literature on this parable is extensive. For a summary of various recent works to 1965, see R.W. Funk, "The Old Testament in Parable. A Study of Luke 10:25–37," *Encounter* 26 (1965): 251–67. Since that article was written, much further work has been done, especially using the methodology of structuralism. See, for example, John Dominic Crossan, ed., *Semeia* 2 (1974), which is entirely devoted to this parable.

2. The home of Martha and Mary

10:38–42

[38]As Jesus and his disciples were on their way, he came to a village where a woman named Martha opened her home to him. [39]She had a sister called Mary, who sat at the Lord's feet listening to what he said. [40]But Martha was distracted by all the preparations that had to be made. She came to him and asked, "Lord, don't you care that my sister has left me to do the work by myself? Tell her to help me!"

[41]"Martha, Martha," the Lord answered, "you are worried and upset about many things, [42]but only one thing is needed. Mary has chosen what is better, and it will not be taken away from her."

In 8:1–3 Luke mentioned several women who traveled with Jesus and the disciples and contributed to their support. Now he tells about a woman who entered into discipleship. Once again Luke portrays the way Jesus transcended the prejudices of his day.

38–40 The travel theme appears in v.38 ("on their way"), but Luke refrains from mentioning that the "village" was Bethany (John 11:1). Possibly he wants to reserve mention of Jesus' ministry in Jerusalem and its environs till later (cf. 13:32–33; 17:11; 19:28; cf. comments on 9:51). The way Martha is mentioned seems to give her the role of hostess (cf. John 12:1–2). It is Mary, however, who takes the place of a disciple by sitting at the feet of the teacher (v.39; cf. Acts 22:3—"under Gamaliel," lit., "at his feet"). It is unusual for a woman in first-century Judaism to be accepted by a teacher as a disciple. Notice that Jesus is called "Lord" (*kyrie*) throughout this passage. Martha was "distracted" (v.40), the verb *periespato* implying that her attention was drawn away by the burden of her duties. One can only speculate about the actual feelings she had toward her sister beyond what she said and about the personal differences between Martha and Mary. Martha's concern seems to have been that she had to work alone rather than that she could not sit at Jesus' feet.

41–42 The Lord shows concern for Martha's anxiety (v.41), but the precise meaning of his saying (v.42) is partly obscured because of a textual problem (cf. Notes). There is no explanation of "what is better" (*tēn agathēn merida*, lit., "the good part"). Some have understood this to be the contemplative life, or placing worship over service. Manson (*Sayings of Jesus*, pp. 264–65) thought it was seeking the kingdom first. This interpretation has the merit of explaining Mary's seeming neglect of household duties, which in comparison with the kingdom would have a radically diminishing demand on her. The word of the Lord has first claim. For the disciple an attitude of learning and obedience takes first place. The preceding narrative and parable establish the importance of priorities in the Christian life—i.e., heeding the commands to love God and neighbor. Martha must now learn to give the Lord and his word priority even over loving service. There are important human needs, whether of the victim in vv.30–35 or of Jesus himself. But what is most "needed" goes beyond even these. The thoughtful reader will recognize, however, that this spiritual priority is not the same as the sterile religion of the priest and Levite in vv.31–32.

Notes

42 As the NIV footnote indicates, there is a textual problem here. Of the several variant readings, none has a clear claim to originality. Among these, the most probable choices resolve into (1) "few things are needed," (2) "one thing is needed," and (3) "few things are needed—or only one." NIV has chosen (2) for its text; the UBS text gives it a "C" rating. The NIV footnote has (3). Reading (1) has slim support from the MSS, but Marshall (*Gospel of Luke*, p. 453) thinks it is worth considering because "it is indirectly attested in the good MSS which have the conflate reading" (i.e., the one reflected in the NIV footnote). Also, if "few" means "few dishes of food," Marshall says, "the change from 'few' to 'one' is comprehensible; scribes were perhaps more likely to think that Jesus would give teaching not about practical hospitality but about the one spiritual goal." In any case the basic meaning is clear—Martha's and Mary's priorities are contrasted.

3. *Teaching on prayer*

11:1–13

¹One day Jesus was praying in a certain place. When he finished, one of his disciples said to him, "Lord, teach us to pray, just as John taught his disciples."
²He said to them, "When you pray, say:

" 'Father,
hallowed be your name,
your kingdom come.
³Give us each day our daily bread.

⁴Forgive us our sins,
    for we also forgive everyone who sins against us.
    And lead us not into temptation.' "

⁵Then he said to them, "Suppose one of you has a friend, and he goes to him at midnight and says, 'Friend, lend me three loaves of bread, ⁶because a friend of mine on a journey has come to me, and I have nothing to set before him.'

⁷"Then the one inside answers, 'Don't bother me. The door is already locked, and my children are with me in bed. I can't get up and give you anything.' ⁸I tell you, though he will not get up and give him the bread because he is his friend, yet because of the man's boldness he will get up and give him as much as he needs. needs.

⁹"So I say to you: Ask and it will be given to you; seek and you will find; knock and the door will be opened to you. ¹⁰For everyone who asks receives; he who seeks finds; and to him who knocks, the door will be opened.

¹¹"Which of you fathers, if your son asks for a fish, will give him a snake instead? ¹²Or if he asks for an egg, will give him a scorpion? ¹³If you then, though you are evil, know how to give good gifts to your children, how much more will your Father in heaven give the Holy Spirit to those who ask him!"

The Lord's Prayer in Luke appears in connection with Jesus' own practice and teaching on prayer. Matthew presents the prayer in somewhat different form as part of the Sermon on the Mount (Matt 6:9–13). The prayer fits each context, and the differences indicate separate traditions. It would be difficult to prove that either Matthew or Luke had significantly changed the prayer from the form in which he knew it. The Matthean form is undoubtedly more "liturgical" in that the successive petitions are parallel, are balanced, and in Aramaic may even have rhymed at points. In Matthew 6 the prayer has petitions that may supplement or substitute for some feature of the Jewish prayers of that day. Luke offers a basic prayer to say what is characteristic of Jesus' teaching.

1–4 Once more Luke speaks of Jesus at prayer (cf. 3:21; 6:12; 9:28). His exemplary practice introduces the exemplary prayer. Since prayer inevitably expresses one's theology, the prayers of the Jewish sects in the first century were distinctive. This was true of John the Baptist (v.1). Jesus responds to the request of "one of the disciples" with a model that, while not to be thoughtlessly repeated (Matt 6:7), provides words disciples can use with the confidence that they express Jesus' own teachings. The words "when [or 'whenever,' *hotan*] you pray" (v.2) imply frequent repetition of the actual prayer.

The word "Father" (*patēr*) expresses the essence of Jesus' message and the effect of his atoning work on our relationship with God. Through the use of this intimate but respectful term of address, the Son of God expressed his own unique relationship to God. It is very probable (so TDNT, 1:6) that in every prayer he spoke to God, Jesus used the Aramaic word *Abba* ("dear Father"), which would naturally be translated *pater* in the Greek text. The notable exception is the prayer of dereliction from the cross (Mark 15:34). Through his atoning death on the cross, the Savior brought about reconciliation with God, making it possible for us to become his spiritual children through the new birth. While we cannot use the term *Abba* on an equal basis with the Son of God, there is a sense in which both he and we may address God as "dear Father" (John 20:17; Rom 8:14–17). (For the originality of the simple term *Abba* as a form of direct address to God by Jesus, see Joachim Jeremias, *The Lord's Prayer* [Philadelphia: Fortress, 1964], pp. 17–21.)

The petitions that follow are two kinds—the first two petitions relate to God, the last three to us. "Hallowed be your name" is an ascription of worship basic to all prayer and is found in various forms in the OT (e.g., Ps 111:9) and in ancient Jewish prayers (the *Kaddish* and the Eighteen Benedictions; see also SBK, 1:406–8). "Hallowed" (*hagiasthētō*) means "let [your name] be regarded as holy." It is not so much a petition as an act of worship; the speaker, by his words, exalts the holiness of God. God's people were told in the OT to keep his name holy (Lev 22:32; cf. Ps. 79:9; Isa 29:33). God told Israel that because they failed to honor his name, he would do it himself so the nations would know that he was LORD (Ezek 36:22–23). The aorist tense here suggests that a specific time of fulfillment is in mind. This may be the coming of the kingdom. The next clause, which is about the kingdom, also contains a verb in the aorist tense.

In the *Kaddish* the petition for the exaltation and hallowing of God's name was immediately followed by a request that we might know the rule of God in our lives now. These requests, that the glory and reign of God may be realized soon, are suitable for the Lord's Prayer because Jesus came to announce and bring the kingdom. Though its consummation is still future, in his ministry the kingdom was inaugurated in power. The form of the prayer in Luke lacks these words in Matthew —"your will be done on earth as it is in heaven" (Matt 6:10).

Thus far, apart from the address "Abba" (see above), the wording has been close to what any Jew expecting the kingdom might pray. The three petitions that follow are closely connected with the "Abba" and give a more distinctive character to the prayer as a whole.

The first of the three petitions relating to us is for "bread" (*artos*), representing food in general (v.3). The meaning of *epiousion* (tr. "daily" in NIV) is obscure (cf. Notes), and so the context of the word becomes crucial. If we transliterate it instead of translating it, the petition can be paraphrased in the Greek word order as follows: "Our bread, the daily, keep giving to us each day" (the verb is in the present tense, indicating continuing, daily provision). This contrasts with Matthew 6:11—"Our bread, the daily, give to us today" (the verb is in the aorist tense, indicating a simple act). "Today" in Matthew and "each day" in Luke are in an emphatic position at the end of the clause. Rather than meaning "daily," *epiousion* may mean "for tomorrow." "Tomorrow" may be literally the next day. This would be appropriate if it were an evening prayer. It could also signify the eschatological bread, that is, God's abundant provision at the consummation of the kingdom. Thus the Matthean form is a request for that kind of bread to be given in advance—on this very day. In Luke, however, any gap between present and future (assuming the future meaning of *epiousion*) is bridged by the substitution of the present imperative "keep giving us" and by the words "each day." Thus the petition, as Luke has it, would then be for the provision of this aspect of the future feast in our own lives now.

The word *epiousion* can also have a more general meaning—"sufficient" or "necessary" (cf. E.M. Yamauchi, "The Daily Bread Motif in Antiquity," WTJ 28 [1965–66]: 147–56). This would make a smoother reading than having two terms that mean "daily" ("each day" . . . "daily"). It would also fit Luke's stress on present needs better than "for tomorrow" (if that means the eschaton). To trust God for sufficient food day by day was important to people in Jesus' time who were hired only a day at a time (cf. Matt 20:1–5). When the people of Israel were in the wilderness, they learned to trust God for manna day by day (Exod 16:4; Deut 8:6).

"Forgive us our sins" (*aphes hēmin tas hamartias hēmōn*) uses the aorist tense (v.4), which may refer to a single declaration of forgiveness, when all accounts are settled. More probably, however, it simply describes a petition repeated as needed. The word "sins" is the familiar *hamartia* rather than the Jewish idiom "debts" (*opheilēmata*) in Matthew 6:12. Since the petitioner has called God "Father," he is a believer, already justified and without guilt through the death of Christ. Therefore the forgiveness he must extend to others is not the basis of his salvation but a prerequisite for daily fellowship with the Father in the sense of 1 John 1:5–10. Conversely, one who does not forgive others may actually be revealing that he has not really known God's forgiveness (cf. Luke 7:47).

"Lead us not into temptation [*eis peirasmon*]" does not imply that God might otherwise entice us to do evil. James 1:1–15 rules this out. God does, however, allow his people to be tested as to their faithfulness (see comments on 4:1–12 and the references there to Deut 6–8). The word *peirasmos* here probably means "testing" rather than "temptation" (i.e., to sin), though severe testing may be the occasion for one to sin. Further, there is a coming *peirasmos* that will severely try all those who undergo it, and this petition may have reference to that. In any case, the request is clearly for the Father to keep his children from falling away in the hour of trial, with a possible allusion to the temptation and fidelity of Christ. With this petition the Lord's Prayer comes to a close, lacking, except in a variant (cf. Notes), the additional words in Matthew.

5–6 Jesus' teaching on prayer continues (vv.5–13) with a parable unique to Luke, the meaning of which has been variously assessed.

The scene is that of a Palestinian home in which the family are all asleep in one room—perhaps the only room in the house—and probably all on one mat. The father could not get over to the door and slide back the heavy bolt that bars it without waking up his family. In such a situation no one would be happy to respond, especially in the middle of the night. Nevertheless the man does respond to his friend at the door (v.5), for a reason to be discussed below.

The midnight arrival of the hungry friend (v.6) has usually been thought normal because "journeys were often undertaken by night to avoid the heat of the day" (Marshall, *Gospel of Luke*, p. 464). Bailey (*Poet and Peasant*, p. 121) maintains that, on the contrary, while this is true in desert areas, the elevation of central Palestine and Lebanon and the sea breeze along the coast made travel during the day customary. The night arrival would therefore be unusual. In either case, a host in that first-century society would be expected to provide a welcome. Rather than insult his guest with too little bread (or with a broken loaf, if it was of the large variety of that area), the host would seek out a person with a good supply, knowing who in his small town had recently done baking. The visitor would have been the guest, not only of the individual and his family, but of the whole community. This placed a great responsibility both on the traveler's host and on the friend he approached at midnight (see Bailey on these customs, *Poet and Peasant*, pp. 121ff.).

7–8 The point of the parable depends partly on the context and partly on the meaning of the word *anaideia* (v.8), translated "persistence" (NIV, NASB) or "importunity" (RSV, KJV). If *anaideia* does mean persistence, the parable would seem to teach that if we persist long enough, God will finally answer our prayers. But since the larger context, especially vv.10, 13, as well as the rest of Scripture, teaches God's eagerness to hear and grant our requests, the meaning persistence has little in its favor. Reference is sometimes made to 18:1–8 in support of the persistence theory.

(But see the comment on that passage.) On the other hand, this parable with its reluctant host and persistent visitor may present not a comparison but a contrast to the way God answers prayer. In that case the point would be that if in human circumstances one will respond to a request, even though reluctantly, if pressed hard enough, surely God will answer and do so far more graciously.

Yet another interpretation has been proposed. The word *anaideia* can mean "avoidance of shame" (Bailey, *Poet and Peasant*, pp. 125–33). While it did come to have the meaning of "persistence," the concept of shame was linked with it in the first century. The parable would thus mean that just as the man in bed would respond so as not to incur shame (for having refused the needs of a visitor to his community), so God will always do what is honorable and consistent with his character.

9–10 In threefold poetic form, Jesus teaches that "everyone who asks" (*pas ho aitōn*, v.10)—not only the persistent—will receive from God. This saying of great assurance is preserved here in Luke and also in Matthew 7:7–8.

11–13 The bizarre examples in vv.11–12 reinforce the point that God will respond to our petitions only in kindness. There are two steps in the argument: (1) God is our heavenly Father (v.13) and will do no less for his children than would an earthly father; (2) God is perfect and will do "much more" than sinful man would. The parallel passage in Matthew 7:11 has the general term "good gifts." Luke specifically mentions the Holy Spirit, who was "promised" (Acts 2:33; cf. Luke 24:49; Acts 1:4).

Notes

2–4 Helpful works on the Lord's Prayer include J. Carmignac, *Recherches sur le "Notre Père"* (Paris: Letouzey & Ané, 1969), R.A. Guelich, *The Sermon on the Mount* (Waco: Word, 1982), pp. 283–97, 307–20; A. Hamman, *Prayer in the N.T.* (Chicago: Franciscan Herald Press, 1971), pp. 103–45; J. Jeremias, "The Lord's Prayer in Modern Research," *Exp. T.* 71 (1960), 141–46; J. Jeremias, *The Prayers of Jesus* (Philadelphia: Fortress, 1978); W.L. Liefeld, "The Lord's Prayer," in ISBE (rev. ed., forthcoming); T.W. Manson, "The Lord's Prayer," *Bull. John Rylands Lib.* 38 (1955–56), 99–113; C.F.D. Moule, "An Unresolved Problem in the Temptation-Clause in the Lord's Prayer," *Ref. Theol. Rev.* 33 (1974), 65–75; J.J. Petuchowski and M. Brocke, *The Lord's Prayer and Jewish Liturgy* (New York: Seabury, 1978); E.M. Yamauchi, "The Daily Bread Motif in Antiquity," WTJ 28 (1965–66), 145–56.

3 Ἐπιούσιον (*epiousion*, "daily") may be derived from a combination of ἐπί (*epi*) used as a preposition or as a prefix with εἰμι (*eimi*, "to be," "to exist") or with εἰμι (*eimi*, with a circumflex accent, "to come," "to go"). Thus it could refer to present or to future time (the latter usage being common in Jesus' time), including the presence of something needed at the moment.

5–6 Jeremias thinks that as Jesus originally told it, the parable was addressed not to the visitor but to the man in bed. The words translated "suppose one of you" (τίς ἐξ ὑμῶν, *tis ex hymōn*, lit., "who [or 'which'] of you?") imply "surely none of you would do what I am going to describe" (cf. Jeremias, *Parables of Jesus*, pp. 157ff.). But though the immediate transition to the third person "he" in v.5 makes for some ambiguity, the hearer of the parable is not to imagine himself as the man in bed but as the visitor.

155

Bailey (*Poet and Peasant,* pp. 124–25) cites as a close parallel Luke 17:7, which he thinks helpful in determining the understood subject of the verb πορεύσεται (*poreusetai,* "goes") here in v.5. If the parallel holds, the hypothetical person ("one of you") is the one who "goes" rather than the friend going to him. Thus the hearer identifies himself with the visitor, who, according to Bailey's interpretation, receives the bread not because of his own persistence but because the man in bed does not want to incur shame.

C. *Growing Opposition* (11:14–54)

1. *Jesus and Beelzebub*

11:14–28

> [14]Jesus was driving out a demon that was mute. When the demon left, the man who had been mute spoke, and the crowd was amazed. [15]But some of them said, "By Beelzebub, the prince of demons, he is driving out demons." [16]Others tested him by asking for a sign from heaven.
>
> [17]Jesus knew their thoughts and said to them: "Any kingdom divided against itself will be ruined, and a house divided against itself will fall. [18]If Satan is divided against himself, how can his kingdom stand? I say this because you claim that I drive out demons by Beelzebub. [19]Now if I drive out demons by Beelzebub, by whom do your followers drive them out? So then, they will be your judges. [20]But if I drive out demons by the finger of God, then the kingdom of God has come to you.
>
> [21]"When a strong man, fully armed, guards his own house, his possessions are safe. [22]But when someone stronger attacks and overpowers him, he takes away the armor in which the man trusted and divides up the spoils.
>
> [23]"He who is not with me is against me, and he who does not gather with me, scatters.
>
> [24]"When an evil spirit comes out of a man, it goes through arid places seeking rest and does not find it. Then it says, 'I will return to the house I left.' [25]When it arrives, it finds the house swept clean and put in order. [26]Then it goes and takes seven other spirits more wicked than itself, and they go in and live there. And the final condition of that man is worse than the first."
>
> [27]As Jesus was saying these things, a woman in the crowd called out, "Blessed is the mother who gave you birth and nursed you."
>
> [28]He replied, "Blessed rather are those who hear the word of God and obey it."

This event shows the real nature of the increasing opposition Jesus faced. Mark and Matthew also include it, but in different contexts. Mark follows it with the parable of the sower, which illustrates the varying responses to Jesus' teaching (Mark 3:20–4:20). Matthew (like Luke) follows it with Jesus' comments on the sign of Jonah but then (unlike Luke) has the parable of the sower, followed by the so-called parables of the kingdom, which also show the contrast between good and evil (Matt 12:22–13:52). In Luke the Beelzebub controversy leads to the sign of Jonah (as in Matthew) and then on to the woes against the unbelieving religious leaders. Each of the other Synoptics also includes a comment regarding Jesus' mother together with a statement that obedience to God's word is more important than even the closest human ties to Jesus.

Whether the arrangement is due to each evangelist's plan or to the order of events in his source, every occurrence of the Beelzebub incident in the Synoptics comes at a crucial point in the narrative. The incident shows that Jesus' hearers must choose between good (Jesus, the Spirit, and God's kingdom) and evil (Satan and his demons).

The issue is nothing less than the source of Jesus' authority and power. This is especially important for Luke, who is deeply aware of the importance of the supernatural as a testimony that Jesus is the promised Messiah (cf. the apostolic testimony he records in Acts 2:22, 43; 4:30; 5:12; 10:38, as well as the miracles in the Gospel itself). The climax of the passage comes in v.20, which, as we shall see, links the display of God's power in the Exodus and the same potential power in the kingdom of God with Jesus' successful attack on the kingdom of Satan. Although Luke continues this theme in vv.21–26, he postpones the issue of blasphemy against the Holy Spirit (located at this point in Matthew and Mark) until 12:19. This may have been the order in his source for this passage.

14–16 The setting of this account of the Beelzebub controversy is the healing (v.14) of a deaf mute (*kōphos*). Such a healing was among the signs of his messiahship that Jesus reminded John the Baptist of (7:22). Once more, as in 4:36 and elsewhere, the crowds are amazed at Jesus' power over demons. The crowd is divided, however, between those who either opposed him outrightly by attributing his power to the head demon, "Beelzebub" (v.15; cf. Notes), or taunted him to give them an even more dramatic sign, which constitutes a "testing" or provocation (v.16).

17–20 Jesus "knew their thoughts" (v.17; cf. 5:22; 7:39–47). The identification of Beelzebub with Satan (v.18) is the basis of vv.17–19. The head of any army would hardly work with the enemy against his own troops. Moreover, if demons are exorcised by the power of their own leader, how do the Jews explain the power their own exorcists (v.19; cf. Acts 19:13–14) are supposed to have? Jesus' illustration shows the drastic antithesis between the powers of evil, darkness, and Satan on the one hand and the power of God the Holy Spirit and the kingdom of light (cf. Col 1:12–13) on the other hand. When the magicians in Egypt were unable to duplicate all the miracles Moses did before the Exodus, they said to Pharaoh, "This is the finger of God" (Exod 8:19). So here Jesus is affirming that the source of his power is "the finger of God" (v.20), i.e., God himself, a statement Matthew specifically identifies with the Holy Spirit (Matt 12:28). If this is true, then Jesus' driving out demons is a messianic sign and "the kingdom of God has come" (cf. Notes).

21–23 Here the imagery is more vivid than in Matthew and Mark, for the strong man (v.21) guards his own house. Jesus' victory against Satan during his temptation may be alluded to here (v.22). In any event, we have in these verses a principal reference to Jesus' tactics in his war against Satan. The ultimate and actual means of Jesus' victory is the Cross. The critical place in Jesus' ministry of his victory over Satan means that we also must take a stand for or against Jesus as the one who brings the kingdom (v.23). Whoever does not "gather" (*synagōn*) the sheep "scatters" (*skorpizei*) them by default and thus works counter to Jesus (so Marshall, *Gospel of Luke*, p. 478). In John 10:11–13, the hired hand neglects his duty and the wolf "scatters" (*skorpizei*) the flock.

24–26 "Evil spirit" (*akatharton pneuma*) is a Jewish term for a demon (v.24). Luke does not say that the demon has been exorcized. When it is, the Holy Spirit in the power of the kingdom will accomplish that work and will indwell the person who has been possessed. In vv.24–26 a spiritual renewal has taken place, but without the indwelling Spirit. Marshall (*Gospel of Luke*, p. 479) suggests that this refers to the work of the Jewish exorcists mentioned in v.19. The evil spirit wanders through the "arid places" (v.24), a description in accord with the popular idea that demons inhabited the desert (cf. the accusation that John the Baptist, who lived in the desert, had a demon [7:33]). Some see Isaiah 13:21; 34:14 as a source for this idea. The demon seeks a human body and, in order to repossess its previous abode, enlists the aid of seven demons even worse than itself (v.26). This combination of seven plus one is reminiscent of the same grouping of spirits in the *Testament of Reuben*, 2 and 3. Contrast the "seven spirits" before the throne (Rev 1:4). The demons "live" (*katoikei*, lit., "settle down") there. The same verb is used in Ephesians 3:17 of Christ's full indwelling. The parallel in Matthew 12:43–45 applies the demons' settling down directly to "this wicked generation" and thus suggests that those who repented on hearing the initial proclamation of the kingdom through John the Baptist but failed to allow Jesus to bring the power of the kingdom into their lives were the ones who were worse off than formerly.

27–28 This saying (v.27) is unique to Luke and provides another instance of his identification of Jesus' sayings (v.28) as the "word of God." It must not be taken as reflecting unfavorably on Mary.

Notes

15 "Beelzebub" is a difficult name to analyze. It has been compared to a similar sounding word meaning "Lord of the Flies." There are several variants of the name. "Beelzebub" (NIV) has come down through the Latin MS tradition. The form "Beelzeboul" (NIV mg.) is the most common one in the Greek MSS—Βεελζεβοὺλ (*Beelzeboul*). Among the various etymologies suggested is that which incorporated a Hebrew word for a dwelling, זְבֻל (*zᵉbul*), which was used in Jesus' day to refer to the temple (L. Gaston, "Beelzebul," *Theologische Zeitschrift* [1962]: 247–55). This would have been a parody of the one who was truly "head of the house" (Matt 10:25).

Whatever its etymology, the significance of the name is clear. The wording in v.18 suggests that Beelzeboul was another name for Satan. That Beelzeboul was more than an ephithet formed for the occasion is not certain. But Jesus' response points to a known and sinister figure. It is possible, though unlikely, that this "prince of demons" (v.15) is to be understood as an inferior being representing Satan's cause (cf. ZPEB, 1:505).

20 In ἔφθασεν ἐφ᾽ ὑμᾶς (*ephthasen eph᾽ hymas*, "has come to you"), we have what is perhaps the strongest single affirmation in the Gospels of the presence of the kingdom. While ἐγγίζω (*engizō*, "approach," "draw near") implies imminent arrival (e.g., in Mark 1:15), the verb here, from φθάνω (*phthanō*), can mean not only to "arrive" but even, in the proper context, to "precede," as in 1 Thess 4:15. The prepositional phrase *eph᾽ hymas* secures the meaning that the kingdom was actually there. See G.E. Ladd, *Theology of the New Testament*, pp. 65–68, for a discussion of the presence of the kingdom, centering on the parallel passage in Matt 12:28.

2. The sign of Jonah

11:29-32

29As the crowds increased, Jesus said, This is a wicked generation. It asks for a miraculous sign, but none will be given it except the sign of Jonah. 30For as Jonah was a sign to the Ninevites, so also will the Son of Man be to this generation. 31The Queen of the South will rise at the judgment with the men of this generation and condemn them; for she came from the ends of the earth to listen to Solomon's wisdom, and now one greater than Solomon is here. 32The men of Nineveh will stand up at the judgment with this generation and condemn it; for they repented at the preaching of Jonah, and now one greater than Jonah is here.

This passage gives us Jesus' response to those who were prodding him for a "sign [sēmeion] from heaven" (v.16). The Gospel of John builds on the premise that Jesus performed miracles as signs (sēmeia). The present passage does not stand in opposition to the meaningful use of signs but rather to the unbelief that resists the testimony already obvious in the messianic works (cf. v.14 above). The Synoptics oppose an inordinate demand for extraordinary miracles beyond those needed for a witness to Jesus' authority. An even stronger statement, though not incompatible with this, occurs in Mark 8:12.

29-30 The transitional phrase "as the crowds increased" (v.29) encourages the reader to understand this comment on "sign" in terms of the previous passage, especially v.16. Only Luke has the phrase, just as only Luke has the reference to a sign in v.16. The "sign" of Jonah is Jonah himself, whose presence and brief message (cf. v.32, kērygma, NIV, "preaching"), though far minimal compared with the preaching of Jesus, triggered immediate and widespread repentance. Matthew 12:40 adds a reference to Jonah's experience in the huge fish as pointing to the duration of Jesus' entombment. This is not mentioned in Luke, and Marshall's attempt (Gospel of Luke, p. 483) to introduce it here may be unnecessary. For Luke the preaching of Jesus—viz., his "word"—carried its authority, especially when affirmed by the power of God in miracles (e.g., 4:32, 36). This does not mean that Jesus' resurrection as a parallel to Jonah's delivery from the fish was not the ultimate sign—only that Luke did not have that part of the tradition.

31-32 The inclusion of the "Queen of the South" (the queen of Sheba) fortifies the judgment on Jesus' generation, because she traveled a great distance to hear the wisdom of Solomon (v.31). A double contrast is implied in these two examples: (1) the response of the audience, (2) the greatness of the preacher. The "one greater" (v.32) than Solomon and Jonah is, of course, Jesus, unless one interprets the neuter form of the word "greater" (pleion) to cover the whole mission of Jesus or perhaps the kingdom (though the latter would call for the feminine form).

Notes

29 On the meaning of σημεῖον (sēmeion, "sign") in Scripture, see Rengstorf, TDNT, 7:200–261 (esp. pp. 233–34 on Jonah); Hofius and Brown, DNTT, 2:626–33 (p. 630 on Jonah).

Hofius takes the sign of Jonah to be the Parousia of the Son of Man; cf. Colpe, TDNT, 8:449–50. Colpe holds that while this would be significant with respect to judgment, it comes too late to validate Jesus' ministry. But in Luke, where the emphasis on judgment is without explicit reference to Jesus' resurrection (cf. Matt 12:40), this would not be as much of a problem and does not require, as clearly as Matthew does, a sign that was observable during Jesus' ministry apart from the very preaching of the word itself. On the tradition-history of the Jonah and sign passages, R.A. Edwards has a major work, *The Sign of Jonah in the Theology of the Evangelists and Q*, SBT, 2d series 18 (Naperville, Ill.: Allenson, 1971). Edwards attributes not only the form of the saying but also its christology to the early church rather than to Jesus.

3. The lamp of the body

11:33–36

33"No one lights a lamp and puts it in a place where it will be hidden, or under a bowl. Instead he puts it on its stand, so that those who come in may see the light. 34Your eye is the lamp of your body. When your eyes are good, your whole body also is full of light. But when they are bad, your body also is full of darkness. 35See to it, then, that the light within you is not darkness. 36Therefore, if your whole body is full of light, and no part of it dark, it will be completely lighted, as when the light of a lamp shines on you."

33 Hearing Jesus' message lays a responsibility on the hearer. The metaphors of light, signs, and judgment (cf. vv.29–32) are akin to what we have in John (e.g., 3:19–21; 9:39–41) and elsewhere in the NT (e.g., Acts 26:18; 2 Cor 6:14–15; Eph 5:5–14). Much of this passage is paralleled in Matthew 6:22–23. There the Jewish concept of the bad eye symbolizing covetousness provides a link with the preceding saying about treasures. In the Lukan context there is no reference to possessions.

34–35 "Good eyes" (cf. Notes) admit light (v.34); bad ones do not. The implication is that the individual is responsible for receiving light. The eye is thus a "lamp" (*lychnos*), not in the sense that it emits light, but that through it (subject to the individual's will) the body receives light. The real source of light is outside the body; if we think we can generate our own light, we must beware lest that inner "light" prove to be darkness (v.35).

36 This seemingly repetitive verse resembles in its repetitiveness and its subject Ephesians 5:13–14a. Its meaning becomes clear in the light of vv.34–35. The body is only completely lighted when a lamp shines on it from the outside. The repetition of two Greek words is chiastic (in reverse order): *holon phōteinon* ("whole body is full of light") and *phōteinon holon* ("completely lighted"). The concluding *holon* is emphatic. The words are repeated to introduce an analogy that describes how the body is fully lighted: "As when [*hōs hotan*] the light of a lamp shines on you." Taking vv.34–36 together, we learn that full illumination only comes when one is willing to receive light from the lamp of God's truth.

Notes

34 The word ἁπλοῦς (*haplous*, "healthy," "sound") can have the idea of "sincere" or "gener ous" (e.g., in Matt 6:22, where, as noted above, the matter of possessions has been discussed). Here it means eyes that see clearly and do not deliberately obscure reality, so NIV's "are good."

4. Six woes

11:37–54

37When Jesus had finished speaking, a Pharisee invited him to eat with him; so he went in and reclined at the table. 38But the Pharisee, noticing that Jesus did not first wash before the meal, was surprised.

39Then the Lord said to him, "Now then, you Pharisees clean the outside of the cup and dish, but inside you are full of greed and wickedness. 40You foolish people! Did not the one who made the outside make the inside also? 41But give what is inside ⸤the dish⸥ to the poor, and everything will be clean for you.

42"Woe to you Pharisees, because you give God a tenth of your mint, rue and all other kinds of garden herbs, but you neglect justice and the love of God. You should have practiced the latter without leaving the former undone.

43"Woe to you Pharisees, because you love the most important seats in the synagogues and greetings in the marketplaces.

44"Woe to you, because you are like unmarked graves, which men walk over without knowing it."

45One of the experts in the law answered him, "Teacher, when you say these things, you insult us also."

46Jesus replied, "And you experts in the law, woe to you, because you load people down with burdens they can hardly carry, and you yourselves will not lift one finger to help them.

47"Woe to you, because you build tombs for the prophets, and it was your forefathers who killed them. 48So you testify that you approve of what your forefathers did; they killed the prophets, and you build their tombs. 49Because of this, God in his wisdom said, 'I will send them prophets and apostles, some of whom they will kill and others they will persecute.' 50Therefore this generation will be held responsible for the blood of all the prophets that has been shed since the beginning of the world, 51from the blood of Abel to the blood of Zechariah, who was killed between the altar and the sanctuary. Yes, I tell you, this generation will be held responsible for it all.

52"Woe to you experts in the law, because you have taken away the key to knowledge. You yourselves have not entered, and you have hindered those who were entering."

53When Jesus left there, the Pharisees and the teachers of the law began to oppose him fiercely and to besiege him with questions, 54waiting to catch him in something he might say.

37–38 In a way typical of his use of material, Luke puts the major discourse in the setting of a dinner (v.37; cf. 14:1–24) Jesus himself attended (cf. the similar discourses in Matt 15:1–20; 23:1–36; Mark 7:1–22). Having accepted table fellowship with a Pharisee, Jesus offended his host, a proponent of ritual separation, by omitting the customary ritual washing prior to eating (v.38). Luke's introduction lacks the details about Jewish customs found in Mark 7:1–4. The reference to Isaiah 29:13 in Mark and in the similar passage in Matthew 15:1–9 is also lacking; and the comments in vv.39–54 have their parallel, not in Mark 7 and Matthew 15, but in Matthew 23:1–36, where the order is different and the comments on each indictment fuller. Luke gives us a concise selection of indictments. These point up some of the most common of the sins that characterize strict religious persons ("churchmen," as Ellis, *Gospel of Luke*, pp. 168f., calls them). These include hypocrisy (vv.39–41), imbalance (v.42), ostentation (v.43), impossible demands (v.46), intolerance (vv.47–51), and exclusiveness (v.52).

39–44 The "Pharisees" (v.39), originally a group of laymen who sought to be separate from impure things and people and attempted to apply Mosaic law to all parts of life, had, for the most part, by the time of Jesus lost the heart of their religion. In vv.41–42b Jesus offered a positive corrective that clearly shows he did not oppose strict attention to religious duties but rather the neglect of caring about people that strict religionists often fall into. This is consistent with his teaching in 6:27–36 and 10:25–37. Seen merely from the religious point of view, to wash externally was in reality only a halfway measure. Moreover, vv.39–41 imply that in their "greed and wickedness" (v.39) the Pharisees had deprived the poor of the very food and drink that were "inside" (v.40) their own carefully washed dishes. Alternatively, "inside" also refers to their inner moral life ("you are full," v.39). Likewise (v.42) they apparently were tithing possessions that they should have shared with (or that rightfully belonged to) the needy. Marshall (*Gospel of Luke*, p. 498) remarks that though it might seem inconsistent that Jesus, while not practicing ritual washing, commended meticulous tithing, tithing was an OT principle. The vivid simile in v.44 is an example of Jesus' use of irony. Though the Pharisees avoided touching a grave for fear of ritual defilement, they themselves, through their own unrecognized corruption, were defiling those who came into contact with them. In Matthew 23:27 the figure is that of whitewashed tombs.

45–46 These verses are directed against the "experts in the law" (v.45). Many of them were Pharisees, and they were often mentioned together. Yet they were distinct groups, and Jesus addressed them separately. Their religious legalism explains v.46. They could interpret the OT and the traditions built on it in such a way as to leave little room for personal moral decisions. As "experts," they could, of course, find ways of circumventing the rules themselves.

47–48 Some lavish tombs were built for royalty and others before and during the time of Christ. It was all very well for the experts in the law to build new tombs for prophets long since martyred by the experts' forefathers (v.47). Yet this very act ironically symbolized approval of their forefathers' crimes against God's messengers (v.48; cf. the longer version of this saying in Matt 23:29–32).

J.D.M. Derrett (" 'You Build the Tombs of the Prophets' [Luke 11:47–51, Matt 23:29–31]," *Studia Evangelica* 4 [1968]:187–93) suggests that the building of tombs was a way of acknowledging guilt analogous to the offering of blood money to a victim's survivors by a relative of one guilty of murder.

49–51 These verses relate the grim truth behind the parable of the tenants (20:9–19). (See Notes on "wisdom" [v.49] and on "Zechariah" [v.51].)

52–54 Jesus directed his final woe against the experts in the law at their sin of taking away not just physical but eternal life. Those who should have opened the meaning of the OT with their "key" not only declined to use it themselves but prevented others from "entering" (v.52). (The present participle *eiserchomenous* may be conative: "trying to enter.") The implied subject of "knowledge" is probably the kingdom of God, which people were seeking to "enter." The connection of "keys" with the "kingdom" in Matthew 16:19 comes to mind here. Jesus charged the experts in the law with dereliction of their most important duty. His series of woes made the violent hostility against him described in vv.53–54 inevitable. His opponents followed him out of the house and fired at him a barrage of difficult questions (v.53), such as those later used to embarrass rabbinic scholars. He had challenged those who professed to be the expert biblical teachers. They were out to defend their reputation by discrediting his (v.54).

Notes

42 In its wild state, πήγανον (*pēganon*, "rue") was exempt from tithing. But Luke is referring to kitchen herbs among which cultivated rue was subject to tithing (D. Correns, "Die Verzehntung der Raute. Lk xi, 42 and M Schebi ix," 1 NovTest 6 [1963]: 110–12).
49 NIV translates ἡ σοφία τοῦ θεοῦ εἶπεν (*hē sophia tou theou eipen*, lit., "the wisdom of God said") as "God in his wisdom said." This interpretation is one way to understand this unusual introduction to a quotation that has no known source in the OT. Some think it is from an apocryphal source. Ellis (*Gospel of Luke*, pp. 170–73) takes it as referring to NT prophets bringing new revelations from the risen Christ. It may embody the essence of several OT passages. Many of the prophets God sent were opposed and even persecuted (e.g., 1 Kings 19:10, 14; Jer 7:25–26; Mal 3:10). The apostles were likewise "sent" on a mission that may be described as prophetic (Luke 6:22–23). Thus the saying applies all that God said "in his wisdom" in the OT to the NT apostles and prophets. Each of the above attempts to understand this difficult saying is plausible, and others could be cited. It is not clear whether there is an allusion to wisdom in its technical sense in Proverbs and other Jewish writings known as wisdom literature. There is no apparent reason for such an allusion, but it is otherwise difficult to explain why wisdom is introduced at all here, since nothing in the saying has a unique "wisdom" characteristic. It may simply refer to the sovereign wisdom of God in allowing evil men to continue and the good (here the prophets) to suffer.
51 Bloodguiltiness is emphasized here by the specific mention of Abel (Gen 4:8–10) and of a "Zechariah" (Matt 23:35—"Zechariah the son of Berakiah"), whose identity is much disputed. Some consider him to be a man, whose father's name was similar to that in Matthew, who was killed in the temple precincts in A.D. 67–68. This assumes that the saying either did not originate in the time of Jesus' earthly ministry or was expanded later. Marshall (*Gospel of Luke*, p. 506) argues that without any reference to Jesus as a martyr-prophet, or to the apostles, the saying cannot be classified as a Christian addition.

It is more common to identify "Zechariah" with the person mentioned in 2 Chron 24:20–25. Not only was that Zechariah murdered in the temple precincts, but the account follows a description similar to those mentioned above, of the prophets whom God "sent" who were resisted (2 Chron 24:19). J. Barton Payne ("Zechariah Who Perished," *Grace Journal* 8 [1967]: 33–35) points out, however, that the murder must have been done in the inner court (1 Kings 6:36; 2 Chron 4:9), in contrast to the location mentioned in 2 Chron 24:20–25; that Jesus is speaking of prophets, a term recalling the minor prophet Zechariah rather than the son of Jehoida the priest; that Jewish tradition favors the prophet; and that taking Josephus's order of the canon, Jesus' placing of Zechariah as last in a series could well refer to the canonical order rather than a chronological order. Further, Matthew adds the detail that the victim was the son of Berakiah, which accords with Zech 1:1. The problem is more vexing for interpreters of Matthew; Luke's version lacks the reference to Berakiah; so neither of the two biblical Zechariahs mentioned above is excluded.

52 Τὴν κλεῖδα τῆς γνώσεως (tēn kleida tēs gnōseōs, "the key to knowledge") could also be understood as an appositive: "the key that is knowledge." The parallel (Matt 23:13) has "you shut [or 'lock up' (κλείετε, kleiete)] the kingdom of heaven." The construction τὰς κλεῖδας τῆς βασιλείας (tas kleidas tēs basileias, "the keys of the kingdom") in Matt 16:19 is grammatically close enough to suggest that NIV's "key to knowledge" is preferable here in Luke 11:52.

53–54 "To besiege him with questions" is perhaps the best translation of ἀποστοματίζειν (apostomatizein), but its meaning is hard to determine. It seems to have connoted "mouthing" something one was supposed to learn and repeat. Here it could have the sense of pressing a series of questions to which certain "correct" answers must be given or the subject is considered heretical. Questions were sometimes used in rabbinic circles of the first centuries of our era to demonstrate one's own superiority over another (a possible clue to the meaning of 1 Cor 14:34–35). But the meaning is not at all certain. BAG (s.v.) says, "Ancient commentators interpreted it (prob. correctly) as *catch* (him) *in someth.* he says = vs. 54; then approx. *watch his utterances closely*" (*emphasis theirs*). The uncertainty led to changes in the Western text. Our problem probably comes from not knowing the development of an idiomatic use that may have had a brief lifespan.

D. Teachings on Times of Crisis and Judgment (12:1–13:35)

1. Warnings and encouragements

12:1–12

¹Meanwhile, when a crowd of many thousands had gathered, so that they were trampling on one another, Jesus began to speak first to his disciples, saying: "Be on your guard against the yeast of the Pharisees, which is hypocrisy. ²There is nothing concealed that will not be disclosed, or hidden that will not be made known. ³What you have said in the dark will be heard in the daylight, and what you have whispered in the ear in the inner rooms will be proclaimed from the roofs.

⁴"I tell you, my friends, do not be afraid of those who kill the body and after that can do no more. ⁵But I will show you whom you should fear: Fear him who, after the killing of the body, has power to throw you into hell. Yes, I tell you, fear him. ⁶Are not five sparrows sold for two pennies? Yet not one of them is forgotten by God. ⁷Indeed, the very hairs of your head are all numbered. Don't be afraid; you are worth more than many sparrows.

⁸"I tell you, whoever acknowledges me before men, the Son of Man will also acknowledge him before the angels of God. ⁹But he who disowns me before men will be disowned before the angels of God. ¹⁰And everyone who speaks a word against the Son of Man will be forgiven, but anyone who blasphemes against the Holy Spirit will not be forgiven.

¹¹"When you are brought before synagogues, rulers and authorities, do not worry about how you will defend yourselves or what you will say, ¹²for the Holy Spirit will teach you at that time what you should say."

The crisis in Jesus' relationship with the teachers of the law at the end of chapter 11 gives rise to a series of strong statements about the eternal issues involved. Jesus' audience must choose sides. He gives promises and warnings, appropriate to each hearer's circumstance. Much of these exhortations is also found in Matthew's account of Jesus' instructions to the Twelve (Matt 10:19, 20, 26–33). Similar ideas occur in the Olivet Discourse (Luke 21:12–19 and parallels). These other passages suggest an application not only to Jesus' immediate audience but also to the future church with its martyr missionaries.

1–3 "Meanwhile" (*en hois*, v.1) specifically connects this section with the preceding one. Again Luke notes the crowds, emphasizing the size of this one by the word "thousands" (*myriadōn*, lit., "of tens of thousands"—viz., an extremely large crowd). The same word in Acts 21:20 designates the great number of Jewish people who were believers, presumably far more than the few thousand mentioned at the beginning of Acts (e.g., 2:41, 47). Jesus addresses the disciples "first" (*prōton*, in an emphatic position). The crowds received his words later (vv.54–59). The key word "hypocrisy" (*hypokrisis*) was triggered by the charges in chapter 11. Jesus compares the insidious way this attitude can influence others to the action of "yeast" (*zymēs*). His next words about concealment and disclosure seem at first to be a warning that what hypocrites try to cover up will be revealed (v.2). But vv.3–4 have a positive thrust. Verse 3 is much like Matthew 10:26–27, where the disciples are encouraged not to be afraid but to declare publicly what they have heard privately from Jesus. This sense also fits the similar saying in the context of the parables of the kingdom (Mark 4:22; Luke 8:17). The idea of disclosure is linked to that of acknowledgment in v.8.

4–7 "Friends" (*philois*) is an expression of confidence (John 15:14–15) and is antithetical to the hostility of the Pharisees (v.4). Jesus does not guarantee protection from death but affirms that (1) God alone controls the final destiny of men, and people should "fear" (*phobēthēte*) him rather than those who can merely inflict physical death (v.5); and (2) God is intimately aware of all that befalls us. "Hell" (*geenna*) is mentioned only here in Luke but several times in Matthew and Mark, where it is clearly a place of torment ("the fire of," Matt 5:22; cf. Matt 18:8–9; Mark 9:43–48).

Geenna is a Greek transliteration of the Hebrew words for "Valley of Hinnom" (*ge hinnōm*), a ravine to the south and southwest of Jerusalem. Because it had been used for infant sacrifices (2 Chron 28:3; 33:6), it was repulsive to the Jews. Josiah attempted to prevent its use in this way (2 Kings 23:10), but apparently its reputation continued. Jeremiah labels it as a place of future judgment (Jer 7:32; 19:6). The idea of a place, of which this valley was an analogy, for punishment after death was developed in the intertestamental period. Jesus taught the reality of hell unambiguously.

Sparrows (v.6) and hairs (v.7) are so insignificant that this kind of argument (from lesser to greater) has a great effect in pointing up the supreme worth of the disciples in God's eyes.

8–9 Jesus underscores the seriousness of the issues by referring to the ultimate issue—whether or not one sides with him (v.8). Although he has already given the substance of this warning in his first passion prediction (9:26 and parallels), the cruciality of the present situation called for its restatement. The reference to "the Son of Man" in the third person has led some to think that Jesus is referring to a

165

coming figure other than himself. But this would make Jesus a personage inferior to him. In point of fact, however, the third-person usage is consistent with Jesus' guarded use of titles. Not until his trial does he publicly combine the terms "Son of Man," "Son of God," and "Messiah" in an eschatological context. "Acknowledge" (*homolgēsei*) and "disown" (*arnēsetai*) are semantic polar opposites (KJV and NASB: "confess" and "deny"). The reference is apparently to a future scene when the Lord Jesus, having achieved victory and honor, acknowledges those who supported him and disowns (v.9) those who repudiated him during the present age. He does this publicly before God the Father (Matt 10:32–33) and the assembled angels.

10 The final one of this progression of warnings relates to the "unpardonable sin." The context of this saying in Luke differs from that of Matthew and Mark and the saying itself is separate from the Beelzebub controversy. This separation not only raises questions of tradition history beyond the scope of this commentary but also makes exegesis of the passage difficult. The separation does allow for the continued buildup of hostility between Jesus and the teachers of the law and for the sequence of warnings in 12:1–9, so that it occupies a climactic place. Nevertheless, it is difficult to determine its meaning without the contextual explanations in Matthew and Mark.

Matthew 12:33–36 and Mark 3:30 make it clear that the blasphemy against the Holy Spirit is the attribution of the works of Jesus to the very prince of demons. Moreover, this oral blasphemy involves not merely careless words but the expression of an incorrigibly evil heart. This background must be kept in mind as an aid to the theological application of Luke's reference to the unpardonable sin. If dishonoring the Son of Man is such a serious matter as vv.8–9 indicate, then total rejection of God by insinuating that his "Holy" Spirit is "evil" is so much the worse. One may reject Christ and later, by God's grace, accept him; but there is no remedy for absolute and complete denial of the one holy God—Father, Son, and Holy Spirit. This is what the "blasphemy" seems to be here. Some would relate this to Hebrews 6:4–6; 10:26–31 and to apostasy, but the Scriptures lack a sufficient interconnection to make this clear. The same caution should be applied to any attempt to connect this sin with the "sin that leads to death" (1 John 5:16–17).

11–12 The foregoing series of warnings and encouragements conclude with this striking contrast to the blasphemy against the Holy Spirit. Far from committing that sin of speaking against him, the believers find that the Spirit speaks through them. Observe the comparison with the mission of the Twelve and with the Olivet Discourse, especially in Matthew 10:19–20 and Luke 21:14–15. The circumstance of the Spirit's speaking through believers is not preaching but persecution, in which preparation of an adequate defense is hardly possible.

2. Parable of the rich fool

12:13–21

> ¹³Someone in the crowd said to him, "Teacher, tell my brother to divide the inheritance with me."
> ¹⁴Jesus replied, "Man, who appointed me a judge or an arbiter between you?"
> ¹⁵Then he said to them, "Watch out! Be on your guard against all kinds of greed; a man's life does not consist in the abundance of his possessions."
> ¹⁶And he told them this parable: "The ground of a certain rich man produced a

good crop. [17]He thought to himself, 'What shall I do? I have no place to store my crops.'

[18] Then he said, 'This is what I'll do. I will tear down my barns and build bigger ones, and there I will store all my grain and my goods. [19]And I'll say to myself, "You have plenty of good things laid up for many years. Take life easy; eat, drink and be merry." '

[20]"But God said to him, 'You fool! This very night your life will be demanded from you. Then who will get what you have prepared for yourself?'

[21]"This is how it will be with anyone who stores up things for himself but is not rich toward God."

Although the narrative flows smoothly, with the word "crowd" (v.13) making the transition from vv.1–12, the change in topic seems abrupt. A comparison with chapter 16 shows a similar placement of controversy with Pharisees alongside teaching about worldly wealth. There the words "the Pharisees, who loved money" (v.14) serve to link the two subjects. Chapters 12 and 16 have much in common. If Talbert (*Literary Patterns*, pp. 51–63) is right, they may be part of an overall pattern in which the two chapters are in a chiastic relationship. In any event, the topic of wealth is prominent in Luke's writing. In this instance, Jesus turns a question into an opportunity for ministry to an individual's underlying need.

13–14 A person who recognized Jesus as a "teacher" (v.13) would naturally expect him to have the ability to render a judgment in ethical matters (v.14). Rabbis were often thus consulted, and in later years some traveled from place to place to render legal decisions. Jesus' refusal to answer is not a denial of his right or ability to answer, nor of his concern for social and ethical matters. Rather he turns directly to an area in which others have no right to judge (cf. Matt 7:1)—viz., the question of motivation. We are not told whether the inquirer had legal ground for his request— a point that is unimportant here.

15 The audience (*autous*, "them") is probably now the whole crowd, not just the two brothers. The issue revolves around the very nature of "life" (*zōē*). Greed seeks possessions, which are not to be equated with true "living." In fact, they become a substitute for the proper object of man's search and worship—God. Therefore, "greed . . . is idolatry" (Col 3:5).

16–21 Since this is a parable (v.16), not an actual incident, Jesus can heighten certain elements that illustrate his point, even to the point of having God speak directly to the rich man. The man expresses in his words (vv.17–19) the attitude Jesus discerns not only in the inquirer but in others (cf. "anyone" in v.21). The word "fool" (*aphrōn*, v.20) is not used lightly but in the OT sense of one who rejects the knowledge and precepts of God as a basis for life. God addresses the man on his own pragmatic terms, dealing not with matters of the kingdom or of life beyond death but with the question of the disposition of the man's possessions. This underscores the fact that he will have to "leave it all." If we read the question "Who will get?" with Ecclesiastes 2:18–19 in mind, there is also the irony that after years of careful management the man's possessions might be frittered away by an incompetent heir.

Verse 21, which uses the contrasting words "for himself" (*heautō*) and "toward God" (*eis theon*), ends powerfully with the participle "rich" (*ploutōn*) as the final word. "Stores up things for himself" resembles Matthew 6:19: "Do not store up for

167

yourselves treasures on earth." Both passages introduce similar encouragements about God's care (cf. vv. 21-22 here with Matt 6:19, 25).

Notes

13 Διδάσκαλε (*didaskale*, "teacher") has the same sense as "rabbi," which Luke does not use in his Gospel. Formerly some thought that the term "rabbi" was anachronistic in the Gospels, as it was only later that ordination was practiced in Judaism. But now it is clear that both terms were used in an honorific sense in Jesus' day (see H. Shanks, "Is the Title 'Rabbi' Anachronistic in the Gospels?" JQR 53 [1963]: 343-44). Jesus' contemporaries recognized that, while he was not rabbinically trained, he was a competent teacher (John 7:15). Luke has already stressed the crowds' assessment of Jesus' teaching authority (4:31-32).

19-20 NIV translates ψυχή (*psychē*) in three ways—"myself," "you," and "life"—thereby showing the broad sense of the word customarily translated "soul."

3. Anxiety over possessions

12:22-34

22Then Jesus said to his disciples: "Therefore I tell you, do not worry about your life, what you will eat; or about your body, what you will wear. 23Life is more than food, and the body more than clothes. 24Consider the ravens: They do not sow or reap, they have no storeroom or barn; yet God feeds them. And how much more valuable you are than birds! 25Who of you by worrying can add a single hour to his life? 26Since you cannot do this very little thing, why do you worry about the rest?

27"Consider how the lilies grow. They do not labor or spin. Yet I tell you, not even Solomon in all his splendor was dressed like one of these. 28If that is how God clothes the grass of the field, which is here today, and tomorrow is thrown into the fire, how much more will he clothe you, O you of little faith! 29And do not set your heart on what you will eat or drink; do not worry about it. 30For the pagan world runs after all such things, and your Father knows that you need them. 31But seek his kingdom, and these things will be given to you as well.

32"Do not be afraid, little flock, for your Father has been pleased to give you the kingdom. 33Sell your possessions and give to the poor. Provide purses for yourselves that will not wear out, a treasure in heaven that will not be exhausted, where no thief comes near and no moth destroys. 34For where your treasure is, there your heart will be also.

This section (vv. 22-34), except for vv. 32-34, is virtually identical to Matthew 6:25-33 in the Sermon on the Mount. As noted in the comment above on v. 21, which forms a transition to this section, both passages are connected with sayings against "storing up" things for oneself. The passage ends (v. 34) with a saying about one's "treasure" (cf. Matt 6:21). The Greek word for "treasure" (*thēsauros*) is related to that for "store up" (*theaurizō*). The passage then both introduced and concluded with a saying about "treasuring" is thereby given its theme. What was implied in the warning parable of vv. 16-20 is explicitly commanded here (note the *dia touto*, "therefore," of v. 22). Believers should not act like the "pagan world" (*ta ethnē tou kosmou*, v. 30), represented by the rich fool of the parable.

22–23 Having addressed the crowds in vv.1–21, Jesus turns to his disciples. The word for "life" in vv. 22 23 (and cf v.20) is *psychē*, which often means "soul." Here the translation "life" is appropriate. Observe the parallelism between v.22 and v.23. A comment on food comes first in each verse, followed by one on clothing. Verse 23 provides the support for the exhortation in v.22: there is more to life than these. The exhortation "do not worry" (*mē merimnate*) stands alongside the implied "do not covet" in this passage and the preceding one (cf. v.15). Actually one can both worry and be covetous whether he is poor or rich. "Do not worry" is the first of a series of four prohibitions. The others are "Do not set your heart on" (v.29), "Do not worry" (again v.29), and "Do not be afraid" (v.32).

24–26 The thrust of the comparison "how much more valuable?" is similar to the argument from the lesser to the greater in vv.6–7. There the sparrows represent birds of little value. Here the ravens (v.24) may represent birds that were considered unclean (Lev 11:13–20, esp. v.15) and therefore unworthy of God's care. Jesus assures us that the God who cares for such birds surely will care for us. Verses 25–26 constitute still another argument from the lesser (adding inches of height or minutes of life [cf. Notes]) to the greater (totality of life and its needs). The point here is that if it is futile to worry about small matters we cannot control, it is even more futile to worry about the larger matters that lie even farther beyond our control.

27–28 Jesus gives a final example of the lesser to greater argument in contrasting the grandeur of Solomon, who could afford the finest clothing, to common flowers, which can do nothing toward making clothes (v.27). His second contrast is between the limited lifespan of flowers and the (implied) eternal life that lay before the disciples (v.28). God's meticulous and lavish care for mere perishing flowers assures us of his unfailing care for his own people. In view of this, the disciples' "little faith" is all the more shameful.

29 "Do not worry" is the third of four prohibitions (cf. comment on v.22). The word for "worry" here (*meteōrizesthe*) differs from that in v.22 (*merimnate*). *Meteōrizesthe* meant in classical Greek "be raised up" or "suspended." While it came metaphorically to mean "worry," the literal meaning might be expressed by "be in suspense" or "be up in the air."

30–31 "The pagan world" (*ta ethnē*, lit., "the nations," i.e., the Gentiles) contrasts with believers. In Matthew's report of the Sermon on the Mount, believers are cautioned three times not to behave as the pagans do: (1) in their relation to people (Matt 5:47), (2) in their relation to God in prayer (Matt 6:7), and (3) in their relation to material possessions (Matt 6:32)—the application it has here in Luke. In Matthew the contrast to Gentiles is especially significant in view of the Jewish slant of that Gospel. Luke 6:32, the equivalent of Matthew 5:47, has "sinners" (*hamartōloi*), a Lukan term. Pagans do not have the same relation believers have with a loving, caring, providing heavenly Father. To know that he knows their needs is sufficient assurance for all believers. Secure in that knowledge, his disciples can turn all their attention to the kingdom they are commanded to seek (v.31).

32 "Do not be afraid" (*mē phobou*) introduces another contrast. The "little flock" (*to* *mikron poimnion*), which now needs to be fed and defended, will one day inherit the kingdom, possessing its benefits and authority. The fatherhood of God and its connection with the giving of the kingdom are themes not only characteristic of Matthew but also foundational in the Sermon on the Mount, of which this passage may have been originally a part. The encouragement not to fear is appropriate in view of the hostility of the "experts in the law" who, instead of opening the way to the kingdom and its truth (11:52), stand in the way of those who seek it.

33 With the injunction to "sell your possessions" (*pōlēsate ta hyparchonta hymōn*), we come to the concluding exhortations on the "treasure" theme. It is difficult to know whether the reason for this exhortation is to benefit the poor or to rid the disciples of encumbering possessions. While the poor are mentioned, the point of the passage as a whole seems to be the total dependence of disciples on God. The second reason, therefore, is probably primary and the first secondary in *this* context but still important in itself and in Luke's thought throughout his Gospel.

The word "all" is neither present nor implied before the word "possessions." As we have seen, the point of Jesus' teaching on treasures is that they are not to be hoarded for one's own selfish pleasure (cf. v.21 and Matt 6:19). Nevertheless the interpreter must be careful neither to blunt Jesus' strong teaching as expressed in Luke regarding a life of abandonment and giving (cf. 6:27–36; 14:26, 33) nor to introduce teachings given to one audience into a discussion with another group. One should live on such a modest level of subsistence that the only "purses" needed (see the metaphor in v.33) are those one needs for heavenly "treasure." By their nature, such purses are never motheaten or stolen.

34 This verse shows the essential thrust of Jesus' teaching. It is not the *extent* but the *place* of one's possessions that is emphasized, because it is the direction of one's "heart," heavenward or earthward, that is all important.

Notes

25 NIV's translation "add a single hour to his life" of ἐπὶ τὴν ἡλικίαν αὐτοῦ προσθεῖναι πῆχυν (*epi tēn hēlikian autou prostheinai pēchyn*) is debatable (cf. NIV mg). *Hēlikia* can mean "age" or "bodily stature" (cf. BAG, s.v.). *Pēchys* means "cubit," a unit of measure the length of one's forearm, roughly eighteen inches. It could be used to describe the extent of the *hēlikia* in either of its senses. NIV takes *hēlikia* in the sense of "age," which fits well with the parable about the rich fool (vv.16–21) who could not add to his life. Yet the words "how the lilies grow" (v.27) suggest the idea of height. A person of normal stature would scarcely want to add another foot and a half to his height; so that meaning may be unlikely. The meaning could, however, be that one normally grows inch by inch without giving it any thought. Even if one thought about it, he could not suddenly gain eighteen inches and be full-grown. While to live on some "borrowed time" may seem important and to grow a foot-and-a-half taller is to gain about an additional fourth of one's stature, these are both insignificant in comparison with the entire scope of one's life, especially considered in its spiritual dimension. At any rate, neither is possible; so why worry at all?

27 Τὰ κρίνα (*ta krina*, "the lilies") may be some specific flower of Jesus' land, but more

probably Jesus was "thinking of all the wonderful blooms that adorn the fields of Galilee" (BAC, s v ; see also Morris, *Luke*, p. 214).

Οὐ κοπιᾷ οὐδε νήθει (*ou kopia oude nēthei*, "they do not labor or spin") receives a cautious "D" rating by UBS. The Western text has οὔτε νήθει οὔτε ὑφαίνει (*oute nēthei oute hyphainei*, "they neither spin nor weave"). Metzger (*Textual Commentary*, p. 161) says the Western reading was rejected "after much hesitation . . . as a stylistic refinement." Marshall (*Gospel of Luke*, p. 528) considers this to be "over-subtle for a scribe" but still finds support by only one Greek MS (D) weak. It is probably best to keep the UBS reading as does NIV.

---

4. Readiness for the coming of the Son of Man

12:35–48

35"Be dressed ready for service and keep your lamps burning, 36like men waiting for their master to return from a wedding banquet, so that when he comes and knocks they can immediately open the door for him. 37It will be good for those servants whose master finds them watching when he comes. I tell you the truth, he will dress himself to serve, will have them recline at the table and will come and wait on them. 38It will be good for those servants whose master finds them ready, even if he comes in the second or third watch of the night. 39But understand this: If the owner of the house had known at what hour the thief was coming, he would not have let his house be broken into. 40You also must be ready, because the Son of Man will come at an hour when you do not expect him."

41Peter asked, "Lord, are you telling this parable to us, or to everyone?"

42The Lord answered, "Who then is the faithful and wise manager, whom the master puts in charge of his servants to give them their food allowance at the proper time? 43It will be good for that servant whom the master finds doing so when he returns. 44I tell you the truth, he will put him in charge of all his possessions. 45But suppose the servant says to himself, 'My master is taking a long time in coming,' and he then begins to beat the menservants and maidservants and to eat and drink and get drunk. 46The master of that servant will come on a day when he does not expect him and at an hour he is not aware of. He will cut him to pieces and assign him a place with the unbelievers.

47"That servant who knows his master's will and does not get ready or does not do what his master wants will be beaten with many blows. 48But the one who does not know and does things deserving punishment will be beaten with few blows. From everyone who has been given much, much will be demanded; and from the one who has been entrusted with much, much more will be asked.

The emphatic use of the personal pronoun "you" (*hymeis*) twice in the Greek text of vv.35–36 sets the attitude of the alert Christian in contrast to that of the pagans (v.30) who seek only the things of this present world. The word "watching" (*grēgorountas*, v.37) expresses the theme of this passage. Luke introduces it earlier in his Gospel than do Matthew and Mark, who use it only in the Olivet Discourse (and in the parables following in Matthew and in the Lord's words to the disciples at Gethsemane (cf. Matt 24:42–43; 25:13; 26:38, 40–41). Luke does not use the actual verb "to watch" in either of the parallel contexts (17:26–30, 34–36; 22:45–46). Here he seems to be impressed by the connection in our Lord's teaching between warnings about future judgment. The verses following the figure about "watching" (vv.39–40) and the next section also (vv.41–46) are parallel to part of Matthew's version of the Olivet Discourse (Matt 24:43–51). They are usually considered to be from Q and interwoven with other material. The scene in vv.36–37 and the parable in v.39 point clearly to the necessity of being ready for the Son of Man (v.40).

35–38 In Jesus' time, a person "dressed ready for service" (v.35) tucked his flowing outer robe under his belt or sash. This was done to prepare for travel, fighting (Eph 6:14), or work (cf. the metaphorical use in 1 Peter 1:13).

Matthew 25:1–13 also describes a time of waiting with burning lamps for the return of a bridegroom for his wedding. In Matthew the lamps are *lampades;* here they are *lychnoi*. There virgins wait for the bridegroom; here servants wait for their masters (v.36). The strong affirmation "I tell you the truth" (*amēn*, v.37) appears for the first time in Luke since 4:24. There is a striking reversal of roles as the master dresses himself to serve (cf. v.35) and waits on the servants. This contrasts with Luke 17:7–10, where a different point is being made. If the return is very late in the night or toward morning, in the "second or third watch" (the middle and last division of the night hours according to Jewish reckoning), the alertness of the servants is even more commendable (v.38).

39–40 The image now changes to one of burglary (v.39). The absence of figurative or parabolic terminology (cf. "like" in v.36) may indicate that this is not a story but a recent incident known to Jesus' audience. Moreover, Jeremias (*Parables of Jesus*, pp. 48–49) notes that the use of the aorist tense in the story gives the impression of a straightforward narrative. It is unusual, but not impossible, for an evil character, such as a thief, to represent a good person (see the unjust judge [18:1–8], who stands in contrast to God). Actually, it is the story as a whole, not the individual characters in it, that provides the comparison here. The concluding exhortation (v.40) to "be ready," because the time of the Son of Man's coming is unknown, is similar to Matthew 24:42–44, in the Olivet Discourse, where the burglary figure is also used (cf. Matt 25:13; Mark 13:33–37). Luke's version of the Olivet Discourse lacks this saying, as well as the saying about ignorance of the day and hour, which is recorded in Matt 24:36 and Mark 13:32. Here Luke is clearly concentrating much of the Lord's teaching on the implications of his sudden return.

41–44 Peter responds, in his accustomed role as spokesman for the apostles, with a question about the extent of their responsibility (v.41). Jesus answers, as often, with a counterquestion (v.42). Although he says elsewhere that exhortations to "watch" apply to everyone (Mark 13:37), in this case the parable that follows (vv.42–46) shows that the apostles have a special responsibility. In the illustration the "manager" (or "steward," *oikonomos*) in charge of the "servants" is a "servant" (or "slave," *doulos*) himself (v.43). This was a common situation in that first-century society. The passage teaches the importance of faithfulness in doing the will of the master. Verses 42–46 emphasize responsibility one has for those who have been placed under his leadership. Conversely, the following paragraph (vv.47–48) focuses on response to the master's command.

45–46 As in 18:7 and 19:12, the clear implication is that Jesus himself would not return immediately but that there would be an interval of waiting and serving (cf. Notes). The attitude of the manager in v.45 is contrary to that commanded in v.40. The word "begins" (*arxētai*, v.45) suggests that the action is interrupted by the master's unexpected return. The severe treatment of the servants may be hyperbolic, but Acts 20:29–30 warns against false leaders who ravage the congregation (cf. the warning in Matt 7:15–23). Likewise the vivid description of the manager's punishment, "cut to pieces" (*dichotomēsei*), stresses the seriousness of his default of responsibility (v.46, cf. Notes). "A place with the unbelievers" applies to the false religious leaders alluded to rather than merely to the secular characters in the story.

47–48 If this punishment seems too severe, the explanation of God's principle of judgment now clarifies matters. The servant in v.47 may represent those who sin "with a high hand," committing "presumptuous sins" (Num 15:30–31; Ps 19:13, RSV). If so, the servant who "does not know" (v.48) sins "unwittingly" and has "hidden faults" (Num 15:27–29; Ps 19:12, RSV). In either case there is some definite personal responsibility and therefore judgment, because the servant should have made it his business to know his master's will. All have some knowledge of God (Rom 1:20), and God judges according to individual levels of responsibility (Rom 2:12–13). The closing statement (v.48) would apply especially to the apostles and church leaders throughout the successive centuries.

Notes

35–48 This passage is important in determining Luke's view of the Parousia. Many scholars have assumed that Luke modified the tradition of Jesus' teaching about his return, reducing the element of imminency to accommodate the fact that Jesus was obviously not returning as soon as expected. A more realistic view, however, is that Jesus not only taught the certainty of his return at an unexpected moment but also implied, through various instructions for his disciples, that the community of believers would continue for an unspecified time serving their Lord till his return in the indefinite future (see comments at 19:11–27; cf Ellis, *Eschatology in Luke*, and Marshall, *Eschatology and the Parables*). There is neither any necessary nor substantial ground for postulating that in the transmission of Jesus' teaching about the Parousia the audience has been changed from the crowds to the disciples so as to make the teaching apply to the church in view of a delayed Parousia rather than to those who need to repent in view of impending judgment (cf. Jeremias, *Parables of Jesus*, p. 48).

46 Διχοτομήσει αὐτὸν (*dichotomēsei auton*, "he will cut him to pieces") seems to be such an extreme punishment to modern readers that various attempts have been made to explain it. Marshall (*Gospel of Luke*, p. 543) surveys some of these explanations, favoring that of O. Betz ("The Dichotomized Servant and the End of Judas Iscariot," *Revue de Qumran* 5 [1964]: 43–58). According to Betz, the original Aramaic statement was "he was cut off," i.e., from the "sons of light" as in the theology of Qumran (cf. 1QS 2.16). The words in v.46 would then express this same idea in different terms.

5. *Division over Jesus*

12:49–53

⁴⁹"I have come to bring fire on the earth, and how I wish it were already kindled! ⁵⁰But I have a baptism to undergo, and how distressed I am until it is completed! ⁵¹Do you think I came to bring peace on earth? No, I tell you, but division. ⁵²From now on there will be five in one family divided against each other, three against two and two against three. ⁵³They will be divided, father against son and son against father, mother against daughter and daughter against mother, mother-in-law against daughter-in-law and daughter-in-law against mother-in-law."

49-50 The Lord's teaching about preparation for his return and impending judgment (vv.35-48) leads to this paragraph about the personal crises Christ precipitates. It is difficult to determine the precise meaning of "fire" (v.49) because the word can signify either judgment or purification, to say nothing of other less probable meanings. The verses that follow v.49 may, consistently with the preceding paragraphs, connote judgment. While Jesus came to bring salvation rather than judgment (Luke 4:19; John 3:17), his coming also meant judgment (John 9:39). A comparison with earlier teaching in Luke, however, suggests that "fire" means purification as well as judgment. The ministry of John the Baptist included not only judgment (3:9, 17) but also the promise that Jesus would "baptize . . . with the Holy Spirit and fire" (see commentary and OT references at 3:16). Luke 9:51-56 shows that Jesus did not intend to bring an immediate fire of judgment on those who rejected him. Since 3:16 links fire with the Holy Spirit, it is possible that this fire was to be "kindled" by the baptism of the Spirit (Acts 2:1-4). This could only occur after Jesus' own "baptism" of death, to which he referred here (v.50). Mark 10:38 mentions baptism as a symbol of Jesus' death, along with the "cup" Jesus spoke of at Gethsemane (Luke 22:42). He felt "distressed" (*synechomai*) in anticipation of that. "The prospect of his sufferings was a perpetual Gethsemane" (Plummer, p. 334).

51-53 Although the Messiah was to bring peace (v.51), this was not his only mission, nor, in the political sense, his immediate one. Isaiah 11:1-9 shows that even in the final period of peace, the Messiah, enabled by the Spirit, will exercise judgment. Already in his earthly ministry ("from now on," v.52), there is division. The parallel to v.51 in Matthew 10:34 has "sword" (*machaira*) instead of "division" (*diamerismon*). In 22:36 Luke reports Jesus' speaking of a "sword" (*machaira*) when the crisis deepens. The expression "from now on" (*apo tou nyn*) is, apart from 2 Corinthians 5:16, unique to Luke in the NT. It is an important part of Luke's vocabulary of time (cf. esp. 5:10; 22:69; also the use of "today" in 4:21; 13:32; 19:5, 9). Luke is stressing the element of crisis, both immediately and at the Lord's return. During this time his disciples must be prepared for a break in their family relationships if others do not concur with their decision to follow Christ (vv.52-53; cf. 14:26). The wording of v.53 is probably from Micah 7:6.

The mention of six people in v.53 does not contradict the number five in v.52, since one person can have two relationships, e.g., a woman can be both a mother and a mother-in-law.

Notes

51 Ἐν τῇ γῇ (*en tē gē*, "on earth") may possibly refer to the "land" of Israel. This meaning of *gē* is possible (TDNT, 1:677-78). "Peace on earth" in 2:14 has ἐπί (*epi*, "on"; so 12:49), not *en* as here. If this was the case, Jesus' words would be referring even more clearly to the Jewish messianic expectations current in his day.

Οὐχί λέγω ὑμῖν (*ouchi, legō hymin*, "No, I tell you") is emphatic.

6. Interpreting the times

12:54–59

> [54]He said to the crowd: "When you see a cloud rising in the west, immediately you say, 'It's going to rain,' and it does. [55]And when the south wind blows, you say, 'It's going to be hot,' and it is. [56]Hypocrites! You know how to interpret the appearance of the earth and the sky. How is it that you don't know how to interpret this present time?
> [57]"Why don't you judge for yourselves what is right? [58]As you are going with your adversary to the magistrate, try hard to be reconciled to him on the way, or he may drag you off to the judge, and the judge turn you over to the officer, and the officer throw you into prison. [59]I tell you, you will not get out until you have paid the last penny."

54–56 Though the text does not link this section with the preceding one, there is a common element of crisis. The words "interpret this present time [*kairon*, or 'season']" (v.56) imply this by comparing the observation of changing weather (vv.54–55) with God's "time" of opportunity and responsibility. This emphasis on the opportune time recurs more emphatically in 19:41–44 (cf. "on this day . . . but now . . . you did not recognize the time"). Here the word "hypocrites" (v.56) shows that the people Jesus was speaking to were not sincere in their professed inability to "interpret this present time."

57–59 Here Jesus' appeal to human judgment regarding a time of personal decision (v.57) is similar to, though not verbally identical with, Matthew 5:25–26. In human affairs one resolves a crisis situation wisely to avoid penalty (v.58). This is a secular illustration, and v.59 should not be applied spiritually in point-for-point detail aside from its basic application of reconciliation with God before the day of judgment.

Notes

54–55 Δυσμῶν (*dysmōn*, "west") is the direction of the Mediterranean, and the νότον (*noton*, "south wind") comes from the desert.

---

7. A call to repentance

13:1–9

> [1]Now there were some present at that time who told Jesus about the Galileans whose blood Pilate had mixed with their sacrifices. [2]Jesus answered, "Do you think that these Galileans were worse sinners than all the other Galileans because they suffered this way? [3]I tell you, no! But unless you repent, you too will all perish. [4]Or those eighteen who died when the tower in Siloam fell on them—do you think they were more guilty than all the others living in Jerusalem? [5]I tell you, no! But unless you repent, you too will all perish."
> [6]Then he told this parable: "A man had a fig tree, planted in his vineyard, and he went to look for fruit on it, but did not find any. [7]So he said to the man who took care of the vineyard, 'For three years now I've been coming to look for fruit on this fig tree and haven't found any. Cut it down! Why should it use up the soil?'

> 8" 'Sir,' the man replied, 'leave it alone for one more year, and I'll dig around it and fertilize it. 9If it bears fruit next year, fine! If not, then cut it down.' "

At this point, dialogue about the problem of human suffering and evil introduces a parable that, like Jesus' teaching in chapter 12, deals with crisis and judgment.

1–5 We cannot be certain as to the exact incident v.1 refers to. The social tension made revolutionary activity in those days possible at any time. Pilate's position as governor of a troubled province far distant from Rome was precarious. Josephus (*Life,* 92 [17]) says that Galileans were especially susceptible to revolt, though see comment at 1:26. Any attack against Jews who had come to offer sacrifices was horrendous whatever its reason. The fact that the people "told Jesus" about the event implies that he was not at Jerusalem when it happened. Jesus (v.4) refuses to attribute tragedy (v.2) or accident (v.3) directly to one's sin as the Jews did (cf. John 9:1–3). On the contrary, he affirms the sinfulness of all people (v.5). "Too" (*hōsautōs*) means "similarly" or even "in the same way," showing that one who flouts God cannot count on immunity from sudden adversity. Whereas the two victims of the calamities referred to in vv.1–5 perished physically, "all" (*pantes*) who do not repent face spiritual death.

6–9 Once more Jesus alludes to Micah 7 (cf. comments on 12:53), this time to Micah 7:1, with its lament over unproductive fig trees. The symbolism, like that of the vine in Isaiah 5:1–7, applies to Israel. Jesus' mention (v.6) of both a fig tree and a vineyard makes the figure doubly clear. Luke includes this parable instead of the cursing of the fig tree (found only in Matt 21:18–22; Mark 11:12–14, 20–25). Here the tree is not immediately destroyed, as it was in the cursing incident, but is given an extra year of grace (v.8), even beyond the three years its owner had already waited (v.7). Israel failed to recognize her season of opportunity (cf. 12:56; 19: 41–44).

Notes

3,5 Oὐχί (*ouchi,* "No!") is the first word in each sentence for emphasis.
4 The tower of Siloam was probably near the Pool of Siloam in the southeastern corner of Jerusalem.

8. *Healing a woman on the Sabbath*

13:10–17

> 10On a Sabbath Jesus was teaching in one of the synagogues, 11and a woman was there who had been crippled by a spirit for eighteen years. She was bent over and could not straighten up at all. 12When Jesus saw her, he called her forward and said to her, "Woman, you are set free from your infirmity." 13Then he put his hands on her, and immediately she straightened up and praised God.
> 14Indignant because Jesus had healed on the Sabbath, the synagogue ruler said to the people, "There are six days for work. So come and be healed on those days, not on the Sabbath."

¹⁵The Lord answered him, "You hypocrites! Doesn't each of you on the Sabbath untie his ox or donkey from the stall and lead it out to give it water? ¹⁶Then should not this woman, a daughter of Abraham, whom Satan has kept bound for eighteen long years, be set free on the Sabbath day from what bound her?"

¹⁷When he said this, all his opponents were humiliated, but the people were delighted with all the wonderful things he was doing.

The Sabbath issue, a major cause of dissension earlier (6:1–11), now reappears. As in 6:6, and for the last time in Luke's narrative sequence, Jesus is teaching in a synagogue. This incident, like the others in this chapter, shows that in spite of the failure of the religious leaders to acknowledge the time of God's working, the kingdom is still being manifested.

10–13 "Was teaching" (*ēn didaskōn*) suggests that as Jesus was speaking (v.10), he suddenly became aware of the woman (*kai idou*, "and look!" untranslated in NIV [v.11], with perhaps some loss of effect). As often in healing narratives, Luke mentions the seriousness and duration of the disease to highlight the greatness of the cure.

The "spirit" (v.11) presumably was a demon, though Luke does not specifically say the woman was demon possessed. Any activity by a demon is ultimately Satan's responsibility (v.16; cf. comments on 11:14–20). The fact that Jesus touched her (v.13) has led some to conclude that she was not demon possessed, on the ground that nowhere else in the Gospels are we told that Jesus touched a demon-possessed person. But the Gospel narratives by no means record every detail of Jesus' actions. Far more important, and emphasized by Luke, is the woman's instant healing and its direct attribution to God. This, of course, shows that Jesus was truly acting with God's authority. "Praised [*edoxazen*] God" reflects Luke's special interest in the glory of God (cf. 5:26). And Luke may have used *endoxois* (v.17), which sounds similar and means "wonderful things," to remind his readers of this theme of praise.

14–17 The controversy over Jesus' Sabbath activities now comes to the fore (v.14), as the synagogue ruler speaks to the people on the ground of Exodus 20:9–10. Notice that he avoids addressing Jesus directly. There was ample evidence of rabbinic precedent for helping animals in emergencies on the Sabbath. So Jesus uses a lesser-to-greater argument to move from helping animals (v.15) to helping human beings (v.16; cf. 12:24). "A daughter of Abraham" means a Jewess. In keeping with Luke's purpose, this designation highlights the priority of the Jews in the program of the Gospel. It also shows that she deserved immediate healing. As he often does, Luke gives us the crowd's reaction (v.17; cf. 4:15, 22, 32, 36–37; 5:26).

9. Parables of the mustard seed and the yeast

13:18–21

¹⁸Then Jesus asked, "What is the kingdom of God like? What shall I compare it to? ¹⁹It is like a mustard seed, which a man took and planted in his garden. It grew and became a tree, and the birds of the air perched in its branches."

²⁰Again he asked, "What shall I compare the kingdom of God to? ²¹It is like yeast that a woman took and mixed into a large amount of flour until it worked all through the dough."

18–21 In Luke's narrative, his presentation of these two kingdom parables comes later than in Matthew and Mark. Isolated from other parables, they receive the added support of the account of the miraculous healing Luke has just described. In Jesus' teaching the "mustard seed" (v.19) represents that which is tiny but effective (cf. 17:6). The full-grown mustard tree may reach ten feet or so in height (see ZPEB, 4:324–25) and thus be quite large enough for birds to settle in its branches. It is not certain whether birds are mentioned as vivid detail in accord with the occasional OT use of birds to symbolize the Gentiles (cf. Notes). The point of the parable is not the growth of the tree, nor a comparison between the seed and the tree, but the power inherent in the seed. This power is implicit in the kingdom (v.18), as Jesus' healing of the woman has just demonstrated. Likewise the point of Jesus' simile of the yeast and the kingdom is not that yeast penetrates the dough but the inherent power— i.e., of the kingdom—that enables it to do this. This interpretation fits Mark's parable of the growing seed (Mark 4:26–29).

Notes

---

19 Πετεινά (*peteina*, "birds") are specifically mentioned in each version of the parable (Matt 13:32; Mark 4:32) and may therefore be significant in symbolizing Gentile nations. Plummer (p. 345) cites Ezek 17:23; 31:6; Dan 4:9, 18[12, 21 MT] as OT evidence for this.
21 Ζύμη (*zymē*, "leaven") when used metaphorically usually symbolizes evil. This is true in both biblical and secular literature. See reference notes on Matt 13:33 in J.J. Wettstein's edition (1751–52) of the Greek NT for examples. But it is difficult without reading extraneous ideas into the text to find anything other than a positive straightforward description of the kingdom here.

---

10. *Entering the kingdom*

13:22–30

> ²²Then Jesus went through the towns and villages, teaching as he made his way to Jerusalem. ²³Someone asked him, "Lord, are only a few people going to be saved?"
> He said to them, ²⁴"Make every effort to enter through the narrow door, because many, I tell you, will try to enter and will not be able to. ²⁵Once the owner of the house gets up and closes the door, you will stand outside knocking and pleading, 'Sir, open the door for us.'
> "But he will answer, 'I don't know you or where you come from.'
> ²⁶"Then you will say, 'We ate and drank with you, and you taught in our streets.'
> ²⁷"But he will reply, 'I don't know you or where you come from. Away from me, all you evildoers!'
> ²⁸"There will be weeping there, and gnashing of teeth, when you see Abraham, Isaac and Jacob and all the prophets in the kingdom of God, but you yourselves thrown out. ²⁹People will come from east and west and north and south, and will take their places at the feast in the kingdom of God. ³⁰Indeed there are those who are last who will be first, and first who will be last."

Jesus' teaching now turns to personal responsibility. Several themes appear in this section that occur in other NT settings in Matthew and Mark (cf., in sequence, Matt 7:13–14; 25:10–12; 7:22–23; 8:11–12; 19:30; 20:16, along with Mark 10:31).

22-23 Here we have one of the few specific travel references in what is sometimes called Luke's "travel section" (9:51-19:44). Nevertheless, the travel theme appears repeatedly in connection with the verb *poreuomai* and its cognates (cf. *dieporeueto*, "went," v.22; see comment on v.33). The words "made his way to Jerusalem" are especially significant because the important element is not merely travel but Jesus' orientation toward that city (cf. 9:51; 13:33-34; 17:11; 19:28, 41 and comment on 19:28). Like the question on divorce (Matt 19:3), this one about whether few or many people will be saved (v.23) was the occasion of differing opinions among the rabbis.

24-27 Jesus' reply (v.24) emphasizes not "how many?" but "who?" The saved are those who seize their opportunity now (in the "year of the Lord's favor," 4:19). Once the time for decision has passed (v.25), attempts to enter into salvation afterward (note the future "will try . . . will not be able," v.24) will be futile. Likewise Esau "afterward" sought his inheritance in vain (Heb 12:17). Does the "narrow door" limit the number of people who are admitted or the opportunities a person has to enter? Verse 24 by itself suggests the former; v.25 with its reference to the closing door suggests the latter. In John 10:9, entrance to salvation is only through Christ, who himself is the gate. The use of the third person in "But he will reply" (v.27) does not refer to anyone other than Jesus as the Son of Man (cf. Matt 7:23: "I will tell them") and simply follows the pattern of v.25. The repetition of "I don't know you or where you come from" (v.27; cf. v.25) heightens the sense of utter rejection (cf. Matt 7:23: "I never knew you"). Familiarity with Jesus (v.26) will be of no benefit then (cf. the even stronger plea in Matt 7:22).

28-30 The contrast is heightened between those inside—note the reference to the patriarchs of Israel—and those outside the door, i.e., outside the kingdom (v.28). Every Jew expected to sit with the patriarchs at the messianic banquet or "feast in the kingdom of God" (v.29). The concept of such a feast in heaven as a celebration with the Messiah is alluded to throughout the OT and other Jewish literature over a long period of time (cf. 14:5). The tragedy would not only be that of looking at the patriarchs from the outside but also that of seeing Gentiles inside with them. Verse 30 describes a total reversal of positions. Here it clearly means the exclusion from future blessings of those who thought they were first in line for them. Its thrust is stronger here than its use in different contexts in Matthew 19:30; 20:16; and Mark 10:31. Exclusion from the kingdom will lead to "weeping and grinding of teeth"—an expression found only here in v.27 but used several times in Matthew (8:12; 22:13; 24:51; 25:30) to express the horror of future doom.

Notes

24 "Make every effort" is ἀγωνίζεσθε (*agōnizesthe*), a word often used in an athletic or a military context. It does not imply working for salvation but rather earnestness in seeking it (cf. its use regarding prayer in Col 4:12).

11. Concern over Jerusalem

13:31–35

> [31]At that time some Pharisees came to Jesus and said to him, "Leave this place and go somewhere else. Herod wants to kill you."
>
> [32]He replied, "Go tell that fox, 'I will drive out demons and heal people today and tomorrow, and on the third day I will reach my goal.' [33]In any case, I must keep going today and tomorrow and the next day—for surely no prophet can die outside Jerusalem!
>
> [34]"O Jerusalem, Jerusalem, you who kill the prophets and stone those sent to you, how often I have longed to gather your children together, as a hen gathers her chicks under her wings, but you were not willing! [35]Look, your house is left to you desolate. I tell you, you will not see me again until you say, 'Blessed is he who comes in the name of the Lord.'"

This is the main passage in Luke in which Jesus expresses a strong sense of destiny in his final journey to Jerusalem. Note the sense of divine purpose expressed by such characteristic Lukan words as "today" (*sēmeron*) and "must" (*dei*). The passage is peculiar to Luke and shows Luke's editorial care in making a significant transition at this point. It marks a stage in Jesus' progress to Jerusalem and prepares the reader for chapter 14 (note v.1).

31 Now the Pharisees warn Jesus of Herod's designs on his life. Later in his Gospel, Luke will speak out in blaming the Jewish leaders for their drastic actions against Jesus but will minimize the role of the people in opposing him (e.g., 19:47). At this point, however, he attributes no evil motive to those who warn Jesus. Apparently these Pharisees have Jesus' safety at heart. "At that time" (*en autē tē hōra*) makes a strong transition from the warning in vv.28–30, which would have caused strong reactions among the Jewish leaders. We do not know where Jesus was at that time; if he was in Herod's territory, he was obviously not near Jerusalem.

32–33 In Luke's last mention of him, Herod was troubled at the reports of Jesus' miracles. By having John the Baptist beheaded, Herod thought he had done away with prophetic opposition. But Jesus, far from being threatened by Herod, called him "that fox" (v.32). Today foxes connote cleverness; in Jesus' day they also connoted insignificance (cf. Neh 4:3; S of Sol 2:15). Either or both connotations may apply here. Jesus' intent was to continue his ministry and manifest the power of the kingdom—"drive out demons and heal people"—but not to do this indefinitely. "Today and tomorrow" (*sēmeron kai aurion*) signifies the time of present opportunity in Jesus' ministry. That time, however, was short. Since "today and tomorrow" are not literal days, so with the "third day," which must have reminded Luke's readers of the day of Jesus' resurrection. Perhaps it was intended to do so. Verses 32 and 33 are parallel, with the idea of "three days" implicit in each. In v.32 "the third day" is followed by "I will reach my goal" (*teleioumai*, "be completed," "be perfected"). In v.33 it is followed by a reference to Jesus' death. Clearly the expressions are equivalent, and there may well be an anticipation of the profound phrase in Hebrews 2:9: "perfect through suffering." In one sense v.33 marks the completion of Jesus' mission, especially in Luke's theology (cf. 9:31). Ellis (*Gospel of Luke*, p. 190) suggests that it refers to consecration to the high priestly work, since the Greek word for "perfected" is used in the LXX of Exodus 29 and Leviticus 8.

The programmatic statement of Jesus' purpose and progress continues in v.33 with two additions: the specific reference to suffering ("die") and the word "must" (*dei*). Luke conveys Jesus' sense of purpose and necessity more strongly than the other Synoptics do. Well over two-thirds of the synoptic uses of *dei* are in Luke (cf. comment on 4:43). Another key word that reappears here is the verb *poreuomai* ("keep going"; cf. comment on "went" at v.22). Luke emphasizes the "way" of Jesus, which led to the cross and on to glory (cf. John 7:35; 14:12, 28; 16:7, 28). Jesus expected to suffer as a "prophet." Jeremias (TDNT, 5:714) says that to a great extent "martyrdom was considered an integral part of the prophetic office" in those days (cf. TDNT, 6:834–35). Stephen's speech (Acts 7:52) accords with this.

34–35 The word "Jerusalem" appears three times in a row: once at the end of v.33 and twice at the beginning of the lament (v.34). The effect is to draw the reader's attention to that city of destiny, both as the place of our Lord's passion and as the pathetic, unwilling object of his love. The "house," perhaps specifically the temple, which had been visited by Jesus as a boy (2:41–50), will now lose him till Psalm 118:26, quoted here ("Blessed . . . Lord"), is fulfilled. The lament and the quotation do not appear in Matthew till after the Triumphal Entry (23:37–39), where Jesus includes the word "again" (*ap' arti*, v.39), apparently to make it clear that there was to be a future fulfillment of the word quoted from Psalm 118:26. The substance of the quotation is recorded by all four Gospels in their account of the Triumphal Entry; but the words are said, not by the Jerusalemites, but by Jesus' supporters. Luke specifies that they were Jesus' disciples (19:37–38).

E. *Further Teaching on Urgent Issues* (14:1–18:30)

1. *Jesus at a Pharisee's house*

14:1–14

> ¹One Sabbath, when Jesus went to eat in the house of a prominent Pharisee, he was being carefully watched. ²There in front of him was a man suffering from dropsy. ³Jesus asked the Pharisees and experts in the law, "Is it lawful to heal on the Sabbath or not?" ⁴But they remained silent. So taking hold of the man, he healed him and sent him away.
>
> ⁵Then he asked them, "If one of you has a son or an ox that falls into a well on the Sabbath day, will you not immediately pull him out?" ⁶And they had nothing to say.
>
> ⁷When he noticed how the guests picked the places of honor at the table, he told them this parable: ⁸"When someone invites you to a wedding feast, do not take the place of honor, for a person more distinguished than you may have been invited. ⁹If so, the host who invited both of you will come and say to you, 'Give this man your seat.' Then, humiliated, you will have to take the least important place. ¹⁰But when you are invited, take the lowest place, so that when your host comes, he will say to you, 'Friend, move up to a better place.' Then you will be honored in the presence of all your fellow guests. ¹¹For everyone who exalts himself will be humbled, and he who humbles himself will be exalted."
>
> ¹²Then Jesus said to his host, "When you give a luncheon or dinner, do not invite your friends, your brothers or relatives, or your rich neighbors; if you do, they may invite you back and so you will be repaid. ¹³But when you give a banquet, invite the poor, the crippled, the lame, the blind, ¹⁴and you will be blessed. Although they cannot repay you, you will be repaid at the resurrection of the righteous."

This passage and the following one incorporate several elements—healing, conversations, and a parable—all tied together in dinner-table conversation—a familiar device in ancient literature. The conversation, except for its opening, revolves around the response and behavior of dinner guests. This leads into the response of would-be followers of Jesus and the cost of discipleship.

1–4 Since this is the fourth time Luke records a controversy over the Sabbath (v.1), it is obvious that this was a major issue between Jesus and the religious leaders (cf. 6:1–5, 6:11; 13:10–17). The host was "prominent"—literally, one of the "ruling" (*archontōn*) Pharisees, possibly a member of the Sanhedrin. The NIV rendering "he was being carefully watched" brings out the durative aspect of the imperfect periphrastic tense, which Luke uses effectively (cf. "was teaching" and "were sitting," 5:17). Luke pictures the Pharisees as watchdogs of the faith as they waited for some theological flaw to appear in Jesus' teaching (vv.1–3; cf. 5:17; 6:7). "There [*kai idou*, lit., "and behold"] in front of him" (v.2; cf. 13:11) draws attention to a man who some commentators think was "planted" there to test Jesus. That would not be improbable, but the text does not affirm it. "Dropsy," an "abnormal accumulation of serous fluid in the tissues of the body" (R.H. Pousma, "Diseases of the Bible," ZPEB, 2:134), may have popularly been considered a curse for sin (Num 5:11–27). As in 6:9, Jesus took the initiative with a question designed to shift the burden of proof to the opposition (v.3). "Is it lawful" may have been intentionally ambiguous, a leading question that could be answered in terms of either OT or rabbinical "law." During the silence of the "Pharisees and experts in the law," Jesus met the man's need (v.4). His condition could have waited another day, but Jesus was concerned to establish a principle. This may be why he dismissed the man without including him further in the conversation and then turned to the Pharisees.

5–6 The phrase "If one of you" (v.5) draws Jesus' listeners into the illustration (cf. 11:5, 11; 12:25; 14:28). "Immediately" (*eutheōs*) stresses the urgency of meeting the need, a pointed reference back to the man with dropsy. The principle exampled in the case of a beast is in accord not only with the OT but with rabbinic law (cf. SBK, 1:629; *Shabbath* 128b, though cf. the forbidding of helping such an animal in the Qumran sect, CD 11:13–17). In the face of this, the silence of Jesus' opponents was no longer by choice (e.g., v.4) but of necessity; they "had nothing to say" (*ouk ischysan antapokrithēnai*, lit., "could not respond," v.6). A dilemma also silences a group of Jewish leaders in 20:3–7 (cf. also 20:26).

7–11 Jesus continued to take the initiative (v.7). In his time the guests at a formal dinner reclined on couches, several on each one, leaning on their left elbows. The seating was according to status. The "head of the table" was the couch at one end, with other couches extending from it and facing each other like the arms of a "U." The important places, the places of "honor" (v.8), were those nearest the head couch position. If an important guest came late, someone might have to be displaced to make room for him (v.9). Jesus' practical advice (cf. Prov 25:6–7) illustrates the spiritual principle he stated in v.11. The significance of this principle—and indeed of vv.7–11—is clarified by Luke's use in the parable of the Pharisee and the tax collector (18:14). The ultimate reference of the principle (v.11) is to God's final judgment. Luke follows the custom of using passive verbs ("will be humbled . . . will be exalted") to avoid direct reference to God, the real subject of this profound sentence. The same may hold for 16:9 (cf. Ellis, *Gospel of Luke*, on both passages; cf. also comment on 15:7 for another way Luke reverently avoids the use of God's name). This practice seems strange to us, but we need to realize that in the culture of that day a name both designated and represented a person. Therefore it was safe to refer to God obliquely by a descriptive title, "Lord"; a phrase, "the Holy One," "Blessed be he"; a circumlocution, "He who sits in heaven"; or a term such as "the heavens," whereas to say the divine Name itself without proper reverence could be blasphemy.

12–14 Having addressed the Pharisee's guests, Jesus turns to his host (v.12). What he says resembles his words in 6:32–36 (see comments)—viz., in view of ultimate reward from God, doing good to those who cannot repay it. Also, v.13 recalls Luke's report of Jesus' concern for the poor and oppressed (cf. 4:18; 6:20–21). As Jesus said (6:35), believers are to do good, not with the expectation of a future reward, but unselfishly. Then God will remember and reward them (v.14). (Scripture distinguishes between the resurrection of the righteous and that of the wicked [Dan 12:2; Acts 24:15; Rev 20:4–5].)

Notes

5 The reason some MSS read ὄνος (*onos*, "donkey," NIV mg.) instead of υἱός (*huios*, "son") is probably because the combination of two animals, donkey and ox, seems more likely than that of a son and an ox. Vaticanus (B) and Alexandrinus (A), significant papyri, and other early MS witnesses have *huios*.

2. Parable of the great banquet

14:15–24

15When one of those at the table with him heard this, he said to Jesus, "Blessed is the man who will eat at the feast in the kingdom of God."

16Jesus replied: "A certain man was preparing a great banquet and invited many guests. 17At the time of the banquet he sent his servant to tell those who had been invited, 'Come, for everything is now ready.'

18"But they all alike began to make excuses. The first said, 'I have just bought a field, and I must go and see it. Please excuse me.'

19"Another said, 'I have just bought five yoke of oxen, and I'm on my way to try them out. Please excuse me.'

20"Still another said, 'I just got married, so I can't come.'

21"The servant came back and reported this to his master. Then the owner of the house became angry and ordered his servant, 'Go out quickly into the streets and alleys of the town and bring in the poor, the crippled, the blind and the lame.'

22" 'Sir,' the servant said, 'what you ordered has been done, but there is still room.'

23"Then the master told his servant, 'Go out to the roads and country lanes and make them come in, so that my house will be full. 24I tell you, not one of those men who were invited will get a taste of my banquet.' "

Jesus continues the figure of the banquet with a striking parable about the "feast in the kingdom of God" (v.15)—the so-called eschatological banquet. Luke 13:28–30 had shown that some who expect to be present will be excluded; this passage teaches that those excluded have only themselves to blame.

15 The exuberant remark seems like a boorish counterpart to Peter's "It is good for us to be here" (9:33); Manson (*Sayings of Jesus*, p. 129) calls it "a characteristic piece of apocalyptic piety." The concept of future celebration in the kingdom is certainly biblical. Jesus does not repudiate it but rather addresses the presumption by some present, perhaps including the speaker in v.1, that they would inevitably participate.

16–17 It is not certain whether the invited guests (v.16) were waiting for the second invitation customary in fashionable circles or whether this was simply to remind those who had already accepted the invitation that it was time to come (v.17). "People had no watches . . . and . . . a banquet took a long time to prepare" (Morris, *Luke*, p. 233.)

18–20 The striking thing is that "all" of them declined (v.18). "Alike" (*apo mias*, a unique expression in Greek) does not mean "in the same way" but probably "with one accord" or "all at once" (Jeremias, *Parables of Jesus*, p. 176).

The excuses are weak. One man "must" go to see a purchased field he probably had seen before he bought it (v.18). Contrast his urgent attention to material things with Jesus' healing a man on the Sabbath (vv.2–4). The second excuse (v.19) is as worthless as the first; would anyone have bought oxen without examining them? Going "to try them out" sounds like preoccupation with a new possession rather than urgent business. In both instances materialism got in the way of honoring an invitation already extended.

The third excuse (v.20) has more validity in the light of Deuteronomy 24:5. Also, only men were invited to banquets (Jeremias, *Parables of Jesus*, p. 177). Yet marriage was not, especially in that society, an abrupt decision and could hardly have been an unexpected factor intervening between the first (v.16) and second (v.17) invitations. With his superb narrative art, Jesus uses these three excuses to show that just as a host may be snubbed, so God's gracious invitation may be flouted.

21–24 The host "became angry" (v.21) because the rejections were a personal insult. A "street" (*plateia*) was broader and traveled by a greater variety of people than a neighborhood road. In contrast an "alley" (*rhymē*) was a small lane or side path, likely to harbor the loitering outcasts of society. Those brought from these places were precisely the same unfortunates Jesus had told his host to invite in v.13 (see comment). With room still available (v.22), the servant is to go outside the town and search even the "country lanes" (v.23). To "make them come in" is not compulsion but "an insistent hospitality" (Manson, *Sayings of Jesus*, p. 130).

Although Jesus does not interpret the parable, it is reasonable to link it with 13:28–30 and find in it an allusion of the extension of the gospel to the Gentiles. Those who had the benefit of the original invitation are perhaps best described by Paul in Romans 9:4–5—Jews with all their heritage and spiritual advantages. "Not one" (v.24) refers to the parable and should not be taken literally but understood as stressing the seriousness of the consequences of rejecting God's invitation.

Notes

16–23 As to the similarity of this parable to the one in Matt 22:1–10, there can be only two explanations. Either there was one original parable handed down in different forms and edited by Matthew and Luke and placed in different settings, or Jesus told similar parables on two different occasions with appropriate variations. Ellis (*Gospel of Luke*, p. 194) observes that the "use of the same parabolic theme to teach different truths is frequent in rabbinical writings." Comparing Luke 15:3–7 with Matt 18:12–14 will show this. The second alternative is reasonable and does not preclude legitimate editing. The same basic story is found in the Gospel of Thomas (Logion 64). For a critical analysis, see Jeremias, *Parables of Jesus*, pp. 63–69. Bailey, *Peasant Eyes*, pp. 88–113, has a number of keen insights into the significance of this parable.

3. *The cost of being a disciple*

14:25–35

²⁵Large crowds were traveling with Jesus, and turning to them he said: ²⁶"If anyone comes to me and does not hate his father and mother, his wife and children, his brothers and sisters—yes, even his own life—he cannot be my disciple. ²⁷And anyone who does not carry his cross and follow me cannot be my disciple.

²⁸"Suppose one of you wants to build a tower. Will he not first sit down and estimate the cost to see if he has enough money to complete it? ²⁹For if he lays the foundation and is not able to finish it, everyone who sees it will ridicule him, ³⁰saying, 'This fellow began to build and was not able to finish.'

³¹"Or suppose a king is about to go to war against another king. Will he not first sit down and consider whether he is able with ten thousand men to oppose the one coming against him with twenty thousand? ³²If he is not able, he will send a delegation while the other is still a long way off and will ask for terms of peace. ³³In the same way, any of you who does not give up everything he has cannot be my disciple.

³⁴"Salt is good, but if it loses its saltiness, how can it be made salty again? ³⁵It is fit neither for the soil nor for the manure pile; it is thrown out.

"He who has ears to hear, let him hear."

The serious tone of the preceding parable continues as attention now turns to those who profess allegiance to Jesus.

25–27 With the words "large crowds" (v.25), Luke again draws attention to Jesus' popularity (see comment on 4:15). These crowds formed an entourage along with Jesus' own group (cf. 8:1–3). They were "traveling," an indication of further progress toward Jerusalem (see comment on 13:22). "Hate" (v.26) is not an absolute but a relative term. To neglect social customs pertaining to family loyalties would probably have been interpreted as hate. Jesus is not contravening the commandment to honor one's father and mother. Moreover, he says a disciple should hate "even his own life," whereas he speaks elsewhere of loving ourselves (10:27; cf. Matt 22:39; Mark 12:31). It is important to understand the ancient Near Eastern expression without blunting its force. (For the meaning of v.27, see comment on 9:23.)

28–32 Jesus uses two different circumstances to illustrate his basic point: discipleship requires a conscious advance commitment, made with a realistic estimate of the ultimate personal cost. The practical nature of the circumstances Jesus so vividly pictures underlines the fact that Christian discipleship is not some theoretical abstract ideal but hard reality.

33 This is clearly a crucial verse. But does it mean that it is impossible to retain any possessions at all if one wants to be a true disciple? The key word is *apotassetai* ("give up"). When used of persons, the verb means to take leave of or say good-by to someone. When used of things, it means to give up or renounce (BAG, s.v.). Here, in contrast to the cares of the rich young ruler (18:22), Jesus does not say a disciple should sell all his possessions and give everything away. His thought probably is that of abandonment of things, yielding up the right of ownership, rather than outright disposal of them. The disciple of Jesus may be given the use of things in trust, as a stewardship, but they are no longer his own. The present tense implies that what Jesus requires in relation to possessions is a continual attitude of abandonment.

In his recent work (cf. n. 34), Pilgrim (*Good News*, pp. 101f.) sides cautiously with those who take the view that abandonment was total only for Jesus' disciples in his lifetime. Pilgrim nevertheless sees this radical abandonment as speaking to the rich of Luke's day, urging them to share their goods with their needy brethren. But the principle of stewardship makes a spirit of abandonment—i.e., the willingness to part with our goods (which are not ultimately ours anyway)—necessary today. This is consistent with the command to *use* our possessions wisely (cf. 16:1–12).

34–35 This saying (v.34) poses two questions: Why does it occur here? and How does salt lose its saltiness? Its place here is due to the common element it shares with the preceding illustrations—the consistent quality of life Jesus expects of his disciples. We do not know with certainty what he had in mind in speaking of salt losing its saltiness. The reference may be to adulteration either by impurities in the beds by the Dead Sea from which salt slabs were taken or by inert fillers introduced by unscrupulous dealers. The point is that tasteless salt is useless. The one who "has ears" is expected to apply the lesson to himself (v.35).

Notes

---

34 On the Aramaic background of μωρανθῇ (*mōranthē*, "loses its saltiness"), see Jeremias, *Parables of Jesus*, p. 168, and Black, *Aramaic Approach*, pp. 166–67.

---

4. *Parables of joy* (15:1–32)

a. *The lost sheep*

15:1–7

> [1]Now the tax collectors and "sinners" were all gathering around to hear him. [2]But the Pharisees and the teachers of the law muttered, "This man welcomes sinners and eats with them."

³Then Jesus told them this parable: ⁴"Suppose one of you has a hundred sheep and loses one of them. Does he not leave the ninety-nine in the open country and go after the lost sheep until he finds it? ⁵And when he finds it, he joyfully puts it on his shoulders ⁶and goes home. Then he calls his friends and neighbors together and says, 'Rejoice with me; I have found my lost sheep.' ⁷I tell you that in the same way there will be more rejoicing in heaven over one sinner who repents than over ninety-nine righteous persons who do not need to repent.

This section begins what Manson (*Sayings of Jesus*, p. 282) has called the "Gospel of the Outcast." The large body of material in chapters 15–19 is unique to Luke and dramatically shows Jesus' concern for the social outcasts of his day (N.B. 15:1; 16:19–25; 17:11–19; 18:1–8; 9–14; 19:1–10). The twin parables (vv.3–7, 8–10) along with the longer one about the lost son (vv.11–32) depend for their interpretation on vv.1–2.

1 "Tax collectors" were among those who were ostracized because their work was considered dishonest or immoral (Jeremias, *Parables of Jesus*, p. 132). NIV appropriately puts "sinners" in quotation marks to show that this was not Luke's designation but the way others, i.e., the Pharisees, thought of them. For an explanation of the attitude of Pharisees to such "sinners," see comments on 5:29–30. "All" signifies either all such persons (wherever Jesus was at the time) or, generally speaking, the large proportion of them among the crowds who usually came to hear him. The imperfect periphrastic "were gathering" (cf. comment on 14:1) could indicate either the process of gathering at the time of the story or the habitual coming of "sinners" throughout Jesus' ministry.

2 In OT times it was taken for granted that God's people did not consort with sinners (cf. Ps 1), but the Pharisees extended this beyond the biblical intent. To go so far as to "welcome" them and especially to "eat" with them, implying table fellowship, was unthinkable to the Pharisees. The parables that follow show that the return of "sinners" to God should be a cause for joy to the religious leaders, as it was to God. Furthermore, "Jesus makes the claim for himself that he is acting in God's stead, that he is God's representative" (Jeremias, *Parables of Jesus*, p. 132.)

3–7 For the phrase "suppose one of you" (v.4), see comment on 14:5. There is a parallel between the expression *tis anthrōpos ex hymōn* (lit., "what man of you") and *tis gynē* ("what woman," v.8, where the lack of the additional words "of you" may indicate that no women were present). The situation described was a common one. One hundred sheep was a normal-sized flock. A count was taken nightly. The "open country" was a safe place to leave the sheep ("wilderness" [KJV, RSV] is misleading), though they would have to be left in someone's care. The frightened, confused, and perhaps injured sheep would have to be carried (v.5).

Two things are striking. First, in the obvious analogy to the search for the sheep, Jesus takes the initiative in seeking out lost people—a major theme in Luke (cf. 19:10). In contrast were some rabbis in the early centuries who hesitated to seek Gentile converts. But that does not invalidate Jesus' comment in Matthew 23:15 about Pharisees who were proselytizing aggressively. They were apparently trying to gain adherents to their sect, rather than compassionately seeking the lost. Second, the climax of the story is not only the return of the sheep but the triumphant rejoicing in its rescue (v.6). Jesus is stressing, both by parable and direct statement (v.7), that his seeking and receiving sinners pleases God.

"In heaven" (v.7) is a customary way of referring reverently to God without saying his name (cf. v.10 and comment on 14:11). The NIV rendering "there will be . . . rejoicing" brings out the future (*estai*, "will be"), which may include the day yet future of gathering and feasting (cf. 13:29). There are none who are truly "righteous" (cf. Rom 3:10); the "righteous persons" referred to in v.7 are devout people (cf. 1:6), or those who seem so (Matt 6:1), who have no gross, open sins to repent of.

b. The lost coin

15:8–10

> 8"Or suppose a woman has ten silver coins and loses one. Does she not light a lamp, sweep the house and search carefully until she finds it? 9And when she finds it, she calls her friends and neighbors together and says, 'Rejoice with me; I have found my lost coin.' 10In the same way, I tell you, there is rejoicing in the presence of the angels of God over one sinner who repents."

8–10 This parable is clearly linked to the preceding one, and the opening words are comparable (see comment on "suppose" at v.4). The "coins" (v.8) are *drachmas* (see NIV mg. on their value). They may have formed part of the woman's headdress, which, being part of her dowry, she constantly wore (Jeremias, *Parables of Jesus*, p. 134; cf. Marshall, *Gospel of Luke*, p. 603). Whether or not that is the case here, the mention of ten coins implies that they were all she had. "A lamp" was needed because the house would have had at best a few small windows or only a low doorway. She would "sweep" the hard earthen floor to find the coin by the sound of its clinking. As in v.6, the extent of joy expressed is striking (v.9). Considering the neighborly feelings in a small village, this is understandable, especially if the coin represented a tenth of the woman's savings. Moreover, Jesus' final comment (v.10) reinforces the point. "In the presence of the angels of God" is, like "in heaven" (v.7), a reverential reference to God. This parable, like that of the lost sheep, justifies Jesus' welcome of sinners (v.2).

c. The lost son

15:11–32

> 11Jesus continued: "There was a man who had two sons. 12The younger one said to his father, 'Father, give me my share of the estate.' So he divided his property between them.
> 13"Not long after that, the younger son got together all he had, set off for a distant country and there squandered his wealth in wild living. 14After he had spent everything, there was a severe famine in that whole country, and he began to be in need. 15So he went and hired himself out to a citizen of that country, who sent him to his fields to feed pigs. 16He longed to fill his stomach with the pods that the pigs were eating, but no one gave him anything.
> 17"When he came to his senses, he said, 'How many of my father's hired men have food to spare, and here I am starving to death! 18I will set out and go back to my father and say to him: Father, I have sinned against heaven and against you. 19I am no longer worthy to be called your son; make me like one of your hired men.' 20So he got up and went to his father.
> "But while he was still a long way off, his father saw him and was filled with compassion for him; he ran to his son, threw his arms around him and kissed him.

²¹"The son said to him, 'Father, I have sinned against heaven and against you. I am no longer worthy to be called your son.'

²²"But the father said to his servants, 'Quick! Bring the best robe and put it on him. Put a ring on his finger and sandals on his feet ²³Bring the fattened calf and kill it. Let's have a feast and celebrate. ²⁴For this son of mine was dead and is alive again; he was lost and is found.' So they began to celebrate.

²⁵"Meanwhile, the older son was in the field. When he came near the house, he heard music and dancing. ²⁶So he called one of the servants and asked him what was going on. ²⁷'Your brother has come,' he replied, 'and your father has killed the fattened calf because he has him back safe and sound.'

²⁸"The older brother became angry and refused to go in. So his father went out and pleaded with him. ²⁹But he answered his father, 'Look! All these years I've been slaving for you and never disobeyed your orders. Yet you never gave me even a young goat so I could celebrate with my friends. ³⁰But when this son of yours who has squandered your property with prostitutes comes home, you kill the fattened calf for him!'

³¹" 'My son,' the father said, 'you are always with me, and everything I have is yours. ³²But we had to celebrate and be glad, because this brother of yours was dead and is alive again; he was lost and is found.' "

The great parable of the lost son speaks even more eloquently than its predecessors to the situation set forth in vv.1–2. The first part (vv.11–24) conveys the same sense of joy on the lost being found the other two parables have; in contrast, the second part deals with the sour attitude of the elder brother. Like the Pharisees, he could not comprehend the meaning of forgiveness. The positions of the two sons would, in a structural analysis, be considered binary opposites, the lost son rises and the elder brother falls in moral state. The central figure, the father, remains constant in his love for both. As in v.2 (cf. comment), by telling the story Jesus identifies himself with God in his loving attitude to the lost. He represents God in his mission, the accomplishment of which should elicit joy from those who share the Father's compassion. The parable is one of the world's supreme masterpieces of storytelling. Its details are vivid; they reflect actual customs and legal procedures and build up the story's emotional and spiritual impact. But the expositor must resist the tendency to allegorize the wealth of detail that gives the story its remarkable verisimilitude. The main point of the parable—that God gladly receives repentant sinners—must not be obscured.

11–12 The "share of the estate" (v.12) that a younger son would receive on the death of the father would be one-third, because the older (or oldest) son received two-thirds, a "double portion"—i.e., twice as much as all other sons (Deut 21:17). If the property were given, as in this case, while the father lived, the heirs would have use of it (cf. v.31); but if they sold it, they could not normally transfer it as long as the father lived. The father also would receive any accrued interest (see Jeremias, *Parables of Jesus*, pp. 128–29). The son may have been asking (v.12) for immediate total ownership, but the parable does not specify the exact terms of the settlement. The property was "divided"; so the elder son was made aware of his share (cf. v.31).

13–16 NIV captures the vivid wording of the account, including "squandered his wealth" and "wild living" (v.13). The famine made employment and food even harder than usual to get. The "distant country" was apparently outside strictly Jewish territory, and the wayward son found himself with the demeaning job of feeding pigs (v.15), unclean animals for the Jews. He would even have eaten "pods" (v.16), which were seeds of the carob tree, common around the Mediterranean and used for pigs' food. He had fallen so low and had become so insignificant that "no one gave him anything"—an indication of total neglect.

17–20 "Came to his senses" (*eis eauton elthōn*; lit., "came to himself," v.17) was a common idiom, which in this Jewish story may carry the Semitic idea of repentance (Jeremias, *Parables of Jesus*, p. 130; cf. Bailey, *Poet and Peasant*, pp. 171–73). Certainly repentance lies at the heart of the words the son prepared to tell his father. The motivation for his return was hunger, but it was specifically to his "father" (v.18) that he wanted to return. The words "against heaven" (*eis ton ouranon*) can mean "to heaven," meaning that his sins were so many as to reach to heaven; more probably the meaning is that his sins were ultimately against God—veiled in the word "heaven" (cf. Ps 51:4). Assuming this latter meaning, we see that the parable is far more than an allegory, with the father representing God, for the father and God have distinct roles. The father in the story does, of course, portray the characteristics and attitudes of a loving heavenly Father. This does not mean that God is heavenly Father to everyone (note John 1:12; 8:42–44). Yet the Jews knew God's loving care was like that of a father (Ps 103:13). The son knew he had no right to return as a son (v.19), having taken and squandered his inheritance. He therefore planned to earn his room and board.

The description of his return and welcome is as vivid as that of his departure, with several beautiful touches. Because his father saw him "while he was still a long way off " (v.20) has led many to assume that the father was waiting for him, perhaps daily searching the distant road hoping for his appearance. This prompted the title of H. Thielicke's book of Jesus' parables, *The Waiting Father* (New York: Harper, 1959). The father's "compassion" assumes some knowledge of the son's pitiable condition, perhaps from reports. Some have pointed out that a father in that culture would not normally run as he did, which, along with his warm embrace and kissing, adds to the impact of the story. Clearly Jesus used every literary means to heighten the contrast between the father's attitude and that of the elder brother (and of the Pharisees, cf. vv.1–2).

21–24 The son's speech was never completed (v.21). Instead the father more than reversed the unspoken part about becoming a "hired man" (v.19). The robe, ring, and sandals (v.22) signified more than sonship (Jeremias, *Parables of Jesus*, p. 130); the robe was a ceremonial one such as a guest of honor would be given, the ring signified authority, and the sandals were those only a free man would wear. Marshall (*Gospel of Luke*, p. 610) doubts Manson's assertion that the robe was "a symbol of the New Age." The calf was apparently being "fattened" for some special occasion (v.23); people in first-century Palestine did not regularly eat meat. Note the parallel between "dead" and "alive" and "lost" and "found" (v.24)—terms that also apply to one's state before and after conversion to Christ (Eph 2:1–5). As in the parables of the lost sheep and the lost coin, it was time to "celebrate."

25–32 It seems strange that the older son was not there when the celebration began (v.25). Jesus' parables, however, are a fictional way of teaching enduring truth; and we may imagine that the celebration began so quickly that the older son was not aware of it (vv.26–27). Or, more likely in view of the dialogue in vv.26–31, his absence showed his distant relationship with his family. Verse 28 contrasts the older son with the father. The son became angry; but the father "went out," as he had for the younger brother, and "pleaded" rather than scolded. The older son's abrupt beginning—"Look!" (v.29)—betrays a disrespectful attitude toward his father. Likewise, "slaving" is hardly descriptive of a warm family relationship. "You never gave me," whether true or not, shows a long smoldering discontent. "This son of yours" (*ho huios sou houtos,* v.30) avoids acknowledging that the prodigal is his own brother, a disclaimer the father corrects by the words "this brother of yours" (v.32). The older brother's charges include sharp criticism of both father and brother. The story has made no mention of hiring prostitutes (v.30).

The father's response is nevertheless tender: "My son" (or "child," *teknon*) is followed by words of affirmation, not weakness (v.31). "We had to celebrate" (*euphranthenai . . . edei*) is literally "It was necessary to celebrate"; no personal subject is mentioned. This allows the implication that the elder brother should have joined in the celebration. The words "had to" (*edei*) introduce once more the necessity and urgency so prominent in Luke (see comment on 4:43).

Notes

11-32 Two issues, one literary and one theological, are often raised concerning this parable. Because the first part of the parable revolves around the younger brother and the latter around the older (and also for other reasons), some have found the parable's literary structure complex—i.e., originally consisting of two independent stories. If so, the resultant unit is well edited; for the older son appears from the very beginning, the two parts complement each other, and the latter part fits as well as the former into the context of vv.1-2. But this view cannot be sustained (cf. Marshall, *Gospel of Luke,* p. 605).

The theological issue centers in the absence of any hint of anything more than repentance and returning to God as Father being involved in salvation. (God's fatherhood is discussed in the comment on v.18.) It must, however, be kept in mind that this is a parable and thus is intended to portray only one aspect of the gospel—God's willingness to receive "sinners" and his joy over their return. Elsewhere in Luke's presentation of Christ as Savior, the Cross has its place (see Manson, *Sayings of Jesus,* p. 286; cf. Marshall, *Luke: Historian and Theologian,* pp. 170–75).

16 Χορτασθῆναι (*chortasthēnai,* "to feed on") has more MS support than γεμίσαι τὴν κοιλίαν (*gemisai tēn koilian,* "to fill the stomach"). NIV appears to have followed the latter but may simply be using a contemporary idiom to express the general idea of both verbs.

5. *Parable of the shrewd manager*

16:1-18

¹Jesus told his disciples: "There was a rich man whose manager was accused of wasting his possessions. ²So he called him in and asked him, 'What is this I hear about you? Give an account of your management, because you cannot be manager any longer.'
³"The manager said to himself, 'What shall I do now? My master is taking away my job. I'm not strong enough to dig, and I'm ashamed to beg—⁴I know what I'll do so that, when I lose my job here, people will welcome me into their houses.'
⁵"So he called in each one of his master's debtors. He asked the first, 'How much do you owe my master?'
⁶" 'Eight hundred gallons of olive oil,' he replied.

"The manager told him, 'Take your bill, sit down quickly, and make it four hundred.'

⁷"Then he asked the second, 'And how much do you owe?'

" 'A thousand bushels of wheat,' he replied.

"He told him, 'Take your bill and make it eight hundred.'

⁸"The master commended the dishonest manager because he had acted shrewdly. For the people of this world are more shrewd in dealing with their own kind than are the people of the light. ⁹I tell you, use worldly wealth to gain friends for yourselves, so that when it is gone, you will be welcomed into eternal dwellings.

¹⁰"Whoever can be trusted with very little can also be trusted with much, and whoever is dishonest with very little will also be dishonest with much. ¹¹So if you have not been trustworthy in handling worldly wealth, who will trust you with true riches? ¹²And if you have not been trustworthy with someone else's property, who will give you property of your own?

¹³"No servant can serve two masters. Either he will hate the one and love the other, or he will be devoted to the one and despise the other. You cannot serve both God and Money."

¹⁴The Pharisees, who loved money, heard all this and were sneering at Jesus. ¹⁵He said to them, "You are the ones who justify yourselves in the eyes of men, but God knows your hearts. What is highly valued among men is detestable in God's sight.

¹⁶"The Law and the Prophets were proclaimed until John. Since that time, the good news of the kingdom of God is being preached, and everyone is forcing his way into it. ¹⁷It is easier for heaven and earth to disappear than for the least stroke of a pen to drop out of the Law.

¹⁸"Anyone who divorces his wife and marries another woman commits adultery, and the man who marries a divorced woman commits adultery.

Chapter 16 follows the pattern characteristic of this part of Luke—viz., a combination of parables and sayings pointing again and again to the need for decision. Here (ch. 16), in spite of obvious diversity, one theme occurs several times. It is that of Jesus' teaching about material possessions—first in the parable of the shrewd manager, then in the comment about the Pharisees "who loved money" (v.14), and finally in the parable of the rich man and Lazarus.

The interpretation of this parable is notoriously difficult. Prior to any overall interpretation and application of it is a series of decisions regarding vv.8–13. Several interdependent questions face the expositor.

1. Is the "master" (kyrios) in v.8 the "master" in the parable (vv.3, 5) or the Lord Jesus?

2. Why did the "master" commend a dishonest manager?—a question that becomes more acute if the "master" is the Lord Jesus.

3. Where does the parable end, before v.8 (in which case the "master" is the Lord), in the middle of v.8 (in which case the sentence beginning "For the people" begins the comment on the parable), or at the end of v.8 (with the words "I tell you" [v.9] initiating the comment)?

4. Finally, are vv.10–12 and 13 part of the same unit or do they represent a separate tradition?

Discussion of these issues will help us interpret the parable. First, the "master" may refer to the Lord Jesus (1) because Luke normally uses kyrios to refer to Jesus and God, (2) because the latter part of v.8 (taking it as a unity) refers to believers and unbelievers rather than to characters in the story, and (3) because in 18:6 kyrios is used to refer to Jesus when he begins the explanation of a parable (see Ellis,

Gospel of Luke, p. 199). On the other hand, it more likely refers to the rich "master in the story, as (1) this would not be an unusual secular use of the word *kyrios*; (2) the religious terminology of v.8 (e.g., "people of the light") seems to refer to real people (in contrast to the characters of the secular illustration) and therefore sounds like the beginning of Jesus' explanation; (3) the real parallel to 18:6 ("the Lord said") may not be in this verse ("The master commended") but in v.9 ("I tell you"); and (4) v.8a seems to form a better conclusion to the parable than v.7 (so Fitzmyer, "The Story of the Dishonest Manager," *Semitic Background*, pp. 161–84, originally published in *Theological Studies* 25 [1964]: 23–42).

Second, even if the "master" of v.8 is the one in the story, the Lord Jesus seems to agree with the commendation; so we are left with the second question in either case: Why was a dishonest manager commended? The answer on the surface is "because he had acted shrewdly" (v.8). But was his shrewd act not dishonest? The text does not say that the manager's action in writing off the debts was dishonest. Rather the word "dishonest" may be used here because it serves a double purpose. First, it refers back to his initial act of mishandling the master's funds. Yet even one who had thus acted could do something commendable. Second, it introduces a chain of words using the same root. "Dishonest" (*adikos*) is recalled by "worldly" (*tēs adikias*) in v.9 and reappears twice in v.10 and once in v.11. Ellis suggests that *adikia* is a "technical theological expression," equivalent to a term used at Qumran describing the character of that age. When *adikia* is applied to people, it is because "they belong to this age and live according to its principles" (Ellis, *Gospel of Luke*, p. 199).

The reason the manager was now commended, though he had previously acted dishonestly, may be that he had at last learned how one's worldly wealth can be wisely given away to do good. This assumption is reasonable if Fitzmyer's suggestion (*Semitic Background*, pp. 175–76) is correct that the amount taken off the bills in vv.5–7 was not part of the debt owed the master but rather represented the interest the manager himself was charging. Though this would have been contrary to Jewish law (Exod 22:25; Lev 25:36–37; Deut 15:7–8; 23:19–20), charging a poor Jew such interest (actually usury) was often rationalized. The bill would be written in terms of the commodity rather than in monetary figures, with the interest hidden in the total. By law a master could not be held accountable for illegal acts of an employee. So the master in the parable was in a position to view the manager's activities objectively. If this explanation is correct, the manager's transaction was not illegal. In any event, the master would lose no money if the amount forfeited was simply the interest the manager would have gained. Furthermore, such a forgiveness of debts would hardly have hurt but would probably have helped the master's own reputation. Therefore, the master admires the manager's shrewdness. The manager knew his job and reputation were gone because of his previous mishandling of funds. He needed friends; and, by foregoing the customary interest, he won friends among the creditors. Jesus then uses this story to show that the "people of the light" could also accomplish much by wisely giving up some of their "worldly wealth."

This explanation follows in the main that of Fitzmyer, who draws on and expands J.D.M. Derrett, "Fresh Light on St. Luke xvi. I. The Parable of the Unjust Steward," NTS 7 (1960–61): 198–219. Even if some details of this view turn out to be unsatisfactory, the basic interpretation remains valid, that Jesus uses the story of the manager's actions not to commend graft but to encourage the "prudent use of material wealth" (Fitzmyer, *Semitic Background*, p. 177). The repetition of the idea of the cessation of the present scheme of things, first in v.4 ("when I lose my job here") and then in v.9 ("when it is gone"), emphasizes the need for prudent preparation for the inevitable.

Some commentators see this parable as an exhortation to act decisively in time of eschatological crisis, just as the manager acted in his personal crisis. This interpretation, while possible, ignores the fact that, though the theme of decision is important in Luke, here, as well as in other passages (e.g., 6:17–36; 13:13–34), the prudent use of material wealth predominates.

Third, the answer to the question of where the parable ends depends partly, as has been said, on who is designated "master" in v.8. It also depends on whether the reference to "people" in v.8b is to those in the world of the story or in the religious world of Jesus' time. In the former case, the reference is part of the story; in the latter, it is part of the commentary on it. If it is commentary, is it by Jesus or by Luke? If by Luke, the opening words of v.9, "I tell you," seem an abrupt reintroduction of Jesus' words. Since v.8b seems inappropriate as part of the story, it is best to assume that the parable ends with v.7 or, more likely, with the "master's" (rich man's) commendation of the manager.

Fourth, whether or not vv.10–13 were part of the original discourse (cf. Notes), as they stand in the text, they provide an integrated sequence of teachings structured around the ideas of dishonesty (see second discussion above) and responsibility ("trusted," *pistos*, "trusted" or "trustworthy," four times, and *pisteusei*, "will trust," once in vv.10–12).

1–4 "Manager" (*oikonomos*, v.1, often tr. "steward") is a broad term for an employee or agent who was entrusted with the management of funds or property. Mismanagement was possible, as in this parable, because strict accounts were not always kept. When word came from others—"What is this I hear about you?" (v.2) —he had to "give an account" (*apodos*, cf. Matt 12:36; Heb 13:17; 1 Peter 4:5). The manager's plight (v.3) was that he had a respectable "desk job" but could do little else. His decision, therefore, is made with a view to his personal security after his dismissal. The word "welcome" (*dexōntai*, v.4) will be dealt with in the comment at v.9.

5–8a As already noted, the bills may have been written in terms of commodities rather than cash, perhaps in order to hide the actual amount of interest. The amounts owed were large; the wheat is said to be equal to the yield of about one hundred acres (Jeremias, *Parables of Jesus*, p. 181). The difference in the percentage of reduction may be due to the difference in the relative value of the two commodities. The actual value of the reduction in each case has been computed to equal about five hundred denarii, roughly eighty dollars, or sixteen months' wages for a day laborer. The meaning of v.8a, as noted above, is not that a manager is commended for an act of dishonesty but that a dishonest manager is commended for an act of prudence.

8b–9 The contrast between those who belong to (lit., "are sons of") this age and those who belong to the light (v.8b) is familiar from Qumran (1QS 1:9; 2:16; 3:13; cf. Eph 5:8). Christians do not belong to this evil age, but they can nevertheless make responsible use of "worldly wealth" (v.9, cf. Notes). The "friends" may not refer to any particular people but simply be part of the parable's imagery (Danker, *Jesus*, p.

174). Usually they have been understood as being poor people, for whom Jesus (and Luke also) had a deep concern, and to whom we are here urged to give alms (cf. 12:33). "Worldly wealth" should not be stored up for oneself (cf. 12:21), since one day it will be "gone." "You will be welcomed" echoes v.4. The future passive of NIV is a good way of representing *dexōntai hymas* ("they will receive you"), which has no expressed subject. Although, if we follow the context closely, the subject may be the "friends," the use of the plural may reflect the Jewish custom of referring to God obliquely.

10–13 The theme of stewardship is now discussed in terms of trustworthiness as over against dishonesty (v.10). "Worldly wealth" (v.11) appears for the second time (cf. v.9). The property here is "someone else's" (v.12), presumably God's, in contrast to the parable's imagery in which, at least in Fitzmyer's view, the amount forgiven was the manager's own commission. Except for the word "servant," v.13 appears in precisely the same form in Matthew 6:24. The verse is equally appropriate in each context; here, however, it is connected to the context, not only topically, but verbally, through the use, for the third time, of *mamōnas* (cf. "worldly wealth," vv.9, 11), this time translated "money" in NIV. The addition of "servant" stresses the point that though one may *have* both God and money, we cannot *serve* them both.

14–15 Money (v.14) links this section (vv.14–18) with the preceding one. The charge that the Pharisees do not have a proper sense of values (v.15) leads to the saying about the value of the kingdom and the law (vv.16–17). In turn, reference to the permanence of the law becomes the context for a specific example of a contested moral standard, divorce and remarriage (v.18). Jesus' charge of greed is not leveled at the Pharisees elsewhere in the Gospels, nor is it intended to be an absolute generalization. Jewish teachers who had been influenced by Hellenistic culture were aware that philosophers often taught for fees. Rabbis in the first centuries of our era often had secular jobs. The Pharisees would not have been immune to desires for remuneration commensurate with their own sense of importance. Later on, Paul was to work at a trade so he could say that he did not "put on a mask to cover up greed" (1 Thess 2:5; cf. 1 Cor 9:12). Self-justification (v.15) is a temptation for religious people (cf. Matt 5:20; 6:1).

16–17 The Pharisees had the truth of the "Law" of Moses (Genesis to Deuteronomy) and the "Prophets" (v.16, here representing the rest of the OT). They failed to respond not only to the Good News of the kingdom but even to their own Scriptures (cf. Mark 7:8–9), whose authority continued into the present age (v.17). Verse 29 also alludes to their failure to heed the Law and the Prophets (see comments). For the relationship of John the Baptist to the kingdom (v.16a), see 7:28 and comment on that verse. Verse 16 appears in slightly different form—and with the sentences reversed—in Matthew's passage about John the Baptist (Matt 11:12–13). The wording in Matthew is notoriously difficult to interpret, but the substitution in Luke (v.16b) of "being preached" (*euangelizetai*) for "forcefully advancing" (*biazetai*, possibly, "suffered violence," see comments on Matt 11:13) limits the meaning here. *Biazetai*, which occurs in Matthew 11:13 though not in Luke 16:16b, does occur in v.16c—"is forcing his way," a translation that takes the verb, probably correctly, to be in the middle voice. Matthew has "forceful men lay hold of it" (*biastai* *harpazousin autēn*), conveying a sense of violence not necessarily implied in Luke's "everyone is forcing his way into it" (*pas eis autēn biazetai*). This could be understood as expressing violence if one interprets it in accord with what Matthew has; otherwise it could simply express the enthusiastic drive of those determined to enter the kingdom (cf. Luke 13:24). However one interprets this difficult verse, it is clear that the Pharisees had missed what was really of value (v.15), while all around them were people whose values were in order and who were energetically seeking the kingdom (cf. Matt 13:44–46). The truth of v.17 is also expressed in the Sermon on the Mount (Matt 5:17–20).

18 This brief excerpt from Jesus' teaching on divorce and remarriage is included as an example of one aspect of the law the Pharisees tended to minimize. The teaching is essentially the same as in Matthew 5:32, except that Luke (1) omits the phrase "except for marital unfaithfulness," (2) says that the remarried man commits adultery rather than that he causes his first wife to do so, and (3) includes a comment about a man who marries a divorced woman. See comments on Matthew 5:32 for the basic teaching.

Notes

4 The use of the aorist ἔγνων (*egnōn*, "I know") rather than the present tense γινώσκω (*ginōskō*) has often been commented on. Exegetes have tended to read too much into the simple aorist and to stress too much its punctiliar aspect. Here it could imply a flash of inspiration, "I've got it!" or, more likely as the culmination of his deliberations, "I've decided."

9 Μαμωνᾶς τῆς ἀδικίας (*mamōnas tēs adikias*, "worldly wealth," lit., "the mammon of injustice" or "of unrighteousness") is probably a Semitic expression used idiomatically to signify money. *Adikias* probably carries the thought, found in the Qumran writings, of that which characterizes the godless world (Ellis, *Gospel of Luke*, p. 199).

10–13 These verses appear to have been independent sayings brought together here by Luke because they share certain catchwords with the preceding verses. This is not impossible; there are no transitional words that indicate that the sayings were given on the same occasion in Jesus' ministry as the preceding. Verses 10–12 are unique to Luke and presumably come from his special source. Verse 13 is found, without the word "servant," in Matt 6:24 and is usually ascribed to Q.

6. *The rich man and Lazarus*

16:19–31

[19]"There was a rich man who was dressed in purple and fine linen and lived in luxury every day. [20]At his gate was laid a beggar named Lazarus, covered with sores [21]and longing to eat what fell from the rich man's table. Even the dogs came and licked his sores.

[22]"The time came when the beggar died and the angels carried him to Abraham's side. The rich man also died and was buried. [23]In hell, where he was in torment, he looked up and saw Abraham far away, with Lazarus by his side. [24]So he called to him, 'Father Abraham, have pity on me and send Lazarus to dip the tip of his finger in water and cool my tongue, because I am in agony in this fire.'

²⁵"But Abraham replied, 'Son, remember that in your lifetime you received your good things, while Lazarus received bad things, but now he is comforted here and you are in agony. ²⁶And besides all this, between us and you a great chasm has been fixed, so that those who want to go from here to you cannot, nor can anyone cross over from there to us.'

²⁷"He answered, 'Then I beg you, father, send Lazarus to my father's house, ²⁸for I have five brothers. Let him warn them, so that they will not also come to this place of torment.'

²⁹"Abraham replied, 'They have Moses and the Prophets; let them listen to them.'

³⁰" 'No, father Abraham,' he said, 'but if someone from the dead goes to them, they will repent.'

³¹"He said to him, 'If they do not listen to Moses and the Prophets, they will not be convinced even if someone rises from the dead.' "

The expositor's basic concern is not the nature and history of this story (cf. Notes) but its primary significance in its Lukan context. It is set in a series of encounters with the Pharisees (cf. 15:1–2; 16:14). Its meaning must be understood in that context. The Pharisees did not follow their own Scriptures, the "Law and the Prophets" (v.16); so they were no better than the rich man's brothers who "have Moses and the Prophets" (v.29). The Pharisees professed belief in a future life and in future judgment. However, they did not live in conformity with that belief but rather in the pursuit of wealth (v.14), just like the rich man of the parable. Even Jesus' resurrection (possibly alluded to in v.31) would not convince them. It is implicit in the account that one's attitude to God and his word is confirmed in this life and that it cannot be altered in the next one.

While the parable does contain a few doctrinal implications, the expositor must keep in mind that one cannot build an eschatology on it. To do that will result in an anachronism; for though Revelation 20:14 places the throwing of death and Hades into the lake of fire at the end of history (the "second death"), in this story the rich man is already in a torment of fire, in his body, while his brothers are still living. It should be understood as a story containing some limited eschatological ideas familiar to Jesus' audience. Thus understood, the story makes a powerful case for (1) the future reversal of the human condition (cf. 6:20–26), (2) the reality of future judgment based on one's decisions in this life, and (3) the futility of even a resurrection to persuade those who persist in rejecting God's revealed word.

19–20 This paragraph vividly pictures the earthly state of the two men and prepares the hearer and reader for the reversal in vv.22–24. The latter is both striking and consistent with Luke's presentation of Jesus' teaching, but it is not in itself the main feature of the story. The fact that Jesus named the "beggar" (v.20) while not naming the "rich man" (v.19) may imply that one was ultimately more important. The naming of a character in the story need not lead to the conclusion some have drawn that Lazarus was a real person, though parables usually do not have named characters. Nor is there convincing evidence that this Lazarus is the same one Jesus raised from the dead (John 11). Admittedly, the similarity is remarkable, since both stories deal with death and resurrection (cf. v.30), and since in both instances resurrection does not convince unbelievers (see Marshall, *Gospel of Luke*, p. 635). Nevertheless, Lazarus was a common name, the Greek form (*Lazaros*) of the Hebrew Eleazar (*'el'āzār*, "[whom] God has helped"). It is probably used symbolically. Tradition has given the name of "Dives," meaning "rich," to the anonymous rich man (cf. Notes).

"Purple" (v.19) was a dyed cloth worn by the wealthy. The Roman soldiers mocked Jesus by putting a purple robe on him in the Praetorium before the Crucifixion (Mark 15:17, 20). In a vivid contrast to the rich man, Jesus depicts Lazarus as neglected and subjected to insult even by "the dogs" (v.20).

21–24 After his death, Lazarus is escorted by "the angels," in contrast to the rich man who was merely "buried" (v.22). Angelic activity is not foreign to the biblical scene (Heb 1:14), but here Jesus' reference to the angels is probably simply an artistic touch.

"Abraham's side" may picture reclining at a banquet, like the "feast in the kingdom of God" at which Abraham will be present (13:28–29). If so, it may contrast with vv.20–21, where the rich man sits at the table while Lazarus longs for the scraps. Otherwise it might be a symbol of reunion with Abraham and the other patriarchs at death. "Hell" (v.23) is "Hades" (NIV mg.). In early classical literature Hades was a term for the place of departed spirits. In the LXX it represents the Hebrew Sheol, the realm of the dead. It occurs ten times in the NT, two of them in Luke (cf. 10:15). In the NT Hades is never used of the destiny of the believer. Neither is it identified with Gehenna (*geenna*), which is usually connected with fiery judgment, as in Matthew 5:22, 29–30 (Luke only in 12:5, q.v.). Here (v.23) Hades stands in contrast to the place and state of Lazarus's blessing. The division between the two is absolute and final (v.26). "Father Abraham" (v.24) expresses the normal attitude a Jew, conscious of his heritage, would have (John 8:39).

25–26 Abraham's response, "Son" (*teknon*, v.25), like the identical term on the lips of the Prodigal Son's father (15:31), conveys something of the compassion God himself shows even to those who spurn him. The possessive pronoun in "your good things" is similar in its force to the words "for himself" in 12:21. In a masterly summary Jesus contrasts the previous states of the rich man and Lazarus with the "now" and "here" of their situations after death. Verse 26 shows the utter and unchangeable finality of their decision.

27–31 This unchangeability comes from a hardness not only toward Christ but toward "Moses and the Prophets" (v.29; cf. John 5:46). Not even a spectacular "sign," like one returning from the dead (vv.27, 30), can change those whose hearts are set against God's word, as the response of many to the resurrection of Jesus was to show.

Notes

19–31 Over the years some commentators have held that this is not a parable but a story about two men, possibly known to Jesus' audience. (For a recent example of this view, see Summers, *Luke*, p. 195.) The usual reasons for supporting this interpretation are (1) the story lacks an introduction similar to the introductions to most of Jesus' parables and (2) at least one of the characters is named. At the other extreme is the view that follows a study by Gressmann (see Creed, pp. 209–10) and assumes that the story originated in Egyptian folklore. A more recent structural approach is more concerned with the structure and contemporary symbolism of the story itself than with any extended history of tradition.

As indicated in the introductory comments to this section, to interpret the story literally introduces a difficult anachronism, that the man is already being tormented by fire, though the event of Rev 20:14 has not yet taken place. The story can be understood as a parable that realistically portrays the fate of those who have rejected the Lord. If Luke had clearly indicated that Jesus was referring to an actual event, we would have to attempt to resolve the anachronism. But since Luke has not done so, and since the story is powerfully didactic, it seems best to interpret it as a parable. However, it is no mere story chosen for its usefulness as an illustration but a rather sober portrayal of yet unseen realities.

The expositor will do best by expounding this passage in its Lukan context, stressing those elements that are clearly affirmed in biblical teaching elsewhere. Issues of source or of background are not as important in this instance as are its immediate purpose and message.

19 The vagueness of ἄνθρωπος . . . τις (*anthrōpos . . . tis*, "a certain man") was intolerable for early readers, and some early "improvements" were made, such as the insertion of the name Νευης (*Neuēs*) in P[75] (see Creed, p. 211, and Marshall, *Gospel of Luke*, pp. 634–35).

---

7. Sin, faith, duty

17:1–10

> [1]Jesus said to his disciples: "Things that cause people to sin are bound to come, but woe to that person through whom they come. [2]It would be better for him to be thrown into the sea with a millstone tied around his neck than for him to cause one of these little ones to sin. [3]So watch yourselves.
>
> "If your brother sins, rebuke him, and if he repents, forgive him. [4]If he sins against you seven times a day, and seven times comes back to you and says, 'I repent,' forgive him."
>
> [5]The apostles said to the Lord, "Increase our faith!"
>
> [6]He replied, "If you have faith as small as a mustard seed, you can say to this mulberry tree, 'Be uprooted and planted in the sea,' and it will obey you.
>
> [7]"Suppose one of you had a servant plowing or looking after the sheep. Would he say to the servant when he comes in from the field, 'Come along now and sit down to eat'? [8]Would he not rather say, 'Prepare my supper, get yourself ready and wait on me while I eat and drink; after that you may eat and drink'? [9]Would he thank the servant because he did what he was told to do? [10]So you also, when you have done everything you were told to do, should say, 'We are unworthy servants; we have only done our duty.'"

As the heading indicates, this unit contains various brief teachings. As with some other parts in this special section of Luke, it is difficult to understand why these teachings are brought together. The introductory words "Jesus said to his disciples" are similar to those in other places where there apparently is no attempt to establish a chronological sequence (e.g., 12:22, 54; 13:6; 16:1). This does not rule out the possibility that the parables in these instances were originally given sequentially, but they could be understood as merely marking a break from the preceding section. Yet it is also possible to see a logical connection between the end of chapter 16 and the beginning of chapter 17, if we understand "the things that cause people to sin" (v.1) to be the sins of the Pharisees, such as those mentioned in 16:14.

Some may feel that logical connections within this passage are difficult to discern, e.g., between v.4 and v.5. However, there is a common unifying theme of attitudes in the Christian community. The connections are no weaker than those that join similar teachings in Matthew 18 about care for the little ones, the problem of sin in the community, and prayer. Actually, though we expect to find material in topical rather than chronological order in Matthew (in contrast to most of Luke), in Matthew 18 the pericopes are joined by chronological indicators, while those in Luke are not. The contexts of the two passages are totally different, and here in Luke the teachings on prayer are not parallel to those on prayer in Matthew 18 but rather to those in Matthew 17:19–20 and 21:21–22. Here, as throughout the Synoptics, each Gospel must be studied and interpreted in its own context.

1–3a Jesus has been addressing the Pharisees since 16:14. Now he resumes his conversation with the disciples. The "things that cause people to sin" (v.1) are the familiar *skandala* (lit., "traps," but symbolically whatever causes people to fall into sin). "Woe" recalls 6:24–26. A "millstone" (v.2) was a stone of sufficient weight to crush grain as it was being rotated in a mill. The "little ones" would seem to be either young or new believers or people the world takes little notice of. There is no mention here of children as in Matthew 18:1–6. There is no antecedent for "these." So if the conversation stands alone, it must be taken to refer to those who were actually standing there with Jesus. In the NIV paragraph structure, v.3a—"So watch yourselves"—is joined with the preceding saying rather than with the following (as in RSV, NASB). Either way makes sense.

3b–4 The two members of v.3b must be given equal weight. Rebuke of the sinner and forgiveness of the penitent are both Christian duties. Verse 4 does not, of course, establish a specific number of times for forgiveness but rather shows the principle of being generous in forgiving others (cf. Matt 6:12). This is the only right response for those who have themselves been forgiven.

5–6 The apostles may have felt that this kind of forgiveness would demand more faith than they had (v.5). The "mulberry tree" (v.6) in Luke corresponds to the mountain in Matthew 17:20; 21:21; and Mark 11:23. In each instance the object is to be disposed of in the "sea" (probably Galilee). The black mulberry tree (KJV "sycamine," not to be confused with "sycamore") grew quite large, to a height of some thirty-five feet, and would be difficult to uproot. The mustard seed is proverbially small, a suitable metaphor for the amount of faith needed to do the seemingly impossible. Jesus' answer to the request for additional faith seems to be that they should use the faith they had to petition God.

7–10 This is one of the passages in which Luke presents Jesus' teaching about the ideal of servanthood. The world's idea of success is to lord it over others; Jesus' way is the reverse—namely, servanthood—which is actually the way to true greatness. Two earlier parables on this theme occur in 12:35–37; 42–48. The circumstances Jesus describes here were normal in that society and the point obvious. In contrast, in the parable in 12:35–37, Jesus presented a reversal of the normal procedure, with the master doing just what 17:7 rules out. The master's extraordinary act depicted in 12:35–37 symbolizes God's grace, while the normal expectation of the master here in Luke 17 symbolizes the proper servant attitude. Jesus did not intend to demean servants but to make their duty clear. In this respect the NIV translation "unworthy" for *achreioi* (v.10) is an improvement over KJV's "unprofitable."

8. Ten healed of leprosy

17:11–19

> [11]Now on his way to Jerusalem, Jesus traveled along the border between Samaria and Galilee. [12]As he was going into a village, ten men who had leprosy met him. They stood at a distance [13]and called out in a loud voice, "Jesus, Master, have pity on us!"
>
> [14]When he saw them, he said, "Go, show yourselves to the priests." And as they went, they were cleansed.
>
> [15]One of them, when he saw he was healed, came back, praising God in a loud voice. [16]He threw himself at Jesus' feet and thanked him—and he was a Samaritan.
>
> [17]Jesus asked, "Were not all ten cleansed? Where are the other nine? [18]Was no one found to return and give praise to God except this foreigner?" [19]Then he said to him, "Rise and go; your faith has made you well."

Not only is this narrative peculiar to Luke, but it also stresses several characteristically Lukan themes. Jerusalem is the goal of Jesus' journey (cf. 9:51; 13:33); Jesus has mercy on social outcasts; he conforms to Jewish norms by requiring that the lepers go for the required priestly declaration of health (cf. Lev 14); faith and healing should bring praise to God (cf. 18:43; Acts 3:8–9); and the grace of God extends beyond Judaism, with Samaritans receiving special attention (cf. 10:25–37).

11–13 That Luke does not mention the particular place where the healing was done implies that he did not consider the exact locale important historically or theologically. What is important is the reminder (possibly to indicate a new phase of his ministry) of Jesus' progress toward Jerusalem (v.11). The "village" (v.12) lies somewhere in the border territory between Galilee and Samaria (cf. Notes); so Jewish and Samaritan lepers share their common misery at its edge. The lepers maintain their proper distance, call Jesus by a term found only in Luke—"Master" (*epistata*, v.13; cf. 5:5)—and ask only for pity without specifying their request.

14–19 Jesus' command (v.14) required obedience based on some faith in the reliability of the speaker (cf. Matt 12:13; Mark 3:5; Luke 6:10). On their way to the priests, the lepers are "cleansed" (*ekatharisthēsan*). Jesus, however, uses the more comprehensive word "made well" (*sesōken*, v.19) on speaking to the Samaritan who returned to give thanks. Though Luke does not say whether the others had faith, it need not be denied them. The stress is on the openly expressed gratitude of the Samaritan, who alone brought praise to God (vv.15–16).

Notes

11 Διὰ μέσον (*dia meson*, "along the border between") is a troublesome phrase. This accusative is well attested, but the Byzantine tradition has the genitive μέσου (*mesou*, KJV, "through the midst"). Conzelmann (*Theology of Luke*, pp. 68–72) considered this a theological use of geography, with Luke trying to establish a travel theme based on an allegedly distorted view of the geographical relationship of Samaria to Galilee. On Conzelmann's assumption, Luke thought that Judea was directly south of Galilee, with Samaria alongside both. On this view, Jesus was going south along this supposed north-south border. Actually, Luke does not state that Jesus made just one journey from north to south but

rather suggests that he crisscrossed the area, making perhaps several trips to Jerusalem before his final stay there. In this case he might have been on his way east to Perea, to turn south on the highway along the east side of the Jordan River.

---

9. The coming of the kingdom of God

17:20–37

20Once, having been asked by the Pharisees when the kingdom of God would come, Jesus replied, "The kingdom of God does not come with your careful observation, 21nor will people say, 'Here it is,' or 'There it is,' because the kingdom of God is within you."

22Then he said to his disciples, "The time is coming when you will long to see one of the days of the Son of Man, but you will not see it. 23Men will tell you, 'There he is!' or 'Here he is!' Do not go running off after them. 24For the Son of Man in his day will be like the lightning, which flashes and lights up the sky from one end to the other. 25But first he must suffer many things and be rejected by this generation.

26"Just as it was in the days of Noah, so also will it be in the days of the Son of Man. 27People were eating, drinking, marrying and being given in marriage up to the day Noah entered the ark. Then the flood came and destroyed them all.

28"It was the same in the days of Lot. People were eating and drinking, buying and selling, planting and building. 29But the day Lot left Sodom, fire and sulfur rained down from heaven and destroyed them all.

30"It will be just like this on the day the Son of Man is revealed. 31On that day no one who is on the roof of his house, with his goods inside, should go down to get them. Likewise, no one in the field should go back for anything. 32Remember Lot's wife! 33Whoever tries to keep his life will lose it, and whoever loses his life will preserve it. 34I tell you, on that night two people will be in one bed; one will be taken and the other left. 35Two women will be grinding grain together; one will be taken and the other left."

37"Where, Lord?" they asked.

He replied, "Where there is a dead body, there the vultures will gather."

Luke contains two major discourses about the future, the present passage and 21:5–33. Both have close parallels in Matthew 24 and Mark 13. (See comments on 21:5–33 for a discussion of interpretive and critical issues a comparison with these parallels involves.) Luke 17 is more uniformly apocalyptic than Luke 21—i.e., no human agency appears here (in contrast to the besieging armies of 21:20); God acts directly from heaven. Also the prohibition against lingering is stronger here than in chapter 21. People on the rooftop when the Son of Man is revealed dare not take a moment to go inside their houses. But those addressed in chapter 21 are threatened by a military siege and should avoid getting caught in the city. The urgency in chapter 17 is greater with less time to spare than in chapter 21.

20–21 The Pharisees' question about the kingdom initiates this new cycle of Jesus' teachings. This includes (1) a saying about the coming of the kingdom that is unique to Luke's Gospel (vv.20–21), (2) the discourse on the coming of the Son of Man (vv.22–37), and (3) a parable of encouragement for those who wait for vindication when the Son of Man comes (18:1–8).

The time of the coming of the kingdom was important to both Pharisees and Christians, though for different reasons. By the time Luke was written, rumors were abroad that the day of the Lord had already come (2 Thess 2:1–2). Later, others would question whether the Lord would return at all (2 Peter 3:3–4). Before this point in Luke, Jesus had made it clear that the kingdom had already come, insofar as God's power was unleashed against demons (11:20). Jesus will shortly indicate by a parable that the full expression of the kingdom does not take place in the immediate future (19:11–27). The present passage is therefore important as a further definition of the nature of the kingdom.

To the question "When?" (v.20; cf. v.37, "Where?"), Jesus says that the kingdom will not come *meta paratērēseōs* (lit., "with observation"). This may have one of three meanings, none of them excluding the others: (1) it cannot be foreseen from signs; (2) it is not an observable process; and (3) it does not come with or through observing rites. The second meaning accords most naturally with the most common usage of *paratērēsis* and with the context, which emphasizes suddenness, though the first meaning may fit the Pharisees' frame of reference better. The NIV "within you" (for *entos hymōn*, v.21) is a questionable translation. Jesus would hardly tell Pharisees, most of whom (especially those who interrogated him) were unbelievers, that the kingdom was within them (cf. Marshall, *Gospel of Luke*, p. 655, who considers the word "you" to be indefinite, though he also rejects the translation "within"). The NIV margin ("among you") is surely right.

Luke's presentation of the kingdom in Jesus' teaching is dynamic rather than psychological, as seen in 11:20: "But if I drive out demons by the finger of God, then the kingdom of God has come to you." The idea behind " 'Here it is' or 'There it is' " is that of the kingdom's authoritative presence. Jesus is thus saying that people are the subjects, not the timekeepers, of God's kingdom. Whether he means here that the kingdom is already present (which was true, in the sense of 11:20), or whether he used the present "is" in a vivid futuristic sense, he is emphasizing its suddenness.

22–25 In this paragraph, which begins with a saying not found in Matthew or Mark, Jesus continues the emphasis on the suddenness of the kingdom's coming. Does "one of the days" (v.22) refer back to the time of his earthly ministry or forward to his return? Does "one" mean any "one" or "the first" of a series as in Matthew 28:1 and parallels? Since Jesus now addresses his disciples, who will have reason to long for his return, and since what follows deals with that return, "one of the days" probably refers to the initiation of the reign of the coming Son of Man (cf. Notes). "You will not see it" implies "not yet" rather than "never." His coming will be obvious, "like the lightning" (v.24); so rumors of seeing him in various places ("here," "there," vv.21, 23) cannot be true. (For Jesus' use of the plural "days" [v.22] and of the third person referring to the Son of Man [e.g., "in his day"] and the combination of these with the passion prediction in v.25, see Notes.)

The inclusion of the passion prediction (v.25) is natural in Luke, who stresses the order of suffering before glory (cf. 24:26, 46; Acts 17:3). "This generation" may obliquely refer back to the Pharisees. Broadly it refers to Jesus' contemporaries, elsewhere called by him "unbelieving and perverse" (9:41) and "wicked" (11:29; cf. 11:31–32, 50–51).

26–29 Jesus' references to Noah (vv.26–27) and Lot (v.28) serve to illustrate the suddenness of the revelation of the Son of Man. The words "eating, drinking," etc. (vv.27–28) describe the usual round of life's activities. NIV accurately represents the Greek use of asyndeton (i.e., a sequence of words without connectives such as "and"). This effectively gives the impression of continually repeated activities. Unexpected destruction came as a judgment on people in the times of Noah and of Lot. God's sudden interruption of human affairs is part of the apocalyptic perspective on the divine ordering of history. The term "apocalyptic" (from the Gr. *apokalypto*, "reveal") occurs in v.30: "the Son of Man is revealed" (*apokalyptetai*). The consummation of history, indeed, of the kingdom of God itself, is realized in the revelation of the Son of Man.

30–36 As already noted, unlike the siege of Jerusalem described in chapter 21, the sudden coming of the Son of Man (v.30) leaves no time even for a quick gathering of possessions from one's home (v.31). This theme of imminency blends into a call for decision between eternal values and present possessions reminiscent of chapter 12. The reason for returning to house or field is to salvage possessions. Lot's wife (v.32), reluctant to leave her old life, looked back to Sodom (Gen 19:26). This leads to the saying in v.33 (used elsewhere in an ethical sense) regarding discipleship (Matt 10:39) but employed here with a very concrete application.

The solemn words, "I tell you" (v.34) introduce a warning that the apocalyptic moment reveals ultimate destinies. Even those closely associated (in bed and at work) are separated. "Will be taken" (*paralēmphthēsetai*, vv.34–35) probably has its normal sense of being taken into fellowship (in Noah's case into safety), rather than being taken into judgment, for which there seems to be no precedent (cf. TDNT, 4:11–14). The one "left" (*aphethēsetai*) is thereby abandoned to judgment. The alternate interpretation, however, is possible in this context. The two illustrations reflect either simultaneous activities early in the morning (Danker, *Jesus*, p. 183) or, more likely, activities selected to show that the Son of Man could come at any time, day or night.

37 The Pharisees had asked "When?" (v.20); the disciples asked "Where?" For us Jesus' reply is somewhat obscure. The hovering "vultures" (*aetoi*, usually tr. "eagles," but here probably meaning scavengers such as vultures [BAG, s.f.]) may symbolize judgment on the spiritually dead. Also they may merely represent the place of carnage.

Notes

21 The phrase ἐντὸς ὑμῶν (*entos hymōn*, "within you") can also mean "in your control," according to an exegetical note by C.H. Roberts (" Ἐντος Ὑμῶν," HTR 41 [1948]: 1–8) and one by J.G. Griffiths ("The Kingdom of Heaven [Lk XVII.21]," ExpT 63 [1951–52]: 30–31 [reprinted in the *Bible Translator* 4 (1953): 7–8]). This would not mean that the Pharisees controlled the kingdom but that response to it was under their control. C.F.D. Moule provides evidence against this view in his *Idiom Book of New Testament Greek* (Cambridge: Cambridge University Press, 1959), pp. 83–84.

22 Μίαν τῶν ἡμερῶν (*mian tōn hēmerōn*, "one of the days") seems to combine both the singular "day" (vv.24, 30) and the plural "days" (vv.26, 28). It seems to be an echo of the Day of the Lord, a term denoting the occasion on which God acts mightily in history, especially the inception of the Messianic Age. A parallel in which both singular and plural are used with the same point of reference is Amos 8:11, 13.

24 Ἐν τῇ ἡμέρα αὐτοῦ (*en tē hēmera autou*, "in his day") sharpens, by its use of the third instead of the first person, the issue as to whether Jesus spoke of himself in such sayings. A common conclusion of recent studies on the "Son of Man" is that the sayings using this designation may be grouped into those that use the phrase as a neutral (or covert) reference to the speaker, those that refer to the expected suffering of Jesus, and those that refer to the future glory of the Son of Man. Some claim that the future (apocalyptic) sayings of Jesus refer to someone else, not him. Jeremias (*New Testament Theology*, p. 276), however, correctly observes that "quite apart from the absence of evidence in the sources, it is impossible that in the 'Son of Man' Jesus should have seen a future saving figure who was to be distinguished from himself. In that case, one would have to suppose that Jesus had seen himself as a forerunner, as the prophet of the Son of Man." Jesus undoubtedly saw himself, not some other, as the one who fulfilled the OT prophecies. The use of the third person is common in all three types of Son-of-Man sayings. (For a fuller bibliography, see note on 5:24). Both the suffering and the apocalyptic type sayings are found in this passage (vv.24–25).

Regarding the textual evidence for "in his day," a variety of significant MSS omit it (e.g., P[75] B D). The omission could have been accidental, if a copyist's eyes mistakenly jumped from the ending of "man" (-πον, *pou*) to the ending of "his" (-τον, *tou*), the last word of the Greek phrase in question. However, the MSS cited are probably correct.

---

10. *Parable of the persistent widow*

18:1–8

> [1]Then Jesus told his disciples a parable to show them that they should always pray and not give up. [2]He said: "In a certain town there was a judge who neither feared God nor cared about men. [3]And there was a widow in that town who kept coming to him with the plea, 'Grant me justice against my adversary.'
>
> [4]"For some time he refused. But finally he said to himself, 'Even though I don't fear God or care about men, [5]yet because this widow keeps bothering me, I will see that she gets justice, so that she won't eventually wear me out with her coming!' "
>
> [6]And the Lord said, "Listen to what the unjust judge says. [7]And will not God bring about justice for his chosen ones, who cry out to him day and night? Will he keep putting them off? [8]I tell you, he will see that they get justice, and quickly. However, when the Son of Man comes, will he find faith on the earth?"

1 This parable must be interpreted with reference to the eschatological theme in chapter 17, as v.8b makes clear. The story is not intended to apply to prayer in general, as though one needed to pester God for every need until he reluctantly responds. The theme is that of the vindication of God's misunderstood and suffering people, as v.7 states. God's people in OT days needed to "wait" on God as he worked out justice with apparent slowness. "Do not . . . let my enemies triumph over me. No one whose hope is in you will ever be put to shame" (Ps 25:2–3). In the final days the martyrs wait for vindication (Rev 6:9–11). Ultimately delay is ended and the "mystery" of God completed (Rev 10:6–7). Meanwhile we wrestle with the problem of evil and with issues of theodicy. Under these circumstances we should "always pray and not give up."

2–3 The designation "unjust judge" (*ho kritēs tēs adikias*, v.6) is similar to the idiom in 16:8, "the dishonest manager" (*ton oikonomon tēs adikias*). *Adikia* ("injustice" or "dishonesty") also appears in connection with wealth in the Greek of 16:9, where it has the connotation of "worldly" (cf. 16:11). Therefore we should probably understand the judge (v.2) to be a "man of the world," who, though crooked, prided himself on shrewd judicial decisions. The judge is typical of a local Gentile judge known throughout the Hellenistic world (cf. *Livy* 22. 3 and comments in Danker, *Jesus*, p. 184). J.D.M. Derrett ("Law in the NT: The Unjust Judge," NTS 18 [1971–72]: 178–91) suggests that as a local secular administrative officer he would be approached by those who could not bring their cases to the high religious court. Being easily accessible and having the authority to make quick decisions, he would naturally be besieged by people such as the widow of the story (v.3).

4–6 The words "wear me out" (*hypōpiazē me*, v.5) are difficult to translate, for they literally mean "strike under the eye, give a black eye to" (BAG, s.v.). Commentators usually give them a figurative meaning. Derrett ("Unjust Judge," p. 191) shows that they are common idiom in eastern countries, where to have one's face blackened means to suffer shame. Probably we can also compare our American idiom "to give a black eye to," meaning "to damage one's reputation." If this is so, the story may be compared to that of the friend at midnight, where, if Bailey (*Poet and Peasant*, pp. 125–33) is correct, the friend responds to his friend's request for fear of public shame (see comment on 11:5–13). In each parable the reputation on the one being petitioned is at stake. Therefore, though God is not compared to a crooked judge, there *is* a partial basis of comparison in that God will also guard his reputation and vindicate himself.

7 "Chosen ones" (*eklektōn*) is a term used throughout Scripture that is especially significant in describing those who, at the end of history, are marked out as on the victorious side (Matt 24:31; Mark 13:27; Rev 17:14). "Will he keep putting them off?" (*kai makrothymei ep' autois*) is one of several possible translations of these words (cf. Notes). The point of the verse is that God patiently listens to his elect as they pray in their continuing distress, waiting for the proper time to act on their behalf.

8 Help is on the way, and the delay will prove shorter than it seems from our perspective (cf. Notes). The noun "faith" (*tēn pistin*) is probably to be understood here in relation to its content or quality. True believers who still wait with patient trust will seem few when the Son of Man comes (cf. vv.24–25). This may reflect the theme of perseverance that Schuyler Brown sees as characteristic of Luke (*Apostasy and Perseverance*, pp. 45–46).

Notes

1–8 For a representative of the older interpretation of the parable that both minimizes the eschatological reference and assumes a strong contrast between God and the judge, see Benjamin B. Warfield, "The Importunate Widow and the Alleged Failure of Faith," ExpT 25 (1913–14): 69–72, 137–39.

7 Καὶ μακροθυμεῖ ἐπ' αὐτοῖς (*kai makrothymei ep' autois*, "Will he keep putting them off ?") is very difficult to exegete. The difficulty is both lexical and syntactical. Does the verb mean to "delay," "put off," or "be patient"? What is the relationship of *ep' autois* to the verb? Does the question anticipate a positive answer or, like the preceding question, a negative one? If the verb means "be patient," if *ep' autois* is taken with it to mean "with them" (as in Matt 18:29; James 5:7), and if it calls for a positive response, the meaning is "He will also be patient with them, won't he?" For a thorough discussion of a number of possibilities, see Marshall, *Gospel of Luke*, pp. 674–75.

8 "Speedily" is a translation of ἐν τάχει (*en tachei*, NIV, "quickly"), which assumes v.7 means that God will not delay his act of vindication. Others think "suddenly" is the meaning here, since a period of time has intervened (recognized especially in Luke). A similar expression, ταχύ (*tachy*), occurs in Rev 22:20. The prophetic scroll is not to be sealed (cf. Dan 12:4, 9), for the time of fulfillment is near (Rev 22:10).

---

11. *Parable of the Pharisee and the tax collector*

18:9–14

9To some who were confident of their own righteousness and looked down on everybody else, Jesus told this parable: 10"Two men went up to the temple to pray, one a Pharisee and the other a tax collector. 11The Pharisee stood up and prayed about himself; 'God, I thank you that I am not like other men—robbers, evildoers, adulterers—or even like this tax collector. 12I fast twice a week and give a tenth of all I get.'

13"But the tax collector stood at a distance. He would not even look up to heaven, but beat his breast and said, 'God, have mercy on me, a sinner.'

14"I tell you that this man, rather than the other, went home justified before God. For everyone who exalts himself will be humbled, and he who humbles himself will be exalted."

Danker (*Jesus*, p. 185) observes that whereas Paul "discusses the *process* of justification . . . Luke describes the nature of the *recipients* of God's verdict of approval" (emphasis his). This is true throughout Luke's Gospel, but it is in this story of "The Churchman and the Politician" (Ellis, *Gospel of Luke*, p. 214) that we see the characteristics of recipients and rejectors most sharply defined. The Pharisee shows the attitude of pride and self-vindication alluded to in Matthew 23:5–7; Mark 7:6; Philippians 3:4–6. The implication of his words is a contractual relationship with God whereby he would accept the Pharisee's merit in exchange for justification. Actually not only this parable but the two following stories (vv.15–17, 18–30) deal with conditions for entering the kingdom. Each stresses human inability.

9–12 Elements of this parable need little interpretation, only careful observation. Luke does not say whom the parable was directed at (v.9) but rather describes the two men (v.10) so that the parable can be understood by his readers. The characters represent extremes, but the sketches are true to life. The Pharisee follows custom in praying in the temple and in standing while praying (v.11). His prayer expresses the essence of Pharisaism—separation from others. This in itself was not reprehensible, because at the inception of Pharisaism there was a need for a distinctive group who would maintain a piety that stood in contrast to the encroaching pagan Hellenism. This initial good hardened into obnoxious self-righteousness on the part of many (not all) Pharisees, as seen not only in Matthew 23 and Mark 7, but in Jewish literature as well. Luke has observed the Pharisees' hostility thus far (cf. 5:17; 6:2, 7; 7:39; 11:37–54; 15:2; 16:14). Pharisees did tithe (v.12), even their herbs (11:42). They did fast, though twice in the week was more than necessary and was only practiced by the most pious. The problem was that this Pharisee's prayer was a farce, being created only in himself (notice the sarcastic phrase "about himself" [v.11] and the mention of God only at the beginning of his prayer).

13–14 The description speaks for itself. The tax collector (v.13), generally thought of as a greedy politician whose very business depended on knuckling under to the despised Roman government, was one of the social outcasts so prominent in Luke as recipients of God's grace (e.g., 5:12, 27; 7:34, 37; 15:1–2; 16:20). His justification was immediate (v.14), granted by God in contrast to the fantasy of self-justification the Pharisee was futilely caught up in. Verse 14b states the principle that is further illustrated in vv.15–17.

The modern reader will probably not feel the impact of this story to the extent a first-century reader would. We already think of the Pharisees as hypocrites and the tax collectors as those who received the grace of God. Jesus' original hearers would have thought, on the contrary, that it was the pious Pharisee who deserved acceptance by God.

12. The little children and Jesus

18:15–17

¹⁵People were also bringing babies to Jesus to have him touch them. When the disciples saw this, they rebuked them. ¹⁶But Jesus called the children to him and said, "Let the little children come to me, and do not hinder them, for the kingdom of God belongs to such as these. ¹⁷I tell you the truth, anyone who will not receive the kingdom of God like a little child will never enter it."

15–17 Luke's special section has now reached its conclusion. With v.15 the narrative rejoins that of Matthew (19:13) and Mark (10:13). Jesus' words about little children provide Luke's second example of the attitude essential for receiving God's grace. It is not age per se that is in view but childlike qualities such as trust, openness, and the absence of holier-than-thou attitudes. Therefore, this passage does not directly bear on the question of infant baptism. Nevertheless v.15 shows through the use of *brephē* ("babies") that Jesus had compassion even on infants too young to understand the difference between right and wrong. The ones he invites in v.16 (*paidia*, "children") include a broader age spread. Only in recent years have we begun to understand the importance of communication through touching, though the instinct has always been present in those who care about other human beings.

13. The rich ruler

18:18–30

¹⁸A certain ruler asked him, "Good teacher, what must I do to inherit eternal life?"

¹⁹"Why do you call me good?" Jesus answered. "No one is good—except God alone. ²⁰You know the commandments: 'Do not commit adultery, do not murder, do not steal, do not give false testimony, honor your father and mother.' "

²¹"All these I have kept since I was a boy," he said.

²²When Jesus heard this, he said to him, "You still lack one thing. Sell everything you have and give to the poor, and you will have treasure in heaven. Then come, follow me."

²³When he heard this, he became very sad, because he was a man of great wealth. ²⁴Jesus looked at him and said, "How hard it is for the rich to enter the kingdom of God! ²⁵Indeed, it is easier for a camel to go through the eye of a needle than for a rich man to enter the kingdom of God."

²⁶Those who heard this asked, "Who then can be saved?"

²⁷Jesus replied, "What is impossible with men is possible with God."

²⁸Peter said to him, "We have left all we had to follow you!"

²⁹"I tell you the truth," Jesus said to them, "no one who has left home or wife or brothers or parents or children for the sake of the kingdom of God ³⁰will fail to receive many times as much in this age and, in the age to come, eternal life."

After the parable of the Pharisee and the tax collector and the incident of the little children, the story of the rich ruler illustrates once more the need for receptiveness if one is to experience God's grace. Then, lest it be thought that this response lies within human power, Jesus makes the point that it is only by the power of God that anyone is saved (vv.25–27). The story thus emphasizes both the responsibility and the helplessness of human kind.

18 "Ruler" (only in Luke) is too broad a term to permit precise identification of the man's background. Only Matthew says that he was young (Matt 19:20). The appellation "Good teacher" is not a common one and called for comment by Jesus. "What must I do?" indicates a desire to discover if any deed has been overlooked in qualifying for eternal life. John 3:3–15 shows that eternal life is life in the kingdom and that it is received only through the new birth.

19 Jesus replies by asking the ruler a question that has puzzled many. Whatever its ultimate meaning, the question does not constitute a denial that he himself is good. Some commentators hold that he is subtly urging the ruler to see that if Jesus is good, and if only God is good, then there is a clear conclusion to be drawn as to his true identity. Whether or not that is Jesus' purpose (the logic is certainly true), his more obvious purpose in this question is to establish a standard of goodness infinitely higher than the ruler supposes it to be. In other words, he brings us close to the principle in Matthew 5:20, 48.

20–21 Jesus now addresses this standard of righteousness. The first step is a summary of several of the Ten Commandments (v.20), omitting the first few that relate to God and the final one about covetousness. The man, like Paul (Phil 3:6), has kept the letter of the law (v.21).

22 Jesus now moves to the heart of the tenth commandment by leading the ruler to face his attitude toward his possessions. Paul recognized his sinfulness when he became aware of the thrust of the command against covetousness (Rom 7:7–8). In Colossians 3:5 he said that greed is idolatry. The ruler had broken the first commandment by breaking the last. Actually, by the act of giving away his goods, he would have shown himself rid of that sin; and by following Jesus, he would have indicated his allegiance to God. Luke's report of this part of the conversation—"You still lack one thing"—corresponds to Matthew's—"If you want to be perfect" (19:21) —in the same way that Luke 6:36—"Be merciful"—corresponds to Matthew 5:48— "Be perfect." In each case the record in Matthew speaks generally of righteousness,

209

whereas that in Luke (and also Mark) concentrates on that which is yet needed in order to produce righteous perfection.

The command to sell everything and give to the poor is difficult to interpret as well as to apply. It goes a step further than 14:33, where Jesus says that whoever does not "give up" (*apotassetai*) everything he has cannot be his disciple (see comments there). Here the ruler must not only surrender all rights to his possessions but must also actually dispose of them. This does not seem to be a universal requirement; it seems rather to be designed particularly for this man to shatter his covetousness. According to Jesus' teaching in 6:30–31, such an act would also benefit others; so his wealth should be dispensed among poor people. Even this is insufficient, however, unless the ruler truly follows Jesus. The command "Come, follow me" (*deuro, akolouthei moi*) means to become a disciple.

23–25 The ruler's sorrow (*perilypos*, only here in Luke; NIV, "very sad") over the decision about his wealth (v.12) recalls the far deeper sorrow rich people who have incurred Jesus' "woe" will experience (6:24). Only Luke mentions that Jesus looked at the man as he spoke to him about the problem of wealth (v.24). This keeps the focus on the ruler even during the transition to the next dialogue. It also limits the application of v.24 to the kind of attitude the ruler had. The vivid hyperbole about the camel (v.25) makes the point unforgettable (cf. Notes).

26–30 If wealth is such a hindrance in respect to salvation, the situation for the rich is hopeless, as the disciples realize (v.26). Jesus' reply about God's power (v.27) provides the assurance the audience needed and evokes an enthusiastic outburst from Peter (v.28), who feels that the disciples have done what the ruler did not do. Jesus acknowledges this with assuring his disciples who have "left all to follow [him]" of abundant recompense, not only in the future age, but also in the present (v.30). In v.29 Luke has "for the sake of the kingdom of God" instead of "for my [name's] sake" (Matt 19:29; Mark 10:29). This again identifies Jesus with the cause of God's kingdom and ties in with v.25. (In Matthew this is accomplished by an added saying [19:28].) Luke lacks the saying about the first and the last (Matt 19:30; Mark 10:31).

Notes

18–29 Luke is following both the Markan sequence of events and, during the first part of this pericope, the Markan wording fairly closely. (See the comments on Matt 19:16–30 for the significant divergences from Mark 10:17–31 in that account.)

24 It is possible, though doubtful, that the original Greek text of v.24 had the words περίλυπον γενομένον (*perilypon genomenon*, "being sorrowful," referring to the ruler). Some Western and other texts have it; UBS puts it in square brackets, showing its uncertainty. See Metzger, *Textual Commentary*, pp. 168–69. The nearly similar words in v.23, however, are original.

F. *Final Approach to Jerusalem* (18:31–19:44)

1. *A further prediction of Jesus' passion*

18:31–34

> ³¹Jesus took the Twelve aside and told them, "We are going up to Jerusalem, and everything that is written by the prophets about the Son of Man will be fulfilled. ³²He will be handed over to the Gentiles. They will mock him, insult him, spit on him, flog him and kill him. ³³On the third day he will rise again."
> ³⁴The disciples did not understand any of this. Its meaning was hidden from them, and they did not know what he was talking about.

This is generally referred to as the third passion prediction because it is basically similar to those in 9:22 and 9:44 (found in fuller form in Matt 17:22–23; Mark 9:31). Luke, however, has preserved other sayings that predict or foreshadow Jesus' death, including, up to this point, 5:35; 12:50; 13:32; and 17:25. Also, he does not follow this saying with the dialogue in Mark 10:35–45 with its further allusions to Jesus' passion. Since Luke normally stresses the role of Jerusalem, it is surprising that he omits the reference to it preserved in Matthew 20:17 and Mark 10:32. This may be because Jerusalem appears in v.31 or because Jesus had already emphasized Jerusalem as the place of his destiny (13:32–33), thereby accomplishing what Matthew and Mark do in this context.

31 Once again Luke, by stressing these words of Jesus, stresses the fulfillment of prophecy (cf. the first two chapters, esp. 2:25–38; 22:37). The parallels in Matthew 20:18 and Mark 10:33 omit any reference to prophecy here.

32–34 In this prediction, Jesus for the first time mentions the Gentiles as his executors (v.32). Luke attributes the ignorance of the disciples (a theme much emphasized by Mark) to what is apparently a supernatural withholding of understanding (v.34; cf. the experience of the two on the road to Emmaus, 24:16).

2. *Healing a blind beggar*

18:35–43

> ³⁵As Jesus approached Jericho, a blind man was sitting by the roadside begging. ³⁶When he heard the crowd going by, he asked what was happening. ³⁷They told him, "Jesus of Nazareth is passing by."
> ³⁸He called out, "Jesus, Son of David, have mercy on me!"
> ³⁹Those who led the way rebuked him and told him to be quiet, but he shouted all the more, "Son of David, have mercy on me!"
> ⁴⁰Jesus stopped and ordered the man to be brought to him. When he came near, Jesus asked him, ⁴¹"What do you want me to do for you?"
> "Lord, I want to see," he replied.
> ⁴²Jesus said to him, "Receive your sight; your faith has healed you." ⁴³Immediately he received his sight and followed Jesus, praising God. When all the people saw it, they also praised God.

This incident shows that Jesus, who was on his way to the royal city of Jerusalem, was actually the "Son of David" (vv.38–39), i.e., the Messiah. It also allows Luke to point again to Jesus' concern for the needy and especially to show his healing of the blind as a messianic work (cf. 4:18). In addition, this miracle emphasizes the importance of faith (v.42) and (in Luke only) the glory that God receives through the ministry of Jesus (v.42).

35-36 Jesus' final approach to Jerusalem is under way. Luke is establishing a very important sequence: the healing of the blind man just outside Jericho (v.35), the call of Zacchaeus in Jericho (19:1-10), and then Jesus' triumphal entry to Jerusalem, his city of destiny (19:11, 28; N.B. the comment on 19:28). Luke apparently makes reference to the crowds here (v.36) to explain how the blind beggar knew that something special was happening (v.37).

38-43 The description of the man's insistent calling (vv.38-39) draws attention to his faith, which was based on the messiahship of Jesus, the "Son of David." So does Jesus' question in v.41, which allows the man to voice his request. Only Luke speaks of the praise both the man who had been blind and the people gave to God after the miracle (v.43). This is a unique Lukan feature (5:26; 17:18; Acts 2:47; 3:9).

Notes

18-43 It is well known that in Matt 20:29 and Mark 10:46, Jesus is leaving, not approaching, Jericho at this point. In Luke's concern to maintain the important thematic order described above (healing, call of Zacchaeus, approach to Jerusalem), might he have described the healing before the Jericho incident in order to prevent confusion within his own narrative? This would have been acceptable to his contemporaries, though it is troublesome to us.

If this were the case, the problem would be cleared up. Luke, contrary to his custom, does not draw attention to the crowds that followed Jesus out of Jericho but only mentions them in passing (v.36). There must be some reason for the unusual omission here, especially when the crowds are stressed in the parallel passages (Matt 20:29; Mark 10:46). If Luke were following a thematic order, rather than a geographical one, so that Jesus is just entering Jericho after the healing, there would be no opportunity for the crowds to follow him out of the city, as in Matthew and Mark. If this suggestion is inadequate, we can turn to one of the various harmonizing suggestions that have been made. The most plausible probably is that Jesus was between the remains of OT Jericho and the new city, with its large Herodian palace to the south of the old city. Thus he could be "leaving" OT Jericho (Matthew and Mark) and "approaching" the NT city (Luke) at the same time.

3. Zacchaeus the tax collector

19:1-10

[1]Jesus entered Jericho and was passing through. [2]A man was there by the name of Zacchaeus; he was a chief tax collector and was wealthy. [3]He wanted to see who Jesus was, but being a short man he could not, because of the crowd. [4]So he ran ahead and climbed a sycamore-fig tree to see him, since Jesus was coming that way.

[5]When Jesus reached the spot, he looked up and said to him, "Zacchaeus, come down immediately. I must stay at your house today." [6]So he came down at once and welcomed him gladly.

7All the people saw this and began to mutter, "He has gone to be the guest of a 'sinner.' "

8But Zacchaeus stood up and said to the Lord, "Look, Lord! Here and now I give half of my possessions to the poor, and if I have cheated anybody out of anything, I will pay back four times the amount."

9Jesus said to him, "Today salvation has come to this house, because this man, too, is a son of Abraham. 10For the Son of Man came to seek and to save what was lost."

This narrative contains what may well be considered the "key verse" of Luke—viz., 19:10. The incident contains several primary Lukan features: the universal appeal of the gospel (vv.2–4); the ethical problem of wealth (v.2); the call of a "sinner" who was in social disfavor (v.7); the sense of God's present work (vv.5, 9); the feeling of urgency ("immediately," *speusas*, v.5), of necessity ("must," v.5), and of joy (v.6); restitution, with goods distributed to the poor (v.8); and, above all, salvation (vv.9–10).

1–4 Zacchaeus was a "chief tax collector" (*architelōnēs*, v.2), holding a higher office in the Roman tax system than Levi did (5:27–30). This system, under which an officer gained his income by extorting more money from the people than he had contracted to pay the Roman government, had evidently worked well for Zacchaeus. His location in the major customs center of Jericho was ideal. Being both a member of a generally despised group and wealthy, he is a notable subject for the saving grace of God. Observe the proximity of this story to that of the rich ruler, whose attitude toward wealth kept him from the Lord (18:27). Zacchaeus's desire to see Jesus, though commendable, was surpassed by the fact that Jesus wanted to see *him*.

5–6 Not only did he want to see Zacchaeus, Jesus had to stay with him—"I must stay at your house today" (v.5). This divine necessity is stressed in Luke (see comment on 4:43). Luke also has the word "today," with its special meaning (see comment on 4:21). The reciprocity of the divine, sovereign call and the human response is striking (v.6; cf. v.10).

7 In chapter 15 Luke gave us three parables Jesus told to answer the "Pharisees and teachers of the law" who opposed his eating with tax collectors and "sinners" (15:1–2). Now "all the people" complain that Jesus was consorting with a sinner. Similar criticism was made of Jesus' visit with Levi the tax collector (5:29–30). In each case table fellowship was involved—something that had a far deeper significance than our dinner parties. (See comments on 5:29–30; 15:1 for the significance of the word "sinner" from the Pharisees' point of view.)

8 Zacchaeus's announcement sounds abrupt and is probably intended to seem so. After all, for Luke (following Jesus) the use of possessions is a major indicator of one's spiritual condition (cf. 14:33; 18:22, and comments). There is no doubt that Zacchaeus had really "cheated" people. "Four times the amount" was far more than what the OT specified for restitution (Lev 5:16; Num 5:7). Whether or not Zacchaeus knew of these laws, his offer was unusually generous and was the sort of "fruit in keeping with repentance" earlier sought by John the Baptist (3:8).

9–10 Salvation did not "come to this house" because Zacchaeus finally did a good deed but because he was "a son of Abraham" (v.9), which may mean because he was a believer and thus a spiritual descendant of Abraham (Ellis, *Gospel of Luke*, p. 220). On the other hand, it may mean that "a Jew, even though he has become one of the 'lost sheep of the house of Israel', is still a part of Israel; the good Shepherd must seek for such" (Marshall, *Gospel of Luke*, p. 698).

Verse 10 could well be considered the "key verse" of Luke. As noted in the introductory comments to this section, the context is rich with Lukan themes, an appropriate setting for a significant verse. The verse itself expresses the heart of Jesus' ministry as presented by Luke, both his work of salvation and his quest for the lost. Luke has portrayed the "lost" throughout his gospel, from Jesus' own statements (e.g., the programmatic statement in 4:18–19) to the disdainful comments of the self-righteous (e.g., the Pharisee in 18:11 and here in v.7). Jesus has sought and found another of the "lost" in Jericho. He uses the occasion and the criticism of the people in v.7 as an opportunity to restate his mission.

This whole incident is the epitome of the messianic mission described in Luke 4.

4. Parable of the ten minas

19:11–27

> ¹¹While they were listening to this, he went on to tell them a parable, because he was near Jerusalem and the people thought that the kingdom of God was going to appear at once. ¹²He said: "A man of noble birth went to a distant country to have himself appointed king and then to return. ¹³So he called ten of his servants and gave them ten minas. 'Put this money to work,' he said, 'until I come back.'
>
> ¹⁴"But his subjects hated him and sent a delegation after him to say, 'We don't want this man to be our king.'
>
> ¹⁵"He was made king, however, and returned home. Then he sent for the servants to whom he had given the money, in order to find out what they had gained with it.
>
> ¹⁶"The first one came and said, 'Sir, your mina has earned ten more.'
>
> ¹⁷" 'Well done, my good servant!' his master replied. 'Because you have been trustworthy in a very small matter, take charge of ten cities.'
>
> ¹⁸"The second came and said, 'Sir, your mina has earned five more.'
>
> ¹⁹"His master answered, 'You take charge of five cities.'
>
> ²⁰"Then another servant came and said, 'Sir, here is your mina; I have kept it laid away in a piece of cloth. ²¹I was afraid of you, because you are a hard man. You take out what you did not put in and reap what you did not sow.'
>
> ²²"His master replied, 'I will judge you by your own words, you wicked servant! You knew, did you, that I am a hard man, taking out what I did not put in, and reaping what I did not sow? ²³Why then didn't you put my money on deposit, so that when I came back, I could have collected it with interest?'
>
> ²⁴"Then he said to those standing by, 'Take his mina away from him and give it to the one who has ten minas.'
>
> ²⁵" 'Sir,' they said, 'he already has ten!'
>
> ²⁶"He replied, 'I tell you that to everyone who has, more will be given, but as for the one who has nothing, even what he has will be taken away. ²⁷But those enemies of mine who did not want me to be king over them—bring them here and kill them in front of me.' "

This parable fulfills four important functions: (1) it clarifies the time of the appearance of the kingdom of God; (2) it realistically portrays the coming rejection and future return of the Lord; (3) it delineates the role of a disciple in the time between the Lord's departure and his return; and (4), while it is similar to the parable in

Matthew 25:14–30 (cf. Notes), it makes a unique contribution at this point in Luke's narrative.

11 The parable of the ten minas is connected with the pericope about Zacchaeus by the clause "While they were listening to this." The transition can be viewed in two complementary ways. First, Marshall, referring back to Jesus' words in v.9, notes that "although salvation has come *today* . . . the End, and the coming of the Son of Man to judgment, still lie in the future" (*Gospel of Luke*, p. 703, emphasis his). Second, "Son of Man" in v.10 of the Zacchaeus incident and "kingdom of God" at the beginning of this parable are conceptually related (cf. Doeve, *Jewish Hermeneutics*, pp. 128, 130, 142f). The one who has the right to reign is precisely the same Son of Man who came to seek lost sheep (v.10).

In addition to its connection with the Zacchaeus pericope, this parable is appropriate to Luke, which, in passage after passage, deals with Jesus' teaching about the future in general, the present and future aspects of the kingdom, and the consummation of God's purposes in history. (On Luke's eschatology, see Introduction: Themes and Theology). Obviously this parable teaches that Jesus predicted an interval of time between his ascension and return. For the time when the kingdom will be restored to Israel, see the beginning of Luke's second volume (Acts 1:6–7).

12–14 The historical background for the parable was the visit of Archelaus, son of Herod the Great, to Rome to secure permission to reign as a so-called client king, i.e., over a territory actually subject to Rome. This petition was opposed by a delegation of Archelaus's own subjects (Jos. Antiq. XVII, 213–49 [ix.3–7], 299–320 [xi.1–4]; War II, 14–22 [ii.1–3]). Similarly, Jesus has gone to the heavenly seat of authority till the time for his return. In the meantime, though his qualifications for kingship are impeccable, he has been rejected by those who should serve him as his subjects (v.14).

The money each servant received was worth about three months' wages (NIV mg.) or perhaps a little more (v.13). Their responsibility was to "put this money to work" in business, trading, or by investment.

15–19 Jesus singles out three of the ten servants as examples. The first two did well (vv.16, 18), one so well as to receive a special commendation for being "trustworthy" (v.17). The test was "small" (i.e., on a small scale), not because the amount itself was so small, but because of its relative insignificance in comparison to the cities awarded the trustworthy servants (vv.17, 19). We need not seek any particular symbolism in the cities other than the contrast between the extraordinary responsibility of ruling them and the responsibility of simply investing the sums of money (minas).

20–23 What some have called the "rule of end stress" leads the reader to concentrate on the last of the three examples. This servant allowed his fear (justified on the basis of experience) of the nobleman's anger (v.21) to prevent him from fulfilling his responsibility of putting the money given him to work (v.20). To be sure, its investment was risky. But he was specifically charged to take the risk of investing the money (vv.22–23). In his case conservatism was born of fear and was wrong (cf. Thielicke, *The Waiting Father*, pp. 143–45).

24–27 The principle of taking from one who has little and giving to one who has much (v.24) strikes us today as strange and unfair (v.25). In the original setting, as similarly in the kingdom parables (Matt 13:12), whether a person has little or much depends on his use of opportunities to increase what he already has.

The nobleman's anger (vv.26–27) is not intended to attribute such behavior to Jesus himself. Rather it does picture the kind of response one might have expected in Jesus' day, especially from the Herodians. It also reveals the seriousness of flouting the orders of the King whom God has appointed Judge (John 5:22; Acts 17:31; cf. 1 Peter 1:17).

Notes

11–27 In structure this parable is very similar to the parable of the talents in Matt 25:14–30. It has been argued, on the one hand, that both go back in tradition history to one story, and, on the other hand, that there were two stories told on two different occasions in Jesus' ministry. The structural similarities seem in regard to the meaning of the story more significant than the differences in detail. Yet while some of the differences—e.g., the number of servants mentioned, the amounts entrusted, and the conclusion (ten cities being mentioned only in Luke)—are relatively minor, the description of the main figure is not. The figure of a king who is rejected is distinctive to Luke and belongs to a deep stratum of his narrative and theology.

5. *The Triumphal Entry*

19:28–44

28After Jesus had said this, he went on ahead, going up to Jerusalem. 29As he approached Bethphage and Bethany at the hill called the Mount of Olives, he sent two of his disciples, saying to them, 30"Go to the village ahead of you, and as you enter it, you will find a colt tied there, which no one has ever ridden. Untie it and bring it here. 31If anyone asks you, 'Why are you untying it?' tell him, 'The Lord needs it.' "

32Those who were sent went and found it just as he had told them. 33As they were untying the colt, its owners asked them, "Why are you untying the colt?"

34They replied, "The Lord needs it."

35They brought it to Jesus, threw their cloaks on the colt and put Jesus on it. 36As he went along, people spread their cloaks on the road.

37When he came near the place where the road goes down the Mount of Olives, the whole crowd of disciples began joyfully to praise God in loud voices for all the miracles they had seen:

38"Blessed is the king who comes in the name of the Lord!"
"Peace in heaven and glory in the highest!"

39Some of the Pharisees in the crowd said to Jesus, "Teacher, rebuke your disciples!"

40"I tell you," he replied, "if they keep quiet, the stones will cry out."

41As he approached Jerusalem and saw the city, he wept over it 42and said, "If you, even you, had only known on this day what would bring you peace—but now it is hidden from your eyes. 43The days will come upon you when your enemies will build an embankment against you and encircle you and hem you in on every side. 44They will dash you to the ground, you and the children within your walls.

> They will not leave one stone on another, because you did not recognize the time
> of God's coming to you."

Luke does not mention Jesus' actual entry into Jerusalem—the Triumphal Entry. Instead, he shows us Jesus only as approaching Jerusalem (v.11), and after the crowd's welcome he is still "approaching" Jerusalem (v.41).

The story comes to its climax, not in Jesus' entering Jerusalem, but in his lamenting over the city (vv.41-44). Therefore, while Jesus deserves a triumphal entry as "king" (v.38), Luke emphasizes that he is moving instead to the place of his rejection. This continues the movement Jesus spoke of in 13:33. It does not contradict Matthew or Mark, for v.45 shows that Jesus did eventually enter the city. Luke simply omits the statement that he entered (cf. Matt 21:10; Mark 11:11) to make his theological point.

28-34 The transition "After Jesus said this" (v.28) links his approach to the city with the parable of the ten minas that denies an immediate appearance of the kingdom and portrays the rejection of its ruler. Luke's mention of Bethphage and Bethany (v.29) locates where Jesus went. Bethany was, of course, important as the home of Mary, Martha, and Lazarus. The Mount of Olives had a significant place in prophecy as the place of the coming Messiah's appearance (Zechariah 14:4). The incident of securing the colt (vv.30-31) "just as he told them" (v.32) reminds us, as did 2:15, 20, 29, of the dependability of the prophetic word. The "owners" are called *kyrioi* by Luke (v.33), which may (as Danker, *Jesus*, suggests) contrast with the one who is supreme Lord (*kyrios*) and rightful owner of all we possess (v.34).

35-38 As does Matthew, Luke shows us the humble king as he portrays Jesus riding on the colt (v.35). (For the custom of spreading cloaks along the path [v.36], see 2 Kings 9:13.) Only Luke mentions the descent from the Mount of Olives (cf. comment above), showing that Jesus was still outside Jerusalem (v.37). The reference to praising God for Jesus' miracles is unique to Luke (cf. comment on 18:43). Luke omits from v.38 the word "Hosanna," which might have been strange to his Gentile readers. He also omits the messianic quotation from Zechariah 9:9 given in Matthew 21:5 but instead stresses the messianic theme with the word "king" (v.38). The word "comes" is reminiscent of the designation "the coming one" for the Messiah. Luke has already quoted v.26 of the festival Psalm 118 in Jesus' previous lament over Jerusalem (13:35). In addition to using the specific word "king," Luke gives us the words about peace, reminiscent of the angels' proclamation at the Nativity (2:14), including the identical words "glory in the highest" (*doxa en hypsistois*). Once again he omits a "Hosanna."

39-40 Here (v.40) is another saying of Jesus found only in Luke. It is a fitting prelude to vv.41-45. Ellis (*Gospel of Luke*, p. 226) suggests that the words about the stones, similar to Habakkuk 2:11, may be a link to the idea of the capitulation of Jerusalem found in the Qumran Habakkuk commentary (1QpHab 9:6ff.).

41-44 Jesus is still outside Jerusalem (v.41) as he utters this lament, which only Luke records. Once more Luke focuses on Jesus' concern for the city and adds his prediction of its destruction, which is not given in 13:34. "This day" (v.42; cf. 4:21, "today," and comment) of peace has arrived; and the city ("even you," *kai su*), whose very name means "peace," has failed to recognize it. For the meaning of "hidden," see comment on 18:34. For a further description of Jerusalem's fate, see 21:20–24. God's "coming" (*episkopē*, v.44) has here the sense of a "visitation" that brings good or ill—in this case, either salvation or judgment.

VI. Concluding Events (19:45–24:53)

A. Teaching in the Temple Area (19:45–21:38)

1. Jesus at the temple

19:45–48

45Then he entered the temple area and began driving out those who were selling. 46"It is written," he said to them, " 'My house will be a house of prayer'; but you have made it a 'den of robbers.' "
47Every day he was teaching at the temple. But the chief priests, the teachers of the law and the leaders among the people were trying to kill him. 48Yet they could not find any way to do it, because all the people hung on his words.

45–48 Luke states—still without specifically saying that Jesus had entered Jerusalem (cf. comments on the previous section)—that Jesus is now in the temple area (v.45). Luke has omitted the episode of the fig tree (Matt 21:18–22; Mark 11:12–14, 20–26). At first thought this is surprising, since through the strange episode Jesus taught the efficacy of the prayer of faith, a matter of particular interest to Luke. However, Luke may have felt that the drastic overtones of the cursing of the fig tree with its relation to the fruitlessness of Israel (symbolized by the fig tree) would be inappropriate here, perhaps because of Jesus' strong words recorded in vv.41–44. The cleansing of the temple lacks the vivid detail in Matthew 21:12–13 and Mark 11:15–17. Luke mentions the importance of the temple as a house of prayer (v.46), though he omits the reference to the nations (cf. Mark 11:17). Verses 47–48 are not in Matthew and are different in form from Mark 11:18–19. Whereas Mark mentions Jesus' "teaching" (noun form of *didachē*) at the end of his brief paragraph (11:18), Luke uses the verbal form of the same word (in a vivid periphrastic construction: *ēn didaskōn*, "was teaching"), evidently to emphasize Jesus' teaching ministry (cf. comment on 20:1). This is appropriate because Luke has consistently portrayed Jesus as a teacher, especially since the beginning of the central section of the Gospel (9:51–19:44). He adds "the leaders among the people" (*hoi prōtoi tou laou*) to those Mark says are trying to kill Jesus, but by careful omission Luke indicates that the people (*laos*) themselves are not hostile to him. On the contrary, they "hung on his words" (v.48). This fits in with Luke's attempt to distinguish between the "people," who were responsive to Jesus, and their leaders and the "crowds" (*ochloi*), who were not. This, in turn, forms part of Luke's attempt to show that Christianity is properly seen as a continuation of true Judaism (cf. 1:68, 77; 2:10, 31–32, and comments).

2. Jesus' authority questioned

20:1–8

1One day as he was teaching the people in the temple courts and preaching the gospel, the chief priests and the teachers of the law, together with the elders, came up to him. ²"Tell us by what authority you are doing these things," they said. "Who gave you this authority?"

³He replied, "I will also ask you a question. Tell me, ⁴John's baptism—was it from heaven, or from men?"

⁵They discussed it among themselves and said, "If we say, 'From heaven' he will ask, 'Why didn't you believe him?' ⁶But if we say, 'From men,' all the people will stone us, because they are persuaded that John was a prophet."

⁷So they answered, "We don't know where it was from."

⁸Jesus said, "Neither will I tell you by what authority I am doing these things."

With this controversy Luke initiates a series of dialogues, most of which are common to all three Synoptics. They include the familiar form in which a question is answered by another question designed to catch the interrogator in his own inconsistency. The controversies are typical examples of the kind of challenges thrown at Jesus by the various sects and parties: "the chief priests and the teachers of the law" (v.1; cf. vv.19, 39), the Pharisees and Herodians (cf. Mark 12:13; Luke alone has "spies," v.20), and the Sadducees (v.27). Jesus also addresses the "rich" in 21:1. These dialogues sharpen the issues so that the reader sees the hostility and the theological errors of the leaders of the people.

Jesus' authority is of paramount importance, and his work as teacher and prophet (especially strong in Luke) requires validation. It is therefore appropriate that each synoptic Gospel begins the controversy section with this question: "By what authority are you doing these things?" (Matt 21:23; Mark 11:28; cf. Luke 20:2).

1–2 "One day" is indefinite in contrast to Mark 11:27, which, unlike Luke (cf. comment on his omission of the actual entry to Jerusalem in 19:28–38) speaks of Jesus' return to Jerusalem. As in 19:47, Luke emphasizes Jesus' role as a teacher. He also mentions the "people" (*laos*), who (in Luke) are always receptive to his teaching (cf. comment on 19:45–48). Luke further adds "preaching the gospel" (*euangelizomenou*), lacking in the other Synoptics. This is consistent with Luke's significant use of that verb (though not the noun *euangelion*).

3–8 The implication of Jesus' question is clear (vv.3–4). Jesus refused to give more light to those who refused to accept the light they had (v.8) and make a decision concerning it (vv.5–7). They refused to live according to what Minear (*Heal and Reveal*, pp. 3–30, 37–38) calls "Consciousness B"—an awareness of the heavenly dimension of life (v.7), choosing to stay on a worldly level, Minear's "Consciousness A." The word "heaven" is a surrogate for God in vv.3, 5.

3. Parable of the tenants

20:9–19

⁹He went on to tell the people this parable: "A man planted a vineyard, rented it to some farmers and went away for a long time. ¹⁰At harvest time he sent a servant to the tenants so they would give him some of the fruit of the vineyard. But the tenants beat him and sent him away empty-handed. ¹¹He sent another servant, but that one also they beat and treated shamefully and sent away empty-handed. ¹²He sent still a third, and they wounded him and threw him out.

¹³"Then the owner of the vineyard said, 'What shall I do? I will send my son, whom I love; perhaps they will respect him.'

¹⁴"But when the tenants saw him, they talked the matter over. 'This is the heir,'

they said. 'Let's kill him, and the inheritance will be ours.' 15So they threw him out of the vineyard and killed him.

"What then will the owner of the vineyard do to them? 16He will come and kill those tenants and give the vineyard to others."

When the people heard this, they said, "May this never be!"

17Jesus looked directly at them and asked, "Then what is the meaning of that which is written:

" 'The stone the builders rejected
has become the capstone'?

18Everyone who falls on that stone will be broken to pieces, but he on whom it falls will be crushed."

19The teachers of the law and the chief priests looked for a way to arrest him immediately, because they knew he had spoken this parable against them. But they were afraid of the people.

The refusal of the leaders to accept Jesus' authority (vv.1–8) leads to this parable that not only clearly affirms that authority but also alludes to Jesus' death and his subsequent vindication. The parable draws its imagery from the Song of the Vineyard (Isa 5:1–7), though Luke's account omits the quotation of Isaiah 5:2 found in Matthew 21:33 and Mark 12:1. The details of the story vary between the Synoptics. In Matthew and Mark, one of the servants is killed; in Luke only the son is killed. The story tends more toward allegory than Jesus' parables usually do. The vineyard may be compared to Israel on the basis of Isaiah 5. The owner represents God; the son, Jesus; the tenants, the religious leaders charged with cultivating the religious life of Israel (as they acknowledge in v.19); and the servants correspond to the prophets.

9–12 The circumstances were not such as to provoke a violent reaction (v.9). Nothing but a sample of the fruit was requested (v.10). In the early years of a vineyard's existence, the tenants would own little if anything (J.D.M. Derrett, *Law in the New Testament* [London: Longman & Todd, 1970], pp. 296ff.).

13 The expression "whom I love" (*agapēton*, "beloved") must be understood with respect to its meaning in ancient Near Eastern family relationships. In the LXX *agapētos* was at times virtually used as a synonym for *monogenēs*, "one and only" (cf. de Kruif, "Only Son" pp. 112ff.) The latter term did not necessarily refer to origin, as the KJV translation "only begotten" in John 3:16 implies, but rather to the unique status of the person as a beloved only child. See Luke 7:12, where the statement that the deceased son was her "only" (*monogenēs*) son shows the widow's desolate situation. The most relevant use in the LXX of *agapētos* is Genesis 22:2: "Take your beloved son, whom you love" (LXX *Labe ton huion sou ton agapēton, hon ēgapēsas*). This is reflected in the Transfiguration account in Matthew 17:15: "This is my Son, whom I love" (*ho huios mou ho agapētos*, cf. Mark 9:7). God spoke similar words at Jesus' baptism (Matt 3:17; Luke 3:22). Luke did not include *agapētos* in his account of the Transfiguration but does include it here in 20:13 (cf. Mark 12:6[Gr.], but cf. Matt 21:38). "What shall I do?" introduces a soliloquy similar to those in 16:3–4 and 18:4–5. Luke's amplification here (cf. Mark 12:6) adds to the pathos.

14–16 Jesus' audience was in a better position than we are to surmise what would have motivated these tenants to kill the son (v.14). But we are in a better position than they to understand the meaning of the story. Certainly the vivid description of the son's murder (v.15) and the father's vengeance (v.16; cf. 19.40–44) evoked from the people who heard the parable a strong "May this never be!" (*mē genoito;* cf. the Pauline use, Rom 3:4, 6, 31 et al.). They sensed the horror of the story and its drastic application, however imperfectly they understood its details.

17–19 The quotation (v.17) is from Psalm 118:22. (In 19:38 the same psalm was quoted.) Luke shows the point of this quotation by referring to the reaction of the people in v.16 (cf. Matt and Mark). Not only will God vindicate his Son, who is the "stone" (v.17, an important NT theme), but those who oppose him will meet destruction (v.18). The point is tacitly acknowledged in the reaction of the leaders (v.19). This carries forward the hostile scheming against Jesus referred to in 19:47.

4. *Paying taxes to Caesar*

20:20–26

> ²⁰Keeping a close watch on him, they sent spies, who pretended to be honest. They hoped to catch Jesus in something he said so that they might hand him over to the power and authority of the governor. ²¹So the spies questioned him: "Teacher, we know that you speak and teach what is right, and that you do not show partiality but teach the way of God in accordance with the truth. ²²Is it right for us to pay taxes to Caesar or not?"
>
> ²³He saw through their duplicity and said to them, ²⁴"Show me a denarius. Whose portrait and inscription are on it?"
>
> ²⁵"Caesar's," they replied.
>
> He said to them, "Then give to Caesar what is Caesar's, and to God what is God's."
>
> ²⁶They were unable to trap him in what he had said there in public. And astonished by his answer, they became silent.

Luke is blunt about the motives of the visitors, calling them "spies" (*egkathetoi*, people hired to lie in wait) and speaking of their insincerity ("pretended" is *hypokrinomenous*, related to *hypokritēs* "hypocrite"). They try to catch Jesus between two positions they considered mutually exclusive and irreconcilable.

20–22 Luke, writing for an audience to whom the distinctions between Jewish parties might be unfamiliar, does not mention the Pharisees and Herodians as Matthew and Mark do. His readers would, however, certainly know about the various forms of the heavy Roman taxation (v.22). These totaled over one-third of a person's income and included a poll tax, customs, and various indirect taxes.

23–26 The portrait on the coin (vv.24–25) represented submission to Rome. Jesus' statement may seem ordinary to us, as we have become so used to the saying. But it was an unexpected and telling response to the question. Jesus' questioners were sure his answer would alienate either the government officials or the pious people and zealots who opposed foreign domination. Actually Jesus appealed neither to those who preached revolution nor to the political compromisers. He stated a principle, not an accommodation or a compromise. This principle appears in the classic passage on Christian social ethics (Rom 13:1–7). To give what the government requires is not only not antithetical to religious duty but part of it. This even goes beyond the idea of dual citizenship. In spite of Jesus' balanced position, he was later accused at his trial of promoting an insurrection against Rome.

5. *The Resurrection and marriage*

20:27–40

> [27]Some of the Sadducees, who say there is no resurrection, came to Jesus with a question. [28]"Teacher," they said, "Moses wrote for us that if a man's brother dies and leaves a wife but no children, the man must marry the widow and have children for his brother. [29]Now there were seven brothers. The first one married a woman and died childless. [30]The second [31]and then the third married her, and in the same way the seven died, leaving no children. [32]Finally, the woman died too. [33]Now then, at the resurrection whose wife will she be, since the seven were married to her?"
>
> [34]Jesus replied, "The people of this age marry and are given in marriage. [35]But those who are considered worthy of taking part in that age and in the resurrection from the dead will neither marry nor be given in marriage, [36]and they can no longer die; for they are like the angels. They are God's children, since they are children of the resurrection. [37]But in the account of the bush, even Moses showed that the dead rise, for he calls the Lord 'the God of Abraham, and the God of Isaac, and the God of Jacob.' [38]He is not the God of the dead, but of the living, for to him all are alive."
>
> [39]Some of the teachers of the law responded, "Well said, teacher!" [40]And no one dared to ask him any more questions.

27 This controversy section continues with still another group challenging Jesus. The Sadducees, who tended to be more conservative than the Pharisees, did not accept what they considered theological accretions to their beliefs. The OT has little specific to say about the future state of the individual after death. Greek thought sharply divided between the soul and the body, the soul's temporary prison, and saw immortality as a quality of the soul. The Pharisees leaned toward a belief in resurrection that owed more to Greek ideas than to the OT. However, the Sadducees refused to even face the clear implications of OT teaching about the future state and were skeptical of the nature of personal future existence related to rewards or punishment.

28–33 This hypothetical case of a woman who had successively had seven husbands rests on the Jewish custom of "levirate marriage" (from the Lat. *levir,* "husband's brother," "brother-in-law"). It provided for the remarriage of a widow to the brother of a husband who died childless, the purpose of the remarriage being to provide descendants to carry on the deceased husband's name (Deut 25:5–6; cf. Gen 38:8). The Sadducees made this custom the basis for an argument ad absurdum that assumed that the idea of resurrection involves sexual reunion with one's earthly partner(s).

34–40 Jesus responded along these lines: It is not legitimate to project earthly conditions into the future state (vv.34–35). Eternal life is actually the life of the age to come (v.36). The believer already participates in that life (vv.37–38); but its full expression, involving the resurrection of the body, must wait till the new age has

fully come. (Note the link in v.36 between "that age" and the "resurrection.")
"Worthy" probably has somewhat the same meaning as in Matthew 10:11, 13,
where it apparently refers to a person or home honoring God and blessed by him.

Though in the new age believers do not become angels (or gods), they do share
certain characteristics of angels. This may refer to the absence of the sexual aspect
of marriage without denying the continuation of mutual recognition and love. The
Greek syntax, however, places the comment about angels nearer to "no longer die"
than to "neither marry." This moves the emphasis from the issue of marriage to that
of the nature of the Resurrection. God's children are also "children of" (i.e., are
characterized by) the Resurrection. Note the repetition of the word "resurrection"
and the absence of any reference to the Greek concept of "immortality." It is not
persistence of life but that "the dead rise" (v.37) that Jesus is teaching. Invoking, so
to speak, the authority of Moses, whom the Sadducees revered (rejecting later oral
tradition), Jesus shows that Abraham, Isaac, and Jacob are also going to "rise."
Therefore their existence does not lie only in the past but in the future; and God is
called, in contemporary terms, their God.

Jesus' answer is approved by some of the teachers of the law (v.39), who are happy
to see the Sadducees lose their argument. Jesus' wisdom has silenced all his questioners (v.40).

6. The sonship of Christ

20:41–47

41Then Jesus said to them, "How is it that they say the Christ is the Son of
David? 42David himself declares in the Book of Psalms:

> " 'The Lord said to my Lord:
>   "Sit at my right hand
> 43until I make your enemies
>   a footstool for your feet." '

44David calls him 'Lord.' How then can he be his son?"

45While all the people were listening, Jesus said to his disciples, 46"Beware of
the teachers of the law. They like to walk around in flowing robes and love to be
greeted in the marketplaces and have the most important seats in the synagogues and the places of honor at banquets. 47They devour widows' houses and
for a show make lengthy prayers. Such men will be punished most severely."

The opponents silenced, the controversy section concludes with a rhetorical question Jesus puts to his questioners—one that is designed to clarify from Scripture
who the Christ is. The interpretation of these three verses has been complicated by
three factors: (1) the paradox inherent in Psalm 110; (2) Jesus' not answering his own
question, thus leaving its significance to be implied; and (3) the reluctance of some
to accept the christological understanding the interpretation of these verses demands.

41–43 The term "Christ" (v.41) is, of course, used here, not as a proper name, but
as a title, "the Messiah." The Messiah was understood by the Jewish people to be a
Son (descendant or "sprout," as in 4QFlor 11). If this is so, the question is Why does
David, in Psalm 110:1, call his descendant his "Lord" (v.42)? In that passage "The
Lord" is the translation of the LXX *ho kyrios*, which in turn represents the Hebrew

Yahweh, the sacred name of God. "To my Lord" represents the same word in the LXX but *'adōnay* in the Hebrew. This word conveyed a sense of dignity and was often used as a substitute for the name of God. Although the rabbis of the first Christian centuries did not interpret *'adōnay* as referring to the Messiah, that is the only meaning that makes sense here.

44 Jesus' question is not intended to suggest that there could not be a descendant of David who was also "Lord" but that the seemingly irreconcilable has meaning only if he is more than just a human descendant. Paul expressed the complete answer to the question in Romans 1:3–4, which says that Jesus was a descendant of David as to his human nature but declared Son of God by his resurrection.

45–47 Having responded with such authority to his opponents' controversial questions, Jesus now comments on those who sought to disprove his authority. His incisive portrayal of them here is shorter than in 11:37–52. Here he stresses their pride and ostentation, as well as accusing them of taking advantage of widows. Apparently they misused their responsibility as legal arbiters (cf. 12:13 and comment) and betrayed the financial trust innocent widows placed in them (cf. J.D.M. Derrett, " 'Eating up the Houses of Widows: Jesus' Comment on Lawyers?" Nov-Test 14 [1972]).

Notes

41–47 This section has occasioned much debate. Among the many alternatives to the interpretation offered above, the most common element is the idea that Jesus was not affirming but specifically denying the apparent teaching of Psalm 110:1 on the identity of character of the Messiah.

For a discussion of these issues, see Marshall, *Gospel of Luke,* pp. 744–47; for an extended critical treatment of the place of Psalm 110 in early Christian interpretation, see D.M. Hay, *Glory at the Right Hand: Psalm 110 in Early Christianity* (Nashville: Abingdon, 1973).

7. The widow's offering

21:1–4

> [1]As he looked up, Jesus saw the rich putting their gifts into the temple treasury. [2]He also saw a poor widow put in two very small copper coins. [3]"I tell you the truth," he said, "this poor widow has put in more than all the others. [4]All these people gave their gifts out of their wealth; but she out of her poverty put in all she had to live on."

The connection between this passage and the preceding one is that both refer to widows: one, how teachers of the law victimized them (20:47); the other, how a poor widow set an example of acceptable giving.

1–4 The "temple treasury" (*to gazophylakion,* v.1) was either a room in the temple or a "contribution box" (BAG, s.v.). Marshall (*Gospel of Luke,* p. 751) argues for the former (following SBK, 2:37–45) and suggests that Jesus would have heard an announcement as to how much was being donated. The widow's "two very small copper coins" (lepta, v.2, the familiar "mites") were each worth only a small fraction of a day's wage. Proportionate to her total financial worth, however, the woman's gift was far more valuable than the gifts of the wealthy (vv.3–4).

8. *Signs of the end of the age*

21:5–38

5Some of his disciples were remarking about how the temple was adorned with beautiful stones and with gifts dedicated to God. But Jesus said, 6"As for what you see here, the time will come when not one stone will be left on another; every one of them will be thrown down."

7"Teacher," they asked, "when will these things happen? And what will be the sign that they are about to take place?"

8He replied: "Watch out that you are not deceived. For many will come in my name, claiming, 'I am he,' and, 'The time is near.' Do not follow them. 9When you hear of wars and revolutions, do not be frightened. These things must happen first, but the end will not come right away."

10Then he said to them: "Nation will rise against nation, and kingdom against kingdom. 11There will be great earthquakes, famines and pestilences in various places, and fearful events and great signs from heaven.

12"But before all this, they will lay hands on you and persecute you. They will deliver you to synagogues and prisons, and you will be brought before kings and governors, and all on account of my name. 13This will result in your being witnesses to them. 14But make up your mind not to worry beforehand how you will defend yourselves. 15For I will give you words and wisdom that none of your adversaries will be able to resist or contradict. 16You will be betrayed even by parents, brothers, relatives and friends, and they will put some of you to death. 17All men will hate you because of me. 18But not a hair of your head will perish. 19By standing firm you will gain life.

20"When you see Jerusalem being surrounded by armies, you will know that its desolation is near. 21Then let those who are in Judea flee to the mountains, let those in the city get out, and let those in the country not enter the city. 22For this is the time of punishment in fulfillment of all that has been written. 23How dreadful it will be in those days for pregnant women and nursing mothers! There will be great distress in the land and wrath against this people. 24They will fall by the sword and will be taken as prisoners to all the nations. Jerusalem will be trampled on by the Gentiles until the times of the Gentiles are fulfilled.

25"There will be signs in the sun, moon and stars. On the earth, nations will be in anguish and perplexity at the roaring and tossing of the sea. 26Men will faint from terror, apprehensive of what is coming on the world, for the heavenly bodies will be shaken. 27At that time they will see the Son of Man coming in a cloud with power and great glory. 28When these things begin to take place, stand up and lift up your heads, because your redemption is drawing near."

29He told them this parable: "Look at the fig tree and all the trees. 30When they sprout leaves, you can see for yourselves and know that summer is near. 31Even so, when you see these things happening, you know that the kingdom of God is near.

32"I tell you the truth, this generation will certainly not pass away until all these things have happened. 33Heaven and earth will pass away, but my words will never pass away.

34"Be careful, or your hearts will be weighed down with dissipation, drunkenness and the anxieties of life, and that day will close on you unexpectedly like a trap. 35For it will come upon all those who live on the face of the whole earth. 36Be always on the watch, and pray that you may be able to escape all that is about to happen, and that you may be able to stand before the Son of Man."

³⁷Each day Jesus was teaching at the temple, and each evening he went out to spend the night on the hill called the Mount of Olives, ³⁸and all the people came early in the morning to hear him at the temple.

Jesus concludes his teaching ministry (apart from the Upper Room Discourse in John 14–16) with this discourse on the end times. It is immediately followed in Luke by the conspiracy by Judas. The corresponding passages in Matthew 24 and Mark 13 are called the Olivet Discourse because, unlike Luke, they tell us that Jesus was on the Mount of Olives when he spoke.

Jesus' teachings in this discourse provide both a realistic warning about future events and a strong encouragement to persevere. They entail some notable difficulties of interpretation and literary analysis. But if the expositor concentrates on the series of exhortations in the discourse, then the supporting teachings along with the problems of interpretation will come into focus. These exhortations are ninefold.

1. Do not follow false leaders (v.8).
2. Do not be frightened by the awesome events associated with the end times in apocalyptic literature (vv.9–11).
3. Do not worry about your legal defense when you are persecuted and face legal charges because of your Christian witness (vv.12–16).
4. When all turn against you, persevere and take a firm stand (vv.17–19).
5. Flee Jerusalem when it is besieged (vv.20–24).
6. When the final apocalyptic events (the portents in heaven and on earth) do take place, take heart at your coming redemption when the Son of Man returns (vv.25–28).
7. Recognize also that these things point to the approach of the kingdom of God (vv.29–31).
8. Be assured that throughout the apocalyptic period the Lord's words endure (vv.32–33).
9. Be watchful and pray so that you will come through all these things in a way the Son of Man will approve of (vv.34–36).

Of these exhortations, only numbers 5–7 are affected by serious interpretive problems. These include the relationship of the destruction of Jerusalem to other future events and the literary problem of the tradition history of this pericope, specifically its relationship to Matthew 24 and Mark 13. (For comment on the latter, see Notes as well as commentary in loc.)

The exhortations can be grouped under five major topics in the discourse: (1) warnings against deception (vv.5–11); (2) encouragement during persecution (vv.12–19); (3) the destruction of Jerusalem (vv.20–24); (4) future events (vv.25–28); and (5) assurances concerning these events (vv.29–36).

5–11 The opening of the discourse resembles, with several exceptions, that in Matthew 24 and Mark 13. Luke does not mention that Jesus himself was at the temple (though the mention of architectural details and the "gifts" shows that Jesus and his disciples were on the premises, v.5). As observed above, Luke does not mention the Mount of Olives. The Matthean part of the question—"and of the end of the age" (Matt 24:3)—is missing. For the temple to be totally destroyed was unthinkable (v.6). Its sanctuary and surrounding structure were huge, solid, and glistening, a symbol of Jewish religion and Herodian splendor. The disciples do not ask for a "sign" (v.7) because they are doubting but because they need a clue as to when the end will come.

The word "deceived" (*planēthēte*, v.8) was frequently used in the early Christian centuries to describe the activities of heretics and false prophets (e.g., 2 John 7; cf. Rev 2:20). Even as late as the time of Origen (died c. 254), pretenders were making such claims as v.8 describes (Origen, *Contra Celsum* 7.9). Certain frightening events (vv.9–11) are typically linked in apocalyptic literature with the end times (e.g., Isa 13:10, 13; 34:4; Ezek 14:21; 32:7–8; Amos 8:9; Hag 2:6; 4 Ezra 13:30 ff.; 1QH 3:29–39). Jesus is teaching that, while such things are indeed to take place as history moves toward its climax, Christians should not be terrified by them (Luke alone has *mē ptoēthēte*, "do not be frightened," v.9). The reason is that wars, revolutions, natural calamities are not a signal that the end of history is to come immediately (*eutheōs*), as is commonly supposed even today. The sample summary of apocalyptic events in v.11 includes the familiar "famines and pestilences" (*limoi kai loimoi*, a literary device called paronomasia, words with similar sound).

12–19 In its content this section resembles Mark 13:9–13 and also the account of the sending out of the Twelve (Matt 10:17–22). Yet the actual similarities are minimal— only thirteen words or syllables (Gr.) in vv.12–16 and all of v.17. It is not certain whether Luke edited Mark or drew on a different source, or whether Jesus repeated this teaching on different occasions. Among the differences between vv.12–19 and the passages in Matthew and Mark are (1) Luke's omission of the preaching of the gospel to the Gentiles (Matt 10:18) and around the world (Mark 13:10, possibly because he has in mind only the period just before the destruction of the temple in A.D. 70 (see Marshall, *Gospel of Luke*, p. 768); (2) a promise of wisdom in time of persecution (v.15) in place of a reference to the Holy Spirit (cf. Matt 10:20; Mark 13:11), an unusual omission for Luke with his strong interest in the Holy Spirit; (3) the addition of the saying "not a hair of your head" (v.18), the idea of which had already appeared in 12:7; and (4) a change in the wording of v.19. Whereas Matthew 10:22 (cf. 24:13) and Mark 13:13 have "He who stands firm to the end will be saved" (which encourages those who are standing firm, because God will bring rescue, cf. Luke 18:7–8), the Lukan expression is stronger: literally, "you will gain your lives" (*ktēsasthe tas psychas hymōn*). Luke uses a different Greek word—*sōthēsetai;* ("shall be saved"). The meaning is close to that of Matthew 16:25; Mark 8:35; Luke 9:24; Matthew 10:39; Luke 17:33, which state, with some verbal differences, that whoever loses his life for the sake of Christ will preserve it, the implication being spiritual survival. If perseverance is indeed a major concern of Luke (cf. S. Brown, *Apostasy and Perseverance*, in loc.), then the particular wording of 21:19 in comparison to its parallels is significant.

20–24 The reference to Jerusalem (v.20) need not be construed as a *vaticinium ex eventu* (a prophecy after the event). It is often pointed out that, were this so, Luke could have included more precise details. Furthermore, the vocabulary was already at hand and well known (cf. 2 Chron 15:6; Isa 3:25–26; 8:21–22; 13:13; 29:3; Jer 20:4–5; 34:17; 52:4; Ezek 4:1–4; Dan 9:26–27; Hos 9:7; 14:1; Zeph 1:14–15).

The description of the siege of Jerusalem, a protracted event, contrasts with the sudden events in Luke's earlier apocalyptic passage (17:22–37). There the one on the roof will not even have time to reenter his house. But here those out in the country are warned not to try to get back into the city during the siege (v.21). *Kykloumenēn* ("surrounded," v.20) refers to the siege itself, not its completion; so reentry was still possible (Morris, *Luke*, p. 298). The vivid description is painful to read. It is certainly possible to assume that Jesus' predictions incorporated two phases: (1) the events of A.D. 70 involving the temple and (2) those in the distant future, described in more apocalyptic terms. The latter takes us back to 17:20–37, where Jesus' words about the end time naturally fit in with the Pharisees' question (17:20). Thus what Luke has there can now be omitted from chapter 21. In its place, using much of the same vocabulary, Luke now substitutes a prophetic oracle on Jerusalem. Among the words common to Mark 13 and Luke 21 are different forms of *erēmōsis* ("desolation")—a fact that suggests that Luke edited this section from Mark. Yet the word "desolation" is a natural one for this passage even if it were not in the source.

Luke's preservation of the saying in v.24, where *plērōthōsin*, another word for fulfillment, occurs, shows his interest in the Gentiles. Verse 24 implies that an extended period of time is needed for this fulfillment—an idea consistent with Luke's twofold emphasis on a period of waiting along with an expectation of Christ's imminent return. It also implies an end to the period when Gentiles are prominent in God's plan (cf. Rom 11:11–27, esp. v.25, "until the full number of the Gentiles has come in").

25–28 The words in Matthew 24 and Mark 13 about false Christs are omitted; Luke has placed them in 17:23. Now he again takes up material from the Olivet Discourse in v.25, where Jesus speaks of apocalyptic signs of the end time. The "roaring . . . of the sea" is reminiscent of Isaiah 17:12; in biblical prophecy the sea often symbolizes chaos or stands for a source of fear. Daniel 7:13 is the main OT source for v.27 and the NT concept of the glorified "Son of Man." "Power," "coming," and "glory" are terms appropriate to Christ as Son of Man and King (cf. Matt 16:27–28; Mark 9:1; Luke 9:26–27; 2 Peter 1:16–17). Luke omits the saying about the gathering of the elect (cf. Matt 24:31; Mark 13:27), which might have followed v.27. Instead he has Jesus' words of encouragement in expectation of redemption (v.28).

29–38 The illustration of the fig tree, found in the parallel passages in Matthew and Mark, is clear. Luke, perhaps to avoid any thought of exclusiveness based on the fig tree's symbolizing Israel, adds the words "and all the trees" (v.29). "Generation" (*genea*, v. 32) could refer here to a span of time or to a class or race of people. In the former sense it could mean the decades following Jesus' lifetime. (Ellis, *Gospel of Luke*, p. 246, notes that in 1QpHab 2:7; 7:2, it includes several lifetimes.) If this whole passage thus referred to the destruction of Jerusalem, the heavenly portents would have to be understood figuratively (so J. Marcellus Kik, *Matthew Twenty-Four* [Swengal, Penn.: Bible Truth Depot, 1948]). If *genea*, still in the sense of a span of time, referred to the period of time following the initial events of the end time, it could indicate that once the sequence began, it would be brought through to conclusion without delay. This does not necessarily demand a predictable time framework beginning with some identifiable event such as would permit setting dates for the Lord's return. The references cited above in the Habakkuk commentary preclude this. The span of time would be too great to calculate precisely.

The other major alternative, "generation" as a class or race of people, would make most sense if understood as meaning the Jewish people. The point then would be that the Jewish people would be preserved throughout the ages till the consummation of history by Christ's return. The usage of *genea* in the Gospels is inconclusive. It frequently refers to Jesus' contemporaries, classing them as evil and unbelieving (e.g., 9:41); but that is hardly the meaning in this discourse. *Genea* here probably means the people living in the end time, who "will be sure that the last events have begun and will be brought to a consummation" (Marshall, *Gospel of Luke*, p. 780). The next most reasonable interpretation would be that it means the Jewish race, but that is hardly the emphasis here. (For a different approach, see comments on Matt 24:34, this volume.)

The conclusion of the discourse again emphasizes faithfulness, with warnings not only against carousing but against the "anxieties of life" (v.34; cf. 8:14; 12:22–26). Only Luke discloses that Jesus taught in the temple by day but spent each night outside Jerusalem on the Mount of Olives (v.37). It is difficult to know whether Luke mentions this to show the danger awaiting Jesus in the city or to show that Jesus dissociated himself from it (see comments at introduction to 19:28–44), or whether it is simply a matter-of-fact statement. He is careful to tell us, just as he did in his earlier narratives of Jesus' ministry (4:14–15, 22, 32, 37, 42; 5:19, 26, 29), how popular Jesus was. Here it is the "people" (*laos*), the responsive group as distinguished from the mere "crowds" (*ochloi*) and from the leaders, who come to hear his teaching "early in the morning" (v.38).

Notes

The problem of the tradition history of this pericope and the issues surrounding Luke's possible editing of Mark 13 is a complex one. A concise summary with careful judgments will be found in Marshall (*Gospel of Luke*, at several points within pp. 752–84, esp. pp. 754–58). An overlooked treatment of the relationship between Luke 17 and Luke 21 is in J. Oliver Buswell, Jr., *A Systematic Theology of the Christian Religion*, 2 vols. (Grand Rapids: Zondervan, 1962–63), 2:368–71. Written before the widespread use of redaction criticism, it contains some original and useful suggestions. Among the major contributions to the problem are V. Taylor, *Behind the Third Gospel* (Oxford: Clarendon, 1926), pp. 101–25, on the possibility of a source other than Mark, and T. Schramm, *Der Markus-Stoff* (cf. n. 17), pp. 171–82, on the same issue. A useful survey is found in D. Wenham, "Recent Study of Mark 13," *Theological Students Fellowship Bulletin* 71 (1975): 6–15; 72 (1975): 1–9. See also Colin Brown, "The Parousia and Eschatology in the NT," DNTT, 2:901–31. An extensive bibliography follows on pp. 931–35.

B. *The Passion of Our Lord* (22:1–23:56)

1. *The agreement to betray Jesus*

22:1–6

[1]Now the Feast of Unleavened Bread, called the Passover, was approaching, [2]and the chief priests and the teachers of the law were looking for some way to get rid of Jesus, for they were afraid of the people. [3]Then Satan entered Judas, called Iscariot, one of the Twelve. [4]And Judas went to the chief priests and the officers of the temple guard and discussed with them how he might betray Jesus. [5]They were delighted and agreed to give him money. [6]He consented, and watched for an opportunity to hand Jesus over to them when no crowd was present.

Luke's passion narrative begins ominously with a description of Judas's plot. Only Luke says that "Satan entered Judas" (v.3). Although Conzelmann's theory that the period between Jesus' temptation and this event is free from satanic activity is wrong (cf. Notes), there is certainly a focus on these two times of heightened satanic opposition. Ellis (*Gospel of Luke*, p. 248) observes, "In the temptation Satan entices; in the passion he threatens."

1–2 The "Feast of Unleavened Bread" (v.1) lasted seven days (Exod 12:15–20). The Jewish dates for Passover were Nisan 14–15 (early spring). The Feast of Unleavened Bread followed it immediately and also came to be included under the Passover.

Earlier the Pharisees were prominent in opposing Jesus (cf. comment on 5:17). Now the "chief priests and teachers of the law" were taking the initiative against him (v.2). In that society the priests were not only religious leaders, but they also wielded great political power. The scribes (teachers of the law) were involved doubtless because their legal expertise would be useful in building a case against Jesus. Matthew, Mark, and Luke all take pains to show that "the people" (*ton laon*) were a deterrent to the schemes of the leaders.

3–6 Among the Synoptics only Luke exposes Judas's plot as the work of Satan (v.3; but cf. John 13:2, 27). Moreover Luke alone mentions the presence of the "officers of the temple guard" (v.4). It was probably their soldiers who captured Jesus (John 18:3). Municipalities had their own officers and so did the Jerusalem religious establishment. Luke alone mentions that, in betraying Jesus, Judas sought to avoid the crowds (vv.4–6).

Notes

1–6 The theory by Conzelmann (*Theology of Luke*, in loc.), alluded to above, about a period in Jesus' ministry that was free from satanic activity, is ably refuted by S. Brown, *Apostasy and Perseverance*, pp. 6–12.

4 Στρατηγοῖς (*stratēgois*, "officers of the temple guard") is literally "soldiers." On soldiers in the ancient world and in Luke's writings, see TDNT, 7:704, 709–10.

6 Ἐξωμολόγησεν (*exōmologēsen*, "consented," "promised") is, contrary to customary usage, in the active, thereby apparently giving emphasis to Judas's eagerness (Marshall, *Gospel of Luke*, p. 789).

2. The Last Supper

22:7–38

⁷Then came the day of Unleavened Bread on which the Passover lamb had to be sacrificed. ⁸Jesus sent Peter and John, saying, "Go and make preparations for us to eat the Passover."

⁹"Where do you want us to prepare for it?" they asked.

¹⁰He replied, "As you enter the city, a man carrying a jar of water will meet you. Follow him to the house that he enters, ¹¹and say to the owner of the house, 'The Teacher asks: Where is the guest room, where I may eat the Passover with my disciples?' ¹²He will show you a large upper room, all furnished. Make preparations there."

¹³They left and found things just as Jesus had told them. So they prepared the Passover.

¹⁴When the hour came, Jesus and his apostles reclined at the table. ¹⁵And he said to them, "I have eagerly desired to eat this Passover with you before I suffer, ¹⁶For I tell you, I will not eat it again until it finds fulfillment in the kingdom of God.

¹⁷After taking the cup, he gave thanks and said, "Take this and divide it among you. ¹⁸For I tell you I will not drink again of the fruit of the vine until the kingdom of God comes."

¹⁹And he took bread, gave thanks and broke it, and gave it to them, saying, "This is my body given for you; do this in remembrance of me."

²⁰In the same way, after the supper he took the cup, saying, "This cup is the new covenant in my blood, which is poured out for you. ²¹But the hand of him who is going to betray me is with mine on the table. ²²The Son of Man will go as it has been decreed, but woe to that man who betrays him." ²³They began to question among themselves which of them it might be who would do this.

²⁴Also a dispute arose among them as to which of them was considered to be greatest. ²⁵Jesus said to them, "The kings of the Gentiles lord it over them; and those who exercise authority over them call themselves Benefactors. ²⁶But you are not to be like that. Instead, the greatest among you should be like the youngest, and the one who rules like the one who serves. ²⁷For who is greater, the one who is at the table or the one who serves? Is it not the one who is at the table? But I am among you as one who serves. ²⁸You are those who have stood by me in my trials. ²⁹And I confer on you a kingdom, just as my Father conferred one on me, ³⁰so that you may eat and drink at my table in my kingdom and sit on thrones, judging the twelve tribes of Israel.

³¹"Simon, Simon, Satan has asked to sift you as wheat. ³²But I have prayed for you, Simon, that your faith may not fail. And when you have turned back, strengthen your brothers."

³³But he replied, "Lord, I am ready to go with you to prison and to death."

³⁴Jesus answered, "I tell you, Peter, before the rooster crows today, you will deny three times that you know me."

³⁵Then Jesus asked them, "When I sent you without purse, bag or sandals, did you lack anything?"

"Nothing," they answered.

³⁶He said to them, "But now if you have a purse, take it, and also a bag; and if you don't have a sword, sell your cloak and buy one. ³⁷It is written: 'And he was numbered with the transgressors'; and I tell you that this must be fulfilled in me. Yes, what is written about me is reaching its fulfillment."

³⁸The disciples said, "See, Lord, here are two swords."

"That is enough," he replied.

7–13 Luke now sharpens his chronology (in v.1 he only mentioned that the Passover was "approaching"). NIV adds the word "lamb" (v.7) as an implication of the text. A kid could also be used. Luke clearly states that it was the day of sacrifice—normally Nisan 14. The actual Passover meal was celebrated after sundown, when, according to Jewish reckoning, the next day, Nisan 15, had begun.

Luke shows that Jesus initiated plans for the Passover arrangements (v.8; Matt 26:17 and Mark 14:12 mention only the disciples' question, v.9). Jesus' instructions guaranteed privacy, indeed, secrecy, perhaps to avoid his premature arrest. Verses 10–12 show his supernatural knowledge. The right person Jesus asked his disciples to follow would be a man carrying a water jar (v.10). Ordinarily only women carried jars; men used leather skins for water.

The "large upper room" (v.12) was on the second story under a flat roof, accessible by an outside stairway. It was "furnished" with the couches for reclining at a Passover meal and with necessary utensils. Things were "just as Jesus told them" (v.13), showing that he was far more than a "teacher" (v.11), though that term was customary.

14–18 Sometimes, as has often been observed, Luke does not use the terminology of vicarious atonement when we might expect him to. Thus in vv.24–27, the passage describing the rivalry between the disciples and the contrasting servant role Jesus adopted, Luke does not include the "ransom saying" in Mark 10:45. Nevertheless, the strong link Luke forges with the Passover underscores the redemptive motif. In the Transfiguration narrative (9:31), he has already used the Greek word *exodos* (NIV, "departure"), with its redemptive connotations, to describe Jesus' approaching death. This passage also exhibits the strong orientation to the future that characterizes Luke's Gospel.

Both of Jesus' opening statements are strongly worded. "I have eagerly desired" (v.15) represents a strong double construction with a Semitic cast—*epithymia epethymēsa* (lit., "with desire I have desired"). The second statement begins with an emphatic future negative: "I will not eat" (*ou me phagō*, v.16). A similar construction occurs in v.18. Together the sentences convey the depth of Jesus' feelings at this time and the immense significance of what is taking place. Grammatically the statements may imply that, though he had greatly desired to do so, Jesus would not partake of the Passover (so J. Jeremias, *The Eucharistic Words of Jesus*, 2d ed. [London: SCM, 1966], pp. 207–18). Luke's placement of the saying may also imply this, as he puts it before the actual meal, in contrast to Mark and Matthew, who place it after the meal (Matt 26:29; Mark 14:25). It is still likely, however, that Jesus actually did partake when, as the host at the meal, he "took" the cup and the bread (vv.17, 19, 20). The word "again" (*apo tou nyn*, lit., "from now on") in v.16 accords with this likelihood. But insofar as it represents the word *ouketi*, it might be better omitted, for the text is uncertain and probably not original here (cf. Notes). In any case, what Jesus would not eat till the coming of the kingdom is described simply as "it" (*auto*, v.16) and probably means the lamb rather than the meal as a whole (Marshall, *Gospel of Luke*, p. 796).

Unlike the other accounts of the Last Supper, Luke mentions a cup before (v.17), as well as after (v.20), the bread. That vv.19–20 are missing from some Western texts complicates this difference. If the words were not in Luke's original account, there would be a difficult problem—the mention of a cup before but not after the bread (v.17). In spite of some arguments to the contrary, it seems reasonable to hold the authenticity of vv.19b–20. Luke has apparently combined his data from various sources to describe both the Passover setting of the supper (vv.7–18) and the institution of the Lord's Supper (vv.19–20) instead of following Mark (cf. Notes). If so, the seeming disjunction and the problem of the two cups are understandable. The cup of v.17 may be the first of the traditional four cups taken during the Passover meal. In this case, Jesus' comments come at the beginning of that meal. This cup was followed by part of the Passover meal and the singing of Psalms 113 and 114. Alternately, the cup of v.17 may be the third cup, mentioned both here in connection with the Passover setting and again in connection with its place in the Eucharist, on which Luke focuses (v.20).

The uncertainties of the passage should not detract from the high significance of the saying itself. The meal is a turning point. Jesus anticipated it; and he likewise anticipates the next genuine meal of its kind that he will eat sometime in the future, when the longed-for kingdom finally comes, or, in Luke's characteristic vocabulary, "finds fulfillment" (*plērōthē*, v.16; the saying in v.18 has a near parallel in Matt 26:29; Mark 14:25). The believer in the present age observes the Lord's Supper "until he comes" (1 Cor 11:26).

19–20 As stated above, the words of institution in these verses may come from a non-Markan source. Similar wording in 1 Corinthians 11:24–25, written before A.D. 60, shows that it was probably an early source, used by both Luke and Paul. This supports the reliability of Luke's research (1:1–4). The suffering motif is consistent with Jesus' understanding of his mission as the Suffering Servant.

The "bread" (*arton*, v.19) was the thin, unleavened bread used in the Passover. "Gave thanks" translates the verb *eucharisteō*, the source of the beautiful word Eucharist, often used to signify the Lord's Supper. Luke alone has "given for you" (*hyper hymōn didomenon*) in the saying over the bread, as well as "poured out for you" (*to hyper hymōn ekchynnomenon*) in the cup saying (v.20).

"In remembrance of me" (v.19) directs our attention primarily to the person of Christ and not merely to the benefits we receive (of whatever nature we may understand them to be) from taking the bread and cup. The final cup, following the sequence of several refillings during the Passover, signifies the "new covenant" (v.20) in Jesus' blood. The disciples would have been reminded of the "blood of the covenant" (Exod 24:8), i.e., the blood used ceremonially to confirm the covenant. The new covenant (cf. Jer 31:31–34) carried with it assurance of forgiveness through Jesus' blood shed on the cross and the inner work of the Holy Spirit in motivating us and enabling us to fulfill our covenantal responsibility.

21–23 Because this saying follows the Last Supper, one might assume that Judas was present at the institution of the Lord's Supper. Matthew 26:21–25 and Mark 14:18–21, along with John 13:21–27, indicate that Judas was there at least for the Passover, for he had dipped the bread in the dish. John 13:30 says that Judas went out immediately after that; so apparently he was not there for the supper itself. But since John does not actually relate the events of the supper, this is only an implication. By mentioning the "hand" of Judas (v.21), Luke draws attention to his participation in the Passover (or supper), thus heightening the tragedy. In each of the Synoptics, this saying about the Son of Man (v.22) includes reference to the "man" who will betray him. The Greek word *anthrōpos* thus appears twice, making a sober play on the word "man."

The use of "decreed" (*hōrismenon*, v.22) emphasizes divine sovereignty, a theme dominant in Luke, though this particular word occurs rarely in the NT (cf. Acts 2:23; 10:42; 17:31; cf. also Rom 1:4). Instead of "decreed," Matthew (26:24) and Mark (14:21) have "it is written" (*gegraptai*). Divine sovereignty is balanced by human responsibility; so Jesus pronounces a "woe" on the betrayer. The same balance occurs in Acts 2:23. Luke alone among the Gospels has v.23, which shows not only the disciples' concern but also the secrecy that still surrounded Judas's treachery.

24–27 Their questions about this treachery leads immediately, in Luke's order of events, to the disciples' argument—shocking on this solemn occasion—about precedence. See also the similar grasping after status that follows the passion prediction in Matthew 20:17–28 and Mark 10:32–45. The differences between the Gospels warrant our treating Luke's account of this argument as distinct from its near parallels. The word "considered" (*dokei*, "seems," "is regarded") in v.24 is well chosen since status has to do with self-perception and with how one desires to be perceived by others. Jesus replies by reminding the disciples of two objectionable characteristics of secular rulers. First, they "lord it over" (*kyrieuousin*) others (v.25). First Peter 5:3 warns elders in the church against this attitude. Second, they are given the title "Benefactor" (*euergetēs*, v.25), which was actually a title, not merely a description (cf. TDNT, 2:654–55). The form of the verb "call" (*kalountai*) may be middle or passive. If the former, it may imply that these Gentile rulers were not passively waiting to be called Benefactor but sought the title for themselves. In Matthew 23:7, Jesus disapproved of a similar kind of status seeking. Actually he himself is the true "Benefactor." In Acts 10:38 Peter uses a verbal form of the word, describing Jesus as going about "doing good" (*euergetōn*).

In v.26 "but you" is emphatic, with the word "you" standing at the very beginning of the clause (*hymeis de*). Jesus makes two points about true greatness. First, one should not seek the veneration given aged people in ancient Near Eastern society but be content with the lower place younger people had. This allusion to youthfulness does not appear in Mark 10:43 and is one of the variations that point to a different setting for Luke's record of the conversation. In v.27 Luke includes another fresh illustration from social custom. The person sitting at a dinner table had a higher social position than the waiter, who was often a slave. This illustration recalls the example of the Lord Jesus, who washed his disciples' feet as they reclined at the table of the Last Supper (John 13:12–17).

28–30 Verse 28 is not in Matthew or Mark; it shows that Jesus' trials kept on between his temptation by Satan (ch. 4) and the passion events. It also recognizes the faithfulness of the disciples during this time. The fidelity of one of them is about to be tested severely (v.31). This theme of testing and faithfulness is prominent in Luke (S. Brown, *Apostasy and Perseverance*). The comparison "just as" (*kathōs*, v.29) is like that Jesus gave his disciples in the commission in John 20:21, which was comparable to the one he received from his Father. Here in Luke the picture is not just that of a commission but of a conferral similar to a testament. There may also be a suggestion of the new covenant referred to in v.20. The verb *diatithemai* ("confer") here (v.29) is cognate to *diathēkē* ("covenant") there. (For a similar promise in noncovenantal language, see 12:32.) The idea of a messianic banquet is reflected in v.30 (cf. 13:28–30 and comments). Matthew's parallel to this verse is preceded by a reference to the "renewal of all things" (*palingenesia*) instead of to the kingdom (Matt 19:28). The parallel in Matthew speaks of twelve thrones, but Luke omits the number, possibly to avoid the problem of Judas's occupying one of them. Since Luke does specify that there are twelve tribes, the omission is not important. (On the role of the Son of Man and the saints in judgment, see Dan 7:9–18.) Specific designation of the number of tribes of Israel with respect to their future role does not appear again in the NT till Revelation 7:1–8.

31–34 Only Luke records these words to Peter, at the same time omitting Jesus' prediction of the disciples' failure and their being scattered (Matt 26:30–32; Mark 14:26–28). He also omits any reference to Jesus' postresurrection appearance in Galilee, likewise omitted in his Resurrection narrative (cf. comment on 24:6). While Luke has stressed the faithfulness of the disciples and might not wish to mention their defection, he does refer forthrightly to Peter's coming defection (v.31), where he attributes it to the direct activity of Satan. In Matthew and Mark there is a transition from the scene of the Last Supper to the Mount of Olives before the prediction of the disciples' defection is given. In Luke, Jesus' warning to Peter comes immediately after Jesus' commendation for the disciples' faithfulness and his promise concerning the kingdom. This makes a strong contrast. The repetition of Simon's name adds weight to the warning. The metaphor of sifting implies separating what is desirable from what is undesirable. Here the thought is that Satan wants to prove that at least some of the disciples will fail under severe testing. The first occurrence of "you" in v.31 is in the plural (*hymas*). This refers to all the disciples in contrast to Peter, who is addressed (v.32) by the singular "you" (*sou*). Notice the use of the name "Simon" for Peter, apparently characteristic of Luke or of his special source.

Jesus' prayer that Simon's faith would not fail (v.32) has occasioned discussion over whether it was or was not answered. The verbal phrase "may not fail" (*mē eklipē*) probably means "may not give out" or "may not disappear completely" (as the sun in a total eclipse). If this is correct, then Jesus' prayer was certainly answered. Peter's denial, though serious and symptomatic of a low level of faith, did not mean that he had ceased, within himself, to believe in the Lord. Nevertheless his denial was so contrary to his former spiritual state that he would need to "return" (*epistrephō*) to Christ. The whole experience, far from disqualifying Peter from Christian service, would actually issue in a responsibility for him to strengthen his brothers. Peter's overconfident reply (v.33) includes a reference to death found among the four Gospels only here and in John 13:37. The prediction of his denial (v.34) is substantially the same in all four Gospels, despite some differences in detail. Luke alone specifies that in the denial Peter will say he does not even know Jesus.

35–38 This short passage is difficult to interpret. The difficulties lie in (1) the syntax of v.36 (cf. Notes); (2) the problem of Jesus' apparent support for using weapons, which is hard to reconcile with his word to Peter when the latter used the sword (Matt 26:52); and (3) the seeming reversal of the instructions Jesus gave the Twelve and the seventy-two on their missions (9:1–3; 10:1–3). Thus there is a question as to which principle regarding the use of force is normative for the church.

It is common to solve difficulties (2) and (3) by taking Jesus' words as ironical. But if that were so, v.38b—"That is enough"—would be hard to understand; for it would seem to continue the irony when one would have expected a correction of the disciples' misunderstanding of it. Any approach to a solution must take into account the fact that later, when the disciples were armed with these swords, Jesus opposed their use (vv.49–51). Moreover, the tone of v.52 is nonmilitant. Verse 36 clearly refers back to 10:4, the sending of the seventy-two; both passages mention the "purse" (*ballantion*) and the "bag" (*pēra*). (See also the sending of the Twelve in 9:1–6, where the bag is mentioned, but not the purse.) Here in v.35 there seems to be an affirmation of those principles in the question "Did you lack anything?" Yet a contrast is also clearly intended. That contrast may imply that Jesus' earlier instructions were a radical statement applicable only to discipleship during his lifetime. On the other hand, however, it more likely indicates, not a reversal of normal rules for the church's mission, but an exception in a time of crisis (cf. "but now," *alla nyn*). Jesus is not being ironic but thoroughly serious. Since he told them not to buy more swords than they had (v.38), and since two were hardly enough to defend the group, the swords may simply be a vivid symbol of impending crisis, not intended for actual use.

Verse 37a is one of several clear quotations of Isaiah 53 in the NT. (The UBS Index of Quotations cites John 12:38; Rom 10:16; Matt 8:17; Acts 8:32–33; 1 Peter 2:22.)

Notes

7–23 The composition of this passage is complex. Verses 7–13 seem to be dependent on Mark 14:12–16. Verse 14 differs from Matthew and Mark and may be from a special source. Verses 15–17 are unique to Luke, with v.18 showing some similarity to Mark 14:25. Except for the first and last phrases, vv.19–20 appear to be from a non-Markan source, possibly one also used by Paul for 1 Cor 11:23–26, modified in the process. If this is so, it reflects a very early form of the tradition that contains the words of institution of the Eucharist. Taken together, the verses constitute an original narrative edited by Luke from different sources.

7 Ἦλθεν δὲ ἡ ἡμέρα τῶν ἀζύμων (*elthen de hē hēmera tōn azymōn*, "then came the day of Unleavened Bread"). It is not certain on what day of the week Jesus celebrated the Passover. Few scholars question that Jesus was crucified on a Friday. There is considerable doubt, however, as to the chronological relationship between the Passover, the Last Supper, and the Crucifixion. Some infer from John 13:1; 18:28; 19:14, 31, 42, that the Passover did not occur till after Jesus was crucified. In that case the Paschal lambs would have been killed in preparation for the Passover at the very time Jesus was on the cross, which would have had strong symbolic significance. But if that inference is correct, then, assuming the chronological reliability of all four Gospels on this point, the Synoptics could not be describing a Passover meal as the setting for the Last Supper, in spite of all appearances that it was. Another approach interprets the Johannine texts above as being consistent with a pre-crucifixion Passover. N. Geldenhuys has a clear discussion of this possibility in *The Gospel of Luke*, NIC (Grand Rapids: Eerdmans, 1951), pp. 649–70.

Most scholars now look elsewhere for a solution. A. Jaubert (*The Date of the Last Supper* [New York: Alba House], 1965) proposed that the Last Supper was held on an earlier evening in the week when sectarians such as those at Qumran (site of the DSS) celebrated the Passover. This would allow more time for the trial of Jesus, as well as solving the Passover chronology. But the theory conflicts with other data. H. Hoehner (*Chronological Aspects of the Life of Christ* [Grand Rapids: Zondervan], 1977, pp. 65–93) suggests that the differences between the Synoptics and John arise from differences caused by different methods of reckoning dates by Jewish groups. If some calculated the date from evening to evening and others from dawn to dawn, both groups could celebrate the Passover on the same *date* but on different *days*. The Judeans (and John) might have followed one method and the Galileans (and the Synoptics) the other. Whether or not any of the schemes mentioned here is correct, at least we have several plausible solutions to this chronological problem.

16 Οὐκέτι (*ouketi*, "never again," "no longer") is not in some of the most reliable MSS (e.g., B or, apparently, P[75]). It may have been added by a copyist who thought it made better sense (cf. Metzger, *Textual Commentary*, p. 173).

19–20 The words τὸ ὑπὲρ ὑμῶν . . . ἐκχυννόμενον (*to hyper hymōn . . . ekchynnomenon*, "given for you . . . poured out [for you]") are found in every Greek uncial MS except D. They are lacking in the Western text and some other sources. Those who have followed the assumption that because the Western text tends to include rather than omit questionable readings and that on those few occasions when it does omit readings it should be given special weight apply that principle here. Also, since copyists have a tendency to include anything they believe may be genuine, any shorter reading is given strong consideration. Furthermore, the wording is similar to 1 Cor 11:24-25, including words unusual in Luke; so there is a suspicion that this was copied from another source, perhaps combining elements from Paul and Mark.

Arguments for the longer text include the judgment that the Western text is not to be given preference (cf. K. Snodgrass, "Western Non-Interpolations," JBL 91 [1972]: 369–79), the weight of all the MSS that include it, the probability that the source of the words is a very old tradition that Paul also followed, and the likelihood that the sequence of cup-bread-cup in the longer reading was perplexing to later copyists, who preferred readings that simplified the narrative. The following are among the more significant discussions: preferring the shorter text: A. Vööbus, "A New Approach to the Problem of the Shorter and Longer Text in Luke," NTS 15 (1968–69): 457–63; preferring the longer text: H. Schürmann, *Traditionsgeschichtliche Untersuchungen* (Düsseldorf, 1968), pp. 159–92; cf. Ellis, *Gospel of Luke*, pp. 254–56; Marshall, *Gospel of Luke*, pp. 799–801.

36 Ὁ μὴ ἔχων (*ho mē echōn*, lit., "the [person] not having"; NIV, "if you don't have") lacks a direct object. It is not clear whether we should (1) supply the same object as in the first clause, "purse," meaning that if they lacked money they should sell their cloaks to get money for swords, or (2) supply the word "sword" from the end of the clause, where it serves as the object of the verb ἀγορασάτω (*agorasatō*, "buy"), since a sword is the needed item. The first is more balanced grammatically, but the final command to buy a sword is the same either way.

---

3. Prayer on the Mount of Olives

22:39-46

[39]Jesus went out as usual to the Mount of Olives, and his disciples followed him. [40]On reaching the place, he said to them, "Pray that you will not fall into temptation." [41]He withdrew about a stone's throw beyond them, knelt down and prayed, [42]"Father, if you are willing, take this cup from me; yet not my will, but yours be done." [43]An angel from heaven appeared to him and strengthened him. [44]And being in anguish, he prayed more earnestly, and his sweat was like drops of blood falling to the ground.

[45]When he rose from prayer and went back to the disciples, he found them asleep, exhausted from sorrow. [46]"Why are you sleeping?" he asked them. "Get up and pray so that you will not fall into temptation."

Luke's account of this prayer differs in several respects from Mark's and Matthew's: (1) Luke does not specify the location as being Gethsemane; (2) he alone includes at the beginning an exhortation to the disciples to ward off temptation by means of prayer; and (3) his account omits much of the narrative included in Mark and Matthew. Such differences raise perplexing questions about Luke's sources—questions that lie beyond the scope of this commentary, though they may bear on Luke's theology. Also there is considerable doubt as to the genuineness of vv.43–44 (cf. Notes). Theologically, there has been much discussion over the purpose of Jesus' prayer. Some have proposed a meaning for the "cup" of v.42 that would avoid any inference that Jesus had difficulty facing death.

39–42 Luke singles out Jesus in v.39 by using a verbal ending in the third person singular (Mark 14:32 uses a plural ending). NIV inserts the name "Jesus" for clarity.

This reminds us of the way Luke focused attention on Jesus' initiative (cf. comments on 19:38). Jesus went to the Mount of Olives "as usual" (*kata to ethos*, cf. the virtually identical *kata to eiōthos*, 4:16), as mentioned in 21:37. He did not change his habits to elude Judas. Luke may have omitted the name "Gethsemane" to direct the reader's attention to the Mount of Olives. But since he did not mention the Mount of Olives as the scene of the eschatological discourse but introduced it only after the conclusion of the discourse (21:37), it may be that in both places he is simply following his practice of omitting names and other words not familiar to his wide readership. That Luke uses geographical features mainly as symbols is doubtful (see comment on 9:23).

While it is natural to think that the "temptation" (or "trial," *peirasmon*, v.40) has something to do with that of the end time, in view of vv.16, 18 (so Danker, *Jesus*, p. 225), Marshall is probably correct that without the definite article the word does not refer to that specific time. The themes of prayer and temptation are common in Luke. So it is not surprising that only he has the saying in v.40. It is repeated in v.46, to which Matthew 26:41 and Mark 14:38 are parallel. Marshall (*Gospel of Luke*, p. 830) interprets it in terms of vv.28–38. Kneeling in prayer (v.41) was not customary in Jesus' time (standing was the normal posture). But this scene is one of intense emotional strain (cf. Eph 3:14). Matthew and Mark say that Jesus fell to the ground (Matt 26:39; Mark 14:35). It is fitting that Luke, who throughout his Gospel stresses Jesus' conscious fulfillment of the purposes of God, should now emphasize Jesus' concern for the will of God. "If you are willing" (*ei boulei*, v.42) is absent from Matthew and Mark at this point, though they do have the rest of v.42.

As in Matthew 20:22 and Mark 10:38, Jesus uses the cup as a metaphor of his imminent passion. Some, however, have imagined that this metaphor implies that Jesus faced death with less bravery than others have faced it. (But to shrink from a painful death is not necessarily cowardice; the highest bravery may consist in being fully cognizant of impending and agonizing death and yet to embrace it voluntarily.) At any rate, it has been suggested that the cup Jesus feared was that he might die from the strain he was under before he could willingly offer himself on the cross. But this view fails to recognize that Jesus would not have been as concerned with the physical pain of his death as with the spiritual desolation of bearing our sin and its judgment on the cross (2 Cor 5:21; 1 Peter 2:24). Moreover, in the OT the wrath of God expressed against sin was sometimes referred to by the metaphor of a cup (e.g., Ps 11:6, where NIV translates *kôs* as "lot" rather than "cup"; cf. Ps 75:8; Isa 51:17; Jer 25:15–17).

43–44 These verses have some formidable textual difficulties (cf. Notes). Since they have a claim to genuineness and are included in most texts of the Greek testament, they require comment. Luke has already mentioned angels (v.43) many times—in the Nativity narrative and elsewhere, e.g., 9:26; 12:8–9; 15:10; 16:22. So the appearance of an angel here in Gethsemane is not strange.

Luke describes Jesus' agony in physical terms, as we might expect a physician to do. The sweating was apparently so profuse that it looked like blood dripping from a wound (v.44).

45–46 Luke does not dwell on the weakness of the disciples, nor does he describe in further detail Jesus' agony. Matthew and Mark refer to another prayer of Jesus and mention two more instances of the disciples' falling asleep. For Luke a single reference to each suffices, with the addition of an explanation for the disciples' sleep: exhaustion from sorrow (v.45). Luke does repeat the injunction for the disciples to pray lest they fall into temptation (v.46).

Notes

43–44 These verses are textually uncertain. Their mention of angels and their description of Jesus' physical agony are not incompatible with Luke's perspective. Also it is unlikely that copyists would have omitted the verses because of their supernatural element, even if they seemed an intrusion into this report of Jesus' intensely human suffering. Yet the MS support is weak. UBS cites "ancient and diversified witnesses," among them P75 ℵ A B, that omit the verses. Their inclusion in square brackets in the UBS text does not indicate that the UBS committee thought them genuine but rather its respect for the antiquity of the verses. Even if vv.43–44 did not appear in the canonical Luke in early stages of the tradition, they may be authentic in their substance and message and may have conceivably been composed by Luke himself at some point.

4. Jesus' Arrest

22:47–53

47While he was still speaking a crowd came up, and the man who was called Judas, one of the Twelve, was leading them. He approached Jesus to kiss him, 48but Jesus asked him, "Judas, are you betraying the Son of Man with a kiss?"
49When Jesus' followers saw what was going to happen, they said, "Lord, should we strike with our swords?" 50And one of them struck the servant of the high priest, cutting off his right ear.
51But Jesus answered, "No more of this!" And he touched the man's ear and healed him.
52Then Jesus said to the chief priests, the officers of the temple guard, and the elders, who had come for him, "Am I leading a rebellion, that you have come with swords and clubs? 53Every day I was with you in the temple courts, and you did not lay a hand on me. But this is your hour—when darkness reigns."

47–48 Luke drops the introductory "and" (*kai*). Thus this pericope "is joined as closely as possible to the preceding one" (Marshall, *Gospel of Luke*, p. 835). All the Synoptics make the point that Jesus was still speaking to his disciples when Judas and the crowd arrived (v.47). This emphasizes the sudden intrusion of Judas and the crowd into the somber scene in Gethsemane. In making the transition to Judas, Luke first refers to the crowd (not mentioned by Matthew or Mark). In Luke "the crowd" (*ochlos*), in contrast to the "people" (*laos*), is sometimes presented as being unfeeling, perhaps even hostile. From the crowd attention moves to "the man who was called Judas" (*ho legomenos Ioudas*, "one called Judas"). The designation occurs only in Luke and seems to be a dramatic way of isolating Judas—holding him off at a distance for a derogatory look and comment, viz., "this Judas person." Each of the synoptic writers feels compelled to say that Judas was "one of the Twelve." The betrayal was accomplished with a kiss. In Judas's scheme of betrayal, the kiss was the way he identified Jesus in the darkness of the night (Mark 14:44). But in the high drama of the actual situation, it was cruelly hypocritical. In the Greek word order, following Judas's name, three elements come together in stark succession— "with a kiss/the Son of Man/are you betraying?" (v.48).

49–51 (See comments on vv.33–38 for the background to this incident.) John 18:10 (but none of the Synoptics) tells us that it was Peter who drew the sword. Luke alone tells us in words a physician might use about Jesus' healing of the ear of the high priest's servant (v.51).

52–53 In v.52 the details regarding the makeup of the crowd—religious, political, and military leaders—are peculiar to Luke. These details may be part of his design to show that it was not the believing Jews who brought about Jesus' crucifixion but their arrogant leaders. Matthew and Mark do not bring this out till later (e.g., Matt 27:20; Mark 15:11, the substance of which is not in Luke). Jesus' comment shows the underhanded nature of their act. "This is your hour [*hōra*]" (v.53) sounds Johannine (e.g., John 17:1 and passim), especially since it refers to the Passion. But Luke also uses the word "hour" frequently, as well as other words designating a time of opportunity or destiny. The verb "reigns" represents the noun *exousia* ("power," "authority"). Satan had previously offered Jesus *exousia* in the Temptation (4:6); but Jesus, who after obediently going to the cross would receive "all authority" from the Father (Matt 28:18), was willing to have Satan exercise his authority for a time under the divine plan of salvation.

Notes

51 Ἐᾶτε ἕως τούτου (*Eate heōs toutou*, "No more of this") means literally "Permit, or let go, up to this [point]." It is usually taken to mean "Stop what you are doing." Marshall (*Gospel of Luke*, p. 837) prefers understanding *autous* ("them") after *eate*, with the meaning "Let them [i.e., the police] have their way," as in NEB.

5. *Peter's denial*

22:54–62

⁵⁴Then seizing him, they led him away and took him into the house of the high priest. Peter followed at a distance. ⁵⁵But when they had kindled a fire in the middle of the courtyard and had sat down together, Peter sat down with them. ⁵⁶A servant girl saw him seated there in the firelight. She looked closely at him and said, "This man was with him."

⁵⁷But he denied it. "Woman, I don't know him," he said.

⁵⁸A little later someone else saw him and said, "You also are one of them."

"Man, I am not!" Peter replied.

⁵⁹About an hour later another asserted, "Certainly this fellow was with him, for he is a Galilean."

⁶⁰Peter replied, "Man, I don't know what you're talking about!" Just as he was speaking, the rooster crowed. ⁶¹The Lord turned and looked straight at Peter. Then Peter remembered the word the Lord had spoken to him: "Before the rooster crows today, you will disown me three times." ⁶²And he went outside and wept bitterly.

Throughout this and the succeeding sections, dramatic tension mounts. A contributing feature is the simultaneous action taking place in the house of the high priest with Jesus (v.54) and in the courtyard with Peter (v.55). Luke separates the two sequences of events instead of intertwining them as Matthew and Mark do. While this literary device differs from his alternation of stories about the births of Jesus and of John the Baptist (ch. 1), it does enable the reader to follow Peter's experience and then Jesus' trial separately. Luke does not tell us anything about a night session of the trial but allows for it in v.54 (cf. vv.63-65; cf Notes). The story of Peter's denial could not have been invented. It presents a sober and utterly real picture of the prominent apostle; and, along with vv.31-32, it offers a deep spiritual lesson about humility and the spiritual conflict.

54-57 A number of problems surround the account of the meeting in the high priest's house (v.54)—possibly the house of Annas, father-in-law of the high priest Caiaphas (cf. John 18:13). But this meeting seems also to have been a trial before the entire Sanhedrin (cf. Matt 26:59; Mark 14:55; cf. the other commentaries in this volume on the verses just cited from Matt and Mark).

Though he followed Jesus at a distance, Peter is the only disciple who, so far as we know, followed him at all. The fire in the courtyard (v.55) was needed because the evenings were—and still are—cool in springtime in Jerusalem. The denial had three phases. All four Gospels identify the first speaker as a servant girl (v.56). As many have observed, the girl and what she said were relatively harmless and did not deserve such a drastic response. Peter, however, realized that many ears were listening. Peter's response is called a denial. The word "deny" (*arneomai*, v.57) is used in the NT as the polar opposite of the word "confess" (*homologeō*). We are to confess (i.e., acknowledge) Christ but deny ourselves (i.e., disown our private interests for the sake of Christ; cf. comment on 9:23). Peter here does the reverse. He denies Christ in order to serve his own interests. While Peter's language may recall the language of the rabbinic ban (SBK, 1:469; cf. "I never knew you," Matt 7:23, and, more distantly, Luke 13:25, 27), this is unlikely to have been in Peter's mind.

58 After a brief time, someone else, not described by Luke, made another charge. Notice that in none of these dialogues as reported by Luke does Jesus' name actually appear. The assumption is that the recent events in Jesus' life were already known to the group in the courtyard. Luke's description of the speakers is also limited. It is only from Peter's response that we know that the second speaker was a man.

59-60 Verse 59 is typical of Luke's way of indicating the passage of time. The third speaker then makes a definite assertion; the verb translated "asserted" (*diischyrizeto*) means to "insist, maintain firmly" (BAG, s.v.). Peter's response is stated more mildly in Luke than in Matthew and Mark, where he accompanies his statement with an oath. Also here (v.60) Peter does not directly deny Jesus but professes ignorance of him, though this amounts to the same thing. Luke emphasizes the fulfillment of Jesus' words about the cock crowing by indicating that the third denial was just being uttered (*parachrēma eti lalountos*, lit., "immediately while he was still speaking") when the cock crowed.

61-62 In telling how the Lord looked at Peter (v.61), Luke uses the word John used (John 1:42) to describe the way Jesus looked at Peter when they first met—*emblepō*.

It "usually signifies a look of interest, love or concern" (DNTT, 3:519; cf. Mark 10:21). Peter's feelings (v.62) need no further comment.

Notes

54–62 Immediately after his description of how Peter and the others made a fire in the courtyard and sat around it, Luke tells us about Peter's denial. Then, without a break, Luke goes on to describe how the soldiers mocked Jesus, after which he gives us his account of Jesus' trial. Matthew and Mark alternate episodes from the denial and the trial. It may be that Luke (1) followed a different source or (2) arranged his material for dramatic effect in bringing Peter's denial closer to Jesus' prediction of it. While there are difficulties in reconciling the accounts of the denial in the four Gospels, Luke's narrative with its designation of the three questioners as "a servant girl," "someone else," and "another" is consistent with the other narratives. Though John 18:25 has a plural verb for the second question, this does not pose a serious problem because it does not exclude the possibility of one man in a group being spokesman.

6. The mocking of Jesus

22:63–65

> 63The men who were guarding Jesus began mocking and beating him. 64They blindfolded him and demanded, "Prophesy! Who hit you?" 65And they said many other insulting things to him.

63–65 Marshall (*Gospel of Luke*, p. 845) says that the beginning of this section is "badly linked" to the incident just preceding. Though the accusative *auton* ("him") in the Greek text of v.63 clearly refers to Jesus (NIV substitutes "Jesus" for *auton*), grammatically it should refer to the subject of v.62—Peter. Again we probably have a matter of sources. Be that as it may, the incident itself is put in a position of sharp contrast between Jesus' sufferings and Peter's attempt to avoid any identification with Jesus. Also, the soldiers' taunting Jesus about prophesying who hit him while he was blindfolded (v.64) contrasts with Luke's clear portrayal in his Gospel of Jesus as a prophet.

7. Trial before the Jewish leaders

22:66–71

> 66At daybreak the council of the elders of the people, both the chief priests and teachers of the law, met together, and Jesus was led before them. 67"If you are the Christ," they said, "tell us."
> Jesus answered, "If I tell you, you will not believe me, 68and if I asked you, you would not answer. 69But from now on, the Son of Man will be seated at the right hand of the mighty God."
> 70They all asked, "Are you then the Son of God?"
> He replied, "You are right in saying I am."
> 71Then they said, "Why do we need any more testimony? We have heard it from his own lips."

This section presents special difficulties of a literary and historical nature. Jesus' trial had several phases. Between them there is some overlapping of persons and charges. There were some irregularities in the proceedings, especially in the light of later evidence from Jewish jurisprudence. Moreover, the Synoptics are not uniform in covering all aspects of the trial; each writer makes his own choice as to what to include or omit in order to fulfill his distinctive editorial purpose. While the Notes will present some details about these things, most of them do not affect the exposition itself.

66–69 Luke has already indicated that Jesus was arrested during the night (see comment on v.47) and has implied that he was confronted by the authorities while in the house of the high priest (v.64). All three Synoptics mention the early morning trial, though the substance of vv.66–71 has already been given in the account of the night trial in Matthew 26:63–65 and Mark 14:61–64. Luke summarizes the crucial exchange between Jesus and the leaders and adds a time note that it was becoming day (v.66). Matthew and Mark refer to the same time of day, when the religious authorities reached a decision, as "very early in the morning [*prōi*]" (Mark 15:1). Luke's way of reporting the questioning separates the questions regarding messiahship and regarding the Son of God (cf. the Matthew and Mark passages just cited).

The word "Christ" (v.67) at this time had not yet become a proper name; so the question is whether Jesus was claiming to be the Messiah (NIV mg.). Jesus' answer, a simple affirmation as in Mark 14:62, is twofold. First, he says that they would not believe him even if he answered them. D. Catchpole (*The Trial of Jesus* [Leiden: E.J. Brill, 1971], p. 195) notes the similarity of this to Jesus' answer to a similar question in John 10:24–25. Jesus also says that were he to question them they would not answer (v.68). The truth of this had already been demonstrated in 20:1–8.

The second part of Jesus' answer (v.69) concerns the exaltation of the Son of Man (who must be identified with Jesus here or the saying is irrelevant) and vindicates Jesus and proves who he is. Luke's report of this differs considerably from its form in Matthew 26:64 and Mark 14:62. Significant among these differences is the phrase "from now on" (*apo tou nyn*), which Mark does not have, though he has "you will see" (*opsesthe*) where Luke has "will be" (*estai*). Thus Mark stresses the future revelation of the Son of Man, whereas Luke stresses the fact that from that very time in his appearance before the council he was to be exalted. This fits in with Luke's emphasis on the present reality of events that may appear, in Matthew and Mark, to have their main significance in the future. Here Luke is concerned with the present vindication of Jesus. Matthew combines both ideas (a fact that complicates the question of sources), though his *ap' arti* is understood by NIV to mean "in the future," or, better, "hereafter" (RSV, NASB).

70–71 Only Luke has this question (v.70). Standing independent of and subsequent to the question about messiahship, it serves to emphasize that Jesus is himself the Son of God and is not merely called such as an honorific title because of his role as Messiah. Jesus' reply—lit., "You say that I am" (*hymeis legete hoti egō eimi*)—while not a direct affirmation, was taken as such, as v.71 shows. The nature of this reply is understandable in view of Jesus' remarks in vv.67b–68.

Notes

66–71 The probable order of Jesus' trial appearances in the four Gospels is (1) before Annas (John), (2) before Caiaphas and the Sanhedrin (Synoptics), (3) before Pilate (Synoptics, John), (4) before Herod Antipas (Luke), and (5) before Pilate (Luke). The charges before Caiaphas and the Sanhedrin were (1) threatening to destroy the temple and (2) blasphemy. The charges before Pilate were (1) subverting the Jewish nation, (2) opposing the payment of taxes to Caesar, (3) claiming to be king, and (4) sedition ("stirs up the people," 23:5).

The procedures at the Jewish trial have been frequently questioned. A brief summary, drawn from Lohse (TDNT, 7:868), of the alleged illegalities in this capital case includes the following: night session, trial on a holy day, failure to wait for a second session on the following day, definition of blasphemy, and holding the trial away from the official chambers. These issues are more complex than appear from this summary. Yet it would appear that the items cited stand in contradiction to the legal procedures in the Jewish Talmud. Out of much recent discussion, the following are some solutions that have been proposed.

1. The Sanhedrin did act illegally. Few, however, would still hold that the situation was clear-cut.

2. The Gospels are in error. Recently, however, scholars have been treating the Gospels with more confidence as to their accuracy in recording these emotionally charged events.

3. The legal procedures described in the Talmud were not all in effect at the time of Jesus' trial. This is probably true to some degree and may help considerably in reconciling the Jewish and Christian positions.

4. There were two Sanhedrins; different rules might have applied to a smaller group meeting first and the whole group meeting later. This is at best uncertain.

5. The trial lasted longer than it appears; so the first three illegalities listed above did not actually occur. The trial may have lasted longer if the Last Supper were earlier, as proposed by Jaubert and others (see Notes on vv.7–23 above). We are not yet certain enough of the facts to accept this proposal without question.

6. Numbers 1, 4, and 5 of the alleged illegalities listed above do not apply to Luke. The Lukan account should be given priority, though its final editing was later than the other Gospels. Not only is it true that the sources Luke followed were early and accurate, it is also true that Luke's account presents fewer problems than the others. But this still leaves questions regarding the other Gospels, as it assumes that they are in error. All things considered, there are enough variables in the different accounts to preclude any blanket accusation against the historical reliability of Luke's account.

The following works represent recent approaches to the problems relating to Jesus' trials: E. Bammel, ed., *The Trial of Jesus* (Naperville, Ill.: A.R. Allenson, 1970); J. Blinzler, *Der Prozess Jesu*, 4th ed. (Regensburg: F. Pustet, 1969); Catchpole, *Trial of Jesus*; A.N. Sherwin-White, *Roman Society and Roman Law in the New Testament* (Oxford: Clarendon, 1963), pp. 24–47; and P. Winter, *On the Trial of Jesus*, 2d ed. (Berlin: De Gruyter, 1974). Of these, Blinzler, Catchpole, and Sherwin-White take the historicity of the Lukan narrative most seriously.

8. *Trial before Pilate and Herod*

23:1–25

[1]Then the whole assembly rose and led him off to Pilate. [2]And they began to accuse him, saying, "We have found this man subverting our nation. He opposes payment of taxes to Caesar and claims to be Christ, a king."

³So Pilate asked Jesus, "Are you the king of the Jews?"

"Yes, it is as you say," Jesus replied.

⁴Then Pilate announced to the chief priests and the crowd, "I find no basis for a charge against this man."

⁵But they insisted, "He stirs up the people all over Judea by his teaching. He started in Galilee and has come all the way here."

⁶On hearing this, Pilate asked if the man was Galilean. ⁷When he learned that Jesus was under Herod's jurisdiction, he sent him to Herod, who was also in Jerusalem at that time.

⁸When Herod saw Jesus, he was greatly pleased, because for a long time he had been wanting to see him. From what he had heard about him, he hoped to see him perform some miracle. ⁹He plied him with many questions, but Jesus gave him no answer. ¹⁰The chief priests and the teachers of the law were standing there, vehemently accusing him. ¹¹Then Herod and his soldiers ridiculed and mocked him. Dressing him in an elegant robe, they sent him back to Pilate. ¹²That day Herod and Pilate became friends—before this they had been enemies.

¹³Pilate called together the chief priests, the rulers and the people, ¹⁴and said to them, "You brought me this man as one who was inciting the people to rebellion. I have examined him in your presence and have found no basis for your charges against him. ¹⁵Neither has Herod, for he sent him back to us; as you can see, he has done nothing to deserve death. ¹⁶Therefore, I will punish him and then release him."

¹⁸With one voice they cried out, "Away with this man! Release Barabbas to us!" ¹⁹(Barabbas had been thrown into prison for an insurrection in the city, and for murder.)

²⁰Wanting to release Jesus, Pilate appealed to them again. ²¹But they kept shouting, "Crucify him! Crucify him!"

²²For the third time he spoke to them: "Why? What crime has this man committed? I have found in him no grounds for the death penalty. Therefore I will have him punished and then release him."

²³But with loud shouts they insistently demanded that he be crucified, and their shouts prevailed. ²⁴So Pilate decided to grant their demand. ²⁵He released the man who had been thrown into prison for insurrection and murder, the one they asked for, and surrendered Jesus to their will.

The trial now moves into its Roman phase. While there had doubtless been more interrogation than the Synoptics report before Pilate declared he found no basis for a charge against Jesus (v. 4), it obviously did not take Pilate long to determine Jesus' innocence. The larger part of this section deals, not with the trial as such, but with the difficulty the authorities had in trying to convict an innocent man.

1–5 Verse 1 links the Jewish and Roman trials. The "whole assembly" is the Sanhedrin. Pilate was Roman governor (procurator) of the province of Judah. His name appears in an inscription found in 1961 at Caesarea, his official residence. Caesarea was a large, magnificent city boasting Roman culture, where Pilate would no doubt have preferred to be at the time of Jesus' trial, were it not the Passover season, when special precautions were needed in Jerusalem against civil disturbances.

The Sanhedrin's accusation contains three distinct charges. The first (subverting the Jewish nation) would have been of concern to Pilate, who wanted no internal strife among the Jewish people. But it was not a matter for Roman jurisprudence. The second (opposing payment of taxes to Caesar) and third (claiming to be king) were more to the point. Luke has already shown (20:20–26) that the second charge was untrue. The third one became the key issue. Jesus' responses to the questions asked him (22:66–71) were understood as being clearly affirmative. It is also clear that the word Christ, or Messiah (v. 2), was deliberately used to imply to Pilate that

245

Jesus was a political activist. The word "king," put in apposition to Messiah, implies a threat to Roman sovereignty to the point where Pilate would have to take action. (In v.5 the Sanhedrin summarized all this by insisting that Jesus was guilty of sedition.)

In Pilate's question (v.3), the word "you" (*su*) comes first in the Greek sentence for emphasis. Jesus' answer, like those in the Jewish trial, implies a positive answer and at the same time returns the issue to Pilate. The answer (*su legeis*, "you say") is the same in all three Synoptics and is virtually similar to Matthew's report of Jesus' answer in the Jewish trial (Matt 26:64, using the synonym *su eipas*, "you say"), which interprets the "I am" of Mark 14:62.

Luke's account lacks the further dialogue in Mark 15:3–5. But Luke is the only Gospel that has Pilate's declaration of Jesus' innocence (v.4). Presumably the source containing that statement was not available to Mark or Matthew, for they would certainly have wanted to make that point. Yet the point is especially important for Luke, who seeks throughout his Gospel and Acts to vindicate Christianity through the vindicating of both Jesus and Paul in their appearances in court. The response from the Sanhedrin is clever. It implies seditious actions by saying that the people are being stirred up by Jesus' (unspecified) teaching.

6–12 Only Luke has this incident. It is appropriate for his narrative; he had more interest in politics than Matthew or Mark and has already mentioned Herod Antipas whereas they have not (3:1; 9:7–9; 13:31). Herod had a more protracted and more intimate experience with Jewish politics and religion than Pilate had. For a long time he had desired to learn more about Jesus (v.8; cf. 9:7–9). Like Pilate, Herod was probably in Jerusalem because of the Passover. For Jesus' attitude toward him, see 13:31–33. Herod's territory, as a local king under the authority of Rome, was Galilee (vv.6–7) and Perea. Verse 11 probably reflects a certain frustration on his part. He apparently had no legal accusation to make; so he vented his anger by echoing the hostility of the priests and teachers (vv.9–11). Mockery (v.11) was an unworthy aspect of the whole trial scene, repeated later on (Mark 15:17–20 and parallel passages). The robe was "elegant" (*lampros*, "bright," "gleaming"—a word used in both biblical and secular literature to describe clothes and other adornments like those of the rich man in James 2:2). This impetuous use of someone's fine clothes contrasts with the later scene (Mark 15:17–20) where the soldiers used a purple robe and other symbols to mock Jesus' claim to kingship.

13–16(17) This section, also unique to Luke, like v.4, demonstrates Jesus' innocence (vv.13–14). As Marshall (*Gospel of Luke*, in loc.) observes, the presence of the people here is "strange," because elsewhere in Luke they are either friendly or neutral. Actually Luke seems to be making a significant point by mentioning their presence. The "people" (v.13) are the *laos*, as distinguished from the crowd (*ochlos*). Throughout his Gospel, Luke has been careful to distinguish these two groups. He has also been careful to show that it is not the people but their leaders who oppose Jesus. Even here the people do not take an active stand against Jesus. Summoned by Pilate, they, like the crowds in v.4, hear a declaration of Jesus' innocence (vv.14–15). The "people" appear again in v.27, following Jesus to the place of crucifixion, and then in v.35, watching Jesus die. Once more (24:19) Luke mentions them as witnesses of Jesus' mighty works. At their first mention in Acts, Luke refers to the "people" as approving the young Jerusalem church (2:47).

English translations usually imply that Pilate punished Jesus (v.16) because he was innocent (e.g., NIV, "Therefore, I will punish him and then release him"). In the Greek structure, the word for "punish" may be a participal (*paideusas*) for stylistic reasons; but it also throws the emphasis on the main verb "release" (*apolysō*). The thought probably is "Because he is innocent, I will let him go with a light scourging [*paideusas*]." In this way Luke shows that Pilate, a Roman official, wanted to treat Jesus as fairly as possible. This would fit in with one of Luke's apparent goals in writing the Gospel and Acts—viz., to show that Christianity deserved to be favorably treated by Rome. The word "scourged" (*paideusas*) is different from the one used by Matthew and Mark to describe the flogging that preceded the Crucifixion (*phragellōsas*, Matt 27:26; Mark 15:15).

18–22 Luke provides only a brief statement about Barabbas compared with Mark 15:6–11 and has nothing about the message from Pilate's wife mentioned in Matthew 27:19. Again the writers are apparently following different sources. While Luke does mention Barabbas's crimes, he does not explain the custom Mark refers to (15:6). Barabbas has been romanticized, but since he was probably only an unimportant leader of a small riot, history has no record of him apart from the Gospels. We see Luke's concern to vindicate Jesus (and Christianity) to his readers again in v.22. He emphasizes Jesus' innocence by noting that this is the "third time" that Pilate spoke on Jesus' behalf, probably counting the appeals after Jesus' return from Herod (vv.15, 20, 22). On the "punishment," see v.16 and comment.

23–25 In vivid Greek (v.23), Luke brings the crowd's action to a climax. Although he does not refer to Pilate as washing his hands of responsibility for Jesus (cf. Matt 27:24), or to the Jews' acceptance of responsibility for Jesus' death (cf. Matt 27:25), or to Pilate's wishing to "satisfy" the people (cf. Mark 15:15), he effectively shifts attention from Pilate to the people by ending the Greek sentence, not with the verb (as in the English rendering), but with a final reference to the crowds, in the words *hai phōnai autōn* ("their voices"; NIV, "their shouts").

Luke omits the incident (Mark 15:17–20) of the soldiers' mockery (cf. v.11 and comment above) and proceeds directly to Pilate's action. He makes it clear in both v.24 and v.25 that Pilate acted in accord with the crowd's wishes. Having emphasized God's plan and will throughout his Gospel, Luke now notes the human factor: Jesus is delivered to the "demand" (v.24) of the crowd. Acts 2:23 shows how God's purpose was fulfilled even in their decision.

9. The Crucifixion

23:26–43

²⁶As they led him away, they seized Simon from Cyrene, who was on his way in from the country, and put the cross on him and made him carry it behind Jesus. ²⁷A large number of people followed him, including women who mourned and wailed for him. ²⁸Jesus turned and said to them, "Daughters of Jerusalem, do not weep for me; weep for yourselves and for your children. ²⁹For the time will come when you will say, 'Blessed are the barren women, the wombs that never bore and the breasts that never nursed!' ³⁰Then

" 'they will say to the mountains, "Fall on us!"
and to the hills, "Cover us!" ' "

³¹For if men do these things when the tree is green, what will happen when it is dry?"

³²Two other men, both criminals, were also led out with him to be executed. ³³When they came to the place called the Skull, there they crucified him, along with the criminals—one on his right, the other on his left. ³⁴Jesus said, "Father, forgive them, for they do not know what they are doing." And they divided up his clothes by casting lots.

³⁵The people stood watching, and the rulers even sneered at him. They said, "he saved others; let him save himself if he is the Christ of God, the Chosen One."

³⁶The soldiers also came up and mocked him. They offered him wine vinegar ³⁷and said, "If you are the king of the Jews save yourself."

³⁸There was a written notice above him, which read: THIS IS THE KING OF THE JEWS.

³⁹One of the criminals who hung there hurled insults at him: "Aren't you the Christ? Save yourself and us!"

⁴⁰But the other criminal rebuked him. "Don't you fear God," he said, "since you are under the same sentence? ⁴¹We are punished justly, for we are getting what our deeds deserve. But this man has done nothing wrong."

⁴²Then he said, "Jesus, remember me when you come into your kingdom."

⁴³Jesus answered him, "I tell you the truth, today you will be with me in paradise."

In their accounts of Jesus' crucifixion, the four Gospels relate essentially the same series of events, but with varied selection of details and of Jesus' words. None of them portrays the physical agony of crucifixion in the shocking details that might have been given. The stark facts are there but are presented with sober restraint. What was most important for the four evangelists was the inner reality of Jesus' atoning death and his spiritual anguish in being identified with the sins of the world. As Cecil Alexander put it in the great hymn "Green Hill": "We may not know, we cannot tell, What pains he had to bear;/ But we believe it was for us He hung and suffered there."

26 Jesus was required, like others condemned to crucifixion, to carry the cross-bar. The wood was heavy, and Jesus was weakened by the maltreatment. The soldiers could press civilians such as Simon into service. Mark 15:21 has the word *angareuō* ("forces"), the same word Jesus used in the famous saying about going the second mile (Matt 5:41). Cyrene is a port in North Africa.

27–31 Once more Luke gives us an incident that is neither in Matthew nor Mark. For Luke it is important because it again expresses his concern for the fate of Jerusalem (cf. 19:41–44). The terrible destruction Jesus was speaking of also reflects his prediction in 21:20–24. Jewish women (v.27) had always considered barrenness a misfortune and children a blessing (v.28). In the day of Jerusalem's destruction, however, women would have the horror of seeing their children suffer and would wish they could have been spared that agony (v.29). A person standing out in the open in Jerusalem, or in the Judean hills, would probably not think of mountains (v.30) as a means of destruction as much as a means of protection. Therefore, Marshall (*Gospel of Luke*, p. 864) is probably right in suggesting that the words from Hosea 10:8 are a plea for protection rather than for quick death. Fire spreads much more rapidly through a dry forest than through a wet one; so Jesus' words in v.31 warn of a situation in the future even worse than the events surrounding his crucifixion.

32–34 It is not certain why, in contrast to Matthew and Mark, Luke mentions the two criminals (v.32) in advance of Jesus' conversation with them. The effect is to emphasize the humiliation of his execution and perhaps also (cf. Hendriksen, p. 1027) his identification with sinners in his death as well as in his life. Luke omits the name Golgotha, either because it would not be significant to his readers or because it was not in his source. His omission of the drink offered to Jesus may be for the latter reason. Luke's narrative is concise (v.33) and effective in presenting the brutal facts. Nor is it surprising that he, who constantly portrayed Jesus as offering God's grace and forgiveness to sinners (e.g., 7:40–43), is the only one who records his prayer for the forgiveness of his executors (v.34; cf. Notes on the textual problem here). Stephen followed his Lord's example and prayed for those who stoned him (Acts 7:60).

35 It is difficult to know whether the connective "and . . . even" (de kai, possibly "but even" or "but also") identifies the "people" (laos) with the sneering of the rulers or whether Luke intends the reader to understand the role of the "people" still to be passive rather than hostile, while everyone else, "even" the rulers, sneered. NIV takes it in the latter sense, which is probably correct. The word "saved" (esōsen) does not mean that the rulers believed in the claim of Jesus to forgive people but alludes to his reputation for restoring the sick and disturbed. Instead of the words "king of Israel" (Matt 27:42; Mark 15:32), Luke has "Christ of God, the Chosen One," which is consistent with his frequent presentation of Jesus as a prophet chosen by God (cf. the words "whom I have chosen," which occur only in Luke's version of the Transfiguration, in 9:35; cf. Isa 42:1).

36–37 The taunts continue. Luke places this incident earlier in his narrative than Matthew and Mark do in theirs, possibly to bring together in one place the people, rulers, and soldiers (Hendriksen, p. 1030). Although in the other Gospels the offering of wine vinegar (v.36) seems to be an act of kindness, the drink being a thirst quencher carried by soldiers, Luke connects it with their mockery of Christ (v.37). It may have been a compassionate act done in the midst of taunts.

38 All four Gospels contain the superscription, with John offering an explanation of the circumstances (19:19–22). The full text of the superscription may be seen by comparing all the Gospels. Luke's record shows the issue as Pilate, Jesus' Roman judge, saw it. Luke reserves the word "this" (houtos) for the end of the sentence, conveying the emphatic idea "The King of the Jews, this one!"

39–43 This conversation, unique to Luke's account, reinforces two characteristics of his Gospel. One (v.41) is the innocence of Jesus (cf. v.22 and comment). The other (v.43) is the immediate ("today") realization of God's saving grace through Christ (cf. 4:21 and comments).

As elsewhere (e.g., with Peter in 5:1–11), Luke focuses on one person in a group. In Matthew 27:44 and Mark 15:32 both criminals insult Jesus; here this attitude is attributed to one in particular (v.39). "Hurled insults" does not express the more serious aspect of the verb eblasphēmei. Marshall, following Beyer (TDNT, 1:623), observes, "To mock Jesus by refusing to take his powers seriously is to blaspheme against him; the use of the verb represents a Christian verdict in the light of who Jesus really is" (Gospel of Luke, p. 871). The criminal's taunt, "Aren't you the Christ?" is "bitterly sarcastic" (Morris, Luke, p. 328).

The other criminal (v.40) recognizes that Jesus is no mere pretender and that he will reign as king (v.42). Jesus' response (v.43) assures this criminal that he need not wait for any future event but that he would have an immediate joyful experience of fellowship with Jesus "in paradise" (*en tō paradeisō*). This Persian word, which had been taken over into Greek, symbolizes a place of beauty and delight. It means "park" or "garden" and refers to the Garden of Eden in Genesis 2:8 (LXX) and to the future bliss the garden symbolizes (Isa 51:3; cf. Rev 2:7). Paul said he was caught up into paradise (2 Cor 12:4), which may preclude the idea that Jesus descended into hell after his death.

Notes

---

34 The familiar words "Father, forgive them . . . doing" may not have been in the original text. While it is (with some variations) in ℵ A C f¹ 13 33, among other MSS, the following are among the significant and diverse MSS that omit it: P⁷⁵ B D W Θ and some versions. Reasons for and against its genuineness are not easy to weigh. Did the idea come from Stephen's prayer in Acts 7:60; or, more probably, was his prayer inspired by Jesus' prayer? Do we take it as a genuine saying of Jesus that was omitted only because later events—viz., the destruction of the temple and other misfortunes of the Jews—seemed to show that they were not forgiven? (The latter view applies the saying to the Jews rather than to the Roman soldiers.) Or did some anti-Semitic feeling cause it to be dropped? Does the fact that it so beautifully reflects what we know both of Jesus' attitude and of Luke's theology and style lead us to conclude that it must be original? Or should we think that it was skillfully woven into the narrative later, since it is hard to suppose that anything so appropriate to the context would have been dropped? Ellis (*Gospel of Luke*, pp. 267f.) and Marshall (*Gospel of Luke*, pp. 867f.) have especially fine treatments of the issue. Ellis argues well that the "ignorance motif" ("they do not know") is "part of Luke's theological emphasis," deriving from the OT. Deliberate and persistent ignorance, far from being excusable, is sinful. Considerations such as this and others mentioned above speak strongly for the genuineness of the saying in its context. The UBS editors concluded that even though they thought it was not originally part of this context, it "bears self-evident tokens of its dominical origin" (Metzger, *Textual Commentary*, p. 180). They therefore included it, but in double square brackets.

42 Εἰς τὴν βασιλείαν σου (*eis tēn basileian sou*, "into your kingdom") presents a double problem, textual and interpretive. While that reading is supported by P⁷⁵ B L, ἐν τῇ βασιλείᾳ σου (*en tē basileia sou*, "in your kingdom") occurs in other significant MSS (e.g., ℵ A C K W X Δ Θ) and a number of minuscules. Also, there is uncertainty as to what either of these readings means when viewed against Luke's other passages on the kingdom. While it is questionable whether a spatial concept of the kingdom is intended by *eis* ("into") and the accusative, the phrase would seem, from the perspective of Luke's eschatology, to indicate that the thief expected that Jesus would in some way assume his reign immediately. See the wording of 22:69 in contrast to the parallels (see comments above). *En* plus the dative would seem to refer to the return of Jesus. Put another way, does the thief speak of Jesus leaving this world for his kingdom? The latter would accord, in Marshall's view, with a Semitism meaning "as king" (*Gospel of Luke*, p. 872). With such a division of MSS and with such uncertainties, not only regarding what Luke might have written, but as to what a thief barely acquainted with Jesus' teaching might be expected to have meant, a firm conclusion is not possible. The balance textually seems to be on the side of *eis* with the accusative.

---

10. *Jesus' death*

23:44–49

⁴⁴It was now about the sixth hour, and darkness came over the whole land until the ninth hour, ⁴⁵for the sun stopped shining. And the curtain of the temple was torn in two. ⁴⁶Jesus called out with a loud voice, "Father, into your hands I commit my spirit." When he had said this, he breathed his last.

⁴⁷The centurion, seeing what had happened, praised God and said, "Surely this was a righteous man." ⁴⁸When all the people who had gathered to witness this sight saw what took place, they beat their breasts and went away. ⁴⁹But all those who knew him, including the women who had followed him from Galilee, stood at a distance, watching these things.

44–46 Luke refrains from giving a precise time ("about the sixth hour," v.44; cf. "about eight days," 9:28) but does imply by the word *ēdē* ("already"; NIV, "now") that the preceding events had filled the morning. Time was less precisely noted in those days, which may help explain some apparent differences between the Gospels. Matthew, Mark, and Luke agree that there was darkness from about the sixth hour to the ninth, i.e., from noon to three o'clock. The whole "land" (*gē*) could refer to all the "land" of Israel or, possibly, to the local area only. Luke does not say what caused the sun's light to fail (v.45; cf. Notes); nor does he say what significance should be given this fact, recorded in all three Synoptics. Certainly it emphasized the somberness of the event; some think it was to symbolize, or possibly to veil, the judgment endured on our behalf by Christ. Hendriksen (p. 1035) lists a number of Scriptures that link darkness with God's judgment.

Like Matthew and Mark, Luke states that the temple curtain was torn apart. This curtain was doubtless the one separating the Holy Place from the inner Most Holy Place (Exod 26:31–33). It might be argued that the word refers to the curtain at the entrance to the Holy Place (Exod 26:36–37), which would have been visible to passersby. The LXX uses the same word Luke does (*katapetasma*) for the curtain in each location. But in this extraordinary circumstance, which would have been accompanied by the sound of the tearing, the priests would have been aware of what had happened even if it had occurred inside the Holy Place. Such questions cannot be settled by typology. Neither can we ignore the allusion to this in Hebrews 10:19–22, where the veil can only be the one hiding the Holy of Holies. Access to the most holy God is now open through the death of Christ.

Normally a person in the last stages of crucifixion would not have the strength to speak beyond a weak groan, but each synoptic Gospel says that Jesus spoke with a "loud voice" (v.46). Jesus' words are from Psalm 31:5 (LXX 30:6), which was used by the Jews as an evening prayer. To the Christian reader who knows that Jesus' death was a voluntary act, they are beautifully appropriate. All four Gospels describe Jesus' moment of death in terse, restrained words.

47–49 All three Synoptics call on the centurion (v.47) as a witness to Jesus' uniqueness. To the modern reader, Luke's words "a righteous man" (*anthrōpos . . . dikaios*) may seem less significant than "Son of God" in Matthew 27:54 and Mark 15:39. The emphasis in Luke is on Jesus' innocence (cf. v.22 and comment); so this form of the saying is appropriate. Also the term "Son of God" might have been misunderstood by Luke's largely Gentile readership, as it was not unusual for pagans to use such terminology with a different meaning. The "people" referred to in v.48 are not the *laos*, who are so significant in Luke, but the *ochloi* ("crowds"), a mixed group. They were deeply affected, as were Jesus' own followers, who endured their inexpressible grief standing at a distance. Luke's Gospel does not name the women (v.49), as do all the other Gospels at this point, probably because he had named some of them in 8:3. All the Synoptics say that the women stood at a distance (cf. Ps 38:11).

Notes

45 Τοῦ ἡλίου ἐκλιπόντος (*tou hēliou eklipontos*, "the sun stopped shining") need not mean that the sun went through an eclipse. While the verb (our English word "eclipse" comes from it) can mean that, it can also mean any darkening or fading of the light. It is the same word Jesus used in his prayer for Peter's faith not to disappear (22:32). It may be that copyists used the variant ἐσκοτίσθη (*eskotisthē*, "was darkened") to avoid the idea of an eclipse. P⁷⁵ ℵ B retain a form of ἐκλείπω (*ekleipō*), while A and others have *eskotisthē*.

11. *Jesus' burial*

23:50–56

⁵⁰Now there was a man named Joseph, a member of the Council, a good and upright man, ⁵¹who had not consented to their decision and action. He came from the Judean town of Arimathea and he was waiting for the kingdom of God. ⁵²Going to Pilate, he asked for Jesus' body. ⁵³Then he took it down, wrapped it in linen cloth and placed it in a tomb cut in the rock, one in which no one had yet been laid. ⁵⁴It was Preparation Day, and the Sabbath was about to begin.

⁵⁵The women who had come with Jesus from Galilee followed Joseph and saw the tomb and how his body was laid in it. ⁵⁶Then they went home and prepared spices and perfumes. But they rested on the Sabbath in obedience to the commandment.

50–54 Luke is careful to assure his readers of the credentials of the man who offered to bury Jesus. Here again Luke presents someone qualified to affirm by word or action that Jesus was a just and innocent man and that by inference the claims of Christianity are valid. He describes Joseph as *agathos kai dikaios* ("good and upright," v.50). He is also a good Jew, "waiting for the kingdom of God" (v.51), and so joins others in Luke whose piety and expectation of the Messiah validates their testimony (e.g., Simeon and Anna, 2:25–38). He was a member of the Council (the Sanhedrin) but had disagreed with their decision against Jesus.

Joseph laid the body in a tomb "cut in the rock" (v.53). We can still see such tombs today in rocky hillsides in Palestine; in fact, one was recently excavated at Tel Midras. They often have more than one chamber, with a special place for initial care of the body. Luke's description of the shroud does not provide enough detail to allow a comparison with the "shroud of Turin." We learn in v.54 that it was Friday (the probable meaning here of the word *paraskeuē*), and the Sabbath was about to begin at sundown.

55–56 Although Matthew and Mark mention the presence of the women at this point (v.55), they do not speak of the women's preparation of the spices in advance of Easter morning, as Luke does (v.56). He carefully notes that the women did not do this on the Sabbath, even though Jewish tradition apparently would have allowed care for the dead on a Sabbath (SBK, 2:52–53). In this way Luke stresses one more time the fidelity of Jesus and his followers to the Jewish laws.

C. *The Resurrection and Ascension* (24:1–53)

1. *The Resurrection*

24:1–12

> [1]On the first day of the week, very early in the morning, the women took the spices they had prepared and went to the tomb. [2]They found the stone rolled away from the tomb, [3]but when they entered, they did not find the body of the Lord Jesus. [4]While they were wondering about this, suddenly two men in clothes that gleamed like lightning stood beside them. [5]In their fright the women bowed down with their faces to the ground, but the men said to them, "Why do you look for the living among the dead? [6]He is not here; he has risen! Remember how he told you, while he was still with you in Galilee: [7]'The Son of Man must be delivered into the hands of sinful men, be crucified and on the third day be raised again.' " [8]Then they remembered his words.
>
> [9]When they came back from the tomb, they told all these things to the Eleven and to all the others. [10]It was Mary Magdalene, Joanna, Mary the mother of James, and the others with them who told this to the apostles. [11]But they did not believe the women, because their words seemed to them like nonsense. [12]Peter, however, got up and ran to the tomb. Bending over, he saw the strips of linen lying by themselves, and he went away, wondering to himself what had happened.

Luke 24 not only presents the climactic event of the Resurrection, but it includes a recapitulation of the saving mission of Christ (vv.6–7, 19–27, 45–47). The Ascension, with which the chapter and the book conclude, is the final goal of Jesus' earthly ministry (cf. 9:51 and comments). It also sets the scene for the church's ministry as recorded in Acts. The first section of the narrative, concerning events at the empty tomb, contains elements that differ from those given in Matthew and Mark. Some of these are often alleged to be discrepancies that invalidate the NT records of the Resurrection as dependable history. Or they have been viewed as redactional (i.e., editorial) changes Luke made to express his own theological perspectives. It is not the purpose of the comments that follow to resolve apparent discrepancies or to deal with Luke's redaction of the resurrection narrative, except as this has clear value for the expositor. The unique features of Luke's resurrection account deserve our attention as his contribution to the reality and meaning of the event.

1–3 All four Gospels specify the first day of the week (v.1) as the day of the Resurrection. This became the day of Christian worship (cf. Acts 20:7). The change from the traditional and biblical Sabbath is in itself a strong evidence of the Resurrection because it shows the strength of the disciples' conviction about what happened on that day. Luke refers to the time of day by the general statement that it was "very early." This fits well with what the other Gospels say, though each Gospel differs from the others. All four Gospels mention the removal of the stone (v.2). While this was not, as far as the NT reports, used as an apologetic to prove the Resurrection, it could not have failed to impress those who heard of it; and its inclusion here is hardly incidental. Only Luke, who has shown particular interest in physical reality —e.g., he is the only synoptic writer to use the phrase "in bodily form" (*sōmatikos*) to describe the Spirit's descent on Jesus at his baptism (3:22)—specifically says that the "body" (*sōma*) of Jesus was gone (v.3).

4–5 Here (v.4), as elsewhere (e.g., 1:29, 66; 2:19), Luke describes someone pondering a remarkable event. Luke speaks of "two men" rather than "an angel" (Matt 28:2) or "a young man" (Mark 16:5). For a writer to focus on just one person when another is also present is not unusual (both Mark and Luke single out one of the blind men at Jericho, Mark 10:46; Luke 18:35; cf. Matt 20:30). Luke's mention of two men at the tomb seems consistent with his other references to witnesses to Jesus (cf. Simeon and Anna, 2:25–38; and esp. 24:48; cf. also the prominence of witnesses in Acts). Two witnesses are the minimum number for validation (Deut 17:6; 19:15; cf. E.G. Bode, *The First Easter Morning*, p. 60, who draws on Morgenthaler, *Die lukanische Geschichtsschreibung*, 1:97–99; 2:7–11). That Luke understands that the two "men" were angels is evident from what he says of them in v.23. Moreover, he describes their clothes as gleaming like lightning (*astraptousē*, v.4), terminology he applies to Jesus' clothes at his transfiguration (9:29; cf. also Acts 1:10—"two men dressed in white"). Luke alone tells us that not only were the women frightened (v.5) but in their fear they bowed face down to the ground. The response of fear in the presence of supernatural visitation occurs elsewhere in Luke (e.g., 1:12, 29 [though in Mary's case not at the angel but at his message]; 2:9; 9:34). "The living" (*ton zōnta*), only in Luke, stresses the factual aspect of the Resurrection Luke also refers to in Acts 2:24: "It was impossible for death to keep its hold on him."

6–8 What Luke gives us here is not in the other Gospels: The angels show the meaning of the empty tomb by repeating the essence of the three passion predictions (9:22, 43–45; 18:31–33, and parallel passages in Matthew and Mark). They begin with the words "Remember how he told you" (v.6), perhaps implying that what the women should have understood earlier the Resurrection has now clarified. The third prediction (18:31–33) was followed by Luke's statement that the saying was obscure, hidden from them (18:34; cf. also 24:16). The Resurrection is the time for revelation and understanding (v.8). Some think the reference to Galilee (v.6) is an alteration of the saying in Matthew 28:7 and Mark 16:7. There Galilee is the place where Jesus would later meet with the disciples; here it is where Jesus had given his passion predictions. Luke obviously centers attention on Jesus' appearances in the vicinity of Jerusalem, the city of destiny in Luke (e.g., 9:51; 13:32–35). His selective focus on Jerusalem is not, however, a major disagreement with the other Synoptics; nor does his different use of the word Galilee contradict theirs.

Luke's frequent use of *dei* ("must," v.7) and other expressions of divine purpose have already been noted throughout this commentary (e.g., 2:49; 4:43; 19:5). It occurs in the first passion prediction (9:22), as it does in the other Synoptics, but then reappears only in Luke in 13:33; 17:25; 22:37. Chapter 24 contains two more references to the inevitable sequence of Jesus' death and resurrection (vv.25–27, 44–46). Luke's stress on God's plan and providence continues throughout Acts, often with d*ei*, but also without it (Acts 2:23–24; see Bode, *First Easter*, pp. 65–67). The term "sinful men" (*anthrōpōn hamartōlōn*) occurs in Jesus' saying at Gethsemane about his impending betrayal (Matt 26:45; Mark 14:41)—a saying Luke does not have. The idea appears again in Acts 2:23 in the term "wicked men" (*anomōn*). Luke often speaks of "sinners," but usually he does so when referring to notorious people Jesus had compassion on. Here, in contrast, the "sinners" are those who opposed him and brought about his death. Only Luke has "on the third day."

9–12 Luke postpones naming the women till this point (v.10), whereas Matthew and Mark name them at the beginning of their resurrection narratives. Luke has already (8:1–3) told of the women who accompanied and supported Jesus in his ministry. (He also mentions the women at prayer with the apostles in Acts 1:14.) While the witness of women was not acceptable in those days, nevertheless Luke records their testimony (v.9). The apostles, in their incredulity, were unable to comprehend the reality the women were trying to convey (v.11). We see this incredulity again in Peter (v.12) and in the disciples on the road to Emmaus (vv.22–24). This reluctance to believe has an important relation to the evidences for the Resurrection. The disciples were not expecting that event (cf. v.25). Thus they cannot be called fit subjects for hallucination as some would have them be.

Verse 12, though omitted by the Western text (cf. Notes), is probably authentic. It is similar, but not identical, to John 20:6–7. Luke does not mention the "other disciple" (John 20:3), probably focusing on Peter as he did in 5:1–11. The strips of linen used in the burial bear their silent but eloquent testimony to the absence of Jesus' body. Peter leaves, "wondering" (*thaumazōn*) to himself about this. In Luke people "wonder" about things that are hard to understand. The word does not in itself imply either belief or unbelief. We conclude that Peter is still incredulous at this point, not because the verb implies it, but because his visit to the empty tomb fails, in spite of the evidence, to evoke a statement of belief from him (cf. John 20:8).

Notes

3 The MSS representing the so-called Western text omit the following: (1) v.3, τοῦ κυρίου Ἰησοῦ (*tou kyriou Iēsou*, "of the Lord Jesus"); (2) v.6, οὐκ ἔστιν ὧδε ἀλλα ἡγέρθη (*ouk estin hōde, alla ēgerthē*, "he is not here; he has risen"); (3) all of v.12; (4) v.36, καὶ λέγει αὐτοῖς, Εἰρήνη ὑμῖν (*kai legei autois, Eirēnē hymin*, "and said to them, 'Peace be with you'"); (5) all of v.40; (6) v.51, καὶ ἀνεφέρετο εἰς τὸν οὐρανόν (*kai anephereto eis ton ouranon*, "and was taken up into heaven"); and (7) v.52, προσκυνήσαντες αὐτόν (*proskynēsantes auton*, "worshiped him"). Because Westcott and Hort concluded that the Western text tended to add words not in the original, they thought that in the opposite circumstance, i.e., when instead of *interpolating* words the Western text *omitted* words found in other MS traditions, such omissions (or "noninterpolations") should be given much weight. In the instances mentioned here, there has been a reluctance on the part of some scholars to reject that reasoning. More recently, however, the tendency has been to examine each case on its own merits, using standard textual principles in making decisions. Verses 23 and 40 present special considerations because they are similar to John's account of the Resurrection. But in these verses, as in the other instances just cited, there are sound reasons for considering each verse a part of Luke's original text. (See Snodgrass, "Western Non-Interpolations," pp. 369–79; cf. Metzger, *Textual Commentary*, on each verse and on the issue of "Western Non-Interpolations," pp. 191–93.)

4 Καὶ ἐγένετο (*kai egeneto*), a familiar expression, properly left untranslated in NIV, is a

Semitic transitional term that generally contributes little to the meaning (cf. KJV, "and it came to pass"). Its significance relates to the reason for Luke's frequent use of Semitic idioms, a matter of slight relevance to preachers and other Bible teachers and therefore not stressed in this commentary. But in this crucial resurrection passage, it cannot be overlooked. The question is the source of Luke's information. Luke's use of Semitisms may, at least in some places, show that he is following early traditions containing Aramaic idioms. On the other hand, he may, whether using such sources directly or adapting material from Mark or non-Semitic sources, introduce Semitic terminology naturally because of his familiarity with the LXX and his desire to represent the ambience of the events he is reporting. This passage contains a number of characteristically Lukan terms and themes, some of which we have already noted. These, along with Luke's use of Semitisms, seem to indicate a mixture of Markan material, early traditions, and original touches of Luke's own editorial skill.

---

2. On the Emmaus road

24:13–35

13Now that same day two of them were going to a village called Emmaus, about seven miles from Jerusalem. 14They were talking with each other about everything that had happened. 15As they talked and discussed these things with each other, Jesus himself came up and walked along with them; 16but they were kept from recognizing him.

17He asked them, "What are you discussing together as you walk along?"

They stood still, their faces downcast. 18One of them, named Cleopas, asked him, "Are you only a visitor to Jerusalem and do not know the things that have happened there in these days?"

19"What things?" he asked.

"About Jesus of Nazareth," they replied. "He was a prophet, powerful in word and deed before God and all the people. 20The chief priests and our rulers handed him over to be sentenced to death, and they crucified him; 21but we had hoped that he was the one who was going to redeem Israel. And what is more, it is the third day since all this took place. 22In addition, some of our women amazed us. They went to the tomb early this morning, 23but didn't find his body. They came and told us that they had seen a vision of angels, who said he was alive. 24Then some of our companions went to the tomb and found it just as the women had said, but him they did not see."

25He said to them, "How foolish you are, and how slow of heart to believe all that the prophets have spoken! 26Did not the Christ have to suffer these things and then enter his glory?" 27And beginning with Moses and all the Prophets, he explained to them what was said in all the Scriptures concerning himself.

28As they approached the village to which they were going, Jesus acted as if he were going farther. 29But they urged him strongly, "Stay with us, for it is nearly evening; the day is almost over." So he went in to stay with them.

30When he was at the table with them, he took bread, gave thanks, broke it and began to give it to them. 31Then their eyes were opened and they recognized him, and he disappeared from their sight. 32They asked each other, "Were not our hearts burning within us while he talked with us on the road and opened the Scriptures to us?"

33They got up and returned at once to Jerusalem. There they found the Eleven and those with them, assembled together 34and saying, "It is true! The Lord has risen and has appeared to Simon." 35Then the two told what had happened on the way, and how Jesus was recognized by them when he broke the bread.

The Emmaus story is a literary and spiritual jewel. It is at once a moving story, a testimony to the Resurrection, an explanation of the empty tomb, and an occasion for Luke to summarize several of his major themes. Despite the fact that it has to a superlative degree the ring of truth—what literary scholars call "verisimilitude"—some have considered it legendary (cf. Notes).

13-16 The opening words of v.13 link this story with the entire Easter event. "Now" (*kai idou*) moves the reader's attention to a new and important phase of Luke's narrative. "That same day" ties the narrative to Jesus' death and resurrection (cf. the sequence in 23:54, 56; 24:1). Two travelers are speaking together (vv.14–15); so a valid witness is provided. A twofold witness is necessary according to Jewish law. Furthermore, the concept of witness is, as we have seen, important to Luke. Two witnesses (Simeon and Anna) bore testimony to the Messiah's arrival (2:25–38); now the two travelers testify to a particular resurrection appearance of Jesus (24:35). The words "of them" (*ex autōn*, v.13) do not clearly identify who the two are. They are not two of the Eleven (v.9; cf. v.33). Probably they are two of the followers of Jesus who had come to Jerusalem for the Passover. So they had been among the "disciples" who lauded Jesus on his triumphal entry to the city (19:39) and were now returning home. At any rate, the phrase "of them," like the opening words of v.13, establishes a continuity with the foregoing events.

The fact that this event occurs when the two disciples "were going" (*ēsan poreuomenoi*, v.13) and "walked along" (*syneporeueto*, v.15) continues the travel theme prominent in Luke, especially in his unique central section (9:51–19:44). That section begins as Jesus "resolutely set out" (*to prosōpon estērisen tou poreuesthai*) for Jerusalem (9:51). Now these two are leaving that same city. Shortly after the earlier journey to Jerusalem began, a man had approached Jesus regarding discipleship "as they were walking" (*poreuomenōn autōn*, 9:57). Now, after the Resurrection, Jesus approaches two disheartened followers as they are walking. Acts continues the theme of Jesus' disciples traveling, going from Jerusalem to Rome (Paul, in ch. 28) and ultimately to the ends of the earth as "witnesses" (1·8). As for the identity of Emmaus, this is uncertain (cf. Notes). It is enough to know that it is a village near Jerusalem.

The two were talking about events surrounding Jesus' resurrection. Between the lines of their dialogue, Luke shows their bewilderment. He uses two different verbs, one of them repeated: "they were talking" (*hōmiloun*, v.14), "as they talked" (*en tō homilein*, v.15), and "discussed" (*syzētein*). So the tension mounts in preparation for Jesus' appearance. Luke introduces Jesus into the story with the emphatic "Jesus himself" (*autos Iēsous*); and his comment that Jesus "walked along with" (*syneporeueto*) them suggests to us, whether or not Luke intended it, Jesus' presence with his disciples in the church age. The passive form in "were kept [*ekratounto*] from recognizing him" (v.16) may be a "divine passive," i.e., a means of connoting that an action, the subject of which is not mentioned, is actually the work of God. This device introduces the structural pattern of nonrecognition and recognition, which is central in this beautiful narrative.

17-18 Still another verb describes their discussion; *antiballete* ("discussed") reflects the exchange of ideas (lit., "throwing back and forth"). The scene in vv.14–17 is of a persistent but rather baffled attempt to understand the meaning of this most momentous weekend in history. Luke now uses a different word for walking (*peripateō*; cf. comments on vv.13–16). Another mention of walking is certainly not necessary merely to convey that fact, and we may assume that there is a deliberate emphasis on that movement. Therefore it is striking that when Jesus addressed them, the two travelers stopped short and "stood still" (*estathēsan*). Their attitude at that point was gloomy, perhaps even sullen. Only one of the two (Cleopas) is named (v. 18), probably because he was known to at least some of Luke's readers. One tradition identifies him as an uncle of Jesus, brother of Joseph, and father of Simeon, who became a leader of the Jerusalem church (Eusebius, *Ecclesiastical History* 3.11; cf. Ellis, *Gospel of Luke*, p. 894). This is not the same man as Clopas (John 19:25), though the two names are variant spellings of each other.

19–24 What follows constitutes an affirmation about the person and work of Christ that is of great significance for our understanding of Jesus and of Luke's perception of him. Concerning the opening words, R. J. Dillon (*From Eyewitnesses to Ministers of the Word*, p. 114) observes, "This characterization, together with the assertion of full publicity amongst the people, contains pointed echoes of Luke's introductory summary of Jesus' ministry [in the power of the] Spirit (Lk 4, 14; cp. Acts 10, 38)." See comments above at 4:14 on the popular response to Jesus. The statement there about his reputation and power precedes the progammatic statement about his ministry under the impetus of the Spirit in 4:18–19. Acts 10:38 is Peter's summary of Jesus' powerful, Spirit-filled ministry (cf. Acts 2:22) and includes the statement "he went around doing good." Peter then tells Cornelius, "We are witnesses of everything" (Acts 10:39), calling to mind Luke 1:2—"eyewitnesses and servants of the word." The importance of the affirmation of the two disciples here in 24:19 must not in any way be underestimated. It is integral to Luke's theology and purpose.

"He was a prophet" recalls the passage in chapter 4 just mentioned, where Jesus clearly identified himself with the prophets (4:24). While in Luke's narrative Jesus is perceived as a prophet (e.g., 7:16; cf. Minear, *Heal and Reveal*, pp. 102–21), the Resurrection affirmed him to be much more, as the two on the Emmaus road are to learn (e.g., v. 26, "the Christ . . . glory"). The word "prophet" does not appear in what Peter told Cornelius about Jesus (Acts 10:36–43). This is probably not because Cornelius was not Jewish, for Jesus was "Lord of all" (Acts 10:36), but because the word "prophet" was inadequate to comprehend all Jesus is. The term "prophet" is then not so much an invalid as an incomplete characterization of Jesus. Another of Luke's favorite terms is "people" (*laos*), used throughout his Gospel for the responsive hearers in Israel (cf. 1:17, 68, 77; 2:10, 31–32). Later Luke will use *laos* of believing Gentiles (Acts 18:10).

The "chief priests and our rulers" (v. 20) stand in contrast to the "people" (v. 21) as elsewhere in Luke. It was they who "handed him over" for crucifixion. In v. 21 the words "but we" (*hemeis de*, emphatic) of the two disciples provide still another contrast. Unlike the rulers, they "hoped" that Jesus would bring deliverance. Observe that the verb is "hoped," not "trusted" (as in KJV); there is a big difference between trusting Jesus as our Deliverer and Savior and hoping that he will prove to be our Deliverer and Savior. The past tense of "hoped" is, under the present circumstances, a pathetic reminder of their inability to recognize Jesus or to believe the report of the empty tomb. Their expectation that he would "redeem Israel" recalls the words of Zechariah in 1:68 (cf. 2:38; 21:28). In view of v. 46 and the passion predictions, the term "third day" had a significance to Luke's readers. What should have been the day of hope realized was for them the day of hope extinguished.

The final ("in addition," *alla kai*) incomprehensible element in the travelers' report was the report of the empty tomb (v.22). This looks back to vv.1–12. Again Luke used the word "body" (v.23; see comment above on v.3). The mention of "angels" shows that this is what Luke meant by "men" in v.4, which is in harmony with the other Gospels. Verse 24 recalls v.12. In the last words in the report, "him they did not see," the word "him" (*auton*) is placed in an emphatic position. The empty tomb without the appearance of Jesus himself was inadequate. It ironically becomes the last sad part of their confused response to Jesus' question, "What things?" (v.19).

25–27 The reader of the Greek text will immediately observe following the pronoun *auton* ("him") in its emphatic position in v.24 that it occurs in v.25 (*kai autos*, "and he"; NIV, "he") to refer (still emphatically) to the same person, though he remains unrecognized. "The Stranger seizes the platform from the confused disciple" (Dillon, *Eyewitnesses*, p. 132). Jesus, who in his transfiguration was superior to Moses and Elijah (9:28–36), now invokes Moses and the Prophets to substantiate the divine plan of his path from suffering to glory (v.27). The word "all" (v.25) is a warning not to treat the Scriptures selectively. Such selectivity could lead to the omission of the Messiah's suffering (v.26). But "the Christ" (Messiah) did "have to" (*edei*) suffer. The verb *dei*, meaning "it is necessary," is one of Luke's key words (cf. 2:49; 4:43; 13:16, 33; 15:32; 18:1; 19:5; 21:9; 22:7, 37; 24:7, 44, along with the basic passion prediction of 9:22 that occurs also in Matthew and Mark; cf. comments on those verses). The future glory of the Christ (v.26) was mentioned in the context of the passion prediction, ascribed there to the "Son of Man" (9:26; cf. 21:27). Some have argued that here "glory" is to be understood as a substitute expression for "was raised from the dead" (cf. Dillon, *Eyewitnesses*, pp. 141ff.). More likely it refers to the honor anticipated in the OT for the Messiah and attributed to the Son of Man in the verses just referred to. The unexpected element in Christ's messiahship was his suffering. On the other hand, one could hardly argue that Christ's glory excludes the Resurrection. Paul quoted the OT to prove the necessity of both the suffering and the resurrection of the Messiah (Acts 17:2–3). "Beginning with" (v.27) probably implies that Jesus drew on all the Scriptures but principally on the Law (Gen-Deut) and the Prophets (Marshall, *Gospel of Luke*, p. 897). The central subject of these OT passages is "himself."

For several reasons vv.25–27 are vitally important. With great clarity they show that the sufferings of Christ, as well as his glory, were predicted in the OT and that all the OT Scriptures are important. They also show that the way the writers of the NT used the OT had its origin, not in their own creativity, but in the postresurrection teachings of Jesus, of which this passage is a paradigm. The passage also exemplifies the role of the OT in Luke's own theology. Although he does not directly quote the OT Scriptures as many times as Matthew does, nevertheless he alludes frequently to the OT, demonstrating that what God has promised must take place and employing a "proof-from-prophecy" apologetic for the truth of the gospel.

28–32 The invitation for Jesus to stay with the two follows the ancient custom of hospitality. As the afternoon drew on and suppertime approached, the stranger would need food and lodging. Jesus had "acted as if" (*prosepoiēsato*) he were going to continue his journey (v.28). The verb *prospoieō*, in spite of well-meaning efforts to weaken it to avoid any thought of deceit on Jesus' part (e.g., Plummer, in loc.), often means "pretend" (BAG, LSJ, MM, s.v.). Such a gesture would, like the invitation itself, be appropriate in the custom of those days. While it is probably true, as Plummer says, that Jesus would have gone on, had he not been invited to stay, this polite action seems intended to draw out a very strong response from Cleopas and his companion, who indeed then "urged him strongly" (*parebiasanto*) to stay (v.29). In other contexts this verb can mean to force someone to do something.

The recognition scene is the third high point in this narrative, the first two being the long reply of Cleopas and his companion to Jesus' question and Jesus' exposition of the OT's teaching about himself. While from a church perspective some have wrongly seen the Lord's Supper in the breaking of the bread, we must also realize that a table scene is characteristic of Luke and probably of his special source material (cf. 5:29; 7:36; 14:1, 7, 12, 15–16; and, less obviously, 10:38–40). What is remarkable is that Jesus took the role of the host and broke the bread, giving thanks (v.30). Of course this recalls the feeding of the five thousand (9:10–17, N.B. v.16) as well as the Last Supper (22:19), though it was not a celebration of the latter.

As to whether it was through the actual breaking of bread or through divine intervention that the moment of truth came and the two disciples recognized Jesus, the answer must be that it was through both. Whether the two noticed the nail scars (Luke does not say they did), Jesus' acting as host led to the recognition. At the same time, the passive verb *diēnoichthēsan* ("were opened") implies divine action (v.31), as was the case when Jesus' identity was hidden from them (v.16). This provides uniformity in the structure and theological meaning, as God is the revealer of the risen Christ. Note the repetition of Jesus' opening "the Scriptures" (v.32) and "their minds" (v.45).

The narrative ends abruptly as Jesus disappeared and Cleopas and his companion reflected on their feelings of intense inner warmth (cf. Ps 39:3; Jer 20:9; the vocabulary differs but something similar may be in mind). (For a survey of interpretations of *kaiomenē* ["burning"], see Marshall, *Gospel of Luke*, pp. 898–99.) The specific occasion of these feelings is the presence of the Lord and his expounding the OT.

33–35 The words "at once" (*autē tē hōra*, lit., "in the same hour," v.33) continue the chronology of the resurrection day (cf. comment at v.13). The reunion with the Eleven brought assurance to all, as the two disciples fulfilled their role as witnesses (vv.34–35). They especially spoke of recognizing Jesus when he broke bread with them (v.35).

Notes

The historicity of the Emmaus story has often been challenged (e.g., H.D. Betz, "The Origin and Nature of Christian Faith According to the Emmaus Legend," Int 23 [1969]: 32–46). There are, indeed, elements of the story many find difficult to accept—not merely the inability of the two to recognize Jesus, but the very appearance of Jesus after his death. But this difficulty relates to the concept one has of the Resurrection itself and of the possibility of a supernatural work of God in the nonrecognition and recognition sequence. There are also similarities to elements in other ancient narratives. We must, however, be careful about drawing conclusions from works written after Luke was. Also, we "must not invoke such parallels prematurely, on the basis of mere resemblance, as instruments of interpretation" (Dillon, *Eyewitnesses*, pp. 73f.). It is impossible to prove or disprove the historicity of a story such as this that exists in no other literature and that, unlike the Resurrection, has produced no effect capable of investigation. Apart from the consideration of alleged legendary elements (remembering that issues of form do not settle issues of historicity, cf. Marshall, *Gospel of Luke*, p. 891), such issues will be decided on the basis of the setting of the story, both in the resurrection narrative and within Luke's carefully researched work, with care not to reject what one may consider, a priori, difficult to accept.

13 The location of Emmaus, "about seven miles from Jerusalem," is of minor concern to the expositor but of historical interest. Attention centers on several possible sites, but certainty is not possible at this time. Two sites are located at an approximately correct distance (one about nine miles away; the other is even closer to Luke's "sixty stadia"— approximately seven miles). They are Abu-Ghosh and El-Qubeibeh. There is little evidence, however, that either is the site.

Another place, Motza-Illit, is only three and one-half miles from Jerusalem. To identify this with the village in Luke, one has to assume that Luke's figure of sixty stadia applied to a round trip. In Jesus' day it was only a "village" (κώμη, *kōmē*), precisely Luke's word. Both Josephus and the Talmud mention it, the first as Emmaus and the second as Motza. It is very possible that the Semitic sound of Ha-Motza became Ammaous or Emmaus. A Roman colony was established there later in the first century, and so it is now also known as Qaloniya or Colonia. Evidence has come to light of a Byzantine church there, indicating that the site was reverenced. This may well be the true location.

There is still another site, much better known: Imwas (by Latrun), known also as Nicopolis probably since the time of Elagabulus (A.D. 218–22). It was prominent as the place of a great victory of Judas Maccabeus in the second century B.C., described in 1 Macc 3–4. The site continued to be well known throughout Christian history, and it naturally has been favored by many as the NT Emmaus. One serious problem is that it is not 60 but 160 stadia away (a problem Sinaiticus and other MSS seem to have addressed by changing the number to 160). This distance, however, seems long, though not impossible, for the two disciples to have traveled in both directions (cf. v.33). It would have meant a round trip total of 30 miles in one busy day, with the return trip started no later than early evening. It is possible that there were actually two places known as Emmaus in Jesus' day: the *village*, hardly known, 3½ miles or 30 stadia away, and the *city*, 160 stadia or 19 miles away. It was perhaps the former to which the disciples went on the Resurrection day. See J. Monson, *A Survey of the Geographical and Historical Setting of the Bible* (Jerusalem: Institute for Holy Land Studies, 1977), pp. 3f., of Benjamin Field Study section; R.M. Mackowski, "Where Is Biblical Emmaus?" *Science et Esprit* 32 (1980): 93–103.

---

3. The appearance to the disciples

24:36–49

[36]While they were still talking about this, Jesus himself stood among them and said to them, "Peace be with you."

[37]They were startled and frightened, thinking they saw a ghost. [38]He said to them, "Why are you troubled, and why do doubts rise in your minds? [39]Look at my hands and my feet. It is I myself! Touch me and see; a ghost does not have flesh and bones, as you see I have."

[40]When he had said this, he showed them his hands and feet. [41]And while they

still did not believe it because of joy and amazement, he asked them, "Do you have anything here to eat?" [42]They gave him a piece of broiled fish, [43]and he took it and ate it in their presence.

[44]He said to them, "This is what I told you while I was still with you: Everything must be fulfilled that is written about me in the Law of Moses, the Prophets and the Psalms."

[45]Then he opened their minds so they could understand the Scriptures. [46]He told them, "This is what is written: The Christ will suffer and rise from the dead on the third day, [47]and repentance and forgiveness of sins will be preached in his name to all nations, beginning at Jerusalem. [48]You are witnesses of these things. [49]I am going to send you what my Father has promised; but stay in the city until you have been clothed with power from on high."

This is the third Easter narrative in Luke. In the first Jesus is not seen; in the second he appears to two disciples; this time he appears to the Eleven. The narrative probably goes back to an older source that also lies behind John 20:19–23. It does not have as many distinctively Lukan touches as the Emmaus story. The events Luke tells us of here also provide the substance for his apologetic for Jesus' bodily resurrection in Acts 1:3–4 and Peter's witness to Cornelius (Acts 10:40–43). Here it is not Jesus' resurrection as such that is being proved but the fact that the sudden visitor was indeed Jesus, present in a tangible body.

36 The care with which Luke connects the events after the Crucifixion chronologically (23:54, 56; 24:1, 9, 13, 33) is again apparent in the words "While they were still talking about this." Once more Luke focuses attention on Jesus by the reflexive pronoun *autos* (i.e., "Jesus himself"; cf. comment on v.25). The next words, "stood among them" (*estē en mesō*), are almost identical to those in John 20:19 (*estē eis to meson*). A sudden appearance is implied (cf. the sudden disappearance in v.31), but Luke does not include the reference to closed doors found in John. "Peace be with you" may not have been in the original but added by a copyist who knew John 20:19. Yet the words may belong to the same tradition John and Luke used (cf. Notes). The characteristically Semitic "peace" (Heb. *šalôm*) would be a striking greeting, if one were expecting the more familiar Greek *chaire* (cf. 1:28).

37–39 Luke's Gospel opened with a terrified Zechariah in the unexpected presence of an angel (1:12). Now, near its end, Luke describes the fright of the disciples at the unexpected appearance of the risen Christ (v.37). One might have thought they would not respond this way, since they had just been hearing about Jesus' appearance on the Emmaus road. But whereas in that case Jesus had walked up to Cleopas and his companion as any traveler might, this time he appeared suddenly. Equally surprising to the reader are their doubts (v.38). These are significant for any who think that the disciples were expecting the Resurrection and projected their hopes into a hallucination. Jesus identified himself very emphatically (v.39): "It is I myself" (*egō eimi autos*, cf. the *egō eimi*, "I am," frequent in John). The methods of crucifixion varied slightly, but Jesus apparently had nails in his hands (the Greek word can include wrists) and feet. Seeing and touching would convince the disciples. Later on John wrote of touching Jesus, not specifically with respect to the Resurrection, but as an argument against docetism (1 John 1:1). As in vv.3, 23, where he mentioned the body of Jesus, Luke drew attention to the physical aspect of the Resurrection.

The argument one sometimes hears that Jesus' appearance in "flesh and bones" here contradicts Paul's statement in 1 Corinthians 15:50 that "flesh and blood cannot inherit the kingdom of God" misses Paul's idiomatic meaning; the human body cannot develop into a resurrection body without the change only God can bring.

40–43 Verse 40 is lacking in some MSS, but it is more likely genuine and is certainly appropriate (cf. Notes). Verse 41a is a beautifully human touch. Jesus provides further evidence of his physical presence by eating (vv.42–43). Commentators refer to instances such as Genesis 18:8 and 19:3 as examples of eating by supernatural visitors, though in these two instances the reason was not, as here, to show that they were not ghosts.

44–49 From time to time Luke has taken care to show that whatever the Lord has said unfailingly takes place (e.g., 2:20, last phrase; 2:26; 19:32; 22:13, 37). That implication is perhaps present in the words "This is what I told you" (*houtoi hoi logoi mou*, lit., "these are my words," v.44). Luke has a double emphasis in these verses, that which the OT predicted (notice the words "must be fulfilled"), and that which Jesus had taught during his ministry. The clause "while I was still with you" is a way of distinguishing between the days of Jesus' earthly ministry and his temporary postresurrection ministry before the Ascension. "Everything" (*panta*, v.44) recalls "all" (*pasin*, v.25); "must" (*dei*) corresponds to "have to" (*edei*) in v.26 (see comment there); "Law . . . Prophets . . . Psalms" expands "Moses and all the Prophets" in v.27 by adding the Psalms as a major component of the third division of the OT, the so-called Writings.

In v.31 the eyes of the two were "opened" (*diēnoichthēsan*). Now Jesus has "opened" (*diēnoixen*) the disciples' minds (v.45). Again Luke emphasizes the "Scriptures." The reader of the Greek text will see this emphasis in the pattern of related words: *gegrammena* ("written," v.44) . . . *graphas* ("Scriptures," v.45) . . . *gegraptai* ("written," v.46). The formula "on the third day" (cf. v.7) goes back to the first passion prediction (9:22). Even the widespread preaching of repentance and forgiveness was predicted in the OT (cf. Acts 26:23). Rabbis in the first centuries of our era debated whether or not they should engage in active proselytization; and some cited OT passages, especially in Isaiah, which referred to the coming of the Gentiles to the Lord. Such Scriptures as Isaiah 42:6; 49:6; 60:3 may underlie v.47 here (cf. Acts 13:47). The fulfillment began in Acts 2:38: "Repent . . . forgiven." Gentiles heard these words in Acts 10:43 and 17:30 (cf. Paul's commission, Acts 26:17–18). The idea of reaching the Gentiles is certainly prominent in Luke (e.g., the mission to the seventy or seventy-two, probably representing the nations of the world [10:1]; see comments). Also, the place of Jerusalem as the base of the mission accords with Luke's constant featuring of that city. Likewise Luke has stressed the place of "witnesses" and will continue to do so in Acts (e.g., 1:8). Therefore, v.48 supports his emphasis. The pronouns *hymeis* ("you") in v.48, *ego* ("I") in v.49, and *hymeis* ("you") again as the subject of "stay" in v.49 (omitted by NIV) are emphatic and in contrast to one another. What the Father "promised" (v.49) is the Holy Spirit (Acts 1:4–5; 2:16–17), who was indeed the promised "power" (Acts 1:8). This "power from on high" (*ex hypsous dynamin*) has been known in Luke from the very beginning of his narrative. The Son of God was conceived in Mary when she was overshadowed by the "power of the Most High" (*dynamis hypsistou*, 1:35).

Notes

<hr>

36, 40 See Notes on v.3 for the textual issue in these verses.

<hr>

4. *The Ascension*

24:50–53

> ⁵⁰When he had led them out to the vicinity of Bethany, he lifted up his hands and blessed them. ⁵¹While he was blessing them, he left them and was taken up into heaven. ⁵²Then they worshiped him and returned to Jerusalem with great joy. ⁵³And they stayed continually at the temple, praising God.

The Ascension is more than the last event in Luke's narrative sequence or a postscript to the Resurrection. He had already mentioned it in 9:51 as Jesus' ultimate goal in his great journey toward Jerusalem (cf. comment on 9:51). The Ascension also has significance in the opening verses of Acts. The brevity of the account here at the close of Luke's Gospel is not the measure of Luke's estimate of its importance. Perhaps he already had in mind an expanded version of the Ascension at the beginning of Acts; perhaps he was simply near the end of an already long scroll (Morris, *Luke*, p. 344). This brevity may also imply a telescoping of the entire closing narrative, thus explaining why Luke did not include sufficient chronological data to indicate how much time had elapsed since Resurrection Day. Nevertheless his words here, though few, are weighty with theological significance and very much in character with the entire book. Of the Gospel authors, only Luke records the Ascension.

50–51 NIV's "to the vicinity of " (v.50) translates *pros* ("toward") and guards against the supposition that they had already arrived at Bethany and so were not actually on the Mount of Olives (Acts 1:12). Bethany was on the other side of the mount to the south. Jesus' action in lifting up his hands and blessing the disciples (v.51) was priestly. The word "bless" (*eulogeō*) was significant at the opening of Luke. Zechariah the priest was rendered speechless in the temple, so that he was unable to pronounce the priestly blessing on the people when he came out (1:22). Such a blessing now concludes the book. Elizabeth blessed Mary and her child (1:42); Zechariah blessed God (NIV, "praising") when, on his declaration of John's name, his speech was restored (1:64); he then blessed (NIV, "praise") God again in his song (1:68); Simeon blessed (NIV, "praised") God in the temple on seeing Jesus (2:28) and then blessed his parents (2:34). This word does not appear again in Luke till Jesus blessed the bread at Emmaus (24:30). Luke immediately uses the word again in v.51 and again in v.53. Thus he places Jesus clearly within the spiritual setting of the temple and priesthood. As resurrected Messiah, Jesus has the authority to bless. This imagery forms an important part of the Letter to the Hebrews, which describes the high priestly intercession of Christ after his ascension into heaven (e.g., Heb 1:3; 4:14; 6:19–20; 7:23–25; cf. Rom 8:34; Eph 1:20). Jesus is also the Prophet of God, and we are again reminded of the prophet Elijah (cf. 4:26). That prophet was "taken up" to heaven (2 Kings 2:11; LXX, *anelēmphthē;* NIV, "went up"; observe the same verb in Acts 1:2 and in Acts 1:11 and the cognate noun in Luke 9:51, though here in 24:51 the verb is *anephereto*). Luke's conclusion points to Jesus as prophet, priest, and Messiah.

52–53 Jesus is also the Son of God, and so "they worshiped him" (v.52). Luke's beautiful Gospel closes with the theme of "joy" restated in v.52 and with the city of Jerusalem and its temple again presented as the true home of Christianity—the origin of the Christian gospel and the Christian church (cf. remarks on Jerusalem throughout this commentary, e.g., 13:31–35; 19:28–44; cf. Acts 1:8). Luke's theme of doxology reappears at the very end, as the disciples are last seen "blessing" (NIV, "praising") God (v.53; cf. note on text), a response to Christ's blessing them in vv.50–51. This is both an appropriate conclusion to Luke's Gospel and a reminder to us to live a life of praise as we wait for the return of the ascended Lord.

Notes

51–52 See Note on v.3 for the textual issue in these verses.

53 There is also a textual issue here. The Byzantine texts have αἰνοῦντες καὶ εὐλογοῦντες (*ainountes kai eulogountes*, "praising and blessing"), a reading that goes back to A f[1] f[13] 33 and other texts. If this is, as most assume, a conflation, one must choose between the highly attested *eulogountes* (P[75] ℵ B, among others) and *ainountes* (supported by the Western text). Internal considerations are somewhat in balance (see Metzger, *Textual Commentary*, pp. 190–91), but the external witnesses give the preference to *eulogountes*. It is possible that the significant use of εὐλογέω (*eulogeō*, "bless") in vv.50–51 may have caused copyists to introduce that reading here. But if, as other considerations make likely, it is the original reading here, it fits in beautifully with Luke's choice of the verb in vv.50–51. Having been blessed by God, the disciples now bless him in return (cf. Eph 1:3 for the same reciprocity). NIV's "praising" may be a nice compromise, representing both verbs, though "blessing" might be preferable and more consistent with vv.50–51.